THE ROMANS

THE ROMANS

AN INTRODUCTION

TO THEIR HISTORY

AND CIVILISATION

by KARL CHRIST

TRANSLATED FROM THE GERMAN

BY CHRISTOPHER HOLME

UNIVERSITY OF CALIFORNIA PRESS
BERKELEY AND LOS ANGELES

Published in 1984 by the
University of California Press
Berkeley and Los Angeles

First Paperback Printing 1985
ISBN 0-520-05634-5

Printed in the United States of America

4   5   6   7   8   9

Contents

List of plates, maps and plans *page* vii
Acknowledgements viii
Preface ix

I THE ROMANS: A CHANGING CONCEPT 1
The people and their city 1
The ages of Roman history 2

II FOUNDATION AND EARLY REPUBLIC 5
Legend and tradition 5
Archaic society and economy 9
The Struggle of the Orders 12
Expansion of Roman rule in Italy 15
System of Roman rule: colonisation 17

III THE CLASSICAL REPUBLIC 23
Social structure and constitution 23
Expansion in the Mediterranean area 33
Crisis and fall of the Republic 38

IV IMPERIUM ROMANUM 49
The Principate established and institutionalised 49
Pax Augusta: a world empire 55
Society, politics and economics 63
    The basic social structure; *princeps, domus principis;* the senatorial
    order; the equestrian order; the municipal aristocracy; the free
    citizens: the Roman army; the freed slaves; the slaves;
    integration policies; economic organisation and development

V WAYS OF LIFE 95
Occupations and means of livelihood 95
Woman in the family and society 99
Education 101

Housing 104
Clothing 106
Food and meals 108
The games 110
Baths 117
Life-styles 118
Disposal and remembrance of the dead 119

VI ROMAN LAW 121

VII LITERATURE, ART, SCIENCE AND TECHNOLOGY,
RELIGION 133
Beginnings of Roman literature 133
Roman historians 135
Roman poetry 137
Peaks of Latin prose 141
Post-Augustan literature 142
Evolution of Roman art 147
Science and technology 154
Roman religion 157
Imperium Romanum and Christianity 165

VIII THE EMPIRE OF LATE ANTIQUITY 169
The Age of the Severans and the Crisis of Empire 169
Late Antiquity and its epochs 175
Government and organisation 179
    Diocletian's tetrarchic system; the empire of Constantine the
    Great; social and economic structure
State and Religion 199
Literature and Art 208
    Introductory; Literature; Art
Fall of the western Roman empire 230

IX THE ROMAN TRADITION 235

THE PLATES 241
Notes on the plates 251
APPENDICES 256
Chronological table 256
Population figures 270
Currency system 270

BIBLIOGRAPHY 271

INDEX 284

Plates, Maps and Plans

PLATES

1 a The Flavian Amphitheatre (Colosseum), Rome; b Residential street, Herculaneum *page* 243
2 Roman senator with toga and ancestral images 244
3 Roman portraits: Caesar, 'Brutus', Marcian (?), and Trajan 245
4 a *Haruspices* examining the entrails of a sacrificial animal, Temple of Jupiter, Rome; b Trajan distributing *alimenta*, Trajan's Arch, Beneventum 246
5 a *Ara Pacis*, Rome; b Decorative band on a *terra sigillata* bowl 247
6 a Gladiatorial contest, floor mosaic; b Gladiator's helmet; c Athletes (wrestler, runner, boxer), floor mosaic 248
7 a Sepulchral chamber (*columbarium*), Via Codini, Rome; b Medical appliances from Pompeii 249
8 a, b Coin commemorating the consecration of Augustus; c, d Silver medallion of Constantine the Great; e Roman ship transporting wine 250

MAPS AND PLANS

1 Early Rome *page* 8
2 Rome in the time of the Republic 8
3 Roman colonies in Italy (up to the time of the Gracchi) 20
4 Italy in 133 BC 40
5 The Roman empire, AD 117 61
6 The Roman frontier in Germany 84
7 The House of the Atrium with a Mosaic, Herculaneum 105
8 Imperial Rome 112
9 The imperial *fora* 149
10 Invasions of the Germanic tribes and Huns 233
Numbers 1, 2 and 4–10 have been adapted from *Atlas of Classical Archaeology*, ed. M. I. Finley

ACKNOWLEDGEMENTS

My original model in writing this book was the study by Sir Moses Finley, *The Greeks*. It was Sir Moses also who first proposed an English edition and whose advice in so many particulars helped it on its way. After him, the translator, Christopher Holme, was responsible not only for an exemplary English version but also for many clarifications of the German original, and beyond that too for his own translations of the passages from Latin and Greek literature. Finally, the arduous task of compiling a new bibliography designed especially for English-language readers was undertaken by Professor Richard P. Saller, of Swarthmore College, and Bernard Frischer, of the University of California. Professor Frischer also offered valuable assistance with the text, and added usefully to the appendix on chronology. As author, I feel myself particularly indebted to these several helpers. It will be due to them if this English edition succeeds in its purpose. But I must also tender my thanks to the publishing houses concerned, to Mr John Charlton and his colleagues at Chatto and Windus, and to the University of California Press with its anonymous experts, for the painstaking realisation of this project, for many original suggestions, and for an unusually rewarding collaborative effort.

Philipps-Universität, Marburg/Lahn   Karl Christ
November 1982

Preface

This introduction to Roman history and civilisation has been written for the reader who would like to know about the main features of Roman society, its politics, economics, and culture; for the traveller seeking to place the monuments of the *imperium Romanum* in their historical context; and for the students of those disciplines which were, and still are, built on Roman foundations.

The composition of the work has been governed by three principles:

First, without attempting to offer a condensed summary of Roman history, or a portrait in miniature of Roman civilisation, it follows the lines of the major historical developments, and reflects the central areas and attitudes of modern research. In the foreground are those historical and cultural phenomena which formed the Roman consciousness, and those sectors of their civilisation in which the Romans recorded special achievements of far-reaching influence – as in architecture, the writing of history, and law, but not, clearly, in philosophy.

Secondly, in none of these areas could I aim at uniform thoroughness. The accents and emphases are placed deliberately: relatively full coverage is given to topics of general importance, whereas names or details important only to the specialist may be omitted altogether. Notwithstanding such limitations, I have tried to encompass the history and civilisation of Rome as a whole, and to convey it in such a way as to avoid the fragmentation which has become usual in the subject. I have made a particular effort to combine the perspectives of constitutional, social, and economic history with those of cultural history.

Thirdly, as a point of method, I have tried to let the Romans speak for themselves. Accordingly, I have included representative texts, not only extracts from classical literature in the narrower sense, but also inscriptions, laws, edicts, and writings of Church Fathers. And I have tried as best I could to make the historical meaning of Roman monuments intelligible. At the back of the book are bibliographical references for further reading, together with the titles of those studies and researches which I gratefully acknowledge as having formed the basis of my own work.

Marburg/Lahn,   Karl Christ
October 1978

THE ROMANS:
A CHANGING CONCEPT

THE PEOPLE AND THEIR CITY

Who were 'the Romans'? To begin with, they were of course the farmers, shepherds, craftsmen, the small-to-middling landowners who originally lived in the 'city' founded on the Tiber. But all who later acquired Roman citizenship were 'Romans' too. Of the most various ethnic origins, they were often in social terms members of the politically and economically dominant strata of Italy. 'Romans' again were the settlers of Roman colonies not only in Italy but also in the provinces; former allies of Rome on whom Roman citizenship had been conferred singly or collectively; later, to an increasing degree, members of the upper classes all over the empire; also soldiers who received full citizenship after twenty-five years' service in Roman auxiliary units; and finally, from the so-called *Constitutio Antoniniana* of the year A D 212/213 onwards, virtually all the free inhabitants of the Roman empire (*imperium Romanum*). In this process the Roman citizen body came to include not only the leading townsmen of Italy but also soldiers of Rome's allies who had distinguished themselves; not only the supporters of the factions in the Roman civil wars but also St Paul; the wealthy Greek merchant as well as the rhetorician; the Arab tribal prince and the German army leader.

Similarly 'Rome' meant very different things in its various epochs. The Rome of the early Republic was a central Italian city community with an extensive identity of political and economic interests. Above all, it was the direct organisation into a state of a self-governing community of free citizens. The acknowledgement of the effective authority of the Senate, the corporate symbol of the governing class, was an essential mark of this process. The 'Rome' of the classical Republic was at the same time the dominant power in Italy. Through purposeful colonisation and a systematically constructed federal organisation, Rome

contrived to achieve and retain rule over Italy with the minimum
exercise of force and without a bureaucracy.

Then came the Rome of the Principate, which became nothing less
than the world-power of the whole Mediterranean area. Leaving on one
side the elements and traditions that were consciously retained from the
Republic, we have a military monarchy 'with a monarchical head of state
and government and a partly monarchical, partly republican administration' (Ernst Meyer). Out of this were developed, after the great Crisis
of Empire in the third century A D, the despotism of Late Antiquity, that
Christian Rome which sought all the more vigorously to renew and
propagate the old traditions the further it moved away from them in
every field.

Some figures may help to clarify this development. The entire citizen
body of the early Republic in the fifth century B C may have been no more
than some 20,000 persons. In imperial times the population of the
empire is estimated to have been some 60–80 million, of whom 5.9
million were Roman citizens in the year A D 48. The territory of Rome in
the fifth century B C comprised about 800 square kilometres; at the time
of its greatest expansion under the Principate, about 3.5 million square
kilometres. Yet despite the variations and contrasts in this process of
development which modern research and writings have revealed, the
continuity and coherence of Roman history are so overwhelming that
there were always older elements of the political tradition available,
whether to legitimate new developments and demands or to combat
them.

THE AGES OF ROMAN HISTORY

The problem of imposing a structure on Roman history and dividing it
into periods has not found a single, generally agreed solution in modern
research. Indeed no such solution can be expected. Developments
in Rome's political, constitutional, social, economic, cultural, and
spiritual history were not in phase with one another. A clean break in
political history, for instance, may not always correspond with anything
in the history of literature, and vice versa. Nevertheless, by way of
introduction I think it may be helpful to set out briefly the usual
subdivisions of Roman history.

The early phase of Roman history comprises the beginnings of the
settlement of Rome from the end of the second millennium B C onwards,
the so-called urbanisation of Rome – probably, in the seventh and sixth
centuries, under Etruscan supremacy or at any rate under strong
Etruscan influence – and the time of the seven legendary kings up to the
foundation of the Republic (about 500 B C). This phase is also sometimes

subdivided into the Iron Age (900–700 BC), the Orientalising Period (700–580), and the Archaic Age (580–480).

The history of the Roman Republic (from *c.* 500 to *c.* 30 BC) was formerly subdivided, predominantly for political and constitutional reasons, into the following periods:

1. The period of the early Republic and Struggle of the Orders (*c.*500–287 BC)
2. The period of the classical Republic (287–133 BC)
3. The age of the Roman revolution (133–30 BC)

Against this, recent sociological analysis has rightly indicated that from about 200 BC, after the end of the Second Punic War, such profound economic and social changes took place that it might be better to terminate the second period in *c.* 200 BC. Grave doubts have also been expressed about the idea of a Roman 'revolution'. This was introduced originally by Theodor Mommsen and given new content by Ronald Syme, but the continuity of Rome's economic and social structures over the period is now felt to be against it. The third period would thus become the late Roman Republic (*c.* 200–30 BC).

The concept of the age of the Roman Emperors for the period from Augustus to Romulus Augustulus (AD 476) or even to Justinian (died AD 565) has now become established. It has also been customary to subdivide this age, primarily on constitutional grounds, into two: the Principate from 30 BC to AD 284, and the Dominate from AD 284 to 476 (or still later).

Here too in recent decades a new terminology and a new division into periods have been introduced. To give a more exact image of the structure of Roman rule from Augustus onwards, emphasis on the changing formal position of the emperor is today widely avoided. The Principate in the narrow sense (30 BC to AD 193) was followed by the transitional phase of the Severan emperors (AD 193–235), while the great Crisis of Empire of the third century AD is generally equated with the period of the so-called Soldier Emperors (AD 235–284).

With the systematic reforms of Diocletian (AD 284–305), or at latest with the succession of Constantine the Great (AD 306), modern studies begin the epoch of Late Antiquity, characterised by wholly new historical forces and forms of expression, a new understanding of the human self, new aesthetic criteria, and also by a new socio-economic structure. In it Roman, early Byzantine and Germanic history overlap. It comprises not only the collapse of the western Roman empire (AD 476) but also the rise of Byzantium and the development of the Germanic kingdoms on the soil of the old *imperium Romanum* during the 'migration of peoples' (*Völkerwanderung*) – the name given in the nineteenth century to the Euro-Asian population movements which for so long challenged Roman rule and finally engulfed Rome itself. In Late Antiquity Roman history fades away, whatever epochal year we choose as the dividing line between ancient and mediaeval history.

FOUNDATION AND
EARLY REPUBLIC

LEGEND AND TRADITION

From the time when Roman history began to be written towards the end of the third century BC there grew up in Rome, out of the most various ingredients of Roman, Etruscan, and Greek origin, a literary tradition about the beginnings and early history of the city. It was systematised by authors like Diodorus Siculus (first century BC), Livy, and Dionysius of Halicarnassus (Augustan period), and it determined the Roman and European view of history up to the beginning of modern times. An intensive criticism of this store of tradition was launched by J. Perizonius (1685), L. de Beaufort (1738), and B. G. Niebuhr (from 1811 on). J. Rubino (1839) and Theodor Mommsen (from 1854 on) sought to establish the priority of the legal sources and textbooks of constitutional history over Roman 'pseudo-history'. In the twentieth century linguistic specialists, historians of religion, and above all archaeologists have proposed new concepts and chronologies of early Roman history which have modified or displaced the ideas of the ancient tradition. A comparison between the ancient and the modern reconstructions of the past will illustrate the problem that faces modern researchers.

At an early date, and no later certainly than the emergence of the literary tradition, the beginnings of Rome were for the Romans associated with the fall of Troy (1184/3 BC, according to the ancient chronology). Aeneas, a son of Venus and Anchises, succeeded in escaping from the burning city of Troy with other fugitives, and after long wanderings at sea landed in Latium. He founded the city of Lavinium, and his son Iulus founded Alba Longa in the Alban Hills. Alba Longa became the capital city of Latium. The connection of its ruling house of Aeneas with the foundation of Rome is enshrined in the Romulus legend. King Numitor of Alba Longa, it relates, had a daughter, Rhea Silvia, who was got with child by the god Mars and bore the twins Romulus and Remus. King Numitor's younger brother,

Amulius, thereupon rebelled and overthrew him, exposing the twins in a basket on the Tiber. They were suckled, however, by a she-wolf, then reared by a shepherd, and grew up to learn their true identity and take their revenge on the usurper Amulius. Their decision to found a new city was marred by a quarrel for precedence, which the omens decided in Romulus' favour. When Remus then ridiculed the height of Romulus' new city wall by jumping over it, Romulus killed him. But the city was built (traditional date of foundation as given by Varro, 753 BC). To attract new citizens Romulus set up an asylum for fugitives, led them in a rape of wives from the neighbouring Sabine people, and, after a joint reign with the Sabine king Titus Tatius, was translated to heaven in a clap of thunder. From then on he was worshipped as the god Quirinus.

The line of the seven traditional kings of Rome began with Romulus. His immediate successor, Numa Pompilius, was said to have created the religious institutions of the city. After him Tullus Hostilius destroyed Alba Longa and considerably increased Roman influence in Latium. The fourth king, Ancus Martius, was credited with the building of the important pile bridge, the *pons sublicius*, at the foot of the Aventine, and with the foundation of an alleged colony in Ostia, to be understood probably as the acquisition of the salt workings at the mouth of the Tiber and a corresponding intensification of trade.

Etruscan influence on Rome, if not more than that, was embodied in the fifth king, Tarquinius Priscus, son of the Corinthian Demaratus and an Etruscan lady. His battles against Sabines and Latins, his development of the Forum, his introduction of the Etruscan royal costume at least betokened a determined will to rule. By contrast, the name of his successor, the Roman Servius Tullius, was coupled with a whole series of institutions fundamental to the organisation of ancient Rome. The creation of a political assembly organised in 'hundreds' (*centuriae*) and the building of the so-called Servian city wall are only the two best known. The measures themselves, however, are in part probably of later date, as was his alleged introduction of the coinage.

Both the achievements and the insolence of the monarchy are colourfully personified in the figure of the last Roman king, Tarquinius Superbus. Great public buildings such as the construction of the *cloaca maxima*, the famous drainage canal, or new successes over the Latins are celebrated in the same breath with the Lucretia episode, as reflections of the ancient picture of a tyrant. These had a part to play in legitimising the overthrow of the monarchy and the aristocratic conspiracy of 510 BC, an event which was later rewritten and disguised as a 'foundation of the Republic'.

Modern archaeological reconstructions have started from systematic analysis and interpretation of the excavation finds and the monuments.

The prehistorian H. Müller-Karpe gave his special attention to the early phase of the settlement's story. He dated the earliest graves found on Roman soil (Palatine, Forum) no later than the tenth century BC, and the finds on the Esquiline and the Quirinal to the ninth–seventh centuries BC. For the excavation deposit itself, especially house-urns, human figurines, and vessels, he looked for analogies in the Aegean area, especially Crete, and sought to prove the existence of close relations with it. In small round house-urns he claimed to recognise the peculiar round form of the oldest Vesta sanctuary, a circular building with a straw roof, which was adorned with pairs of horns, had a pair of forequarters of birds over the entrance, and coloured bands. On the whole, it must be said that he left open the question whether there was any connection between the earliest traces of settlement and the later foundation of the city, and if so what.

It is above all the Swedish archaeologist Einar Gjerstad who has concentrated on this question, in his monumental work, *Early Rome*. Meticulous investigations of the entire archaeological material on the early history of Rome, especially the remains of buildings and installations on the Forum, Palatine, and Forum Boarium (in the neighbourhood of the Church of S. Omobono), produced a self-consistent conceptual model. According to this, the earliest traces of settlement in Rome date from the eighth century BC, and the Palatine was the centre of modest village settlements on the hills of Rome. Later, in the years between c. 625 and 575 BC, these formed a loose federation called the *Septimontium*. It was Etruscan kings, about 575 BC, who first, according to this account, brought about its organisation into a city. The most important archaeological elements in this urbanisation process were considered by Gjerstad to have been the change of habitation style from the old straw-roofed huts to the first buildings with tiled roofs, the erection of monumental temples, the installation of a paved city market-place in the area of the Forum, the planned laying out of new streets such as the Via Sacra, and the building of a citadel on the Capitol. For him it was a specific and characteristic trait of Roman development that the 'foundation' of the city of Rome precisely did not begin with a fortification but with the systematic formation of a new centre for the citizenry in the Forum. The 'foundation' of Rome was seen by Gjerstad, moreover, as part of the great Etruscan urbanisation process in central Italy, and he pointed with special emphasis to the intensity of distant trade, revealed particularly by vase fragments, which in the phase between 575 and 450 BC linked archaic Rome with Greece.

This is not the place to comment on the efforts that have been made to reconcile the ancient literary tradition with the reconstructions of archaeologists, or to offer opinions on the fascinating, imaginative, but

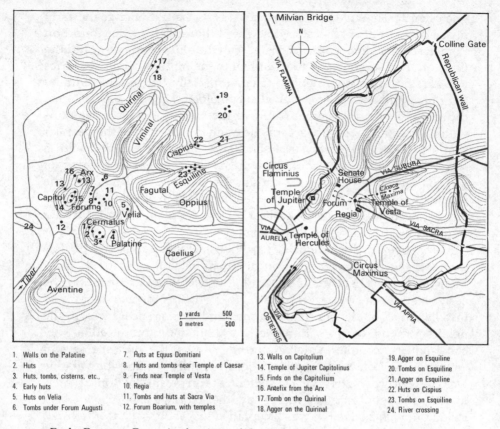

1. Walls on the Palatine
2. Huts
3. Huts, tombs, cisterns, etc.,
4. Early huts
5. Huts on Velia
6. Tombs under Forum Augusti
7. Huts at Equus Domitiani
8. Huts and tombs near Temple of Caesar
9. Finds near Temple of Vesta
10. Regia
11. Tombs and huts at Sacra Via
12. Forum Boarium, with temples
13. Walls on Capitolium
14. Temple of Jupiter Capitolinus
15. Finds on the Capitolium
16. Antefix from the Arx
17. Tomb on the Quirinal
18. Agger on the Quirinal
19. Agger on Esquiline
20. Tombs on Esquiline
21. Agger on Esquiline
22. Huts on Cispius
23. Tombs on Esquiline
24. River crossing

1 Early Rome; 2 Rome in the time of the Republic

often unverifiable attempts to bring the early history of Rome into agreement with general Indo-European traditions (G. Dumézil) or very concretely to fit them into Eurasian patterns of mythical and religious thought and social structure (A. Alföldi). At a time when there is not even a consensus among scholars as to the beginnings of the city's foundation and its dating, when the model of a 'pre-Etruscan' Rome is as roundly affirmed as it is denied, or a longer-term evolution upheld as widely as a definite foundation act, the once widespread assumption of a uniquely Roman special development giving way to more general interactions, it is perhaps better to fall back on the very existence of a Roman tradition and its far-reaching importance.

The 'mixture of ancient memories and political convictions', as Ranke once defined the Roman tradition, that interweaving of legend, poetry and truth which could scarcely any longer be unravelled, was for the later Rome – however it might be rationally criticised – the foundation of political and historical self-awareness. The events leading to the foundation of the city were like a consecration which gave the beginnings of Rome an incomparable sanctity. How deeply such a figure as Romulus was implanted in the Roman consciousness may be seen not only from Octavian's deliberations about himself taking the name of Romulus but also from St Augustine's words in discredit of the fratricide. The figure of the *rex* debased to a tyrant became a regular trauma for the Roman imagination. The attempts to lure Julius Caesar from dictator closer to kingship, made by both followers and opponents, are evidence of how critical and how fateful but also how strong this tradition still was.

The decision whether or not to accept the existence of a pre-Etruscan city of Rome depends on the dating of the archaeological finds. In any event, sixth-century Rome was under strong Etruscan influence. The previous units of settlement at about this time lost almost all their individual existence, and certainly any genuine political function. They lived on only within the framework of the cult associations, as for instance in the *Salii Palatini* and the *Salii Collini*, the communities of Leapers which performed their peculiar cult-dancing ceremonies in honour of Mars. The city area itself was formed as a first step into four city quarters: the *regio Suburana*, the *regio Palatina*, the *regio Esquilina*, and the *regio Collina*. The inhabitants after the union were called *Romani*, although for a time the special name for the inhabitants of the Quirinal was also preserved, the *Quirites*, a fact which was most clearly expressed in the stereotyped formula, *populus Romanus Quiritium*.

ARCHAIC SOCIETY AND ECONOMY

Despite the Etruscan element within the community, the population as a whole was still characterised by its basic Indo-European stock. Probably all that happened was that individual Etruscan families joined it. The city's social fabric was early on moulded by the ideas and authority of a strong aristocratic class. It is not clear how comprehensive the powers of the king (*rex*) at the summit of the city-state really were: in Rome, as in other Etruscan cities, they may have been strictly limited at this period.

In any event, the leading social class consisted of the members of a hereditary aristocracy, the *gentes*, or clans. Already in the age of the kings the Senate was an assembly of the heads of families of the aristocracy, who were later called the *patricii*. For political and military purposes, however, early Rome was divided into three great associations: the *tribus*, or tribes, of the *Ramnes*, *Tities*, and *Luceres*. These units bore Etruscan names. Every tribe consisted of ten *curiae*, or corporations of men. Under the *curiae* were the *gentes*, extended families or clans, and under them the individual families.

The military organisation was constructed in corresponding fashion. Every *curia* put into the field one hundred (*centuria*) of infantry, and every tribe consequently ten hundreds, so that a *populus*, or infantry mass, totalled three thousand men. This was complemented in analogous fashion by a cavalry force of 300 *equites* or *celeres*. It follows that *populus* in the narrower sense meant the militarily organised infantry of the citizenry, and such a definition clearly points to an army assembly which could also be politically effective. The *curiae* correspondingly emerge as the associations of greatest political importance. They form the fundamental unit of which the community is initially composed. It was they who took the oath of allegiance to the king, and it was they who delegated their authority, their *imperium*, to the senior magistrates.

What became more important, however, than the formal character of this relationship was the opposition between the patriciate – the aristocracy – and the *plebs* – the mass of the people. The aristocracy, being hereditary, was originally a class closed from below. It could probably admit patricians from other cities, but in principle did not tolerate marriages with non-patrician Romans. At first all political and all religious rights of any consequence were in the hands of this aristocratic class. Originally the patrician families or clans were bound to one another not only by living together but also by common cults. And from the very beginning every *gens* had its *clientes* – client members of the clan who were juridically free citizens but economically and socially dependent in the widest degree.

The main features of the social structure of archaic Rome were defined by specifically Roman phenomena: first, the family, the fundamental unit of Roman society; and secondly, the client institution. The structure of the Roman family was characterised by the uninhibited power of its male head, the *pater familias*, whose position of authority was as firmly documented in law as it was in matters of economics or cult. The *pater familias* originally had the right of life and death over every member of the family. He could sell his own children as slaves. The Roman family was in its beginnings essentially a logically organised rural community of life and home. For its children the duty of religiously sanctioned obligations towards the parents corresponded to that of the relations between men and gods. And this duty was designated by the same word, *pietas*.

The institution of clienthood, *clientela*, is still more important for the understanding of the Roman social order. It assumes on the side of the weaker, the *cliens*, a fundamental acknowledgement of dependency; on that of the stronger, the *patronus*, a conscious acceptance of responsibility for the weaker. With this the *patronus* had also a helping and protective function. He must never be ruthless in exploiting his [own] advantage over the weaker. The relation of trust which existed in such cases was called *fides*. It imposed on the client the duty of attendance, of forming part of the patrician's retinue in his public appearances. In special cases, too, the client had to render physical services. Against that, the patron was obliged to stand up for his client in many different ways, not least in court. Thus the relation of trust was mutual. By the Law of the Twelve Tables a patron who betrayed his client was proscribed.

Such sources as we have do not permit a clear account of how the *clientela* originated. The differentiation of landed property, influence and power, the fall of free farmers into dependency, the influx of artisans, the cession of arable land in usufruct subject to arbitrary recall – these are the usual suggestions. There have been attempts to deny that the client relationship had any economic basis at all, but these are not convincing. On the contrary, it is more likely that the institution had its beginnings in a conscious admission of economic dependence such as might easily arise in an early subsistence economy built around the family. A second conditioning factor was of legal character, since in early times the client had no possibility of making good his rights by due process of law without the support of a patron.

On this view the *clientela* must originally have depended on direct, permanent, personal ties between one person or family and another. Such ties could be heritable and thus pass to the next generations on both sides with all their rights and duties, although not with quite the same strength as when they were first created – as, for instance, in the case of freed slaves. The *clientela* of a patrician family could sometimes outnumber its members by ten to one. According to Livy, for instance, the *gens Fabia* in the year 479 BC had 306 members of the clan (*gentiles*) and as many as four to five thousand clients.

For a long time the *clientela* remained in its original form, but later, with the process of Roman expansion and the development of Rome's internal politics, there were considerable changes. While the relationship at first was entirely personal, later whole villages and cities and also kings would join the *clientela* of individual Roman aristocrats. These were often the very Roman army commanders who had subdued them and then became the representatives of their interests in the Roman Senate. In this way, in the words of J. Bleicken, the *clientelae* began to 'lose their personal identity'.

Changes brought about by internal politics in the composition of the circle of patrons were no less important in their consequences. This was originally identical with the closed group of patricians, but in the course of the Struggle of the Orders in the fifth and fourth centuries BC wealthy 'plebeians' were also moving up into the circle of patrons, as citizens whose material circumstances enabled them to assume the functions of aristocrats. Moreover, the *patroni* themselves, from being at first large landowners exclusively, had subsequently been joined by outstanding lawyers and politicians, and in the later republican age also by the great generals. While the network of *clientelae* at first formed a system of dependency with many centres, later on, as it became further and further expanded in membership, the office of patron became increasingly confined to the dominant politicians and generals, until during the Principate it was practically monopolised by the emperor.

The effects of the *clientela* on the formation of political objectives can hardly be over-estimated. In the early and classical Republic the client was as a matter of course bound by his patron's decisions in elections and plebiscites. There was thus a concentration of political objectives which also prevented political fragmentation. The patrons so to speak assumed the role of the modern political parties. Not until the secret ballot was introduced by the *leges tabellariae* of the second century BC (that is, the moment it was made impossible to control the actual casting of the vote) did the client's voting obligations begin to be loosened and finally to disintegrate.

THE STRUGGLE OF THE ORDERS

The abolition of the monarchy was bound to lead to internal antagonism between the two great social groups, patricians and *plebs*, in the Roman state. Unlike the patriciate, the Roman *plebs* was not at all homogeneous. For the period of the early Roman Republic it would be quite wrong to see it as an amorphous metropolitan population without adequate possibilities of work and subsistence. This would be to project back features which began to be characteristic of Rome only in the late Republic and Principate. For the Roman *plebs* of the early Republic included not only the clients – predominantly small peasant producers – but also farmers, artisans and traders, all equally independent, and, beyond that, non-patrician citizens of substance and property enough to be able to afford the equipment of a heavy-armed soldier. The revolution in the technique and tactics of warfare involved in the transition from cavalry squadrons fighting from chariots or horses to the hoplite phalanx, a massed battle array of heavy-armed infantry, made this last group of particular importance. The heavier the burdens they were called on to bear, with their years of service in the numerous military confrontations of the early Republic, the more vigorously they pressed for political equality with the privileged patricians.

For the broad mass of the *plebs*, however, there were other issues in the foreground. The main anxiety for them was the provision of arable or pasture land, if for no other reason than for their later-born children. Next in importance was an acceptable settlement of the debt problem. By the early Roman credit law in the form of the *nexum*, the creditor had a virtual right of arrest against the person of the debtor. The danger of enslavement for debt resulted above all from the very high rates of interest, which, in the view of many interpreters, at times amounted to one-twelfth of the capital. Not until the enactment of the *lex Poetelia* of 326 B C were the confinement and sale of the debtor forbidden, and after that the whole institution of the *nexum* fell into disuse.

In almost all the social disturbances of the Graeco-Roman cultural world, land distribution and the cancellation of debt were primary demands. It may therefore be that our ideas about what happened in early Rome are in some sense a reflection of later Roman or Greek developments incorporated in the tradition handed down from the ancient world. It can hardly be doubted, however, that even in the early Roman Republic there were great abuses. These were aggravated in the beginning by the manner in which justice was administered by the leading magistrates. Evidently this was quite uncontrolled and opened a wide door to abuses, so that the demands for protective measures against arbitrary power were widely supported.

There has so far been no analysis of the beginnings of the Struggle of the Orders in Rome that rests on secure foundations. We must suppose that successive popular leaders looked back into the past for a revolutionary tradition as a long-established sanction for their current demands. As a consequence, later events and even the contents of later legislation were reflected back into the early period, where they often seem much less appropriate. In the year 287 B C, for instance, a *secessio plebis* occurred. The *plebs* left the city and refused to serve in the army. There are legendary tales of similar happenings in the year 494/3 B C – 200 years earlier. Were these a case in point? The so-called 'repetitions of laws' are another case. It can hardly be doubted, for instance, that in the year 300 B C recognition was accorded to the right of *provocatio*; that is, the right of every free Roman citizen to appeal to the people against a sentence of death or other severe penalty by a Roman magistrate. But tradition dates juristic analogues of this law to the years 509 and 449 B C, which can hardly be correct.

The Struggle of the Orders in Rome is usually said to have begun with the first 'secession' of the *plebs* in the year 494 B C, and to have been concluded with the *lex Hortensia* of the year 287 B C, which invested the resolutions of the independent popular assemblies with the force of law for the whole Roman state. Its most important stages and peaks were the Decemvirate of 451/450 B C, when the law code of the Twelve Tables was enacted; the attempted plebeian uprisings under Marcus Manlius Capitolinus in 385 B C; the enactment from 367/6 B C onward of the *leges Liciniae-Sextiae*, which included the admission of the *plebs* to the highest offices of state; the practical abolition of enslavement for debt by the *lex Poetelia* of the year 326 B C; and the recognition in the year 300 B C of the *provocatio*.

During the fifth century B C the conflicts between *plebs* and patricians were intensified. As patrician pretensions grew, so did the awareness of the plebeians. The antagonism at times overshadowed the client system, because certainly in a political respect but also to some extent in legal help the leaders of the *plebs* were coming to assume the functions of the *patroni*. At the same time it is characteristic of the Roman development that again and again individual patricians took up the defence of plebeian interests – such as, to mention only a few examples, Spurius Cassius (486 B C), Marcus Manlius Capitolinus (385 B C), Quintus Publilius Philo (339 B C), and Appius Claudius Caecus (censor 312 B C).

The dispute lasted more than two centuries and was characterised by phases of bitter internal conflict, with long periods of compromise under the necessity of self-defence against common external dangers. When it ended, the complete equality of all plebeians at civil law had been recognised, the laws in force had been codified, and the constitution reformed. This reform will be discussed more fully below, but it found its most striking expression in the so-called centuriate constitution as finally worked out. It also provided for the participation of the *plebs* in the election of magistrates, in political trials, in decisions of war and peace, and in the enactment of laws. Finally, a system of legal protection had been established against arbitrary behaviour by magistrates, and the authority of the people's court in capital cases had been recognised. At the same time, by painful degrees, the richer plebeians won admittance to an expanded ruling class, now called *nobiles*, as one by one the right of election to the different offices of state was accorded them (366 B C, first plebeian consul; 356 B C, dictator; 351 B C, censor; 172 B C, both consuls plebeian for the first time).

As a first step, from 494 B C onwards, a special organisation of the *plebs* had come about, so to speak a state within a state. The main feature of this development was the institution of the tribunate of the people. At first two, then five, and from 449 B C ten people's tribunes represented the special interests of the plebeians against the ruling patrician order. All these tribunes' actions were originally assertions of rights, and that was the very reason why in a community held together by religious obligations the inviolability (*sacrosanctitas*) of their persons was requisite, why they must be hedged around with a taboo, as representatives of the people's interests. In the *intercessio* ('getting in between') of the tribunes of the people, in their organisation of crowd protests when the patrician magistrates exceeded their duties, or in a walk-out of the *plebs*, we see the forms of battle taken by the Struggle of the Orders.

The tribunes of the people were originally also the military commanders of the *plebs*. Later their military origins receded completely into the background, behind the continuous exercise of their legal protection, their conduct of the assemblies of the people, and their far-reaching right of eliciting motions (*plebiscita*). Taken altogether, the powers of the tribunes of the people were largely negative. A tribune of the people could effectively block a magistrate's exercise of his office but he could not take it over himself. At the end of the Struggle of the Orders, the powers of the tribunes of the people, originally usurped, were fully legalised and incorporated in the republican constitution. This is the most striking expression of the fact that the two constitutional levels, the patrician and the plebeian, which had become separated during the Struggle of the Orders, had again been combined in a uniform system at its end. By the *lex Hortensia* of 287 B C, what had once been a special organisation of the plebeian opposition was raised to the rank of an organ of state with official functions. For a considerable time after that, it is true, the tribunes of the people themselves became constructive promoters of senatorial policy. All the same they did now hold, in the words of Theodor Mommsen, 'the holiest, highest, and freest of all the magistracies', which for that reason too in the crisis of the late Republic offered itself as a basis for new oppositional objectives.

EXPANSION OF ROMAN RULE IN ITALY

The elimination of the monarchy and the emergence of the Roman patrician state from Etruscan control at once confronted it with a severe crisis of foreign relations. Rome had now lost its security in respect not only of the Etruscans but also of the Latins. The first Roman–Punic treaty from the first year of the Republic is no doubt to be understood as an expression of this situation. For Rome everything depended on maintaining its position in Latium. With hindsight and from a great distance it may be said that this was the beginning of the continual process of expansion by which the Roman Republic up to the beginning of the First Punic War (264 B C) was able to extend its area of control over the whole of central and southern Italy.

Yet this process was also scarred with heavy defeats and catastrophes. In its struggles with Etruscans, Latins, Celts and Samnites, to name only the most important opponents, Roman power seemed more than once to have been shattered. Rome's 'heroic' period is characterised by a rapid alternation of crisis and success. The legends about the battle of Lake Regillus, Coriolanus (allegedly 491 BC), Cincinnatus (allegedly 462 BC), the capture and destruction of the old rival Veii in the year 396 BC, the disaster on the Allia river and the sack of Rome by the Celts (387 BC), the great Latin rebellion (340–338 BC), the three wars against the Samnites (I, 343–341 BC; II, 327–304; III, 298–290) and finally the struggles against King Pyrrhus of Epirus (280–275 BC) mark the most important stages in an expansion that was by no means uninterrupted.

Yet the very severity of the relapses and crises which do interrupt the expansion and organisation of Roman power is an indication of the unique character of the process. Its continuity and inexorable logic were dictated corporately by a governing class which at the same time acted predominantly in the interests of the majority of all free citizens. The most important achievement of the patriciate, and later of the nobility, was its creation and consolidation of a broad identity of interests against the other Italian powers. In this context it would be quite unrealistic to close our eyes to the elementary economic and social causes and consequences of Roman expansion. This was the only way in which both patricians and plebeians could assuage their land hunger, the only way in which they could provide a living for the younger sons of the free small proprietors, the farmers, herdsmen, artisans and merchants, the only way in which the social system of the city could continue to reproduce itself.

In its later phase, however, this process of expansion could only be continued and consolidated because the Roman governing class was once more successful in forming a broader community of interests with their own social fellows in the Italian cities and among the tribes. Because the advantages of the Italian federal association organised by Rome obviously outweighed the loss of local privileges and traditions, this politically crucial social group at first acquiesced in Roman supremacy and then identified itself with it completely. In any case in the long term there was no realistic alternative to the growth of Roman power. In the Italy of the sixth to third centuries BC there was no other political power which, over so long a span of time and with such consistency and lack of compromise, had pursued a comparable process of expansion and consolidation. In many cases, moreover, the acceptance of Roman rule must have seemed the lesser evil, at times when the free communities and cities of Italy on their own had proved unable to withstand the intrusions of the Oscan-Sabellic mountain tribes or the Celts or the neighbouring states.

On its way to Italian hegemony there were power configurations enough in which Rome found its own potential strength simply inadequate. Only by the continuous concentration of all its available forces and, very early on, by the comprehensive mobilisation of those of its allies was it able to match the occasional superiority of its opponents, fragmented as these mostly were. Both politically and militarily, the triumph of the Roman collective leadership is all the more astonishing in view of the severe internal crises which it was simultaneously required, again and again, to surmount. We can thus understand that this active process of expansion, maintained so tenaciously, and so unparalleled in the evolution of national states or among general ideas of human progress in modern times, was for a long time judged solely for its positive aspects and results, especially in the overcoming of particularism. Yet for all the glorification of the political and military successes of the Roman Republic it must not be overlooked that, as Herder was the first to point out, they were at the same time synonymous with the destruction of the civilisations of ancient Italy.

SYSTEM OF ROMAN RULE: COLONISATION

The Roman Republic gave the area of its rule in Italy a new type of political and legal order. Constitutionally the Roman citizens, whose assembly was invested with the sovereignty of the state, formed its inner base. Not all the inhabitants of Rome, however, were Roman citizens with full rights, nor did all such citizens live in the city of Rome. Instead, Rome like no other city-state of the ancient world used the right of citizenship as a political instrument, a means to consolidate its rule. With the growth of Roman territory, the *ager Romanus*, the annexed regions were permeated with scattered settlements of Roman citizens who had received grants of land by the method of individual apportionment, the so-called *assignatio viritana*. In contrast with these, the concentration of Roman settlers in the colonies (which will be discussed below) was considerably stricter. In their constitutional rights both categories of citizens were entirely dependent on Rome, although in practice, in view of the steadily increasing radius of Roman rule, they could hardly exercise their citizen rights politically any longer.

The constitutional structure of Italy meanwhile was being changed not only by new Roman settlements but also by the abolition of once independent communities and the granting of Roman citizenship rights to the conquered. Yet there were limits to this kind of indirect incorporation. By extending the process to tribes and communities of foreign origin and language, the Roman citizen body ran the risk of being outnumbered. So the need was to find a system of organisation and law which would guarantee to the individual the civil rights involved in Roman citizenship without burdening the very small official staff of the city of Rome with yet further administrative duties, or incurring the political dangers of a wider extension of Roman citizenship. The solution was found in the *civitas sine suffragio*, a category of citizenship which excluded its holders only from the active and passive electoral and voting rights in the Roman popular assemblies but afforded them complete equality in all areas of civil law. In return they were required to serve side by side with the full citizens in the legions.

Such graduated communities were left to administer their own local affairs themselves through their own freely elected officials. It was merely their military sovereignty and their right to a 'foreign policy' of their own which were transferred to Rome. The recipients of this status were principally Rome's neighbouring cities, which stood on a similar social and cultural level, especially those in Latium and Campania, but also the Etruscan Caere, which in the year 342 BC was the first city to receive it.

In contrast with this constitutional and political nucleus were the Roman allies, who again were strongly differentiated. The most important and most highly privileged group were Rome's Latin confederates, who originally enjoyed equal rights with Rome. Initially the so-called law of Latium (*ius Latii*) was valid for all the Latin cities, being thus confined to a definite geographical area and a definite people. With the defeat of the great Latin insurrection (340–338 BC) there was a decisive change. At first *ius Latii* was limited to a few special cases, like Tibur and Praeneste, but then later it was extended also to communities and citizens not belonging to the Latin people.

The law of Latium first of all recognised the autonomous position of the communities concerned. Not only were its citizens given equality with the full citizens of Rome in matrimonial law and commercial law, *conubium* and *commercium*, but in the event of their moving to Rome to settle there permanently they received full Roman citizenship. However, this provision was later qualified, until finally in the second century BC a different procedure was introduced which was to become of special significance for the social and legal structure of the *imperium Romanum*. This procedure extended full Roman citizenship to the former officials of the *ius Latii* communities, thus sytematically attaching the Italian upper middle class to Rome.

At the same time, in giving statutory form to the higher standing of Roman over Latin citizenship in these communities, it marked the Latin citizenship as a preliminary step towards the Roman. In this form Latin citizenship, detached from all regional or ethnic ties, continued right into imperial times to be awarded to cities, peoples, and whole provinces. As a legal intermediate stage in the Romanisation process it came into very wide use.

The group of the *socii*, the allies of Rome, was a very diverse one, comprising as it did cities and peoples of the most different sizes, structures, traditions, and abilities. After the conclusion of a treaty of alliance, the *foedus*, all remained substantially independent. Yet in reality the pre-eminence of Rome was recognised. All the allies had renounced the right to have relations independent of Rome with other states, and moreover the alliance was for ever and could not be dissolved. On occasion, too, it contained the so-called majesty formula, which meant that the ally formally and freely undertook to acknowledge the *maiestas* or sovereignty, of the Roman people. In addition, the allies were obliged in the case of war to supply a contingent of troops, which however remained under the command of the city concerned and were not absorbed into the legions.

Roman rule was thus organised as a network of sharply differentiated states and territories. The pillars to which the system was anchored were the Roman and Latin colonies. Originally Rome had a hand only in the founding of the Latin colonies. The members of Rome's lowest classes who settled in these colonies gave up their Roman citizenship and exchanged it for that of the Latin colony concerned. But while as unpropertied citizens of Rome they could not be called up for army service, as members of the Latin colony they were obliged to serve as soon as they had received their land allotment, so that Rome's military potential was considerably strengthened by this means.

The main object of all colonies was to secure the conquered territories. They generally had a supervisory function assigned to them, over frontiers, roads, river crossings, passes and harbours. The earliest Roman citizen colonies (Ostia after 350 BC; Antium 338; Tarracina 329; Minturnae 295; Sinuessa 295; Castrum Novum *c.* 289; Sena Gallica 283; Pyrgi 264?) were as a rule situated near or on the coast as *coloniae maritimae*. Their main task was coastal protection, and they also explain why Rome did not assemble a war fleet of any size until the First Punic War. These early Roman citizen colonies were relatively small. As a rule their male population was only about 300, with land allotments of 2 *iugera* (about 5000 square metres or 1¼ acres) each and, in addition, with access to the common land, the *ager publicus*, especially for pastoral purposes. The colonists were subject to strict rules of attendance. They were never allowed to leave their colony for longer than thirty days. They were however exempted from service in the Roman legions. At first in these small defence posts there was nothing but the rudiments of an independent administration. The administration of justice was in the hands of prefects who came from Rome.

Latin colonies before 338 BC were founded in consequence of a decision of the Latin Federation, and after that only on the initiative of Rome. Both in size and in number they greatly exceeded the Roman

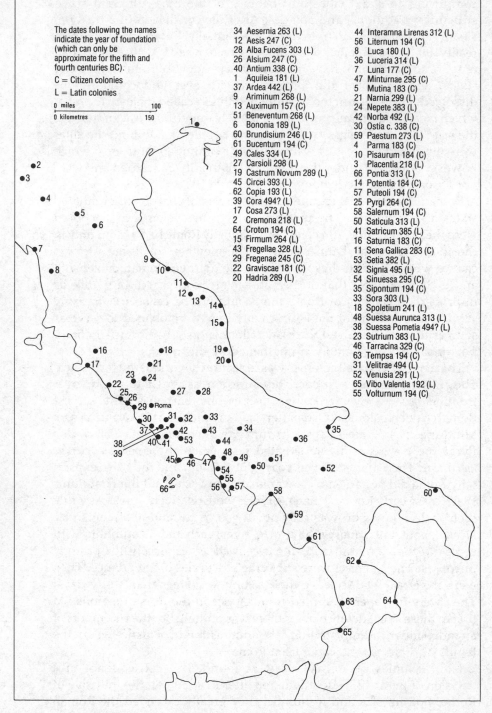

The dates following the names
indicate the year of foundation
(which can only be
approximate for the fifth and
fourth centuries BC).

C = Citizen colonies
L = Latin colonies

0 miles   100
0 kilometres   150

34 Aesernia 263 (L)
12 Aesis 247 (C)
28 Alba Fucens 303 (L)
26 Alsium 247 (C)
40 Antium 338 (C)
1 Aquileia 181 (L)
37 Ardea 442 (L)
9 Ariminum 268 (L)
13 Auximum 157 (C)
51 Beneventum 268 (L)
6 Bononia 189 (L)
60 Brundisium 246 (L)
61 Bucentum 194 (C)
49 Cales 334 (L)
27 Carsioli 298 (L)
19 Castrum Novum 289 (L)
45 Circei 393 (L)
62 Copia 193 (L)
39 Cora 494? (L)
17 Cosa 273 (L)
2 Cremona 218 (L)
64 Croton 194 (C)
15 Firmum 264 (L)
43 Fregellae 328 (L)
29 Fregenae 245 (C)
22 Graviscae 181 (C)
20 Hadria 289 (L)

44 Interamna Lirenas 312 (L)
56 Liternum 194 (C)
8 Luca 180 (L)
36 Luceria 314 (L)
7 Luna 177 (C)
47 Minturnae 295 (C)
5 Mutina 183 (C)
21 Narnia 299 (L)
24 Nepete 383 (L)
42 Norba 492 (L)
30 Ostia c. 338 (C)
59 Paestum 273 (L)
4 Parma 183 (C)
10 Pisaurum 184 (C)
3 Placentia 218 (L)
66 Pontia 313 (L)
14 Potentia 184 (C)
57 Puteoli 194 (C)
25 Pyrgi 264 (C)
58 Salernum 194 (C)
50 Saticula 313 (L)
41 Satricum 385 (L)
16 Saturnia 183 (C)
11 Sena Gallica 283 (C)
53 Setia 382 (L)
32 Signia 495 (L)
54 Sinuessa 295 (C)
35 Sipontum 194 (C)
33 Sora 303 (L)
18 Spoletium 241 (L)
48 Suessa Aurunca 313 (L)
38 Suessa Pometia 494? (L)
23 Sutrium 383 (L)
46 Tarracina 329 (C)
63 Tempsa 194 (C)
31 Velitrae 494 (L)
52 Venusia 291 (L)
65 Vibo Valentia 192 (L)
55 Volturnum 194 (C)

3 Roman colonies in Italy (up to the time of the Gracchi)

citizen colonies. Cales, founded in 334 BC, is said to have had 2500 settlers, and Venusia (291 BC) as many as 20,000. We have documentary evidence of 30 Latin and 10 Roman citizen colonies before 218 BC. These Latin colonies, too, were a considerable help in preventing the accumulation of a landless and impoverished peasantry in Rome itself. The dual function of the Roman colonisation process can hardly be better described than it was by Max Weber, who called it 'the incomparably effective means of securing Roman rule and, alongside all the many negative measures such as corn procurement and remission of debt, the only positive measure of social politics in the grand manner . . . with which the Roman state countered the convulsive symptoms of the sickness of its body politic' (*Die römische Agrargeschichte in ihrer Bedeutung für das Staats- und Privatrecht*, 1891, 7).

Taken all in all, the Roman system of allies was a completely new form of organised rule. In it Rome, the ruling city, succeeded in transcending the limitations of the ancient city-state, the *polis*, the self-governing community of free citizens. At the same time those dependent on Rome were left with the highest possible measure of administrative authority and local government in the original city-state framework. Later on too, within the *imperium Romanum*, the area of Roman power, this remained the basic pattern of the power structure. It was still the case in imperial times, long after the establishment of an effective provincial administration, that while the central function of Rome was still insisted on, at the same time the cities continued to be the most important administrative cells of the Roman empire.

The sociological structure of Roman rule was fundamentally incapable of supporting any other form of ruling organisation. The Roman governing class had to adopt an indirect form if only because, unlike the Hellenistic monarchies, especially in Egypt, they neither possessed a bureaucracy nor wanted one, and also because the city-state of Rome could simply not afford the means for a direct administration over the whole area of its rule. The many defects of such a rule without an adequate administrative basis came to light only later. For the moment both sides saw only the advantages of such a solution.

The Roman form of ruling organisation had a stabilising effect that helped the local and regional governing classes. The groups of propertied city aristocrats from then on found in Rome the strong support they needed to secure and strengthen their position in their internal city disputes. Just as in Greece at the time of the Peloponnesian War the aristocratically ruled *poleis* joined Sparta and the democratically ruled *poleis* sided with Athens, so now in Italy the Roman Republic became the guarantor of the existing social order.

There was yet another respect in which the members of the Roman system of allies shared a community of interests. Its consolidation was fostered by the great common enemies – the Celts, King Pyrrhus of Epirus with his mercenaries, and finally the Carthaginians. The common defence against all these powers, and with it the common burden of military tasks enduring for long periods of the fourth and third centuries BC, did more than anything else to bind the allies to Rome, and to forge a sense of community which otherwise would have been very much more difficult to attain and give life to.

THE CLASSICAL REPUBLIC

SOCIAL STRUCTURE AND CONSTITUTION

The classical Roman Republic is usually dated to the period between 287 and 133 BC. In its internal development it was marked by an astonishing compactness and stability. Once the Struggle of the Orders was concluded the nobility consolidated its rule. In the structure of society there seem to have been few fundamental changes. As before, we find in the family and the *clientela* the most important social cells of the state. And yet the continuity and lack of change in many of the constitutional features of the Republic mask the onset and extent of profound changes. These were later, in the second century, to become more and more conspicuous.

The tempestuous expansion begun by the three Punic Wars (I, 264–241 BC; II, 218–201; III, 149–146) had far-reaching effects on the social and economic existence of the Roman Republic. Changes were brought about by an interplay of mutual influences, a tangle of factors, foreign and domestic, military and economic, social as well as religious and intellectual. Only their wars, successful despite losses and setbacks, can explain how the power of the Roman governing class came to be reinforced, how Rome's productive capacity expanded, how substantial masses of slaves became available. The transition to new forms of industry and new production goals cannot be understood except in terms of Rome's new access to Sicilian corn and Spanish silver or its new-found acquaintance with the refining industries of Magna Graecia and Carthage. The spread of pastoral farming and the *villa* system of agriculture, which both depended on a continuous supply of slaves, cannot be understood without an appreciation of the deep wounds inflicted on Italy by the wars – the ruin of many smallholder families by death and devastation, the long absences of many free farmers and artisans. The reasons for the progressive differentiation of Roman society can only be sought in the growth of the money economy, the new possibilities of enrichment open to the governing class, and the economic activities of a new generation of profiteers able to exploit the traditional ties of senators with the land. These examples will give some idea of the context in which developments from the third century BC onward can be explained at least in outline.

At no time were the influence and power of the Roman governing class in the narrow sense, the nobility that is, so important as in the classical Roman Republic. This newly constituted group was an enlargement of the old patriciate, by the addition of the families of all those Romans who had held the highest office of state, the consulate. Against that it must be observed that only very few 'new men' (*homines novi*) in fact got as high as the consulate – from the passage of the Licinian-Sextian Law to the time of Cicero, not more than a dozen. As a general rule only members of families already noble were elected to the consulate.

After the Samnite Wars, the circle of leading families thus became rigidified. Evidently even the plebeians, once the new ruling class had been fixed, wanted to keep it exclusive. The promotion of qualified 'new men' was made very difficult in practice. C. Flaminius (consul 223 and 217 BC), M. Porcius Cato (consul 195 BC), C. Marius (consul 107, 104–100 and 86 BC), and M. Tullius Cicero (consul 63 BC) are the best-known examples from the late Republican period, and the list of names shows how wide a political span they represented. While Flaminius and Marius were as often as not fighting the Roman aristocracy, Cato and Cicero represented its traditions and policies with particular keenness.

By reason of its traditions and pretensions the Roman nobility was obliged always to keep alive the legitimacy of its hold on all Roman citizens, especially those of their own order. The holding of office by an individual member of their class, they felt, and indeed any successes and achievements in the public service, the *res publica*, must never fall into oblivion. The fulfilment of norms, in the sense of a vigorous effort in the common cause, a satisfactory performance in offices of state and public duties, must be not only achieved but seen to be achieved, must be repeatedly vaunted at elections and in political debates, dilated on at funerals, inscribed on gravestones. This was the only way in which political and social prestige could be maintained.

Thus it is that we have the parade of ancestral deeds and customs, together with an individual's own achievements, which often seems so obnoxious to modern taste – the boasting of magistracies held, cities taken, territories conquered, booty brought in, down to the cult of pedigrees, often forged, and family traditions with their one-sided overstatements, also often invented, and yet finding their way into late annalistic histories. There also evolved a code of behaviour, a system of values and ideals, to fix the governing class's conception of itself.

At first the 'customs of our forefathers' (*mores maiorum*) had force only as binding moral categories. But from the second century BC onward there were more and more attempts to give the force of law to the ancient norms of behaviour. The sumptuary laws (*leges sumptuariae*), to limit luxurious living, were a case in point. In other instances the censors would intervene with rebukes and reprimands. Such measures often ignored the fact that particular modes and manners of behaviour and life-style were a product of particular economic and social circumstances. The whole of Roman history is swept by the tension between the world of the *mores maiorum*, so soon transfigured and translated from history to mythology, and the necessity of meeting the demands of new social and political realities. Tacitus is as much shaped by it as Symmachus.

The Roman governing class offered a wide field of employment, usually at a very early age, to politicians, generals and administrators who were both gifted and experienced. As is shown by the age stipulations of the *leges annales*, the members of this class were already reaching the higher stages of their careers in their thirties and forties. The Roman consuls were no dotards but men in their prime. The reaction of the governing class was downright allergic, however, if ever one of their number by reason of his achievements and authority grew 'taller than the average', or if even the remotest danger appeared of an individual's continuance in any position of extraordinary power. It was then quite enough to hint at the trauma of monarchy or tyranny in order to topple anyone with rank or ambitions of that kind. P. Cornelius Scipio, the conqueror of Hannibal, and the Gracchi were victims of this mentality.

The Roman Senate had once been constituted as the assembly of the heads of patrician families. Now it became practically speaking an assembly of former senior magistrates (consuls, praetors), but the censors who supervised its composition could also co-opt persons who had not held office, just as they could annul the membership of those who had. The number of senators was limited to 300. The Roman Senate was thus not equivalent in membership to the nobility. On the one hand there were Roman politicians belonging to it whose families had not yet held a consulate, while on the other not all the male members of noble families had a seat there. In practice, however, it was the nobility who controlled it. It was their most important instrument for enforcing the political will of their majority.

By reason of the initial uniformity, economically speaking, of a landed aristocracy, the Roman governing class was characterised by an astonishing social homogeneity. In itself, however, it was differentiated by the offices held, currently or previously, by its members, by their achievements, the size of their *clientela*, their property, and their connections. The *princeps senatus*, the most distinguished member of the Senate, the former censors, consuls and praetors, constituted in accordance with the hierarchy of magistracies an important ladder of rank. Every individual senator had his place in the corporate body. Thus it was necessary to regulate each career of public office exactly in the *leges annales*, and to protect the conduct of every election from irregular influence – especially from the bribing of groups of voters – by the *leges de ambitu*.

Inside the Senate political disputes were governed by the differences between various groups of aristocrats, formed either by kinship or connections of political friendship (*amicitia*). For a long time our understanding of the structure of policy-making in the Senate was obscured by the importation of ideas from modern parliamentarianism. What we have to realise is that the Roman Senate did not contain 'parties of peers' defined by political programmes but groupings which remained constant for a considerable time by virtue of the ties just mentioned or of shared objectives; nevertheless, next to this we often find political alliances representing very short-term interests, for example during elections.

The Roman Senate was the competent authority in almost all spheres of political life; or it could at any rate take under its notice almost any public matter, with the exception of those powers specifically assigned to the Assembly of the People during the Struggle of the Orders (decisions about war and peace, election of magistrates, legislation, political trials). Even with these limitations, however, it must be understood that senate initiatives would have been responsible for many of the bills laid before the Assembly. Central to its own activities, however, were matters of 'foreign' policy, of the conduct of war, the administration of finance, taxation, the provinces, but also public order in the widest possible sense. The *auctoritas senatus* at all times represented for the Romans the highest concentration of political authority. For the representatives of foreign powers, the Senate was the Roman Republic's decisive organ of power.

The proceedings of the Roman Senate were transacted in accordance with a very simple rule strictly governed by precedent. The magistrate conducting the session introduced the points on the agenda one by one. His report (*relatio*) as a rule concluded with a proposal, on which the senators could each give their opinion according to the prescribed hierarchical order, which roughly corresponded to modern rules of seniority. In the course of this debate alternatives or amendments to the chairman's proposal were worked out. The voting was by simple walking over, that is, every senator stepped across to the group of persons to whose views he wished to 'accede'. The senate resolution thus arrived at was taken into protocol and filed.

The achievements of the senate aristocracy speak for themselves. Even Theodor Mommsen, who branded the 'Junker rule' of the late Republic with scathing disapproval, gave an emphatic appreciation of the Senate of the classical Republic:

'Embracing in it all the political intelligence and practical statesmanship that the people possessed; absolute in dealing with all financial questions and in the guidance of foreign policy; having complete power over the executive by virtue of its brief duration and of the tribunician intercession which was at the service of the Senate after the termination of the quarrels between the orders – the Roman Senate was the noblest organ of the nation, and in consistency and political sagacity, in unanimity and patriotism, in grasp of power and unwavering courage, the foremost political corporation of all times – still even now an "assembly of kings", which knew well how to combine despotic energy with republican self-devotion.' According to Mommsen, 'the Roman people was enabled by means of its Senate to carry out for a longer term than is usually granted to a people the grandest of all human undertakings – a wise and happy self-government'. (*The History of Rome*, tr. W. P. Dickson, Vols. I, III).

The Roman offices of state, the magistracies, were unpaid short-term honorary offices. Their functions were so wide-ranging that, in order to secure self-control and restraint in the exercise of official power (*potestas*), responsibilities had to be corporately shared (by the principle of *collegium*). At the same time the term of office had to be strictly limited to one year, or in the case of a dictator to half a year, and in that of the censor to a year and a half. These principles of 'collegial responsibility' and annual tenure were very likely a reaction to experiences under the monarchy. In the Roman magistracy there was no separation between civil and military commands. A praetor could just as well preside over a court of justice as command troops or administer a province.

By the principle of collegial responsibility every magistracy was as a rule simultaneously occupied by at least two persons. Moreover, every magistrate had a right of *intercessio* against measures of his colleagues in the same magistracy. This requirement was originally derived from the idea of equal authority and equal responsibility among the persons simultaneously occupying a magistracy. On all important questions it made it essential either that a consensus should prevail or that proposed measures should be dropped if there were no consensus.

The strict order of precedence among magistracies led to the systematic subordination of the lower magistrates to the higher, so that the occupant of a higher magistracy could actually veto the measures and decrees of the occupant of a lower. The magistrates had at their disposal only a very small number of subordinates to carry out their orders (lictors, scribes, messengers, etc.) so that nothing in the way of a bureaucracy developed, nor did the magistracy become dependent on its staff. Instead, the magistrates had to fall back on the help of members of their own families, their own *clientelae*, or their friends. They were supported in all questions of principle by a *consilium* on which friendly politicians or – in the provinces and theatres of war – all available *nobiles* were consulted. Further, continual attention had to be paid to the recommendations both of the Senate as a collective body and of its envoys, representatives and commissions.

In this way the holders of magisterial *potestas* were systematically prevented from becoming isolated or independent. At the same time the continuous exercise of power was hindered by a compulsory two-year interval between the holding of one magistracy and another, by impediments against the repeated holding (*iteratio*) of the same office, and by a ban on the simultaneous combination of different offices (*cumulatio*).

At the head of the continuously manned magistracies were the consuls as chiefs of the executive, both in war leadership and in general state administration. They were supreme representatives of the entire state. The praetors, as I have said, could function as judges, army commanders and governors. The aediles, of which there were two kinds, 'curule' and plebeian, had supervisory functions over the markets and business centres situated by the temples, and directed the market police. They were also required to manage the great games and festivals. The quaestors served as special administrative officials specialising particularly in the financial sector and, from 267 B C onward, as naval quaestors.

The dictatorship and censorship were not continuously manned posts. The dictatorship was an intermittent but regular emergency office of the whole Roman Republic. In its classical form it was an ultimate resort in the critical phases of great military conflicts between the Samnite Wars and the Second Punic War, on the last occasion in 202 B C. When Sulla and Julius Caesar later revived the dictatorship, its constitutional power base had nothing but the name in common with the original office. Originally the dictator was appointed for the term of half a year by a consul after a senate debate, and he himself then appointed his most important assistant, the master of the horse (*magister equitum*).

The primary task of the censors was to carry out the internal classification, registration and assessment of the entire population (*census*), a responsibility which in view of the increasing differentiation of Roman society became of greater and greater importance. Through their reprimands or deletions from the list of senators the censors deeply influenced the composition of the governing class. They were also responsible for supervising the entire property of the state, the fixing of payments and award of contracts in the fields of finance, taxation and public building. As a rule, a *census* was held every five years.

The total number of Roman magistrates was always extremely small, and it was kept so as a matter of principle. To achieve this, the Senate adopted the institution of the so-called pro-magistracy. Initially this involved an extension of office for a Roman magistrate who served on after completion of his term instead of being replaced in the normal manner, as for instance in a distant theatre of war. The *prorogatio*, or extension of command, was decided by the Roman Senate, which thus had a means of maintaining in decisive positions persons whom it trusted.

In economic terms the Roman nobility always considered itself an aristocracy of landowners, even though in the first century BC this function was more of a show than a reality for many of its members. One decisive step, however, towards the preservation of this homogeneous character of land ownership among the senatorial aristocracy was the *lex Claudia de nave senatorum* of 218 BC, which practically excluded senators from participation in sea freight and transport business and thus in overseas trade. The subsequent expansion of land ownership among senators was among the consequences of this law, coupled with the fact that the strongest economic initiatives, especially large-scale mercantile and financial business, were from now on conducted by the *equites* ('knights').

Originally, any Roman citizen serving in the Roman army on horseback was designated an *eques*. Owing to the fact that both the army and the voting system were 'timocratic' – based on property qualifications – the group of *equites* included the members of the nobility and the rest of the senators, but it also took in all those wealthier citizens who belonged to the cavalry but not to the Senate. As Roman society differentiated, a separation came about between senators on the one hand and 'knights' on the other. Not all *equites*, however, were big businessmen, bankers and tax-collectors. They also included the ruling class of the Italian country towns, who had acquired their property mostly in agriculture. As a social group the *equites* thus had an economic base appreciably less uniform than that of the Roman senators. The *lex reddendorum equorum* of 129 BC compelled the senators to give up their cavalry horses, and thus outwardly distinguished them from the *equites*. Their further development as an 'order' occurred in the time of the Gracchi, when the *ordo equester* was consciously brought into politics as opposition to the Senate.

The free Roman citizen who did not belong to the Senate could give effect to his political will only within the framework of the different kinds of popular assembly, the *comitia curiata*, the *comitia tributa* and the *comitia centuriata*. Of these the *comitia curiata* was the most ancient system of ordering the Roman people, which it divided into 30 *curiae*, clan and family associations. This system was retained for certain sacral procedures.

In the course of the Struggle of the Orders, the *comitia curiata* (which at first was completely controlled by the patricians) was confronted by the *comitia tributa (plebis)*, developed in opposition to it. These assemblies of the plebeians were originally organised according to residential districts. From the third century BC onward the number of tribes was fixed at 35, but most citizens of the city of Rome were enrolled in only four of these. For reasons of organisation, membership of a tribe was so important for a Roman citizen that it virtually became a part of his name. After recognition had been accorded in 287 BC to the resolutions of assemblies of the people as valid for the whole state, it was this type of assembly in particular which rapidly gained importance because of its relatively simple structure. In the tribal assemblies directed by the tribunes of the people not only were the more junior magistrates elected but also the laws were passed, although it must be realised that these *leges* included quite a number of *ad hoc* measures to deal with a particular situation.

The most important type of assembly, however, was undoubtedly the *comitia centuriata*, composed of 'centuries' corresponding to military units. These were once simply army assemblies, and were accordingly divided into military troop categories (cavalry, heavy infantry, light infantry, special units, non-property-owning citizens). I have already pointed out that the Roman practice of making each man responsible for his own arms and equipment led to a differential system of voting. An order of society based on property qualifications found its most obvious expression in the centuriate assembly.

In its fully developed form, from the fourth century BC onward, the centuriate assembly comprised the following units, which were at the same time voting corporations:

horsemen	18 centuries		
1st Class	80 centuries	(40 *iuniores*,	40 *seniores*)
2nd Class	20 centuries	(10 *iuniores*,	10 *seniores*)
3rd Class	20 centuries	(10 *iuniores*,	10 *seniores*)
4th Class	20 centuries	(10 *iuniores*,	10 *seniores*)
5th Class	30 centuries	(15 *iuniores*,	15 *seniores*)
technicians	2 centuries		

bandsmen	2 centuries
capite censi	1 century

Total	193 centuries

Thus the eighteen centuries of cavalry were followed by a total of 170 centuries of infantry organised in five different classes, and there were five special groups at the end. At the same time the number of centuries making up the individual classes was not uniform. The eighty centuries of the 1st Class, originally identical with the heavy infantry phalanx, were balanced by the 2nd to 4th Classes of twenty centuries each and the 5th Class of thirty centuries. The classes themselves were divided into two age groups each, 46 being the dividing year, so that the 'juniors' were those from 17 to 46 years old, and the seniors those from 47 to 60.

We cannot tell exactly what property limits determined the respective classes. All we have are the figures given by Livy and Dionysius of Halicarnassus for the first century BC, the minimum property qualifications for Classes 1–5 being respectively 100,000, 75,000, 50,000, 25,000 and 11,000 sesterces.

The total of the five classes was then followed by the five special centuries. First were two of *fabri*, carpenters and smiths, men of special aptitudes like the modern pioneers. Then came two centuries of horn and trumpet players, corresponding to the military bandsmen of nineteenth-century armies, to blow the commands and play the troops into battle. Finally there was one last century for the proletarians, who fell short of the property qualification for the 5th Class and in the event of war were employed as batmen and orderlies.

To understand the ordering by centuries, particularly in its political effects, the important point is that the centuries had nothing at all to do with units of a hundred men. The eighty centuries of the 1st Class were undoubtedly much smaller, those of the remaining classes each many times greater than a hundred. Politically, however, their weighting was uniform and unambiguous. In voting on elections or measures, each century had one vote. They voted in order of their class, and a simple majority decided the result. In practice a decision was usually reached by the time the centuries of *equites* and wealthier citizens of the 1st Class had cast their votes. The mass of the poorer population was only infrequently called on even to give a vote.

The assemblies of the centuries, over which the consuls presided, could vote only on proposals laid before them, elect candidates regularly proposed and examined, or condemn or acquit those on trial. Thus they had no right of initiation. Yet however limited the responsibilities of these assemblies of the people may have been, they were not merely courts of acclamation, and the nobility did have to convince the entire people of the rightness of their policies in a continuous process. Thus as a matter of course the differences between different groupings among the nobility were imported into the assemblies of the people. This was where they had their wider impact, and this, again and again, was where the decision on the power and influence of the different groups was reached.

The classification by centuries was closely bound up with the whole development of the Roman army. In its early stages Rome had learnt from the Etruscans the Greek battle tactics of the phalanx, the close battle-line, and undoubtedly the Roman army had used these tactics up to the Samnite Wars. Correctly employed, the heavily armed legion was supposed to beat down all resistance by the shock of its closed impact. In the course of the wars in central Italy, however, the Roman army was not only increased in its mere numbers of men but at the same time introduced to a new tactical system. The legion was divided in depth into three fighting units. The first of these was made up of ten 'maniples' (detachments of 120–200 men) of *hastati*, who took their name from the old thrusting spear, the *hasta*. The second unit consisted of the ten maniples of the *principes*, the third of the ten maniples of the veteran *triarii*. In battle the maniples took up a chessboard-like position and were grouped each around a small field standard. Battle in general was begun by the flight of the throwing spears, with the maniples storming after, so that the fighting at close quarters with the short Roman sword usually started before the enemy had recovered from the shock of the missile hail.

When the ancient legion had attacked as a closed phalanx, the individual legionary was carried along by the impetus of the great mass of men in which he was embedded. But this older formation could only develop its full dynamism on open and level ground, and consequently was a direct invitation to outflanking or encircling manoeuvres. As an archaically primitive unit formation, however, it was easy to command. By contrast, the legion fighting in maniples could perform military operations only when all its members worked in co-ordination as a team. Its subordinate officers had to be continuously on the alert to give orders from moment to moment in the interest of the whole. Rightly handled, the maniples could combine a maximum of flexibility with an impact responding elastically to the situation. They enabled the Roman legion not only to operate on blind and broken terrain but also to set up shifting centres of gravity for attack and defence. The manipular tactics show how far the leadership of the Roman state could build on Roman discipline, and how absolutely it could rely on the individual in the service of the group. These were the tactics with which the decisive campaigns of the Republic were fought.

EXPANSION IN THE MEDITERRANEAN AREA

In the long, fierce wars against the Samnites (343–290 B C) and Pyrrhus of Epirus (280–275 B C) the Roman Republic had achieved the domination of southern Italy and at the same time established its system of alliances. Even these successes, however, were not followed by any lengthy period of consolidation. The expansion continued, extending over a larger and larger radius, leading to the destruction of all the Mediterranean great powers, and finally ending in the establishment of the great *imperium* that encompassed the whole Mediterranean area. This dramatic process cannot be described here in all its details. Only its most important stages and principal issues can be indicated.

Carthage had long been the leading commercial and maritime power of the western Mediterranean. It had monopolised large sections of the entrepôt trade, yet this did not endanger the Roman system of alliances in Italy. On the contrary, the Roman–Punic treaties (suggested dates 508/7, 348 and 278 B C) had regulated relations between the two powers, and in the struggle against Pyrrhus they had formed a common front, even though there were some causes of friction between the Greek allies of Rome in southern Italy and Carthaginian mercantile interests. All this was brushed aside, however, when the Mamertini, mercenaries who had seized control of Messana (modern Messina) in Sicily, requested Roman help and thus offered the chance of a Roman assault on the wealthy city of Syracuse, which promised easy and abundant spoils.

Seldom has an initially limited operation led to such escalation of its forces or had such far-reaching consequences as this step. The intended attack on Syracuse became a great war against Carthage, which, seen as a whole, after several eventful passages at arms, only ended in 146 B C with the destruction of the enemy. The minor attempted landing developed into an embittered large-scale war of attrition, forcing Rome to build fleets and embark on dangerous adventures. With a surprising victory in the sea battle of Mylae (260 B C) Rome joined the company of the great sea-powers. But the loss of four great naval squadrons containing a total of some 650 war and transport ships was due above all to the nautical incompetence of the Roman naval officers. The tale of Roman reversals and anxieties was further marked by a catastrophic invasion of North Africa (256–255 B C) and by casualty-laden sieges and mountain warfare in Sicily against such able Carthaginian mercenary leaders as Hamilcar Barca. Yet these too were surmounted after a phase of exhaustion. In a last access of voluntary effort, Rome in the year 242 B C built a Roman war fleet which finally, a year later, won the decisive victory off Aegates Insulae.

Even this victory, however, which led to the annexation of Sicily, did not satisfy Rome. Only three years later the great insurrection of the mercenaries of Carthage was exploited in the massive pressure by which Rome forced the surrender of Sardinia and Corsica. In 227 BC both here and in Sicily the Roman provincial administration was introduced and the first step thus taken towards the setting up of an imperial administration no longer contained within the Italian system.

The Roman expansion was not halted there. In northern Italy the process of colonisation was intensified; the Celts were once more put down; in the two Illyrian wars (229 and 219 BC) the first Roman bridgeheads were established across the Adriatic; and Roman concern with the Iberian peninsula was demonstrated in the Ebro treaty of 226 BC, aimed at checking the spread of Carthaginian influence in Spain, and in the conclusion of an alliance with Saguntum.

The Second Punic War which was thereupon launched by Hannibal (218–201 BC) at first plunged Rome in mortal crisis. The disaster of Cannae (216 BC) with its battle of annihilation, the conclusion of an alliance between Hannibal and Philip V of Macedon (215 BC), the mobilisation of former Roman allies (Capua, Syracuse, Tarentum) against the Italian federation, and not least the years of bitter campaigning in central and southern Italy seemed to be destroying Rome and its federal system. Yet after Roman counter-offensives in Spain and Italy and a new invasion in North Africa, P. Cornelius Scipio finally succeeded in defeating Hannibal at Zama (202 BC). He forced the relinquishment of all Punic colonial possessions, the surrender of all but ten units of the Carthaginian war fleet, and the payment of a high war indemnity calculated to impose a heavy burden on Carthage's finances for half a century.

But the Roman victory was dearly bought. Even one who does not accept the metahistorical connections propounded by Arnold Toynbee in the great work of his old age, *Hannibal's Legacy*, must take some account of the drastic changes produced by this war in the whole economic and social system of Rome. These I shall discuss below in greater detail. The generation which so successfully fought to a conclusion the heroic fight of the classical Roman Republic thereby opened the door to a development which was to change the whole structure of Rome.

However conscientiously Carthage might struggle to fulfil the peace conditions, the quarrelling with Rome's North African allies under the Numidian king Massinissa did not abate. When Carthage in the end took arms against these provocations it launched the Third Punic War (149–146 BC). This ended with the total destruction of the city, the enslavement of its inhabitants and the foundation of a Roman province of Africa.

The will to halt the power in Spain of the Barcids (Hamilcar Barca, Hasdrubal, Hannibal) and then to crush it had firmly attached Rome to the Iberian peninsula. But the take-over of the Barcid possessions and the establishment in 197 BC of two new provinces (*Hispania Citerior* in the north-east and *Hispania Ulterior* in the south) was not enough. The Celtiberian and Lusitanian tribes in particular offered a fanatical resistance. They combined a savage and embittered guerrilla war, in which their fortified hilltop settlements were defended to the last, with mass onslaughts destroying whole detachments of the Roman army. Famous for the latter was the undefeated Lusitanian, Viriathus. For decades Rome found itself involved in the most costly military actions.

The manner in which the Romans waged this war was especially vile. Terror, treachery, massacre of the disarmed, cheating, extortion, looting and exploitation were all in evidence. The failure of the generalship was obvious, and the reluctance of the troops very great. In 151 BC there was a mutiny of Roman conscripts destined for the Spanish theatre of war. And yet even here the determination and persistence of the Roman effort triumphed in the end. With the capitulation of the stubbornly defended city of Numantia (133 BC) the fighting, in which a great part of the Roman smallholder class had bled to death, was brought to a temporary end.

As the Greek historian, Polybius, had already seen (*c*. 200–120? BC), it was the Second Punic War especially which brought together the western and eastern power zones of the Mediterranean, so largely isolated before. Since his alliance with Hannibal, Philip V of Macedon had become Rome's greatest enemy in Greece. The peace of Phoenice (205 BC) ended the First Macedonian War, in which Rome had won the Aetolians to its side. When Philip V with the Seleucid ruler king Antiochus III began to annex the foreign possessions of the weakened empire of the Ptolemies, Rome was persuaded to act by Pergamum and Rhodes and thus got itself entangled in the quarrels of the Hellenistic states. A chain of interventions was the consequence.

In the Second Macedonian War (200–197 BC) Philip V was defeated, but the Romans again withdrew from Greece after the 'declaration of freedom' by T. Quinctius Flamininus (196 BC). In fact, however, Greece had already become a Roman protectorate, and Rome's commitment was so strong that an intervention by Antiochus III was answered with a declaration of war. Through a victorious campaign conducted in the main by L. Scipio and P. Scipio Africanus (191–188 BC) the Seleucid empire was much reduced. A notorious action by Manlius Volso against the Galatians of Asia Minor demonstrated the cruelty and rapacity of which Roman armies were capable. They enriched themselves in these areas without scruple.

For the very reason that Rome did not want to be burdened with a direct and continuous administrative and peacekeeping organisation in the Hellenistic East, what occurred was a profound process of fermentation and disintegration, further complicated by social tensions, all over the Greek and Hellenised world. There were repeated Roman interventions. After the Third Macedonian War (171–168 BC) against Perseus, the Macedonian monarchy was finally destroyed. On a single day in Epirus no less than seventy small towns and villages were demolished and their populations enslaved; in Aetolia some 500 supporters of Macedonia were slaughtered; and about a thousand members of the governing class of the Achaean League were taken to Rome as hostages, Polybius among them. When there were fresh disturbances in Macedonia and Achaia, Rome answered with the creation of the Province of *Macedonia* (148 BC) and with the destruction of Corinth (146 BC).

The radius of Roman power had long since extended to Egypt and Cyrenaica. As early as 273 BC Ptolemy II had entered into diplomatic relations with Rome, and out of these an official bond of friendship developed. The unstable kingdom of the Ptolemies, on the so-called 'day of Eleusis' when the Seleucid king Antiochus IV was subjected to brutal Roman diplomatic pressure, was thus saved from extinction at a word from Rome. It seems only logical therefore that the thoughts of Hellenistic monarchs when their dynasty was dying with them should turn to bequeathing their lands to Rome. This is how in 129 BC *Asia*, the first Roman province on the soil of Asia Minor, arose out of the bequest of Pergamum in 133.

In the accounts of Roman expansion it is noticeable that for a long time the fundamental problems were less intensively explored than the questions about the 'guilt' or responsibility for the outbreak of particular wars. Yet even Polybius had already distinguished between the occasions and the causes of the Second Punic War. Only limited results could be expected from isolated modern discussions of 'war guilt'. The key question is not whether the Romans in this or that case were justified on juridical or moral grounds, but how the continuity of Roman expansion is to be explained.

Quite recently 'the feeling of being permanently under threat' was described by W. Hoffmann as the 'fundamental experience' of the Romans of the early Republic, and he went on to discuss the constant factors in such a psychological condition. Of course we can point to the many serious threats to the city by neighbouring tribes, Etruscans, Celts, Samnites, and later by Pyrrhus and Hannibal. But it is a very one-sided conception of 'security' to regard it as the sole objective of the entire foreign policy and military actions of the Roman Republic. This view, moreover, implies that Rome gave its own need for security an absolute value, that on principle it did not recognise powers of equal rank with itself, neither their interests, nor their spheres of influence, nor their security needs, and that the city in the course of a more and more vigorous preventive elimination of every opponent, whether actual, potential or merely imagined, established a 'world empire against its will'.

This notion of 'defensive imperialism', for all the support given to it by Theodor Mommsen, is wrong in its very inception. It is indeed true that the Romans in many cases were primarily interested in the smashing of power-centres (Carthage, Macedonia, Syria). They did indeed start as masters of destruction. But they were totally unprepared to complete the integration of the areas they conquered, and at first had not even the means to perform the administrative and political duties thrust upon them.

The argument that recurs so frequently with Cicero, that the Romans waged their great wars particularly to defend their allies and won their world empire for that reason, is just as unconvincing (*De Imperio Cn. Pompeii*, 14; *De Officiis* 2, 26; *De Republica* 3,35). The *fides* Cicero so often swears by was not honoured altruistically. There was an astonishing lack of proportion and extreme over-reaction in the fact that the respect for *fides* in the case of the Mamertines led to the annexation of Sicily, in that of Saguntum to the annexation of Spain.

Polybius, by contrast, already understood the expansion of Rome as a logical power-forming process. Even though we allow with Theodor Mommsen that 'the policy of Rome throughout was not projected by a single mighty intellect and bequeathed traditionally from generation to generation; it was the policy of a very able but somewhat narrow-minded deliberative assembly, which had far too little power of grand combination, and far too much of a right instinct for the preservation of its own commonwealth, to devise projects in the spirit of a Caesar or a Napoleon' (*The History of Rome*, tr. W. P. Dickson, Vol. II, p. 522), we still have to take account of the fundamentally action-seeking attitude of the Romans and their will to power. The existence of their governing class did after all rest on their continued regard for *virtus*, their ambition for *gloria* and *honos*, their permanent rivalry with all the other members of their own social group in the pursuit of reputation, authority and influence. In a later phase these motives for action were joined by more material ones, which explain their readiness to seize any chance of intervening or increasing their own areas of sovereignty.

From the beginning of the First Punic War onwards there is always a noticeable readiness to take major risks in the representation and defence of Roman interests. The consequences of intervention in the various geographical areas could perhaps not be foreseen in every case, yet once the way had been taken it was followed with single-minded consistency wherever it might lead. Where territories once occupied had to be evacuated, as under T. Quinctius Flamininus in Greece or under the Scipios in Asia, it soon turned out that this apparent retreat and the indirect rule which followed it were no less fateful for the areas concerned than an immediate incorporation in the *imperium Romanum*, which then always proved just as inevitable in the end.

The use of the modern term 'imperialism' for the process of Roman expansion is not advisable. It is a concept with too many implications that are not relevant to the conditions of Rome. Loaded with political experiences and phenomena of the nineteenth and twentieth centuries, associated with features of modern capitalism and colonialism, frequently steeped in elements of Marxist theory, it arouses anachronistic associations and tempts us to unhistorical ideas. The quest for raw materials or the slave trade had in the beginning as little to do with Roman expansion as the search for new markets or investment possibilities.

CRISIS AND FALL OF THE REPUBLIC

From the beginning of the second century BC onwards there was an increase in that general sense of crisis expressed in particular by the elder Cato. Starting with such individual phenomena as luxury, depravity, corruption, moral degradation, the emancipation of women, it contrasted the decadent present with a glorified past. The profound economic, social and political changes were for a long time not recognised to their full extent or in all their consequences. The prepossession in favour of ancient norms and values, and the obstinate insistence on ancient privileges, had the effect of making it a 'crisis without alternative'.

In all this there were layers of tension and antagonism. Optimate senate politicians defended their corporate authority against the *populares*, members of their own order who, with the support of the Assembly of the People, were trying to bring in reforms. The Senate was struggling to keep within bounds the holders of the great military commands it could no longer dispense with. The occupants of common land opposed the agrarian reforms which sought to help the landless free citizens; privileged full Roman citizens resisted the claims of the Italian allies; slave-owners fought rebellious slaves. All these conflicts were matched by others in the provinces and on the frontiers, and they all intermingled.

And yet no revolution ever came. The aristocratic state of the late

Republic, still dominated as it was by the nobility, was transformed into the Principate, the specifically Roman form of a 'masked monarchy' (M. Rostovtzeff); and yet in the end this brought about neither a violent inversion of property relationships nor a systematic shift in social stratification. It was a long time, moreover, before the goal of this historical progression could be discerned.

The most far-reaching in their consequences at first were the developments in agriculture, the branch of the economy in which it is estimated that ninety per cent of the Italian population were still engaged. The devastation of the Second Punic War and the campaigning demands of the second century BC had brought about an extraordinary weakening and overstrain of the free smallholders who still provided the core of the Roman army. The changeover to pastoral and *villa* farming by the great landlords put them at a further disadvantage. This new type of villa enterprise was a specialised, rationally organised, market-led business. Its medium-size estates, each with one to two dozen slaves, produced olives and wine especially, but around towns also vegetables, fruit and other provisions with a ready sale. The members of the governing class generally had several such villa farms. By the second century BC the land owned by individual senators was already scattered across Latium, Campania, the Sabine country, Etruria and Lucania. By contrast, *latifundia* in the proper sense of the word, great estates with hundreds of slaves, did not at this time exist in Italy.

The preconditions for such far-reaching changes in agrarian structure were the great increases in the holdings of the big landlords, the continual availability of slaves, and the ruthless and one-sided exploitation of the common land, the *ager publicus*. It was for this reason that the reforms of the Gracchi (133, 123/2 BC) started at this point. They had become aware that the existing social, military and economic structure could only be preserved by the intensification of a policy of settlement and colonisation. Through them the tribunate of the people once more became an important power-base and instrument of opposition to the Senate majority.

Tiberius Gracchus was already aware of the close connection between agrarian structure and military organisation. The class of the small and medium farmers was subject to constant excessive demands. In their long absences it was their wives who had to manage the farms and household, though their difficulties were hardly ever noticed by historians. To relieve this situation, the basis of recruitment had to be widened, and this was done by constantly reducing the property qualification until it was finally abolished altogether and military service extended to the landless proletarians, the *capite censi*. This step is

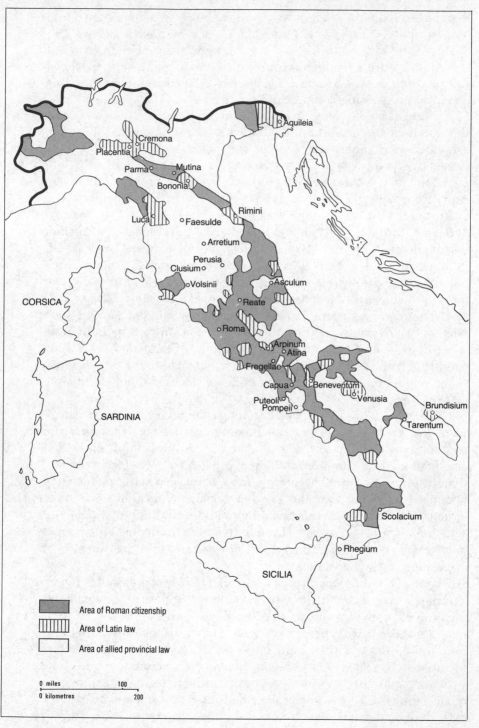

Aquileia

Cremona
Placentia

Parma   Mutina
        Bononia

Luca   Rimini
    Faesulde

    Arretium

    Perusia
Clusium
    Volsinii   Asculum

CORSICA   Reate

        Roma

            Arpinum
            Atina
        Fregellae

        Capua   Beneventum
    Puteoli   Venusia
    Pompeii

SARDINIA   Brundisium

                Tarentum

            Scolacium

        Rhegium

    SICILIA

▓▓▓ Area of Roman citizenship

||||| Area of Latin law

☐ Area of allied provincial law

0 miles   100
0 kilometres   200

4 Italy in 133 BC

associated with the name of Marius, and formed part of his comprehensive military reforms.

With it, however, the problem of maintenance for the troops became much greater and more acute. Hitherto the legionaries, each time they left the service, compensated with wages and a share of booty, had been able to return again and again to their old livelihood, usually that of a smallholder.But from now on, for the longer-serving landless soldiers when dismissed by the army commanders, a means of livelihood had still to be created. In this way, in attachment to the commanders, the great 'vassal armies' of the later Republic came into being, and this was how the old client system became swamped by the formation of a mass *clientela*. For Marius, Sulla, Pompey and Caesar, the problem of providing for their army units was a first priority. They either had to solve it for themselves, like Sulla and Caesar, or become dependent on politicians who promised to solve it, like Marius and Pompey.

At the same time the problem of the confederates was giving more trouble. Resentment at the heavy burdens imposed on them by the continual warfare waged by Rome was increased by the arrogance of Roman magistrates and the aggravating discriminations due to the reforms of the *ager publicus* and changes in criminal procedure in military courts. After the failure of some initiatives by the conservative reformer M. Livius Drusus came the great crisis of the Social War (91–88 BC), as the war against the allies (*socii*) has been called. The defecting Italians, especially the Samnites and Marsi, drew up their own war constitution and founded a state of their own. For the first time, a new political counterweight to Rome came into existence in Italy.

Only after several losses and far-reaching concessions was the Roman Republic able to surmount the crisis. In the year 90 BC all Italians who had remained loyal received full Roman citizenship, and in 89 BC this was extended to all who laid down their arms. The question of the admission of the Italians to the Roman citizen tribes remained in dispute, it is true, and the practical exercise of Roman citizenship rights still called for a citizen's personal presence in Rome, but the decisive step had been taken towards the levelling of political rights over the whole area of the state up to the Po, and it was accompanied, what is more, by a general standardisation of the Italian municipal constitution.

There is no denying that the period of the late Republic, like the age of the Struggle of the Orders long before, was dominated by problems of internal politics. Yet these were closely bound up with developments in the provinces and frontier areas of the *imperium*. The Jugurthine War (111–105 BC), a Numidian 'war of succession' in North Africa which showed up the corruption of the Roman aristocracy, and the struggles against the Cimbri and Teutones (105–101 BC) brought Marius to the peak of his career. The war against Mithridates VI of Pontus, who had practically extinguished Roman rule in Asia Minor and Greece, and in the year 88 B C had ordered the slaughter of tens of thousands of Romans and Italians, brought Sulla not only fame but also the military potential which he was subsequently able to throw into the scales against the adherents of Marius and Cinna.

In the years of fighting in Spain against Sulla's opponent Sertorius (77–72 B C), and in his great army commands, first against the pirates (67 B C) and then to establish a whole new order in the east (66–62 B C), Pompey won his high reputation as a general and administrator. Caesar similarly established his position by his campaigns in Gaul. Both cases, it is true, demonstrated the extent to which provinces and frontier areas multiplied the inner political disputes of Rome itself. Conversely, the conflicts of the late Roman Republic involved the whole Mediterranean area in their effects. The cities of Spain were drawn in no less than the German warrior king Ariovistus, Egypt no less than Athens. For quite a number of Rome's allies, their very survival depended on which side they were on in the civil wars.

The social development of the late Republic was marked by a progressive differentiation of all its social groups. Particularly striking was the concentration of wealth inside the governing class. The tendency for 'more and more to be owned by fewer and fewer' took on extreme forms in consequence of the various possibilities of enrichment open to the leading politicians. The compulsion to luxury and impressive display produced a provocative materialism in the life-style of the successful, while lack of success in a political career could be the ruin even of a great fortune owing to the cost of public games and rigged elections – as was shown in particular by the conspiracy of Catiline (63 B C).

In economic terms, however, it was now increasingly the new social groups, the *equites* and freedmen, who came to the fore. Since the *equites* were excluded from the offices of state, the *cursus honorum* of the senate aristocracy, they found themselves entirely confined to the economic sphere. They took over, either as individuals or through participation in companies, the distant trading, big business and large-scale money transactions made possible by Rome's dominating role in the entire economy of the Mediterranean area. They profited above all by the intensification of the money economy which now characterised the whole system; they assumed all those administrative and economic tasks which the Roman Republic with its rudimentary administrative machinery was quite unable to perform – tax farming, big building, military supply, procurement of materials, transport. Thus it was the *equites* and freedmen who developed the organisational, economic and financial skills which were first systematically used for the administration of state under the Principate. Such developments were a further demonstration of the deep-seated antagonisms of Roman politics. It was, for instance, the order of *equites* in particular to which C. Gracchus first quite deliberately assigned a political role, and it was the *equites* who assumed judicial functions in the trials of senatorial governors accused of extortion.

While the population of Rome became more and more concentrated in the city itself, there was no corresponding increase in the number of jobs. Although new business possibilities were opened up by public and private building, and by the demand for luxury objects, works of art, refinements of life-style, and services of every kind, yet the economic circumstances of the *plebs* in the city of Rome visibly deteriorated. The oft-lamented transition to an all-providing state began with the law introduced by C. Gracchus in 123 BC, guaranteeing every qualified proletarian a monthly ration of about three-quarters of a hundredweight of wheat at a preferential price. This finally led to the free distribution of grain to the poorer population of Rome. The whole development can also be partly explained by the fact that Rome itself never became a great centre of industrial production.

In the early Roman Republic there was no marked distinction between slave and free. Nor was there at first a need for additional hands, which is often taken as a prerequisite for the introduction of slaves. In the small workshops of free landowners, the required labour could be performed without difficulty by the members of the *familia*; and in the larger ones of the patriciate, by the clients on whom such services were obligatory. Prisoners of war, who at the beginning were probably killed, were later as a rule put up for sale, just like citizens enslaved for debt, and 'sold across the Tiber' (*trans Tiberim*). Thus in the time of the early Republic slaves were present only in very small numbers. In the mode of 'patriarchal' slavery, they were completely absorbed into the family and perhaps supplemented the free labour but were not the decisive element of the production process. Even in the Struggle of the Orders, the slave group played no significant part, which is one more indication that they were only of minor importance in society.

From the third century BC onward, however, these conditions altered visibly. Above all in the reconstruction phase of the Roman economy after the Second Punic War, the spread of the villa system in agriculture, and the social changes which accompanied it, led to a big jump in the number of slaves. New forms of economic organisation in many areas of agriculture and handwork isolated the slave from the owner's family. In not a few cases exploitation took intolerable forms, and the great slave risings were the consequence. The tens of thousands of slaves who joined them are evidence, too, of the importance already assumed by slave labour in the Roman economy.

The total number of slaves in Italy increased finally to such an extent that modern estimates for the time of Augustus amount to a figure of some three million slaves (P. A. Brunt) out of some seven and a half million inhabitants. To ensure the continuous supply of such a great quantity of slave labour, it soon became impossible to rely on the arrival of war prisoners in batches (in 209 B C 30,000 from Tarentum, in 167 B C 150,000 from Epirus, in 146 B C 50,000 from Carthage, to mention only a few examples). Consequently regular slave markets were set up, like that in Delos, for instance, which was equipped to handle a daily sale of some 10,000 slaves. At the same time there was an increase in the number of slave children reared by the slaveholders. This particular category of slaves (*vernae*) was regarded as specially docile and reliable.

The position of slaves was anything but uniform. While the state slaves working in mines and quarries, and the greater number of those employed in agriculture, led dull, strictly supervised lives, the herd slaves enjoyed greater freedom. Individual qualified slaves might be entrusted with supervisory functions, like the *vilicus*, the slave administrator, on whose abilities the yield of a villa estate was largely dependent. Still more favourable conditions were enjoyed by the artisan and house slaves, who often held regular positions of trust and became confederates of their masters. A variety of work incentives, and the concession of a precarious right to private savings or personal property (*peculium*), which could at any time be withdrawn, were designed to keep these qualified slaves contented. From this point it was only a short step to manumission. The class of freed slaves, however, was characterised like that of the *equites* by vigorous economic activity, often at the expense of the free citizens. For the freedmen generally owed their great influence to the connections of their former masters.

The part played by slaves in the economic sphere increased to such an extent that the development and consolidation of the new forms of economic organisation would be unthinkable without the institution of slavery. While the importance of the client relationship declined even in the organisation of labour, and at the same time the completely owner-dependent relationship so characteristic of slavery came to count more and more, a measure of state intervention such as might be applied to any group of free workers, as for instance through military service, was here as a rule not possible. Thus the institution of slavery actually strengthened the position of all citizens of property, and especially those of the governing class.

Against that, the gulf between slaves and the free poor was almost unbridgeable. The possibilities of turning Roman citizenship rights to material account had never been so great as in this period. Only the full Roman citizen was eligible for the grain rations and allocations of land; only he had the opportunity, by joining the legions, of acquiring a small property; only he could receive the presents of patronage (*sportula*), the material rewards of a client. Even among the slaves of different groups, the solidarity of a 'class' was lacking. How much more so was this the case between slaves and the free poor. Only now it was no longer unusual for freedmen and slaves in particular cases to command more resources and greater influence than the free poor.

The great slave wars in Sicily (I, 136–132 BC; II, 104–100 BC) and Asia Minor (the Aristonicus rebellion, 133–129 BC), a considerable number of almost simultaneous risings in southern Italy and Greece, and finally the rebellion of Spartacus (73–71 BC) shook the Roman state. Yet it would be wrong to infer that the structure of Roman society was finally stabilised by the suppression of these revolts. In Rome's great civil wars and internal political disputes the slaves became a courted instrument of power against the free. Marius and Cinna, Clodius, the opponents of Caesar and Sextus Pompeius, mobilised the slaves for their cause without scruple. In contrast Sulla, Catiline, Caesar and Augustus 'took the master's view', and in general refrained from infringing the priority of common interests among all slaveholders. Yet even here there were some striking contradictions. Sulla did not hesitate to give the ten thousand slaves of his proscribed opponents their freedom and employ these freedmen, his *Cornelii*, to strengthen his power. On the other hand, Augustus styled the civil war against Sextus Pompeius a 'slave war'.

Yet the socio-economic system of the late Republic was not only put in question from below, by the slave risings, but in a manner of speaking also from above, through the involvement of slaves in intrigues of power politics, especially during the civil wars. In fact it was the Principate which first sought to prevent such excesses and to achieve a new consolidation of the traditional structure of society. Yet it would be mistaken to regard Augustus merely as an agent or 'tool' of the slaveholding aristocracy (Staerman).

The efforts of the Gracchi had intensified the differences between *populares* and *optimates*. Neither group, however, was a constant political block, a party, as it were, of democrats confronting one of conservatives. It was primarily, as I have already indicated, a contrast of political method, because the leaders of the *populares* were also as a rule aristocrats, who were often prompted by strong personal ambitions. But the political equilibrium inside the governing class had been destroyed ever since the elder Scipio, and neither Sulla nor Pompey nor Caesar could in the long run be contained by it.

One thing which had particularly grave consequences was the increasing embitterment of differences in internal politics and the radicalisation noticeable from the time of the Gracchi onward. The appeal to force found an all-too-ready response, and the atmosphere was poisoned by the street fighting, political terrorism, and political perversion of justice. Sulla's proscriptions put method into political revenge on a scale never previously known. The personal and material obliteration of opponents became an example which was copied. It is true that Sulla's dictatorship (82–79 BC) also offered one last chance for a systematic restoration of the traditional aristocratic state. Yet comprehensive though this great re-organisation of the Republic might be, with its enlargement of the Senate to 600 members, its reform of the *cursus honorum*, provincial administration and criminal justice, it was much too late for any long-term stabilisation.

In the years following, Gnaeus Pompeius was at first the dominant figure. But the 'imperial commander' was less successful as a politician than as a general, and with the First Triumvirate of the year 60 BC, when Pompey, Caesar and Crassus were already demanding that 'nothing should happen in the state to displease any of the three' (Suetonius, *Divus Iulius* XIX, 2), the final phase had begun of the accelerated, dynamic process of crisis in the Roman Republic. Soon Caesar seized the initiative. After the conquest of Gaul (58–51 BC) he was victorious also in the Civil War (49–45 BC). The adherents of Pompey and the Senate were defeated and dispersed in all parts of the empire. Caesar, ultimately dictator for life, became furiously active. A new enlargement of the Senate to 900 members, the speeding up of colonisation and urbanisation in the provinces, the utmost generosity in the award of citizenship to his adherents, extensive building schemes, the reform of the calendar and countless other projects testify to his tireless energy. But however many of his numerous political opponents might be treated to Caesar's clemency, on the whole his style of exercising authority, his quite open, often directly brutal assumption of all the powers he needed, more and more provoked the opposition forces.

The years between 60 and 44 BC were marked by an increasing polarisation. The establishment of Caesar's dictatorship would have been unthinkable except on the basis of his great army *clientela* and the mobilisation of a broadly based party of adherents at all social levels. Caesar's officer corps was recruited from the whole of Italy. Unlike Pompey, who had tried to win over adherents of the old nobility, Caesar was joined by numbers of social climbers, members of families not long in the Senate, *equites*, members of the Italian municipal aristocracy. While the optimate leaders of the senate aristocracy were concerned to keep their ranks closed – of the sixty-one consuls of the years 78–49 BC only seven belonged to non-consular families – Caesar did away with the old restraints. While up till then membership of the old families and patronage from within the optimate circle had been essential requirements of a political career, now the only decisive factor was Caesar's favour.

For Caesar it was always personal rather than institutional ties which counted. He had already based his rule in Gaul solely on individuals and had bound these individuals to him by friendship (*amicitia*) and favours (*beneficia*). His power stood or fell with their loyalty. In Roman domestic affairs the case was much the same. Here, it is true, Caesar adopted the tradition of the *populares*, it is true that he profited from the cause and prestige of Marius. But here too Caesar was not primarily concerned with abstract programmes, with positions or institutions, the interests of closed social groups, least of all with those of a class, but once again with the courting or elimination of individuals.

Above all, he had given an absolute value to his own person – and at the same time isolated it. As a result, his opponents too so to speak personalised the political and social crisis, and embraced the illusion that all they had to do in order to restore the republican order was to remove the 'tyrant' – the title which they had very cleverly pinned on Caesar. While Caesar undoubtedly failed to recognise the importance and the strength of the republican traditions which he openly trampled under foot, and which his opponents were able to mobilise against him, for their part the 'heroes' of the Republic, Brutus and Cassius and their sympathisers, unquestionably exaggerated the load-bearing capacity of the foundations of the nobility with which they identified themselves. The conspirators flaunted the words 'tyrant-slayer' and 'freedom', but the tyrannicide of the Ides of March (15 March 44 BC) was no *coup d'état* and no seizure of power. And yet neither was the freedom demanded by the group by any means a democratic freedom for all Romans or all citizens of the empire. This *libertas* was freedom according to the traditions and interests of the senate aristocracy, freedom for the governing class to practise politics once more according to the forms of the aristocratic state.

In face of a *plebs* systematically spoiled and corrupted by Caesar, in face of an army *clientela* and its numerous adherents, the conspirators with their political outlook could never find a broad social and political power base in Rome and Italy. There was no movement of broad sections of the people to identify themselves with their deed. However splendid the moral and political protest of the Caesar slayers might appear, it served a lost cause. The conspirators themselves, moreover, soon had to resort to measures contrary to the rules and spirit of the old Republic. The civil war, at first delayed by compromises, did in the end break out. In a quick alternation of power groupings, it soon encompassed the whole empire and led to an unimaginable and seemingly never-ending escalation of terror and violence (44–30 BC). In these murderous battles first between Caesar's adherents and the defenders of the old Republic, who were finally destroyed at Philippi (42 BC), then between the forces of Octavian and Sextus Pompeius (defeated in 36 BC), and last of all between those of Octavian and Antony (who lost the decisive battle of Actium in 31 BC), the Republic collapsed. From the creeping paralysis of these civil wars, from a sea of human suffering and personal disasters in all sections of the population of the empire there finally emerged a new, durable political order, the Principate of Augustus.

IMPERIUM ROMANUM

THE PRINCIPATE ESTABLISHED AND INSTITUTIONALISED

C. Octavius (born 63 BC), Caesar's great-nephew, whom the dictator in his will appointed principal heir and also adopted as his son, was called Octavian by his opponents. In the year 27 BC, however, he was honoured by the Roman Senate with the surname Augustus, which was also to become the name of a historical epoch, the Augustan age. The young man who, as Antony put it, owed everything to his name, in a revolutionary situation entered on Caesar's heritage. By giving political force to Caesar's will, by the ruthless application of material power, the mobilisation of Caesar's *clientela*, by unscrupulously changing sides but also consistently legalising his position each time, by the systematic broadening of his political and military base in a structure of solid permanence, and with a wide-ranging idealisation of his personal will to power, he was victorious in Italy and throughout the empire.

The senator Cornelius Tacitus, the greatest Roman historian, looking back one and a half centuries later, thus described this rise to power:

'After the death of Brutus and Cassius there was no longer any state army. [Sextus] Pompeius had been crushed off Sicily, Lepidus eliminated and Antony murdered. Even the Julian party no longer had any leader but Caesar [= Octavius], who thereupon resigned the triumvir title, assumed the consulate and contented himself with the full tribunician authority for the protection of the common people. He won over the soldiers with gifts, the populace with a guaranteed food supply, everybody with the delights of peace. And then, little by little, he began to climb, to gather to himself the functions of the Senate, the magistrates, of legislation. There was no opposition. The bravest had fallen in battle or been removed by the proscriptions. As for the rest of the nobles, the more slavishly they behaved, the more they were loaded with wealth and honours, and those who had benefited from the new state of affairs of course preferred the safety of the present to the dangers of the past. The provinces too were not displeased with the turn of affairs. They had been turned against republican rule by the conflicts of those in power and the greed of the magistrates. The laws had failed, having been rendered ineffectual by violence, intrigue and downright bribery.' (Tacitus, *Annals* I,2)

It would be a mistake to see in Octavian merely the great genius of individual action on the scale of world history, a man who, so to speak, by a single act of will decreed a new political system. On the contrary, Octavian-Augustus established and maintained his autocracy step by step in a lengthy dialectical process in which even the year 27 BC, the year when his position was legalised on a long-term basis, was merely one stage. Precarious though his situation was to start with, yet the erosion of the republican constitution was far advanced. A whole series of elements were lying ready to hand for him to use and incorporate in a new system under his own control. Among these were not only his military *clientela* but also the great emergency commands, conferring the supreme administrative power (*imperium*) for several years, such as Pompey and Caesar had held. They included also the separation of office from function, the erosion of the old principle of annual magistracies by prolonging their powers through extension (*prorogatio*) or repetition (*iteratio*). Finally too they included the practice to which Pompey had already resorted of entrusting administration of provinces to personal deputies – legates.

Paradoxically enough, all the great consolidator achieved to begin with was a series of new polarisations, first among the Caesarians themselves, then against the Caesar murderers, and finally against Antony, who had joined with Cleopatra VII of Egypt in setting up a personal regime, on the Hellenistic model, in the east. With ruthless opportunism Octavian himself was always changing sides in the process. The Senate was obliging enough to legalise his usurped position, as was Antony to defeat the Caesar murderers and give repeated assistance against Sextus Pompeius. But any return obligation, in good Roman *fides*, towards these associates was far from Octavian's thoughts.

The unfaltering success of Octavian's consolidation of power is surprising for the very reason that he himself was not a great general with the charisma of an Alexander or a Caesar. The peculiarity of the Augustan Principate can be most clearly seen in comparison with the dictatorships of Caesar and Sulla. Each of these was a short-term, logically imposed framework of government with the unconcealed use of force. But the Principate was a medium-term political process in which opposites were reconciled and force was most carefully camouflaged. The construction and expansion of the Augustan Principate were not a simple matter of piling up spheres of responsibility. On the contrary, Augustus ostentatiously contented himself with a few, decisive elements of authority, an *imperium proconsulare* which gave him the supreme command of far the greatest part of the army, an *imperium consulare* for the city precincts of Rome (from 19 BC onward) and the expanded powers of the tribunate of the people (from 23 BC onward). Even the *imperium proconsulare* was for a limited term; the years of the *tribunicia potestas* were specified; provocative assignments 'for all time' – like Caesar's *dictator perpetuo* – were avoided. Augustus used to boast that he had not taken a single magistracy in conflict with ancestral custom or ever possessed greater official powers than his colleagues in the office concerned. He was able to reject the dictatorship, or the consulship for life or other offices, and trust merely to his all-surpassing *auctoritas*.

In the establishment and consolidation of the new political system, we must not underestimate the importance of the Augustan ideology. From the very beginning it helped to justify and legitimate his own claims, and to make propaganda for his own achievements. It was thus in line with ancient traditions of the Roman governing class, who had always been obliged to make a parade of the grounds on which they based their own social prestige. Literature, coins, architecture, public games had been from time immemorial called in aid by noble families to keep alive in the minds of all the citizens the achievements of their respective *gentes*. What was new, however, in Augustan propaganda was the size of the 'tool kit', the scale of manipulation of views, the monopolisation of public opinion, and the gradual identification of one man and his family with the sovereignty of the state, the *maiestas rei publicae*. But it was not only claims and achievements which the Augustan ideology indoctrinated. Its slogans also preached integration; they helped to strengthen the system and make it fast; they gave prominence to the chosen successors of Augustus, and were a decisive factor in identifying the family of the *princeps* with the state.

Octavian had first taken to the field with the motto 'revenge for Caesar'. He appealed to *pietas*, his own sense of filial obligation, to his adoptive father. Then his fight against Sextus Pompeius and Antony was launched under an all-Italian banner. His opponents were systematically discredited as enemies of the Italian tradition and the existing social order which he claimed to represent. The restoration and maintenance of peace, the re-establishment of ordered government (*res publica restituta*), and the cleansing of military honour were central elements of his propaganda. It would be quite wrong to dismiss all the formulations of this ideology as lies. Their appeal to broad sections of the population whose hopes and wishes they systematically idealised was no small ingredient in their success.

However we define the principate of Augustus constitutionally and politically, whether as a 'masked monarchy' or a 'constitutional monocracy', it is clear that after the failure of Caesar's undisguised dictatorship Augustus was bound to respect the strength of the republican tradition and take great care to camouflage his own rule. It is characteristic how much trouble he took in his own chronicle, the *Res Gestae*, to plant the idea of continuity with the traditional state system, to hammer home the legality of his own position, and to cloak the basis of his power. It is easy to understand the Augustan method in the light of the historical experience of decades of civil war, and especially the lessons of Caesar's murder. But the new political system was heavily encumbered by its contradictions between façade and reality. It was to be a long time before the principate had become so thoroughly institutionalised that the naked exercise of power to the fullest extent became possible.

Under Tiberius (A D 14–37) the peculiarities and special features of the new system emerged more openly, for the very reason that this Claudian emperor was much more deeply impregnated with the aristocratic traditions of the Republic than Augustus. The old campaigner got into deeper and deeper embarrassments because he had no feeling for the subtleties of Augustan camouflage and political method. The extended family of the *princeps*, the *domus principis*, was as much disrupted by the ambitions of its women, however, as by the status-seeking efforts of a designated heir to the throne. The system became more and more heavily encumbered with rivalries of this kind. At the same time 'treason trials' were an indication of the compulsion to flattery and deceit which it seemed impossible to avoid.

The inexperienced Gaius, nicknamed Caligula (A D 37–41) next faced Rome with absolute rule in the style of the Hellenistic monarchies. All the offices and honorary privileges which had been held by Augustus and Tiberius were transferred to him *en bloc* on his accession, and the Principate thus confirmed as a complete institution. By his excesses in the abuse of power and his identification of himself with a variety of gods, Gaius then became the prototype of 'Caesar madness'.

Next Claudius (A D 41–54), dragged to the throne by the Praetorian Guard, a sort of clownish antiquarian, an over-zealous and well-meaning reformer, was never able, for all his good will and appeals to the achievements of his family, to achieve genuine authority. The administration of the empire drifted under him into the hands of qualified freedmen, on whom the *princeps* became just as dependent as on his women folk. With Nero (A D 54–68) at first a 'golden age' seemed to be dawning, but only so long as the young man allowed himself to be guided by Seneca and the praetorian prefect, Burrus. Soon his emancipation from his mother, Agrippina, who had helped him to the throne, and from his first advisers turned into an eccentric and uninhibited despotism. In Nero the fantasies of an autocrat were realised and their possibilities exploited to their fullest extent, in the declaration of freedom for the Greeks and the Corinth canal project no less than in the persecution of Christians and the excesses of public games and festivals. This was the *princeps* who above all others impressed himself on the imagination of his own and later ages, the one who fancied himself primarily as an artist but is remembered as matricide, tyrant, antichrist, agent of Satan on an apocalyptic scale, the lyrist who played to Rome's burning, the circus performer and idol.

Vespasian (AD 69–79), after a chaotic civil war, led the house of the Flavians to the Principate. These, in Suetonius' words (*Divus Vespasianus* I, 1), were 'a family of obscure origins and without important ancestors'. They were indeed a family of the Italian citizenry whom the power of the Syrian troops and the Danube legions hoisted over every social obstacle to the summit of the state. From the *lex de imperio Vespasiani*, the so-called 'certificate of appointment' of the Emperor Vespasian which has been partly preserved in an inscription, we learn that the new *princeps* assumed, in one flagrant bundle, all the rights, offices and privileges previously held by Augustus, Tiberius and Claudius.

This massive accumulation was all the more provocative for the very reason that Vespasian in other respects appealed ostentatiously to the example of Augustus. In reality his very idea of the principate was diametrically opposed to that of his already idealised predecessor. While Augustus had maintained the appearance of being still bound by the old republican rules of precisely limited terms of office and collegial sharing of magistrates' powers, Vespasian together with his son Titus (AD 79–81) year after year assumed the consulate, together with *tribunicia potestas* and *imperium proconsulare*, and in AD 73–74 also the censorship. Titus in addition not only acted as praetorian prefect but practically speaking as co-regent, and Vespasian moreover had quite openly declared that he would be succeeded in the principate either by his sons or by no one at all.

The enormous consolidation of functions for the *princeps* had thus already been introduced by Vespasian. It reached a new peak with his youngest son Domitian (AD 81–96). The youngest of the Flavians, who was at first not qualified by personal achievements, again adopted Hellenistic forms of monarchy in order to elevate and strengthen his own position. The accumulation of offices, the adoption from AD 85 onwards of the position of a *censor perpetuus*, the demand for exaggerated honours, or their toleration (like the style of address *dominus et deus* even among intimates, triumphal dress when attending the Senate, an escort of 24 lictors etc.), court recital of laudatory poems and intensification of emperor-worship were characteristic elements of a ruthless autocratic regime which, with its flamboyant exaggerations, aroused a strong resistance. For his successors, Nerva (A D 96–98) and Trajan (A D 98–117), it therefore became prudent formally to dissociate themselves from Domitian's style.

The 'adoptive emperorship' was the ideological answer to the new crisis of the system. Instead of the purely arbitrary rule of a despot who had attained the principate by natural descent, the regime of an adopted 'best man' was to be substituted; instead of a reign of terror and excesses, a humanitarian form of government devoted to the well-being of the state, devoted to all its citizens, especially the Senate; instead of an aloof, arrogantly isolated autocracy, a principate of justice, of modera- tion, of a decidedly civil character (*civilitas*). Tradition and the needs of the time were to be fully respected, but at the same time the Roman *princeps* must satisfy the ideals of a Stoic kingship. The ruler as a Herculean figure, at once father and benefactor of all men – these were the key notions which could newly establish the Roman Principate, even in the Hellenistic East. They cast an ideological spell under which it was possible for the crisis to be surmounted. An important contributory reason, however, was the fact that Trajan, by means of an expansionist frontier policy (A D 106 annexation of Dacia and Arabia, 114–117 Parthian campaign), was able to prove his legitimacy as *optimus princeps*. The soldier who came of the colonial élite strengthened the authority of the 'pinnacle of empire' more than most of his predecessors. The system of the Principate was stabilised once more.

Hadrian (A D 117–138), the philhellene more than usually receptive of new ideas, inherited a legacy of over-ambitious military offensives. In the intensification of frontier defence, civil and judicial administration and social policy, he became a 'restorer of the globe', while at the same time, by a variety of cultural and religious impulses, he gave new life to the riches of Graeco-Roman culture. The perambulating style of government of this tireless traveller was among the reasons why the special needs and qualities of every constituent branch of the empire received his full recognition. Only the Jews, who in the great Bar Kochba insurrection once again rebelled, were excluded by Hadrian from his synthesis of ancient civilisation in the *imperium Romanum*.

Under Antoninus Pius (A D 138–161), a pacific, righteous character, the empire enjoyed the peaceable rule of a pedant who made the Principate 'inconspicuous' (J. Burckhardt). With his social policy of moderate reforms, his strengthening of frontier defence, the correctness of his administrative procedures and dispensation of justice, and his markedly harmonious relations with the Senate, he was yet unable to ward off the new crisis which did then come to a head under the rule of the philosopher Marcus Aurelius (AD 161–180). While a new Parthian war and ceaseless irruptions of German tribes along the whole Danube front and down to Italy were shaking the *imperium*, while an epidemic of plague, insurrections, currency collapse and economic crisis merged in an almost endless chain of catastrophes, the Stoic *princeps* stood firm against all his trials. Filled with the ascetic rigour of the philosopher, Marcus Aurelius had grasped the narrow limits of human action. So in his meditations he declared his faith in Rome as in the Cosmos, without any possibility, however, of actually realising his vision of a rule which should respect the freedom of the ruled.

Paradoxically, it was Marcus Aurelius of all men who returned to the principle of pure dynastic succession. His son Commodus was already declared co-regent in AD 177, and when he became sole ruler (AD 180–192) his reign degenerated into an appalling exhibition of pathological and unbridled despotism. In excesses of bestial sensuality, an apotheosis of the *princeps* as gladiator, the perversion of the Hercules idea, the Augustan form of the principate was systematically debauched and destroyed.

PAX AUGUSTA: A WORLD EMPIRE

After his victory over Antony and Cleopatra, after the great triple triumph of the year 29 BC, after the demonstrative resumption of a 'republican' form of rule and the consolidation of his political power at home, Octavian on 13 January 27 BC laid down his special powers in the Senate and returned provinces, armies, and civil administration to the hands of the Roman Senate and people. When the Roman Senate thereupon transferred to him, at first for a term of ten years, the responsibility for the endangered or not yet wholly pacified areas of Spain, Gaul and Syria – in Roman terminology as his *provincia* – this decision constituted the foundation of the peculiar constitutional and administrative structure of the *imperium Romanum* under the Principate. The agreement between the Senate and Octavian was immediately made law by a resolution of the people, and therewith received the broadest conceivable juridical and political basis of support.

The decision conclusively legalised the dominant position in the state of Octavian, who since 16 January 27 BC had borne the honorific title Augustus. At the same time it transferred to the *princeps* the supreme command of almost the entire Roman army. It was the public acknowledgement by the old governing class that it no longer felt itself capable of solving the complex problems of the *imperium* without Octavian-Augustus, without his support, without his troops, and, last but not least, without his immense material resources. From that moment on, the new administrative organisation of the *princeps* took its place beside the old one of the Republic. This situation could not in fact ever lead to a genuine competition of rival powers. For while the administration of the principate was always unilaterally fanning out into new spheres, the 'republican' administration was more and more strongly dominated and penetrated by the *princeps*.

But the solution of the year 27 BC was in another respect, too, a compromise. Even Octavian was restricted in his own possibilities by the power of the Roman tradition. It confined him to definite constitutional and adminstrative norms, and restricted him by the limited number of qualified and loyal persons available for his far-flung tasks. This is the explanation for the continuance of relatively large areas of authority under senate administration, as also for the reluctance to intervene in local constitutional structures at a lower level. But what was decisive over all in the new political system of the Principate was that the functions legally transferred to the *princeps* took on permanence at the same time as they expanded and grew into independence.

The principle of delegation which was here basic, and which from now on remained characteristic of large sections of the imperial administration, had from the very beginning been a constitutive principle of the Roman Republic. From quite an early date it had been usual to delegate for a term tasks involving the sovereignty and authority of the state. Even the Roman magistracy relied on this basic conception. Thus in the formation of the *imperium* delegation played an ever larger part. As already described, parts of the tax administration in the provinces, together with a variety of economic tasks, were transferred to the associations of *publicani*, and there were encroachments on the chain of command which obviously infringed the principle of collegiality, of mutual trust and shared authority among office-holders, while as early as 55 BC under Pompey provinces were already being administered by legates – that is to say, indirectly. The important thing, however, was always the time limit set upon such delegation, which could never be without a term. The delegation of duties in the maximal form which it took in the case of Augustus of course entailed further delegation. But although at the lower levels of the system the individuals on whom the *princeps* devolved duties and authority were regularly changing, in his own case the term put on his appointment was side-stepped by successive renewals of his *imperium* and later, as the Principate became generally institutionalised under his successors, was altogether ignored.

In the administration of the *princeps* and in army affairs the fact of delegation was openly expressed by official titles. While the governor of a senatorial province under the Principate always bore the title *proconsul*, and did so moreover even when he governed a praetorian province and had held only the office of praetor, the official designation for the governor of a province subject to the *princeps* was *legatus Augusti pro praetore provinciae* . . . , that for the commander of a legion *legatus Augusti legionis* . . . . At the same time, provincial governorships and legionary commands were only some of the top positions which the administration of the *princeps* was in future to provide. Numerically speaking, far more significance must be attached to the recruitment of large groups of senators, *equites*, officers, and non-commissioned officers, together with the freedmen and slaves of the personal household, to staff the various areas of the administration, the courts of justice, and the army. These groups, which will be discussed individually below (pp. 66ff.), were immediately subordinate to the *princeps*.

The administration of the provinces was thus characterised from the time of Augustus by the coexistence of both imperial and senatorial provinces. At first no more than a few 'great' provinces – Lusitania, Tarraconensis, Gallia, Syria, Cilicia, Cyprus, and Aegyptus – had been assigned to the *princeps*, whereas the Senate kept control of a far greater number of provinces: Asia and Africa, both governed by former consuls, Sicilia, Sardinia, Baetica, Macedonia, Achaia, Dalmatia, Creta et Cyrene, Bithynia et Pontus, all of which were governed by former praetors. But alongside these two main categories there were also smaller administrative districts, subject either to prefects, as for instance the Cottian Alps and the Maritime Alps, or to procurators, as Judaea for instance, which in A D 6 was made into a procuratorial territory dependent on Syria. In these territories the influence of the *princeps* was dominant, just as it was in the client kingdoms which, from being partly integrated in the *imperium* and partly annexed to it, often in the course of further development were converted into provinces.

In the context of the administration of the Roman empire as a whole, one of the most important features of the Principate was the systematic evolution of a separate financial administration for the *princeps*, with its own range of specialised functions. Of course even for Augustus it was not possible to alter the existing principles and forms of administration at one blow. As before, indirect taxes, customs and harbour dues continued to be collected largely by private agents, but in distinction from the excesses of the later Republic, the rates of levy were precisely laid down, the collection itself was supervised, and the tax-farming associations of the *publicani* were gradually eliminated, although partly, it is true, not until the second century A D. Procurators of the *princeps* in every province began to assume supervision of the financial management of all moneys and property accruing to the *princeps*. It was in practice always possible for them to report directly to the *princeps* on anything they found amiss.

The interweaving of the responsibilities of Senate and *princeps* is shown even more impressively in the management of the central funds of the imperial treasury. The traditional state treasury, the *aerarium Saturni*, remained as before in the Senate's hands and was managed by two praetors. In practice, however, all that they handled were the surpluses from the accounts of the individual senatorial provinces and the general account settlements, whereas the great part of the available revenues of the Roman state were now administered by the new finance offices of the *princeps*, introduced by Augustus. The most important of these was the *aerarium militare*, a supply fund for the whole of the armed forces. It had been funded originally by Augustus with an initial gift of 170 million sesterces. Later it received the proceeds of particular taxes, such as the 5 per cent inheritance tax, the *vicesima hereditatum*, and the 1 per cent sales tax, the *centesima rerum venalium*. Alongside this, however, increasing importance became attached to the *fiscus (Caesaris)*, the real exchequer of the *princeps*, with its many public offices for receiving taxes, fines, the proceeds of sequestered property, and the like. Strictly separate from that was the *patrimonium*, the private property of the *princeps*.

Thus the year 27 BC was also a decisive watershed in the history of Roman administration. More important here than the detail of the many procedural novelties and shifting responsibilities is the fact that from the time of Augustus onwards the provinces as never before were systematically organised as continuously administered units of the *imperium*. Until then the coherence of the *imperium* had been merely a claim, now it became a reality. In most departments of the administration, successive short-term improvisations gave way to continuous responsibility and control. The increase in administrative efficiency, however, was not only a powerful means of incorporating all the non-Italian territories in the *imperium* but at the same time the way by which the new political system constantly widened its base.

Even under Augustus the development, as I have said, was characterised by a continual increase in the range of the *princeps'* responsibilities. But this did not mean that the *princeps* of his own accord had been seizing one new responsibility after another; rather that, in some crisis or through the inadequacy of the senatorial administration, new tasks were thrust upon him. Let me give just one illustration of the burdensome consequences such a commission could have. In the year 22 BC, in a dangerous procurement crisis, the *cura annonae*, the responsibility for Rome's grain supply, was delegated to Augustus. By the direct take-over of this sensitive and critical branch of the administration, Augustus was not only compelled to limit the number of those entitled to a monthly ration of corn (to 320,000 persons) and to subject the distribution procedure to supervision by his own prefects, the *praefecti frumenti dandi*; much more than that, he was soon faced with the task of guaranteeing a continuous and adequate supply of corn to Rome. Augustus put this under the management of his own *praefectus annonae*, one of the highest equestrian functionaries of his whole administration. But the radius of necessary action extended still further. It involved the building of great granaries, the enlargement of transshipping harbours, the safeguarding of transport capacities, and the acquisition of grain in areas of surplus. It is easily seen how the *annona* became a pivot of the economic administration of the *imperium*.

Joseph Vogt once demonstrated that the idea of Roman rule embracing the whole *oikoumene*, the whole inhabited and known world, was derived from Greek thinking of the second century BC, and he proved that the idea of Roman world rule, as so variously expressed, above all by Cicero, was in entire accord with the Romans' conception of themselves in the late Republic. In whatever way Roman rule was legitimised, whether as a gift of the gods in return for the scrupulous exactness of Roman respect for their will, or as the reward of superior Roman morality, the proverbial *mores maiorum* and the Roman virtues, or as a consequence of the well-balanced constitution of the Roman Republic, the conviction of the legitimacy of this rule was deeply grounded and generally held. The Roman idea of the just war (*bellum iustum*), that is, of a war declared in legitimate form, a war intended in self-defence, for the protection of a people's own rights, its own honour, or the support of its allies, contributed substantially to the fact that no doubts were ever entertained about the legitimacy of the extension of Roman rule. It was without a hint of cynicism that Cicero could say: 'Our people by defensive wars on behalf of its allies has taken possession of the whole world' (*De Re Publica* III, 35).

The idea of Roman world rule, however, was not only an element of political terminology but at the same time a result of historical experience. By Pompey, 'the Great', the Alexander ideology had been resuscitated; under him a Roman army had penetrated the region of the Caspian Sea. Then Caesar in the west reached the boundaries of the *oikoumene*, and forced open the gates to Britannia and Germania. The destruction of the Dacian kingdom under Burebistas and the overthrow of the Parthian kingdom seemed only a matter of time. Of course there had been setbacks in the East under Crassus and under Antony, but there was never a doubt that the Parthian kingdom could not withstand a Roman assault, if only all the Roman forces were thrown into it.

Long-range expectations and sober analysis conflicted with one another under Augustus. Augustan literature contains a number of indications that far-flung military operations on a Caesarian scale were expected also from Caesar's heir after 30 BC. Would not such campaigns moreover furnish the best opportunity of launching against a common foe the legions fragmented by the civil wars and thereby weld them together once again? Even the criteria and standards of the older governing caste, to say nothing of the high expectations entertained of the leaders of the great vassal armies of the late Republic, seemed a direct compulsion to further conquests.

In fact, later *principes* in comparable situations did yield to the compulsion of 'justifiable' military or political action of an external kind, especially when their own qualifications were in doubt, or when their succession to the throne was in question or they had to establish it through civil war. Cases in point can be seen in the annexation of Britain under Claudius (AD 43), the over-reaction of Vespasian and Titus in putting down the Jewish rebellion (AD 70), the opening of a new offensive in Germany by Domitian (AD 83), the destruction of the Dacian kingdom and the occupation of Arabia by Trajan (AD 106), and the new offensives of Septimius Severus in Parthia and Britain.

Augustus was not, however, the man for great visionary plans of campaign in the style of Caesar. After 30 BC he gave precedence to the internal political stabilisation and the consolidation of the *imperium*. By so doing he was able not only to satisfy the motherland's longing for peace but at the same time to profit from the fact that the maintenance of his power base could more easily be justified by military and political tasks still to be undertaken and still unfinished. A direct reference was in fact made in the Roman Senate, on 13 January 27 BC, to the tasks still awaiting performance. At the same time Augustus saw to it, by every means and in every form of propaganda, that the conclusion and maintenance of peace was celebrated as his decisive achievement. The *princeps* had thus become the personal guarantor of peace. The *pax Romana*, the reign of peace created by the Roman Republic within its area of influence, became the *pax Augusta*, so that any opposition to the new reign of peace could at the same time be labelled as a threat to peace itself.

Pax is a relatively late Roman abstraction. It was Caesar who first introduced it as an element of political terminology. It was represented for the first time on his coins in the year 44 BC, but there are indications that he wanted to bring in a cult of *Pax* to the *imperium*. Octavian did then celebrate peace with special emphasis as early as 36 BC, after the overthrow of Sextus Pompeius, and again after his return from the east, when in 29 BC he ordered his first closure of the temple of Janus

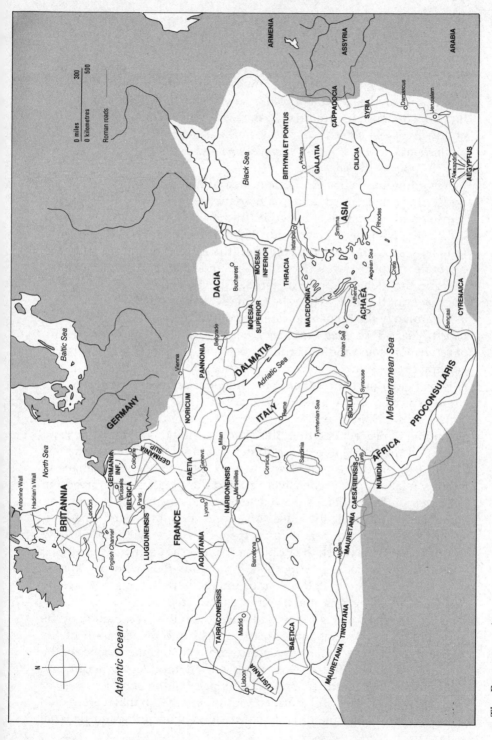

5 The Roman empire, AD 117

as a symbol of the peace won by land and sea throughout the Empire.

Peace and concord were thus placed under the protection of the goddess *Pax*, who was often identified by the herald's wand, the *caduceus*, though also by the olive branch and the horn of plenty. It was particularly in her beginnings, however, that the image of clasped hands appeared as a symbol of the new abstraction. Thus *Pax* always had two dimensions. Internally, she was closely connected with the goodwill of all citizens to one another, *concordia*. Externally, the attainment of peace was always associated with the supremacy of Roman power, the *imperium*.

According to the ancient Roman idea of the *pax deum* (peace of the gods) the achievement and maintenance of peace lifted Augustus himself into the sphere of the gods. In the Greek parts of the empire it linked him with the Alexander ideology. The dedication in Rome on 30 January 9 BC of the *Ara Pacis Augustae* (the Altar of Augustan Peace) to celebrate Augustus' safe return from Gaul and Spain, and the many variations on the theme of peace in Virgil, Tibullus and Horace, document the power of the idea. When the Cumae calendar celebrates Augustus as Guardian of the Roman Empire and of the Peace of the Globe (*custos imperii Romani pacisque orbis terrarum*), it is bringing together the *imperium Romanum* and the order of peace in an association which, according to the Romans' conception of themselves, had always existed. It is no matter of chance, therefore, that *principes* as different from one another as Nero and Vespasian both adopted this conception of peace.

The contradictions and tensions between world dominion and the dominion of peace inherent in the historical situation of the year 30 BC pervaded the whole age of the Principate, until finally, from the last third of the second century AD onward, the fundamental changes in foreign relations comprehensively altered the situation and forced the *imperium* on to the defensive. But ideological constructs, fictions and illusions maintained the idea of world dominion and made it coterminous with the *pax Augusta*. It was the very synthesis of these contrary elements which the Principate claimed as its own. Thus, too, it was not only quietist *principes* like Antoninus Pius who proclaimed policies primarily of defence and integration, but also far-seeing experienced soldiers as able as Tiberius and Hadrian.

Of course the *pax Augusta* was identical with the preservation of the new political system of the principate, with the preservation of the existing social and economic structure, and with the maintenance of the primacy of Rome. But it was in no way a product of deceit and exploitation. For centuries, in almost all parts of the *imperium*, the *pax Augusta* was accepted and affirmed for the very reason that it offered an effective and stable rule of law; that it stood above local and regional conflicts of interest and party, and was not involved in everyday disputes; and, last but not least, because it must have had the effect of a deliverance after the aristocratic misrule of republican provincial administration and the excesses of the civil wars. The sober recognition of Roman achievements, the permanent military security, and the high standard of administrative, judicial and fiscal efficiency did more to identify a public with the Roman system than any manipulation of minds through panegyric, cult or ideology. The Roman empire as a power system was not an invention of ideologues but an experience of every day. The *pax Augusta* was not only a propagandist slogan but a wide-ranging reality.

SOCIETY, POLITICS AND ECONOMICS

The basic social structure

With the conclusion of the Struggle of the Orders, the gradations of Roman society became more and more strongly marked. They corresponded with the classes of the centuriate system, ranked according to property qualifications, as we have seen, and combining military with social and political duties. But what remained decisive about this system was that it originated in the single Roman *classis*; it was an association of the phalanx, the Roman citizen-army. It grew, that is, out of a unit which became more and more subdivided, not out of an original cleavage of society itself, not out of an antagonism of different classes. Of course there were political and social polarisations, like the oppositions we have discussed between patricians and plebeians, patron and client, optimate and *popularis*. But it was the political and social union of all free citizens that mattered, not the antagonism of different classes as defined today. The Roman concept of *classis* is based upon the inclusiveness and domination of a unified, if differentiated, primary structure, whereas the fundamental antagonism between different classes is implicit in modern definitions of class.

This fundamental idea of a system of social grades determined both the political order inside the Roman state and the constitutional relationships of political power within the whole area of its rule. It was not till Late Antiquity, by contrast, that levelling ideas of race, religion or social class came to polarise Roman society. Then such abstract extremes as 'Roman' and 'Barbarian', 'Christian' and 'Pagan', *honestiores* and *humiliores*, simply dominated the whole picture, even though the antagonisms themselves had been planted earlier. For the Republic and Principate on the contrary, within the determining units of the *res publica* and the *imperium Romanum*, what mattered was the pluralism of the *ordines* and the legal gradations of both, the cultural and the economic and political units. It is characteristic that when the Roman Principate was at its peak in the second century A D, it was not general abstractions which figured on the official coins of the empire, the most important vehicles for portraying the state's own conception of itself. What strikes us is the very multiplicity of images representing deities and powerful beings, of virtues and values, of the armies, provinces and branches of empire.

At the centre of the area of Roman power, at the Roman–Italian core of the *imperium Romanum*, the progressive economic and social differentiation in the period of the late Republic led to an increasingly clear demarcation of the *ordines* of the governing class, the orders of senators and *equites*. In parallel with this, however, there were increases in the importance of the municipal aristocracy and the long-serving military garrisons; there came the 'massing of the *clientelae*', the loss of social status by the *plebs urbana* and the *plebs rustica*, and the consequences, disastrous even in the short term, of the rapid increase in the proportions of slaves and freedmen in many sectors of the Roman economy.

Adjoining this central core, there were large territories with what were often completely different social class systems and economic foundations, formed by ancient traditions of the region. The Roman–Italian social structure did indeed assert itself, if often only in rudimentary form, in the intensively Romanised districts of northern Italy and also in Provence and southern Spain, but in other parts of the *imperium* the old structures remained dominant. In the interior of Gaul and in the Rhine zone, the role of slavery was quite secondary, as also in extensive parts of the Danube region. In the cities of Greece, Asia Minor and Syria, the structure of society changed just as little under Roman rule as in the tribal associations inhabiting backward territories only half-civilised, in the village communities of the Arab–Syrian frontier and in the interior of Asia Minor, in the priestly states incorporated in the empire, or in the client kingdoms allied with it.

But Augustus never pursued the aim of overturning or levelling social stratifications of this kind; he preferred to maintain them, remodel them, and above all make them work in the context of his own political system.

The varied structure of society in the *imperium Romanum* was further complicated by its accumulation of social levels and layers of civil law rights. The position of the individual in this society was defined not only by his wealth and family but also by his legal status. On the first count, he might belong to an old family of the governing class or to a new family of social climbers; he might rely on the prestige of great ancestors, or on the mere fact of being a *homo novus*, a newcomer who, thanks to his own talent and achievement but also to promotion by the *princeps*, had surmounted traditional social barriers. Of equal importance, however, was the second count, his legal status. He might be a full Roman citizen, or a member of an allied community with Roman citizenship rights, or a free provincial with citizenship of some reputable or not so reputable city or one with Latin citizenship rights, or he might be a freedman or a slave. A freedman of the household adminstration of the *princeps* during the first century A D might make a great fortune, or reach the highest levels of the state administration and himself have critical influence on the *princeps*, yet none of that could cancel the inferiority of his personal status at law, whereas any free Roman citizen, however poor and degraded, still enjoyed considerable legal privileges both in Rome and in the provinces. His appeal to the *princeps* (*Caesarem appello . . .*) withdrew him from the competence of the usual provincial course of justice, and guaranteed him the advantages of a Roman citizen court or even the judgement in final instance of the *princeps*.

Princeps, domus principis

In the system founded by Augustus, the *princeps* in the end became the sole commander of the army, the direct or at any rate indirect head of the administration, the governing statesman and ruler with such enormous funds and immense property at his disposal that he could personally take on the tasks of state. According to the appendix of the *Res Gestae*, the sums given by Augustus to the old state treasury, the Roman people and the veterans totalled 600 million *denarii*. This amount was in any case greater than the minimum property qualifications of all Roman senators put together. The expenses (*impensae*) provided by Augustus for public games, measures of relief and the support of individuals are described as simply uncountable. As is proved by the numerous preserved documents, petitions, enquiries and requests for legal assistance, acts of clemency or compensation, the *princeps* was also the source of justice, favour and social advancement.

All the same, the new political system was not identical with the rule of a single individual but with that of the *domus principis*, the family and dynasty of the ruler, his women, children, advisers, stewards and intimates. It was a characteristic feature of the new system that Livia, Augustus' wife, ended by seeking to share the rule with her son Tiberius; that Agrippina the elder, wife of Germanicus, in the crisis of A D 15 on the Rhine, took on herself the responsibilities of military command; that even a friend of Livia's, Urgulania, usurped an authority beyond the law; that the authority of state was again and again infringed by the ambitions and rivalries of the ladies of the *domus principis*.

But this happened not only in the beginning of the Julio-Claudian dynasty; later, too, female figures like Messalina, Agrippina the Younger and Poppaea Sabina were able to seize the initiative in the family of the *princeps* and, at least for a time, to determine the course of events in a way similar to that of the so-called Syrian empresses at the beginning of the third century A D. Paradoxically, the influence of the womenfolk in the *domus principis* was conspicuous in the very period of the Principate when, ideologically speaking, it ought to have been least so, that of the adoptive Roman emperors. It is true, Trajan, the *optimus princeps* himself, had his entourage of senior officers; but his wife Plotina, with his sister Marciana, his daughter Matidia and Matidia's daughter Sabina, formed a group which exercised an influence not perhaps so spectacular but in practice no less important than that of the first-century ladies. Both Plotina and Sabina came to bear the title *Augusta*. According to ancient tradition, Hadrian's advancement was attributable to the favour of Plotina, and women have never appeared so frequently in coin portraiture as the Faustinas in the time of the Antonines. But also forms of address and ideological constructs are evidence of the tendency to glorify the wives of the *principes*. The mother of the dynasty at a given moment was raised to the rank of *mater patriae*, not to mention individual honours of a still more exalted kind.

But it was not only the women and children of the *princeps* whose new status advertised the changing social realities. They were evident also in the status of his assistants and agents. In so far as the advisers of the *princeps*, especially his privy council, the *consilium principis*, were members of the governing class, there was nothing repugnant to Roman tradition in such influence. But obviously the old rules were no longer in force, as when the *eques* Sejanus rose to be second man in the state, or when Tacitus records that, because of his personal influence, Sallustius Crispus had greater power than many generals who had been awarded triumphs, and many former consuls, although he himself was not even a member of the Senate. Most provocation, however, was caused by the influence of the freedmen of the *princeps*. It must at the same time be well understood that the Roman *principes* of the first century A D simply could not have performed their functions without the qualified assistants of their private domestic staff. It was not until the growth, during the second century A D, of qualified personnel in all branches of administration that a decisive shift could occur in the staffing system.

The senatorial order

Politically and socially the most important group of the governing class within the *imperium Romanum* was still the Roman Senate. The functions of Roman senators were given by their newly regulated career of office, their so-called *cursus honorum*. The young member of a senatorial family, assuming he could prove the requisite minimum property holding of one million sesterces, would as a rule expect to embark on a senatorial career himself. If so, he would in general begin between the ages of 18 and 20 with a post on the vigintivirate, as one of the twenty who served on the commissions for the mint, for road management or for legal duties. This would be followed by service for two to three years as a military tribune in a legion and then, usually at 25, as a quaestor, the office which involved immediate admission to the Senate.

After the quaestorship there was a two-year breathing space. After that, the ex-quaestors could stand either for a tribunate of the people or for an aedileship, a step in the career of office which members of patrician families were not as a rule obliged to take. Then, at the age of 30, they became eligible for the praetorship. Under the Principate the need of praetors and ex-praetors in the administration and the army was especially great, so that senatorial careers from this post onward fanned out widely in accordance with the qualifications and interests of individual senators, but also with the staffing decisions of the *princeps*. As a rule, a senator would hold three praetorian offices after the praetorship, or in individual cases even twice as many, before he finally reached the consulate – or else had reached the end of his career. Among the posts open to ex-praetors was the legate who commanded a legion; the *legatus Augusti pro praetore* who governed one of the lesser provinces – *Aquitania*, for instance, or *Iudaea* or *Cilicia*; the prefect who superintended one of the central state treasuries; the *curator viarum* responsible for one of the great Italian public roads; the *iuridicus* or justice who presided over a court of middle instance; or finally the officer in charge of grain distribution or public works.

Only a small circle of all the senators, not even half of them, finally reached the consulate. The age at which a senator of plebeian origin could do so, even under the Principate, was normally 43, whereas a patrician could be as young as 33. The reason why the chances were so small was that in the second century A D only about 8–10 persons yearly could become consuls. Anyone reaching this office belonged to the governing élite of the *imperium* in the most restricted sense. After that he could become governor – usually for about three years – of one of the larger provinces, in which anything from two to four legions might be stationed, so that the governorship always involved an important military command. Besides that, the former consuls occupied key posts in the civil administration, such as city prefect, manager of the metropolitan water supply (*curator aquarum*), or controller of the Tiber basin, embankments and sewers (*curator alvei Tiberis et riparum et cloacarum urbis*). These last two offices were both responsible for sensitive sectors of the administration of the metropolis.

Although the *principes* made a big show of encouraging the members of the old patrician families and also created new patricians, the composition of the Senate body underwent fundamental changes. The select gathering of the Roman–Italian aristocracy became more and more an assembly of the governing class of the whole *imperium*. It is true that a recent analysis of the origins of Roman senators finds that, under Antoninus Pius (A D 138–161), of the senators whose origins are known over 57 per cent came from Italy. (Of those from the provinces 23.9 per cent were from the western, 46.5 per cent from the eastern, 26.8 per cent from the African, and only 2.8 per cent from the Dalmatian provinces.) Yet even more important is the fact that the proportion of Italian consuls declined from about 56 per cent under Antoninus Pius to about 43 per cent under Marcus Aurelius.

This glance over the senatorial career also indicates that all the important positions of the *cursus honorum* were subject to the direct or indirect influence of the *princeps*. From his twentieth to his fiftieth year the Roman senator was again and again dependent on the *placet* of the *princeps*, and that not only in the cases where the *princeps* expressly proposed a candidate as his own or caused him to be admitted to the Senate, as for instance when he had had him appointed *praetor*, but also in those cases where it was a question who was to govern such and such a province and for how long. It is true that the governors of the senatorial provinces *Africa* and *Asia* drew the top salaries of one million sesterces per year; yet long-term employment in suitable senior posts, and the consequent high salary, could only be expected by a senator who proved his loyalty to the *princeps*.

An essential condition of social prestige in a senator was to have been employed at least formally in a religious capacity. We know from a number of senatorial inscriptions that it was usual for members of the Senate to stand for one of the major ancient priestly offices, either *augur* or *fetialis* (member of the priesthood responsible for issues concerning international law) or *pontifex* or, like Tacitus, *XV-vir sacris faciundis* (the guardians of the Sibylline Books and trustees of non-Roman cults), or *VII-vir epulonum* (the college responsible for preparation of religious feasts). Undoubtedly the personal beliefs of the man concerned had in many cases very little to do with the holding of such a priestly office, but it was still an essential ingredient in his social standing.

Under the Principate as before it, landed property remained the essential economic foundation of a senator's position. In general, we are struck by the enormous disparities of properties and incomes. The two largest private fortunes of the age of the Principate, those of the senator Cn. Cornelius Lentulus and the freedman Narcissus, amounted to 400 million sesterces, which is to say that they corresponded in value and purchasing power to about 1,500,000 tons of wheat. According to R. Duncan-Jones, the value of the greatest private fortune in England around 1700 was no more than 20,000–40,000 tons of wheat.

Of the Roman senators under the Principate, the one whose property we know most about (as Duncan-Jones has shown) is the younger Pliny. His total fortune can be estimated at about 20,000,000 sesterces, which puts him twenty-first in the list of known rich men of that period. Of this amount, investment in land represented not less than 17,000,000 sesterces. Even though the property structure known from Pliny's case cannot be generalised – his property had been considerably increased by three marriages – yet its distribution gives us some important indications of the economic foundations of the senatorial class as well as its income and expenditure.

The younger Pliny owned three villa farms of large extent in the region of Lake Como, a town house on the Esquiline, a country house 17 miles from Rome near Vicus Laurentium, and probably two other villas near Tifernum Tiberinum. On this property Pliny employed a total of 400 slaves, and in his will he made provision for 100 freedmen. We know from Pliny's correspondence that this rather influential man who was a friend of Trajan's received, like many leading politicians of the late Republic before him, a great number of legacies and bequests which still further increased his property. On the other hand, an aristocrat of his calibre was expected to make considerable donations if he wished to maintain his social prestige. The younger Pliny indeed distinguished himself in this respect by a quite remarkable generosity – donations of 1,800,000 sesterces for his freedmen, 500,000 for a private foundation in Como providing for the support of 175 children, 200,000 for the establishment and running costs of a library in Como, with considerable further sums for temples and private gifts.

Although such disbursements might do something here and there to bridge social gaps, the basic trend towards accumulation of property remained. In the words of Ramsay MacMullen, 'Beginning approximately with the birth of Cicero (i.e. about 100 BC) the tendency of socio-economic development in the *imperium* for the following five hundred years can be summed up in three words – "fewer possess more"' (*Roman Social Relations*, p. 38). This was in fact the decisive development affecting the Roman governing class under the Principate, quite apart from all internal differentiations and displacements. It is a tendency which goes far to explain the acquiescence in the Principate by the governing class, indeed its inward affirmation, for it was the Principate which guaranteed and ensured this development in the first place. It is, however, also a tendency which explains the elimination of politics from a society lacking an organised political opposition. In this society it was all the newly ascending groups from the provinces which profited from the principle of achievement. Consequently they had no wish to alter the system themselves on their own account but, on the contrary, wanted to keep it functioning and to stabilise it.

The equestrian order

Not only the Senate, but the order of *equites* too was carefully reconstituted under the Principate. In contrast with the relatively homogeneous class of great landowners and public service nobility which made up the 600 senators, the composition of the equestrian order was substantially more varied, its range of interests broadly based. The actual numbers of *equites* have been much disputed in recent research. Estimates for the Augustan period vary between 10,000 and 20,000 over the whole empire, with a considerable increase of this total in the following decades. There are, however, two more important numbers. From a systematic study of inscriptions, it is calculated that around the middle of the second century AD there were some 550 equestrian officers' posts, and that at the same time some 110 procurators' posts, or headships in various branches of the civil, finance and tax administration, were also held by *equites*. This has two important consequences. First, of over 20,000 Roman *equites*, only a fraction was at any time on long-term service in the administration of the empire. Secondly, the proportion of *equites* in the administration of the *imperium* was many times greater than that of senators.

Appointment to the order was in every case individual, by the *princeps*. The requisite qualifications were membership of a family which could prove free birth for at least two generations, and possession of a fortune of at least 400,000 sesterces. The sons of *equites* were not automatically admitted to the order, but usually they were. The coupling of the equestrian with the senatorial order remained close. Quite a number of members of equestrian families were promoted to the Senate under the Principate. There were also very close relations with the order of decurions, the municipal aristocracy. Quite often Roman *equites* were found as the most respected members and patrons of the city councils in the provinces, where they served side-by-side with the decurions.

An equestrian career in the imperial service usually began with a lengthy spell as an army officer. In contrast with the senators, these postings were usually to the command of auxiliary troops, and thus also in the smaller garrisons and frontier forts. The civil career would follow, with a post as *procurator*. The young *eques* had a chance to shine in a variety of managerial posts in finance, tax, customs and general administration. He could, for example, head the department administering inheritance tax over a group of several provinces, or the entire tax administration of a province, or be a leading treasury official in the service of the Principate. As with modern salary grades, the posts in an equestrian career were arranged in different salary groups of 60,000, 100,000 and 200,000 sesterces, with a top grade towards the end of the second century A D of no less than 300,000 sesterces. These grades were borne as titles, the individual *eques* belonging first to the *sexagenarii*, then rising to the *centenarii, ducenarii* or *trecenarii*.

Beyond this the *equites*, like the senators, were distinguished by status symbols and ostentatious external marks of rank. One group of them was still distinguished by the *princeps* with the so-called horse of state, the *equus publicus*. Under Augustus, it is said that at the yearly mounted parade of 15 July there were still 5000 *equites* taking part. Besides that, the *equites* were distinguished by a narrow purple stripe on the tunic, a gold ring, a special parade uniform, and seats of honour in the theatre.

It was among the *equites* especially that the progress and distinction of a career were determined by the trust of the *princeps*. Any equestrian *cursus* could of course end in the tangled undergrowth of the administration, but it could, with necessary achievement, especially in the closer reaches of the household administration of the *princeps*, lead to positions at the top, which in breadth of function, power, authority and influence far exceeded the highest senatorial offices. Among these especially were the posts always filled by *equites*: *praefectus classis*, commander of the fleet; *praefectus vigilum*, commander of the security police in Rome; *praefectus annonae*, the official responsible for the entire procurement and supply of food for the capital; *praefectus Aegypti*, whose position could be described as that of viceroy of Egypt; and finally *praefectus praetorio*, the commander of the Praetorian Guard. Such names as Sejanus and Burrus give an indication of the heights which an *eques* in such positions could reach.

Indeed, the career of Burrus is a typical example of the way these peaks could be climbed. From an inscription dedicated by the inhabitants of Vasio (Vaison-la-Romaine in Provence) to Burrus as their patron (CIL XII 5842), we learn that, after serving as military tribune, he was *procurator* in the households successively of Livia, Tiberius and Claudius, until he finally became praetorian prefect and thus occupied a position in which he acted jointly with Agrippina and Seneca as a virtual regent for the young Nero. Although Burrus' official standing was only that of a 'knight', he thus became one of the two most influential men in the empire, and his advancement was in due course confirmed by the award of the highest social dignity of all, the *ornamenta consularia*. Burrus was therewith adopted as an honorary member into the consular order, at the very peak of Roman society, although he had neither had a senatorial career nor held a consulate.

It was in the equestrian órder that the social mobility of the *imperium* was most clearly evident. From the time of Augustus onward, qualified freedmen who enjoyed the emperor's special favour, as well as younger aristocrats from the provinces who had commanded detachments of troops, were raised to the rank of *equites*. Arminius became the best-known example of this group. Particularly in the military sphere, moreover, there was a realistic chance, after a long spell as a centurion, of reaching the equestrian order. Nonetheless, varied though the careers of Roman *equites* may have been in the army and in the state administration, taken altogether this group of *equites* on empire service was only a fraction of the whole order. The overwhelming majority of the *equites* consisted of medium-to-large landowners, successful businessmen of the most varied kinds, bankers, overseas merchants, men who had made their often substantial fortunes in the most diverse ways. In their ranks above all, the knowledge and experience of economic organisation were concentrated. It is thus significant that this order in particular was the one to be systematically integrated into the new political structure of the Principate during its great process of internal growth. Finally we may notice in passing that the knights too could act as priests. Among the lesser priestly offices they could hold were that of *haruspex* (a priest specialised in augury from animal livers and the general reading of omens) and *lupercus* (originally the priesthood of 'wolf-averters', later specialised in animal sacrifice and purification ceremonies).

The municipal aristocracy

A specially important but at the same time remarkäbly heterogeneous social group was formed by the *ordo decurionum*, the order of city councillors, the municipal aristocracy. It must be emphasised that the social quality of this group was locally determined and that for that reason, according to the size, importance and economic function of the city concerned, there were considerable differences in the property, professions, rank and influence of the members of city councils. This heterogeneity results first from the mere fact that the minimum property qualifications for members of the *ordo* varied greatly from city to city. Thus to be a city councillor of Comum (Como) a census qualification of 100,000 sesterces, or a quarter of that for a knight, was required. That for other Italian cities was probably similar. But it is also known that to be a city councillor in one of the smaller North African cities 20,000 sesterces was enough.

The differences are due to the fact that the smaller cities found it extraordinarily difficult to muster the target figure of 100 decurions at all. Against that, the existence of every city depended on the competence of its council. To be a *decurio* was a double-edged honour. To be sure, it was only open to one who had been a free citizen from birth, who practised no dishonourable trade, was of good repute and 25–30 years old, and who was in possession of the minimum property qualification already mentioned, with its variations from place to place. Yet the position was accompanied by ever-increasing financial burdens. These the decurions seem to have been for a long time ready to shoulder, to such an extent that they were obliged to reduce their family property in the interest of their city. The decurions were not only obliged to volunteer for a year's duty without pay for the city offices of aedile (chief of police and superintendent of public order), *duumvir* (mayor) or quaestor (head of treasury). On first joining the city council they were each expected to make a public donation (*summa honoraria*) of some thousands of sesterces. After that, several more contributions to public amenities were expected, according to the old principle of public compulsory donations (the 'liturgies' or *munera*) – an entire public building, for instance, or parts of one, public baths, an amphitheatre, a temple, the adornment of market places and city centres, and of course public games, festival banquets, the provision of oil for bathers and so on. Local government, city management, the administration of justice, food supplies, cult provision, public works, diplomatic missions, for all these they might be responsible, to say nothing of a variety of special expenses, such as contributions to gifts and testimonials for the *princeps*, members of his house or other influential persons. In return for such expenses, which were often considerable and, in the larger cities, might amount to tens of thousands of sesterces, the decurions were distinguished by conspicuous privileges, seats of honour at the games and in the theatre, free and preferential water supply, meals at public expense and the like, and finally also legal privileges.

Several modern analyses of the social structure of the Roman Principate start from the basic notions that the orders so far described here, of senators, knights, and decurions, together formed the upper class of the *imperium*. We read in such accounts of a 'trinity' or 'social continuum'. There are emphatic references to the fact that in ancient literature each of these three social groups is expressly designated an *ordo*; that is, a juridically and precisely limited social group. However numerous the cross-connections between the three groups, this manner of viewing them overlooks some critical differences. For the senatorial and equestrian orders, the decisive point of reference is always Rome, so that the *princeps* is always involved in the structuring of these two orders, directly or indirectly. This is not the case, however, with the *ordo decurionum*. The senator is always a Roman senator, the *eques* a Roman *eques*; the careers of both are critically determined by the assent

or encouragement of the *princeps* concerned. By contrast, the member of
the *ordo decurionum* owed his social rank to local criteria, connections,
conditions, to local co-option or election. It is a mistaken inference to
count as a member of the upper class of the Roman empire the decurion
of a small North African city who, with great difficulty, has got together
his fortune of 20,000 sesterces and with it in Rome would be counted
only among the poorer citizens or at most the lower middle class. It is
probably more correct to distinguish between an imperial governing
class and a local governing class. The imperial would comprise the most
important members of the *domus principis*, the senatorial and equestrian
orders, leading military officers, and also, at least in the first century A D,
a few specially influential freedmen. The local would consist of the
municipal aristocracy, to which, by reason of their place of residence or
origin, individual members of the imperial governing class might also
belong.

The free citizens: the Roman army

In all its ideological publicity the Principate again and again made
official obeisance to the *populus Romanus,* but this must not deceive us
into overlooking the fact that the community of Rome's own free
citizens had been subjected to a process of systematic elimination from
politics. The centuriate assemblies, once the most important political
cells of the *plebs,* even in the days of Julius Caesar had still been a scene
of vigorous political self-expression. Under the Principate they degenerated into conventions of yes-men. Practically, all they could then
do was to confirm the candidates for the magistracies who had been put
forward by a very complicated electoral process, the *destinatio.* From
Nerva (A D 96–98) onward, the responsibility of the assemblies of the
people for legislation lapsed. The well-worn slogan *panem et circenses*
gives the most telling description of the 'common law' rights which
more and more dominated the thoughts of the *plebs urbana* with all the
privileges it still, even then, enjoyed. The distributions of grain and
money were still carried out, even in the middle of the greatest crises, as
when under Marcus Aurelius every free citizen of Rome received a total
of 850 *denarii.* At the beginning of the first century B C in Rome there
were public games of the most varied kinds on a total of fifty-seven days
in the year, whereas the calendar of the year A D 354 actually showed 177
games days.

The lack of industrial sites and jobs in the capital was not corrected
even under the Principate. In contrast with all modern state administra-
tions, the work in Rome was done with a minimum of subordinate staff.
The importance of the Roman army was all the greater for that reason.
Some 150,000 free Roman citizens, predominantly members of the *plebs*

rustica, served in about thirty legions. The wages of an ordinary legionary in the first century A D amounted to 900 sesterces a year. On termination of service the legionary could expect a further 12,000 sesterces. In addition there were extraordinary material rewards, at first infrequent but later at shorter and shorter intervals – the donatives. It is true that according to modern estimates some 50 per cent of all Roman soldiers died in service, but those who did survive belonged as veterans to the privileged class of their city's inhabitants. Veterans and sons of veterans gradually acquired the same social rank as the decurions. In modes of punishment, for instance, they were distinguished from other Roman citizens, and could not be condemned to shameful methods of execution, like fighting wild animals in the arena.

While a working life in the capital enabled only a few specially qualified Roman citizens to climb the social ladder, the Roman legion on the contrary, with its abundance of private soldier and non-commissioned officer ranks, offered regular preferment with dozens of promotion possibilities. The most important group in the hierarchy were the centurions, who in their origins and careers corresponded to modern professional non-commissioned officers but in their position to the company commanders of modern armies. Their period of service as *centurio* was normally twenty years, and their ranks were graded accordingly. At the age of about 50 a centurion could finally become a *primus pilus*, that is, commander of the first century of a legion. This made him the centurion of longest service and highest rank over all the sixty centurions of the legion. After one year's service in that rank, the *primipilus* could retire from the army with 600,000 sesterces, or continue his military career with promotion to still higher posts.

The *primipilares*, as they could then be called, had not only reached the social census rank of *equites*, but their particular prestige as members of a relatively small group of the active military governing class with long troop service had become even greater than that of an ordinary *eques Romanus*. This also explains the fact that among those who served as career centurions were not only non-commissioned officers of the legions and the guard but also, in individual cases, members of the equestrian order.

Service in the army always remained, even in its material conse-quences, a privilege of the free full citizen hardly to be over-estimated. This was particularly the case with the units of the Praetorian Guard which, from A D 23, were concentrated in Rome. They had only to serve sixteen years, whereas the legionaries were as a rule twenty years under arms, sometimes longer, and the praetorians got three times the salary of citizens serving in the legions. While the *plebs* gradually sank to the level of a passive substratum of government, the Praetorian Guard and the army units concentrated on the periphery of empire emerged more and more as the key organs of power. In this militarised form the political will of the Roman people, so to speak, became more and more concentrated. From Augustus onward, all the *principes* therefore endeavoured by all conceivable means, material and psychological, to secure the devotion of these units and to repress rival influences like that of the Senate. It thus became a political factor of the first importance that ultimately only the *princeps* was entitled to celebrate a triumph or receive acclamations of the troops and surnames of victory. The monopolisation of the military supreme command in one hand remained the decisive basis of the whole political system. The highest military honours formed the core of the ideology of the Principate.

The greater part of the free population of Rome eked out a meagre livelihood with craft work, service trades or small shopkeeping. The tombstone inscriptions tell us these people's conception of themselves and their working philosophy. Lucius Nerusius Mithres, for instance, a goat's wool merchant of the city of Rome, says of himself: 'I dealt in popular goods, my rare honesty was praised always and everywhere. My life was happy, I built myself a tombstone of marble, I lived free from care, always paid my taxes, was honest in all my contracts, just to all men so far as I could be, often helped a petitioner . . .' (*Inscriptiones Latinae Selectae* 7542, H. Dessau, Berlin). At the same time Rome bristled with every kind of parasite. There was the poor client who had to put up with every imaginable humiliation, even at the hands of the slaves of his patron, in order to get his meagre alms, the *sportulae*. There were thieves and criminals of every sort. For a senator historian like Tacitus, it was therefore natural to try to discredit the Roman city *plebs* as a whole. He often enough identified it with the mob. Unreliability, treachery, poor judgment, pleasure-seeking, above all fickleness were the terms of his abuse.

While the Roman Republic in its systematic colonisation process had carried out an effective measure of social policy with the deliberate regeneration of society in view, under the Principate there was an extension of almsgiving by the state, with distributions of free food in Italy or military service instead. Yet it was particularly for the free population that social expenditure by the state under the *imperium* remained inadequate and ineffective. Where the aged, widows, disabled, sick, children and orphans were not provided for within the family, they fell as often as not into destitution. Among the decisive secular reasons for the victory of Christianity – as Edward Gibbon saw – was that the Christian communities stepped into the breach. Not the least of the reasons for the Christian church's final victory was the fact of its being an effective social institution.

The free citizen of the city of Rome was the one who bore the brunt of the change when the capital of the *imperium* became a world city under the Principate; became the 'Greek Rome', as Juvenal in one of his Satires has vividly described it:

All the dregs of Greece are pouring into our city.
Here's one from Sicyon's heights, another from Amydon,
from Samos another, from Tralles and Alabanda,
all bound for the Esquiline, bound for the Viminalis.
Now heart and soul of our great houses, soon their masters!
Their quickness of wit, bold sallies are our despair,
their gift of the gab would put Isaeus to shame.
Is that why you keep the fellow? because any trade you name he'll offer?
language teacher, rhetorician, painter, masseur, surveyor,
rope-dancer, soothsayer, magician, doctor –
nothing your hungry Greek can't do.

(Juvenal, *Satires* III, 69ff.)

The total population of Rome in the first two centuries A D is estimated at some 800,000 to one million inhabitants, but these figures are disputed. Augustus partitioned the total area of the city into 265 city precincts, the *vici*, easily controllable units in which the community feelings of the inhabitants could develop more strongly and neighbourly relations have more concrete effects. Among the new cells of social life which developed in Rome, as in the provinces, were the *collegia*. Originally these were trade associations of distinct craft groups, as for instance the carpenters, fellowships which in cities of the provinces often functioned as fire brigades too. They might also be cult associations or burial clubs, anything else in fact but forerunners of trade unions. Labour conflicts were not among the activities of these bodies with their privileged rights of association.

It has become usual to divide up the lower classes of Roman society into a town and country *plebs*, the *plebs urbana* and the *plebs rustica*, and further to subdivide each half into *ingenui* (free born), *liberti* (freed slaves) and slaves. If logically pursued, however, this arrangement is scarcely true to the facts. Certainly, in Rome itself from the time of the Gracchi onward, there was a divergence of elementary interests, because the Roman city *plebs* gave precedence to food supply laws, while the country *plebs* wanted land settlement laws. Yet the many free inhabitants of the numerous small towns often differed very little in their ways of life and work from the neighbouring free rural population. However, all the essential phenomena of ancient civilisation were bound up with the city. For the *plebs rustica* under the Principate, social conditions had changed very little. It is true that the importance of the smallholder class had diminished with the increase of *villa* agriculture and the extra-territorial *latifundia* which were now forming (the great independent estates whose privileged owners were no longer integrated in the cities and communes). In large areas of Italy, however, and also in the Danube area the status of the small farmers remained as before. But the spread in the second century of the *alimentatio* showed that there too impoverishment threatened the children of free farmers and land workers. This was a semi-philanthropic institution by which a piece of private land was mortgaged to the state for a fraction of its value, and the landowner's interest payments distributed officially as maintenance grants to poor children.

The freed slaves

The case of the freedmen has similarities with that of the *equites*. They too achieved power only as isolated individuals. After reaching the summit of their power under Claudius and Nero, their importance in the top positions of the imperial administration declined. Moreover they never seem to have exerted power as a self-contained corporate whole. It is particularly important, with this group above all, to make an exact assessment of its social and economic position. Of course it included men of the Pallas or Trimalchio type who are so often mentioned in the literature (Pallas, 'finance minister' under Claudius, a man who could afford magnanimously to refuse a testimonial gift of 15,000,000 sesterces offered him by the Senate, a man who actually received the *ornamenta* of a praetor; Trimalchio, immortalised by Petronius in his satirical novel, an outrageous parvenu bursting with possessions and wealth). Yet both cases were provocative exceptions, in no way representative of the group as a whole. More truly typical were the tens of thousands of qualified craftsmen, reliable employees and tireless shopkeepers who often enough had to give support to their former free masters.

For them, too, the inscriptions are an important indication of their mentality and their qualifications. Of a freedman silversmith, for instance, we read: 'He never said an angry word in his life and did nothing unless by his master's will. He always had a quantity of gold and silver by him and never coveted any of it for himself. He excelled everyone in the craft of silverwork' (*ILS* 7695). Or a freedman teacher says of himself; 'I lived as long as I could without litigation, quarrel or dispute and without debts. To my friends I was always honest, poor in fortune but rich in spirit' (*ILS* 8436). It was from the circles of men like these, after all, that so many successful and wealthy freedmen came. They frequently did sterling service to their residential community, or to the cities in which they had gained their wealth, or to their original home towns. Such freedmen, who on occasion would publicly donate many thousands of sesterces, rivalled the decurions and were sometimes themselves invested with the *ornamenta decurionalia*. They often took a prominent part in the city rites of the emperor cult, as members of the corporation of the *augustales*, in which there were often three freedmen and three free-born citizens serving together as *seviri*, with joint responsibility for the maintenance of the cult. Emperor worship was of course a conspicuous demonstration of the political loyalty of the community.

The proportion of freedmen to the total population, and therewith also the proportion of those free citizens who had once been slaves to all free Roman citizens, considerably increased under the Principate. If Peter Brunt's estimate is correct, that in Augustan Italy there were no fewer than 3,000,000 slaves in a total population of some 7,500,000 inhabitants, this must also mean that the 3,000,000 slaves were to a considerable extent potential freedmen; or in other words, that generation after generation tens of thousands of new freedmen were changing the overall relation between free-born citizens, freedmen and slaves. This automatic route from slave to free via the status of freedman was unknown in the Greek cities.

If more recent hypotheses are confirmed, that a city slave could as a rule expect to be freed between the ages of 30 and 40, this is unlikely at first to have meant much more for him than a change in his personal status at law. For the new freedmen, many material and moral ties with their ex-master and his family would remain, while against that the ex-master's obligation to support the ex-slave would lapse. It must be strongly emphasised that not every freedman rose clear of his ex-master's economic range, which might be very restricted. Not every freedman achieved the jump or long slow climb from former slave to rich shopkeeper, merchant, craftsman or specialist. Yet the freedmen were in effect the economic and social climber class. In contrast with the members of the upper class and the free-born citizens, for them the only path of social ascent lay in their professional qualifications, their expertise, industry, skill, adaptability and reliability. One markedly special group in their whole class was that already mentioned, the freedmen of the *familia Caesaris*, the men and women employed in the administration of the *princeps'* household. In individual cases during the first century A D they must be counted among the governing class of the *imperium*, and on occasion rose even to the equestrian order.

The slaves

The proportion of slaves to the total population of the *imperium Romanum* in the age of the Principate cannot be exactly determined. Conditions varied greatly from one part of the empire to another. We have a statement of Pliny the Elder that the greatest number of slaves belonging to a single master (a rich freedman) was, according to his personal knowledge, 4116. From Pliny the Younger's letters we learn that it was evidently nothing extraordinary for a large landowner of his own calibre to possess several hundred slaves. Yet in the province of Noricum the greatest number of slaves so far known in one man's ownership, as determined by G. Alföldi, was six. Galen, the great second-century doctor, records of Pergamum that only 40,000 of its 120,000 inhabitants, or about one-third, were free citizens, but this proportion cannot be generalised. Altogether it is probable that the proportion of slave to free in the total population gradually declined from the time of Augustus onward, but it must nonetheless have remained for a long time considerable. The institution was in principle never questioned. Individual rhetorical and philosophical quotations to the contrary should not deceive us. Even Christianity, generally speaking, never threw doubt on it. Economically, the slave condition retained the part it had played from the late Republic onward. Only in agriculture did its importance in certain districts decline, especially in North Africa, in favour of free tenant farming, the colonate. Generally speaking, slavery remained the social basis of the Roman empire.

Like Augustus, his successors in the Principate systematically safeguarded the institution of slavery and kept it working. Either because of the inhumanity of labour conditions or because of other forms of exploitation and excesses by many slaveholders, isolated slave risings did still occur during the Principate. But taken altogether there were no large-scale rebellions like the Sicilian slave wars. Instead, considerable numbers of slaves took part in the new civil wars and in what were primarily national insurrections.

Against that, the escape of individual slaves was relatively frequent. In such cases the slaveholders' self-help usually proved inadequate, although rewards of up to 500 sesterces were sometimes offered for denunciations, and in the end there were professional slave-catchers, the *fugitivarii*. But the great landowners resisted enquiries on their own estates, and the magistrates and governors also shrank from too zealously engaging in the recovery of fugitives. Consequently, from the second century onwards, it was more and more the central administration that concerned itself with these problems. From the reign of Marcus Aurelius in particular, several decrees are known by which the governors and magistrates were ordered to use the military garrison and do everything to help a slaveholder in pursuit of a fugitive. Slaves who were recovered were threatened with savage penalties – flogging, enchainment, consignment to the *ergastulum* (the slave prison), branding and crucifixion. Early Christianity did not in general approve of slaves running away. As we learn from St Paul's letter to Philemon, the slaveholder's rights were in principle recognised.

Apart from the many personal motives which an individual slave might have for running away, one objective circumstance was the scarcity of labour in agriculture. One good reason why so many slaves did risk flight was that they scented a real chance of hiding on the great estates, with their labour shortage, and knew that a considerable number of slaveholders would not hand them over. This state of affairs is thus a further indication of the looming crisis in agriculture in certain areas.

The *principes* on their side tried to bolster up the system of slavery not only by repressive action or precautionary security measures but, in parallel with them, also by trimming the excesses. It was probably under Tiberius that the *praefectus urbi* became a court of appeal for harassed slaves, who could by this means at least obtain their sale to another master. In addition, the custom rooted itself more and more firmly that ill-treated slaves fled to the statues of the *principes* and made their complaints under their protection. As we learn from rescripts of Antoninus Pius, the rights of slaveholders were only curtailed, as for instance by threatening to sell the slave, when the slaveholder put the whole system in question by cruelty or providing insufficient food.

Integration policies: citizenship, the auxiliaries, the provincials

For any overall estimate of the connections between the social structure, the economic development and the political system of the *imperium Romanum* under the Principate, the fundamental facts are that of the 60–80 million inhabitants of the empire at the beginning of the first century AD, only some 5,000,000 were free and full Roman citizens; that according to modern estimates nine-tenths of the population did not live in cities, yet Rome's political supremacy was nonetheless primarily based on the *imperium*'s more than a thousand urban settlements. Thus a Roman social policy conceived, for instance, on the systematic plan of extending the Roman–Italian model of social structure to the whole *imperium* was, all things considered, out of the question.

The continuity of the existing social class system therefore prevailed not only in the Roman–Italian geographical core – as was obvious in the situation of the late republic and, beyond that, was ostentatiously promoted by Augustus – but just as much in the provinces. Against that, both in Italy and in the provinces, all social groups were affected by the new political system and subordinated to it. Not only the functions, social mobility and social status of individual inhabitants of the empire but also their material basis were more and more, directly or indirectly, determined or at least decisively influenced by the *princeps*.

The central problem in organising Roman rule was the incorporation of the free-born non-Romans, especially their upper classes on which Roman rule usually leaned for support, into the political system of Rome. To achieve this purpose, three methods were normally used. They were: 1) the continued pursuit of a consistent but cautious policy of citizenship rights; 2) the organisation of auxiliary formations of the Roman army, constituting at the same time an important vehicle of romanisation; 3) the consolidation and development of the cities as the most important social and political cells of the *imperium*. I will take these one by one but first note that, although the means employed proved for a long time successful, yet they also brought about changes in the relations that existed when the Principate was founded. On the one hand, the greater the number of citizens the less important Roman citzenship became, and it lost almost all its value to the individual when by the *Constitutio Antoniniana* of A D 212/213 it was extended to nearly all free-born inhabitants of the empire. On the other hand, the advancement of the members of the governing class from the provinces to the old Roman orders and to the leading positions of the *imperium* worked ultimately to the prejudice of their home cities. For since the *imperium* in its heyday during the first two centuries A D was to a considerable extent financed in the provinces by the social élite of the cities, in the end the whole system was at risk if its members shirked their responsibilities or were put under too great a strain. But this is exactly what happened in the second half of the second century A D. It also follows, however, that social status became more important the less important citizenship rights became.

1. Citizenship policy. It is important to bear in mind that by Roman standards the dominant notion was that of the concrete legally determined community, not that of an abstract nationality as understood in modern times. It was therefore an elementary principle of the Roman conception of citizenship that a foreigner could in time perhaps win Roman citizenship without losing his own, but that the converse was not permitted. When we consider the award of Roman citizenship or of its preliminary stage, Latin citizenship, we must distinguish between collective and individual awards. The former were at first very infrequent. They occurred under Julius Caesar with the obvious additional motive of widening the basis of recruitment to the legions, but later especially when the adaptation of a territory to Roman ways was far advanced. That, for instance, is how the award of Latin rights to the inhabitants of Spain by Vespasian is to be understood.

Individual awards of citizenship are attested as early as the Second Punic War, but for a long time they were extremely rare and required that the recipient should have personally and publicly engaged himself on Rome's behalf, or later for one of the parties in the Roman civil wars, like the Seleukos of Rhosos, in Cilicia, on whom an edict of Octavian's in 41 BC conferred citizenship and exemption from taxes. Under the Principate there were changes with momentous consequences. The first thing to go was the insistence on Italo-Roman origin as a precondition of Roman citizenship; next was the requirement that the individual should at least be rooted in the Latin civilisation, which had long been the *condicio sine qua non* of any grant of Roman citizenship to foreigners. At the same time the interweaving of citizen rights with citizen duties was done away with in important respects. That which, under the Republic, had been the central duty of a citizen, to render many years' military service in the legions, was no longer exacted under the Principate owing to its standing army. Foreigners were now more and more frequently awarded Roman citizenship in recognition of active proofs of loyalty to the *imperium Romanum*.

It is obvious that, in the Greek East as well, Claudius and Nero were already quite generous with individual awards of citizenship. The point is made in sharpened burlesque form in Seneca's *Apocolocyntosis* ('The Pumpkinification of the Divine Claudius'). Claudius was determined, it says, to see every Greek, Spaniard and Briton wearing a toga – that is, to make Roman citizens of them. In any case, the dangers of a policy of being too free with the gift of Roman citizenship were recognised and criticised early on. The complexity of the problem, however, lay in the fact that the steady increase in Roman citizens was not only due to the institution of 'Roman cities' and collective or individual grants of citizenship but much more to the continual freeing of slaves of Roman citizens. A restrictive citizenship policy towards free foreigners, especially the members of the governing class in the provinces, was bound to seem absurd and out of date when at the same time, year after year, freedom was given to thousands of slaves whose offspring would be promoted, in a comparatively short time, to fully qualified Roman citizens. These complications had already been well understood by Augustus, who however had only been able to impose a short delay on a development that was already clearly marked during his reign.

2. The auxiliaries. The new organisation of the regular auxiliary detachments of the Roman army was another important step in fastening Roman rule on the provinces. Free provincials served in auxiliary infantry and cavalry units of 500 or 1000 men each, the cohorts and 'wings' (*alae*), which were generally designated by the name of the tribe from which the formation was originally recruited. These units often provided the garrisons of the frontier forts on the *limes*, but to some extent also they served with the legions in the great encampments.

6 The Roman frontier in Germany

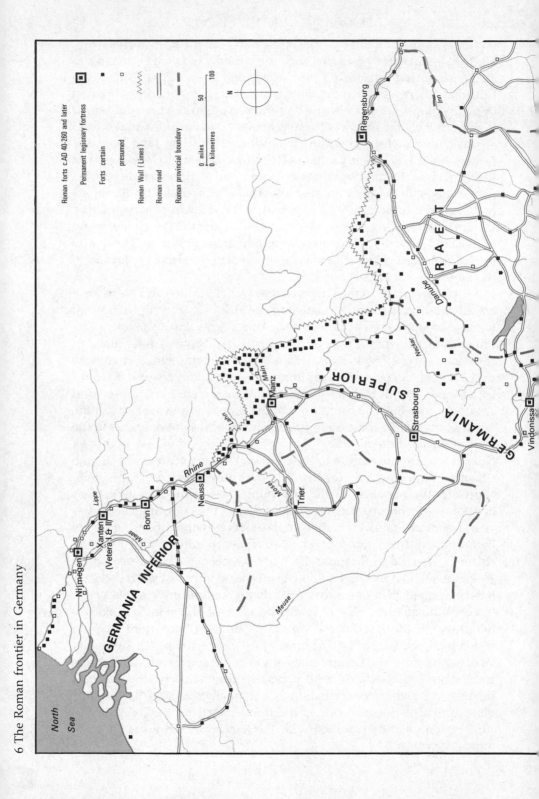

Roman forts c.AD 40-260 and later

Permanent legionary fortress

Forts   certain
         presumed

Roman Wall (Limes)

Roman road

Roman provincial boundary

0 miles   50   100
0 kilometres

N

North Sea

GERMANIA INFERIOR

Nijmegen

Xanten
(Vetera I & II)

Lippe

Maas

Bonn

Neuss

Rhine

Meuse

Trier

Mosel

Mainz

Main

Lahn

GERMANIA SUPERIOR

Strasbourg

Neckar

Vindonissa

RAETI

Danube

Regensburg

Inn

The members of auxiliary formations were awarded full Roman citizenship, with their children and descendants, after the completion of twenty-five years' service with honourable discharge. At the same time the marriage of the discharged to the wife he was living with at that time, or, in the case of a bachelor, a wife whom he might subsequently marry, was legalised, 'for the individual only one at a time', as the stereotyped formula has it. All this is known from the so-called 'military diplomas' – a pair of bronze tablets issued to each such soldier, of which a number survive. In this way the military potential of the provinces was made available to the *imperium* for its own purposes, and the old policies of the Roman Republic towards its allies were continued and institutionalised on a broader basis, with new forms. The total number of soldiers thus recruited became as high as the number of legionaries; that is, of the free Roman citizens under arms.

3. The cities: the provincials. The relatively small circle of people who embodied the central administration of the *imperium Romanum* and the modest staffs available to the governors of the provinces were inadequate for the complex tasks of public business and the administration of justice imposed on the Roman Republic and the Principate by the formation of the *imperium*. Since no systematic territorial rule could be organised by such a work force, the *imperium* had to support itself on the existing social and political nuclei of the cities. They alone were capable of undertaking, with their autonomous bodies, all the tasks of state, with due regard to the interests of the entire body politic and the system of Roman rule. Thus, in its fundamental structure, the *imperium Romanum* was an association of over a thousand cities, 'a conglomerate of cities' (A. H. M. Jones), ruled by Rome. Only in certain inland areas were other types of community to be found – tribal structures (*civitates*) or villages, or dispersed or isolated settlements, though these last were as often as not administratively assigned to cities. It is important to remember too that the ancient city-state even under Roman rule, besides its own central urban settlement, often included a considerable hinterland. A further point is that Rome in the eastern provinces found a dense and ready-built network of cities which, under the rule of Hellenistic monarchs, had often enough experienced submission to the higher interests of a far-flung state. In the west, however, beside cities of Phoenician and Greek foundation the Romans encountered, at least in the districts of late La Tène civilisation and Celtic mould, the urban settlements known as *oppida*. But where Roman rule could not build on nuclei like these, as for instance in 'free Germany', it was frequently a failure.

The majority of the cities of the *imperium* had populations of 10,000 to 15,000 inhabitants, but we often hear of smaller cities with no more than a few thousand. Against that, the *imperium* had only a few great cities of several hundred thousand inhabitants each. Of these, the most obvious examples were Alexandria, Antioch and Carthage. The accumulation of urban settlements, by contrast, varied greatly from one region to another. The concentrations were mostly near the coast or along the great rivers of Greece, the fringes of Asia Minor, Syro-Palestine, Italy, Sicily, North Africa, southern Gaul and Spain. They contrasted with the great stretches in the interior of Spain, Gaul, the Alpine regions, Britain, the Danubian Balkans, the highlands of Asia Minor and the Syro-Arabian and African borderlands where urban settlements were almost completely absent.

Just as the existing variations in civil law at first persisted within the *imperium Romanum*, so the juridical variations from one urban settlement to another arising in the course of the expansion and colonisation process under the Republic were systematised and expanded under the Principate. Especially privileged were the cities of Roman citizenship in the narrower sense; that is, the colonies and municipalities under Roman law, two categories which approximated more and more closely to one another in practice. According to a preliminary estimate by F. Vittinghoff, the *imperium Romanum* contained over 600 cities of both groups. Of these, 160 were in Spain, about 200 in North Africa, some 50 in Dalmatia, but in the whole Danube region from Raetia to Moesia and Dacia there were only 60. In the British and German-Gallic provinces (except in Narbonensis) and in all the eastern provinces there were strikingly few Roman colonies and municipalities. In the east, the network of originally free city-states (*poleis*) or royal foundations of the Hellenistic era was already so dense that only a few isolated colonies were inserted, the settlement structure and the city constitutions being left generally unchanged.

Originally, the *coloniae* were always colonies of settlement by Roman citizens, with a standard Roman city constitution. Under the Principate, beginning probably with Claudius, it also became usual to confer the title and status of *colonia* on existing communities of different origin. This practice then became widespread under Hadrian and his successors. In the case of the *municipium*, the usual practice was for already existing urban settlements in which a considerable number of Roman citizens were resident to be distinguished as cities with full citizen rights, including an administrative autonomy enshrined in their own *lex*. Thus local government and jurisdiction, including in particular the entire process of law at lower levels, were transferred to the citizens of the *municipia* and their institutions, the city council and people's assembly. In return, they were bound to render military service and active political loyalty to Rome, and were also liable for contributions to state expenditure in the general interest. In the provinces, however, still further privileges could be conferred by means of the *ius Italicum*. Units of settlement governed by this law probably enjoyed *immunitas*, the freedom of the soil from all state taxes, as also their own freedom from any form of supervision by the governor concerned, together with both exemption from all billeting liabilities and certain citizenship privileges regarding the law of property.

At one step lower than these *coloniae et municipia civium Romanorum* were the colonies and municipalities of 'Latin rights'. Originally a grade of community with historical antecedents, which in their ancient meaning had become obsolete on the conclusion of the Social War in 89 BC, these rights had then come to be awarded as a special grant of citizenship privileges. Under Hadrian they underwent a remarkable subdivision, when the so-called *Latium maius* was introduced. This was an enhanced form of the Latin citizenship rights by which not only the magistracy of the city but also all the members of its governing council automatically received Roman citizenship.

The last category of urban settlements was numerically largest. These cities of foreign law were in variously graded groups, tributary, free and allied (*civitates stipendiariae, liberae* and *foederatae*). Their varying status was generally a consequence of the historical and political circumstances in which the cities entered into relations with Rome. The most numerous among them was the group of *civitates stipendiariae*, while that of the cities exempt from tribute was markedly infrequent.

Not all the inhabitants of a particular city had the same personal grade of citizenship. Beside the privileged holders of Roman or Latin citizenship there were the free residents and immigrant strangers, the *incolae*, and of course here too freedmen and slaves. But, in addition, there was an occasional Roman *eques* and, still less frequently, a senator retaining his local residence. As I have noted, the city constitutions for the categories of Latin or Roman colony or municipality were grounded in a Roman *lex*, which then laid down the graded rights of the individual citizenship groups, together with the functions, responsibilities and privileges of the magistrates. At the same time, they often detailed with astonishing precision the methods of administration of justice, of taxation and finance, leasehold regulations, elections, religious cult and public games. The *leges* for the Caesarian colony Urso in Spain (*ILS* 6087) and for the Domitianic *municipia* of Latin rights Salpensa (*ILS* 6088) and Malaca (*ILS* 6089) are the best known documentary examples of such constitutions.

Following republican tradition, Caesar and Augustus opened wide the doors to a systematic policy of urbanisation within an imperial framework. While Caesarian colonies were placed especially in Spain, in the Narbonensis, in Greece, in Africa and in north-western Asia Minor, Augustan foundations, both *coloniae* and *municipia*, were concentrated, in a far greater total number, in Spain, North Africa, Sicily and Dalmatia, but additionally also in Greece, Galatia and Pisidia. After such powerful encouragement, the process of urbanisation proceeded in an anything but uniform manner in the different parts of the empire. While municipalisation in the Danube region, with special emphasis under Trajan, came to resemble a continuous process, as it did also in Africa right into the third century A D, in the Spanish provinces the possibilities had evidently been exhausted as early as the first century A D; after the Flavians, no new colonial foundations and no new *municipia* are recorded, although both Trajan and Hadrian came from Baetica. On the whole, the dominant feature of the Principate was the gradual ascent of the civil rights ladder by existing nuclei of city settlement, whereas the foundation of genuinely new colonial settlements petered out.

Roman policy towards the cities of the *imperium* was designed to keep them functioning, and especially to strengthen the position of the city councillors. As long as it was at all possible, the governors and the central administration refrained from any direct intervention in city concerns. From the beginning of the second century B C onwards, however, there was an increase in the number of cases in which agents of the *princeps*, either as legates on special mission like the younger Pliny in Bithynia (about A D 111) or as special commissioners, *curatores rei publicae*, took charge of financial or other local concerns of the cities which had run into difficulties and could no longer be solved by the cities on their own. Trajan's written reply to one such question of Pliny's shows how the central offices of the *imperium* wanted to have as little as possible to do with such matters, and urged the mobilisation of the province's own resources:

'What is to be done about the unfinished theatre at Nicaea can best be considered and decided by yourself on the spot. I shall be content with a report from you as to what view you adopted. Then when the theatre is finished you can make sure that the private donors put in hand the buildings they have promised in connection with it. Your Hellene has a weakness for gymnasia, which is no doubt why Nicaea started this project, perhaps a little too enthusiastically in the first place. But they must be content with what is practicable on the old site. As for your advice to Claudiopolis on the baths they have begun to build on what, as you inform me, is an unsuitable site, decide the matter yourself. You can have no lack of architects. Every province has experienced and talented people. Do not make the mistake of supposing it easier to send to Rome for them. Usually it is from Greece that they come to us.'

(Pliny the Younger, *Letters* X, 40)

When, in A D 156, Aelius Aristides told how the cities did nothing but vie with another 'to be considered the finest and most beautiful, everywhere building gymnasia, fountains, colonnades, temples, workshops, schools . . .' (*On Rome*, 97), we at once realise the source of the difficulties which sometimes occurred. Rivalry in the building of larger and larger and more and more splendid public buildings, and the steadily increasing claims on public expenditure, at a time when the imperial administration was also making extraordinary demands on them in consequence of wars and defence emergencies, was bound to strain city finances and provoke serious crises. Not only were the citizens with property faced with increasing compulsory levies and, in parallel with that, the *ordo decurionum* transformed into a compulsory association, but at the other extreme there was the abuse of *immunitates*, the exemptions from state obligations enjoyed by specially privileged groups such as higher officials, but also persons engaged, for instance, in the sea transport of grain for the state procurement agencies. The compounding of such injustices led in the end to the decline of city autonomy.

Above all, in the cities of the Hellenistic East, Rome was confronted with more and more far-reaching social and political conflicts. These did not primarily originate in any way with disputes between Romans and non-Romans, or between slave-holders and slaves, nor were they merely expressions of the opposition between rich and poor, or between town and country, but with special frequency they were conflicts between long-settled full citizens and underprivileged groups such as former free foreign immigrants or members of certain social classes like the linen weavers fighting for equality in the Cilician capital of Tarsus. In addition, there were the old ethnic rivalries, like that between the Greeks and Jews of Alexandria, which for decades on end kept the Roman administration on tenterhooks. Indeed, the class of 'provincials' was by no means a homogeneous one.

Economic organisation and development

Rather as in city government so also in economic affairs the *imperium Romanum* under the Principate was very far from the type of standardisation that we associate with a modern area of industry in the large. It was neither systematically coordinated nor made up of partial economic sectors, each with its own individuality but continuously interdependent. There was no economic policy methodically pursued by the state, not even the obligatory coordination of production by the various sectors. The *imperium* on the contrary consisted of a whole series of widely varied economic landscapes, which to a large extent clung to their traditional methods of production and production goals, and were only very loosely connected with one another. The constant imports into Rome of great quantities of Sicilian corn, African oil and Spanish fish sauce (*garum*), are the exceptions which prove the rule. Nor should the often astonishing extent of long-distance trade in luxury goods (silk, glass, art objects and ornaments, delicacies for the table) blind us to the elementary fact that in all essential products of daily need the agricultural and handicraft production for the local market, and therewith the local trade, far exceeded it.

The impact of the *imperium Romanum* on the world of economics was of a different kind. Its strengthened political framework created sheltered conditions which had a lasting effect on economic development. The *imperium* guaranteed security, especially security of transport, on a wide scale; it guaranteed existing property relationships, and also the economically fundamental institution of slavery. It set up a currency system, including the local coinages long current in the Greek East, and coordinating them with a relatively stable imperial currency; it contented itself with fairly modest rates of tax and customs which did not hinder the economic development of the provinces. Finally, it stimulated new markets in the frontier zones and created there new economic regions of military administration which for quite a number of territories represented their first systematic exploitation of mineral resources and other production possibilities.

It would be hard to over-estimate the importance of these economic consequences of the development of the entire Roman army with its auxiliaries on the periphery of the *imperium*. In Roman times, the irrigation of numerous North African and Arabian frontier areas reached a standard which in many ways was not to be reached again till the present day. This was just one consequence of Roman security policies. Another was the shift of production centres to the newly arising markets which was made necessary by the technical inefficiencies of land transport. M. I. Finley has rightly pointed out that, according to figures quoted in Diocletian's maximum prices edict of AD 301, 'a shipment of grain by sea from one end of the Mediterranean to the other would cost less (ignoring the risks) than carting it 75 miles (120 kilometres)' (*The Ancient Economy*, 126). The consequence was that the transport of bulk goods in general did not occur by land but was confined to the range of sea and river traffic. The Roman merchant ships, though they mostly preferred to hug the coast, could after all hold over 3000 *amphorae*, as underwater archaeology has shown.

The peripheral placing of new markets meant on the whole that centres of production also moved to these areas. The businesses of the Arezzo region, for instance, found themselves unable in the long run to compete with the great potteries of Gaul (La Graufesenque, Lezoux) and of the Rhine zone, which had far better local conditions for supplying the Gallo-Germanic area. This fact alone is enough to show that we cannot equate the economic development of the *imperium* with exploitation in favour of Rome and Italy. In many respects it was quite the opposite, and worked out wholly to Italy's disadvantage.

It is not possible here to analyse the development of the individual economic territories of the *imperium* systematically, and the following sketch of the essential features must be confined for the most part to Italy and the Roman West. Under the Principate agriculture was still the dominant factor. However great on the one hand the tenacity of the free small producers, whose total numbers should not be under-estimated, and the success on the other of the intensive management methods of the medium-sized villa estates newly organised under the late Republic, taken as a whole it can be said that difficulties in agriculture again increased.

In his *On Agriculture*, a work composed in A D 50, Columella rejected contemporary complaints about the infertility of the fields, the unfavourable nature of the climate, and the exhaustion of the soil. Instead, he criticised the fact that agriculture was handed over to 'the very worst type of slaves', while the practical knowledge and economic competence of landowners was declining. 'And so it has come to this, that we today in "this Latium and land of Saturn", where the gods themselves have taught their offspring the fertility of the fields, negotiate public contracts to ensure the supply of grain from provinces overseas, so that we do not have to endure famine, and import the vintages from the Cyclades and the Baetic and Gallic lands' (*Praefatio*, 20).

In all this the connection between productivity and conditions of ownership was recognised early on: 'The ancients thought that moderation should be observed in land ownership because they thought it better to sow less and plough better. . . . To tell the truth, the *latifundia* have ruined Italy and indeed will soon bring the same ruin on the provinces. Six landlords were in possession of one half of the provinces of Africa at the time when the Emperor Nero had them all removed' (Pliny the Elder, *Natural History* XVIII, 35).

The spread of large estates in Italy under the Principate had many causes. First, landed estate had always been the safest form of property. Under the stable conditions of the Principate, a yearly income of some five to six per cent could be counted on; indeed with vineyards the annual profit could be set as high as seven to ten per cent. On the one hand, the members of the old governing class liked to plough back into good Italian land the salaries they received in the *princeps*' service, very high as these sometimes were. On the other, from the reign of Trajan onwards even those senators who originated in the provinces were obliged to invest at least a third of their property in Italian land. In addition, there was a quite deliberate interweaving of land ownership with the capital market. Theodor Mommsen was among the first to discuss the far-reaching consequences of the fact that the investment of money at interest in Rome and Italy was allowed only up to a certain proportion of the creditor's capital investment in Italian landed estate (*Boden- und Geldwirtschaft der römischen Kaiserzeit*: reprinted in *Römische Geschichte*, 7, 1976, 358).

In Italy under the Principate the large estates were preponderantly in private hands. It is true that in the environs of Rome, the holiday country around Baiae and other attractive Italian resorts, the *princeps* had at his disposal a whole series of often luxurious villas set in substantial grounds. But the great areas of state-owned land were in the provinces, with remarkable concentrations in the Fayûm, in the area south-west of Carthage, and in the river valleys and interior of Asia Minor. A point to notice in this context is the tendency to concentrate in the *princeps'* hands as many brickyards, mines and marble quarries as possible.

The Italian governing class too made successful efforts to own great estates in the provinces. It is symptomatic of this development that under Claudius the senators received permission to visit Sicily and Narbonensis without special leave, in order to inspect their estates there. The systematic archaeological investigation of Roman villas in the provinces is in many places only just beginning, and the question who owned them has not always been answered. However, some essential light has been thrown on the diffusion of the great villa farms by the fact that the Gallo-Roman villa of Montmaurin (Haute-Garonne) obviously commanded an estate of many hundreds of acres, while air photographs in the Somme basin have discovered dozens of villas often only a few kilometres apart.

A similar regional variation in the sizes of large estates is attested for Italy too by the documents of poor relief 'mortgages' (*alimenta*) from Trajan's time. In North Italy the large estates were a good deal more widely distributed than for instance in the Beneventum area, where medium and smaller properties continued to be more in evidence. Moreover, the large estate in the Italy of the Principate was not necessarily managed as a closely coordinated whole. Very frequently it would be subdivided into smaller units, each of which would then be entrusted to an agent (*actor*). According to Columella, however, the letting of land to free leaseholders generally gave a better return than handing it over to slave bailiffs. Things developed to the point where the term *colonus*, originally simply the Latin word for farmer, became identical with the now prevalent type of independent small tenant farmer, besides whom there were of course still free agricultural labourers who would be taken on principally at harvest time. The changes thus occurring were once described by Theodor Mommsen as a substitution of small farmers for smallholders, and his opinion was that this 'small tenant farming' was essentially of a more humane stamp than the perfect rationalisation of a villa farm with slaves in Cato's sense. At the same time it must be acknowledged that this last form of farm management also continued on a considerable scale in Italy.

The new farming institution of the colonate, however, appears in a strikingly coarsened development in the colonial possessions of the *princeps* in North Africa. The large territories there under his ownership were described as *tractus*, the individual estate as *saltus*. At the head of a *tractus* stood a *procurator* of the administration of the Principate, while the estates were leased one by one, each to a *conductor*, a responsible entrepreneur who in turn sub-let each individual parcel of land on the estate to a *colonus*. The rents and obligations of the *coloni* as a rule followed the directions of the *lex Manciana*. According to these the amount of the rent was a third of the grain and olive harvest, plus an annual corvée of three three-day periods of unpaid labour on the home farm of the *saltus*.

In handicrafts too it was small production which predominated under the Principate, often coupled with producer trading. The direct sale of his own products by the craftsman was the rule, as we may often observe in the Mediterranean to this day. It applied as much to the baker as to the silversmith, to the halter-maker as to the basket-weaver or cobbler. The step to mass production in huge workshops, with hundreds of workmen and the greatest possible division of labour, was not taken. Production remained decentralised, in easily controllable units. Even in the well-known potteries of Arezzo, at most sixty slaves were employed in a workshop. Even in Gaul small businesses, in this case with free labour, predominated. The 'atomisation' of production (R. MacMullen) was to a considerable extent due to the often detailed specialisation of the craftsman and producer merchant. The combination of small workshop with store open to the street may be regarded as typical of this development. Such *tabernae* were often operated by slaves or freedmen. The latter not only practised the trade of their former master and patron but quite often carried on his business. The beginnings of production on a larger scale were to be found, but only in a few sectors, in ceramics for instance, oil lamps, glassware and bricks.

In all cities of the *imperium*, tradesmen formed associations. It may indeed be that the native craftsmen's fellowships had pre-Roman origins. The same applied to the river and sea transport trade, where the *corpora* of the inland boatmen, or *nautae*, and the shipowners, or *navicularii,* guaranteed the regular maintenance of transport services. The high prestige of the Rhône and Saône boatmen, who at the same time were engaged in the oil and wine trade, can be judged from the fact that in the amphitheatre of Nîmes forty seats of honour were reserved for these *nautae Rhodanici et Ararici.*

Banking and lending businesses had been developed in Gaul early in Julius Caesar's time by Roman *negotiatores,* but intensified development of the Roman provincial administration reduced their activities. Under the Principate, the term *negotiatores* then came to be used synonymously with that of the merchants in the narrower sense, the *mercatores,* though these mostly had more extensive businesses, often with central offices and depots serving a number of shops, and took pains to distinguish themselves from the small shopkeepers and craftsmen. They included also the wholesalers and distant traders whose inscriptions giving their professional qualifications often record wide-ranging continuous trading connections inside the *imperium.* Citizens of Cologne, for instance, are recorded as Dacian and Transalpine traders; a citizen of Trier as a trader with Britain; while a Syrian boasts that his trading activities reached from Aquitania to Lugdunum.

Even contemporaries were impressed by the scale on which long-distance trade was at that time conducted. In his fourteenth satire, Juvenal writes: 'Look at the harbours and the sea crowded with great keels. Already there are almost more men there than on the land. Wherever the hope of profit calls, there come the great squadrons, threading the Archipelago and the African waters, even leaving Gibraltar far behind them to hear the sun's hiss as it sinks beneath the wave' (XIV, 275ff.). More prosaic, but more important historically, are some of the indications given by the elder Pliny in the *Natural History.* For instance, in mentioning the commercial traffic in Dioskurias in the Crimea (Sebastopol), he notes that there too were Romans doing business with the help of 130 interpreters (VI, 5). In another place, he writes on the India trade: 'The merchants have found a shorter way (from Egypt to India across Arabia) and the greed for profit has brought us closer to India. Every year journeys are made to India under military protection, because pirates have always been dangerous there. It is worthwhile describing the whole route from Egypt, of which we now have certain knowledge. It is worthwhile, because India receives yearly at least 55 million sesterces from our empire and sends us goods in return which are sold here for a hundred times as much' (VI,101). Besides these literary evidences, however, we also possess from all over central, northern and eastern Europe a rich archaeological deposit giving us a picture of the whole range of Roman exports in metal goods, ceramics, glass, and wine casks.

WAYS OF LIFE

OCCUPATIONS AND MEANS OF LIVELIHOOD

Work, service, social function, obligations – these were what principally determined the life of the Roman, as they did his institutions. A classic passage of Cicero provides a reliable guide to the esteem in which various forms of occupation were held in the late Republican period and also during the Principate:

'Let us now turn to the various trades and occupations. The question which of them are suitable for a free man, which base, we have learnt to answer somewhat as follows. First, all those occupations are disapproved which tend to incur men's dislike – those, for instance, of tax gatherers and moneylenders. Then all trades in which payment is made merely for the labour and not for the skill are regarded as illiberal and base, for the wages thus received are a slave's hire. Base too are middlemen who immediately re-sell what they buy from a dealer. Such people can earn nothing except by lying and there is really nothing baser than deception. All artisans too must be considered base, for what can be suitable for a free man about a workshop? Least of all can we approve of trades which only cater for sensual appetites – "fishmongers, butchers, cooks, poultrymen, fishermen", as Terence puts it. So far as I am concerned, you can include also perfumers, dancers and the whole pack of low-grade performers. But those professions which require a more serious training and aim at higher things, such as medicine, architecture and teaching at a decent level, are respectable enough for anyone of appropriate rank. Small trading is reckoned base, but if the business is large and substantial, procuring goods in quantity from everywhere and disposing of them without deception to a large body of customers, it is not so much to be condemned. It can even be, quite rightly, applauded if such a man, as does often happen, after making his little pile, "leaves the high seas and runs for port", retiring immediately to his landed estates. For of all lines of business agriculture is the best, most productive, most pleasant and worthiest of a free man.' (Cicero, *De Officiis* I, 150ff.)

Cicero's pronouncements echo the prejudices and attitudes not only of an educated man philosophising but above all those of the ancient Roman governing class. There is more elementary sobriety in the advice given a century and a half later by Martial:

'What tutor you should entrust your son to, Lupus, you have long been anxiously exploring and asking. Avoid the grammarians and rhetoricians all, I warn you, and let him have nothing to do with Cicero's or Virgil's books. Just leave [the advocate] Tutilius to his fame! If your son makes verses, just disinherit the poet! If he wants to learn arts that make money, let him be taught the guitar or flute. If the boy has a thick head, make him an auctioneer or an architect!' (Martial, *Epigrams* V, 56)

Whatever form life in Rome might take, the ideal form of existence for the governing class was that of an educated landowner, even though it had long since moved very far from Cato's 'simple life'. One of Pliny the Younger's letters gives a glimpse of 'country life' as led by an intellectually active aristocrat:

'You ask how I divide up my day on my Tuscan country estate in summer. I wake up when I like, mostly at six, often earlier, seldom later. The shutters remain closed for the time being. . . . I think over what I am at the moment working on and concentrate on it as if I were writing it down word for word and then revising it – sometimes less, sometimes more, depending on whether the subject is difficult or easy to handle and whether the words can be correctly memorised. Then I send for my shorthand writer, we let in the daylight, and I dictate to him what I have composed. He goes, is sent for again, again dismissed. About ten or eleven – I don't keep to a strict timetable – I go out to the flower garden or the covered walk to think out the concluding section and dictate that. Then I go for a drive. Yet even in the carriage I occupy myself just as when I was walking or lying in bed. Mental work can go on because it is stimulated by change. I go back to sleep a little, then I go for a walk. After that I read a Greek or Latin speech, aloud and with emphasis, not so much to exercise my voice as to improve my digestion, but it's true too that the voice is strengthened by it as well. Once more I take the air, then oiling, gymnastics, bath. At table when I'm alone with my wife or with a few friends, I have a book read to me. After the meal there's a comedy played or a lyrist performs. Finally I walk in the open air with my people, some of whom are educated. In such a manner, with all kinds of conversations, we pass the evening, and even the longest day draws quickly to a close.

'Sometimes this arrangement of the day is slightly changed. When I've lain long in bed or in the open air, after sleeping and reading I don't take the carriage but go on horseback. It's quicker and takes less time. Meanwhile friends from the neighbourhood come visiting and take up a part of my day, and often when I am tired after work I find this a welcome interruption. Sometimes too I go hunting, but never without my writing tablets, so as to bring something home at least, even when it's not game. Some time too I give to my tenants, not enough indeed in their opinion. You may imagine how gladly I return from their farmers' grumbles to the labours of authorship and public affairs.' (Pliny the Younger, *Letters* IX, 36)

In Rome itself, however, the 'public business of the city' imposed its frantic demands even on a nature as easy-going as the younger Pliny's. These involved social and political obligations of vast range, especially if the senator still had ambitions or wanted to prove his social prestige by action. The early morning hours in Rome were reserved for levees and courtesy calls of every kind. As an office-seeker, bearer of congratulations, pressure group representative or confidant of the *princeps*, the aristocrat was just as much obliged to run from house to house as was the poor client to dance attendance in antechambers. In the most favourable case he could receive visits himself and listen to the non-committal phrases of his own clients, whom he was obliged to support in return.

The Principate restricted the functions and reduced the importance of the ancient social cells of Rome, the family and the client body, by curtailing the rights of the *pater familias* and those of the *patronus*. Yet it is characteristic of the tenacity of these institutions that they continued to determine social life in Rome as they always had done. Even though deprived of all political significance, the *clientela* persisted as the virtually indispensable social basis of the aristocracy. At the same time, the relationship had been reduced to a largely material one. For every attendance the client could claim his little basket, the *sportula*, with provisions and, besides that, regular small presents. There were attempts to regulate the patron's donations by converting them into cash. In Trajan's time, for instance, the rate was $6\frac{1}{4}$ sesterces per day. One reason why this sum was unsatisfactory for the clients was that during their attendance they were required to wear the toga, the expensive 'robe of state', and moreover quite often had to spend hours in following the patron around on his rounds of engagements and duty visits as his background figures, escorts and 'extras'.

The poet Martial was one who had long experience of this kind of existence, and his poems are full of complaints about the impositions involved. After his two-mile morning walk, he discovers that his patron is already out or 'not at home' to visitors, or bluntly refusing to receive him personally. Then, if his patron is hunting legacies or pursuing amorous adventures, he must escort him on visits to ten widows. Then, on a temporary break for refreshment, he finds that the client's little basketful, his payment in kind, is an inferior meal to the patron's. The older the client becomes, the more oppressive his lot.

While the morning duties of free citizens and freedmen, rich or poor, were governed by the client system, their activities for the rest of the day were very different. A critical observer like the doctor Galen might exclaim at the numbers of Roman citizens attending the judicial proceedings which took place in the Forum for all to hear, or the even greater numbers of people at the chariot races and games, or the time spent on love pursuits or playing dice, or in the monumental public bathing establishments, followed by evenings at long dinners. All this may have been very true, but such sweeping moral judgments on life in the great city were far from telling the whole story of its occupations and labours.

If we believed only such authors as Martial, Juvenal and Petronius and their spectacular accounts, the only people to gain a livelihood in Rome were procurers, legacy hunters, tavern scroungers, confidence men and parasites, gigolos and seducers, claqueurs, courtiers and informers. They tell us little of those who were 'worthy and poor and honest of heart'. Martial himself is the very type of the one-sided ancient critic who tells us more about the legacy hunter or client than about the whole working population of artisans and shopkeepers whose lives were beneath his notice and whose occupations were rated as base and ignoble by the spoiled aristocrats with whom he consorted. Yet one rich wholesale baker, Marcus Vergilius Eurysaces, proudly got his own back. His striking grave monument still preserved today in front of the Porta Maggiore has the form of a huge oven carved with the most important scenes from the bread-making process.

The variety of such monuments and inscriptions gives us a most vivid picture of the lives of these ancient Romans, actively absorbed in their occupations and their work. They are remembered in tombstone reliefs and ornaments, paintings, working equipment and tools, legal texts but, only in exceptional cases which we must never generalise, literary, dramatic and poetic compositions. The Roman working day was confined by the inadequacies of artificial light to the hours of sunlight, and the high noon temperatures of summer imposed a lengthy break and siesta in the middle of the day. The consequence was that all important engagements were crowded into the mornings. Those who could afford it contented themselves with the six or seven working hours of the forenoon. As a matter of course, however, the shops were all reopened after the noon break and then kept open till sundown.

During these working hours, for the governing class especially, the Senate and the courts of justice were in session. These they attended as representatives of their order and in defence of their clients' interests. Then too began the activities of the commissions and priestly colleges to which they belonged, as also did their private and commercial conferences and consultations. It may well have been the case that, apart from such specially committed persons as magistrates and judges and active men of business, a good deal of these activities, as Seneca and Pliny describe them, was social and society freewheeling. But all the same it was important to take part, to be informed, to look after the interests of your own friends and clients in order to be respected by your peers. Anyone who drew back or shut himself out had to be strong enough to live by his own resources without the support of others.

The Roman artisans and small traders wherever possible moved their business on to the street. Since the streets and alleys of Rome were extremely narrow, and even the main exit roads like the Via Appia, the Via Latina and the Via Ostiensis had a width of no more than 4.80 to 6.50 metres, by a decree of Julius Caesar vehicular traffic with a few exceptions was banned during the day. It was thus transposed to the night hours, which in consequence were anything but quiet on the main through roads. In the confined uproar of lanes and alleyways pedestrians, shoppers and strollers jostled and squeezed their way between traders of every sort, until Domitian brought relief:

'Bold as brass the huckster had taken over the whole city
And not a threshold kept within its own limits,
But at your command, Germanicus [= Domitian], the alleys widened
And what was no more than a track has become a road.
And not a wineshop post is now hung with chained jars,
Nor is the praetor forced to walk in mire,
Nor does the barber blindly wield his razor in the crowd,
Nor the soot-blackened cookshop block the passage.
Tavern-keeper, cook, barber, and butcher now have each their threshold:
Now it is Rome, where only yesterday was one great shop.'

(Martial, *Epigrams* VII, 61)

WOMEN IN THE FAMILY AND SOCIETY

Even though the Roman woman of every order was completely absorbed in her household, yet from the beginning her position in the family and in society was incomparably better and more free than that of Greek women, for example. She lived in the main room of the house and attended the guest meals and shows. In the household itself she held the respected position of the mistress. Wherever possible she did not personally do any rough work but managed the house and children, and spun. Spinning and weaving ranked as the principal occupations of a Roman lady right into Augustan times. The loom became the symbol of womanly industry. The trite phrase of the grave inscriptions, 'She was of civil speech and noble gait, looked after her house and span', is an accurate statement of the expectations of the Roman husband.

The husband's *patria potestas* (paternal authority), or that of his father if still head of the family, did not in the reality of daily life take the heroic form of legend in which the father for whatever reason killed grown children. Also, it was rarely shown in such excesses as the deliberate terrorisation of the wife, children and other members of the *familia*, but mostly, and first and foremost, in the power of disposal of the property in cases where the marriage was of the *manus* type that is discussed below. It did however show itself in the form most hateful to any mother, the power of the *pater familias* to decide on the exposure of those new-born children which the father could not or did not want to rear, whether because they were bastards, or girls, or mentally deficient, or just could not be fed. The inhuman exposure of new-born babies on public rubbish dumps, resulting in their death or at best their sale into slavery, was legal throughout the Roman world until AD 374 and grounded in the absolute validity of the *patria potestas*.

Roman girls were considered fully adult at 12 years old, boys not till 14. As a rule, girls were married between 13 and 17. Out and out love matches for a long time formed the exception. With children of the governing class especially, marriages were on the whole political and based primarily on social and material interests. It would not be safe to generalise from those cases in which relations of deep human affection sprang from such unions, as in the marriage between Pompey and Caesar's daughter, Julia.

At first, the so-called *manus* marriage was the dominant form. In this, the woman left the *patria potestas* of her own *pater familias* and transferred to that of her husband or his *pater familias*. In this way she brought her entire property into the new marriage *familia*, and she herself could no longer dispose of it. Since this legal form of marriage was of material disadvantage not only to the woman but also, on her death, to her own kith and kin who were excluded from the inheritance, from the time of the late Republic onward the form of marriage without *manus* came to predominate. In this, the woman no longer passed under the complete *patria potestas* of her husband or his *pater familias*. Instead, by a marriage contract concluded before witnesses, she remained in possession of her own fortune. Moreover, in this new legal form of marriage, which soon became general, it was relatively easy to obtain a divorce, in fact simply by a declaration of will by one of the partners. It must be acknowledged that the old patriarchal forms of marriage in the Roman family were thereby shattered. Martial's assessment of marriage with a richer wife can so be understood:

'Why I don't want to marry a richer wife, you ask?
Well, I don't want to be wife to my wife, but husband.
The married woman, my dear Priscus, must always be subordinate to her man.
Else man and wife can never be a match.'

(Martial, Epigrams VIII, 12)

Alongside the legally concluded marriage, *matrimonium* in the narrower sense, there existed a form of living together without legal bonds, the *concubinatus*, which gained a steadily increasing hold on all social classes.

Yet the Roman ideal of womanhood remained the unsullied wife and mother who, after she had born her third child, was distinguished with a special gown (*stola*) and looked up to as a *femina stolata*. The highest ideal of womanhood was ultimately the *univira*, the woman who throughout her life had been 'only one man's wife and loved one', as the inscriptions have it. In reality, it is true, this style of life was less and less often achieved. It may have been an exaggeration of Martial's to grumble that in Rome no woman ever said No, yet promiscuity was the rule and, particularly in the governing class, a colourful succession of marriages and divorces was quite usual.

Tacitus, it is true, still openly exalted in his ideal of womanhood the qualities of purity (*pudicitia*), noble birth (*nobilitas*), fertility (*fertilitas*), wealth (*opes*), but also beauty (*forma*). He wanted a wife to bring up his children and to be the unflinching companion of her husband in good times and bad, bad especially, a woman who must refrain from mixing herself directly in politics. He was shocked by female lasciviousness and greed for power, female ambition and wantonness – the affairs and excesses he had to record and the picture conveyed by other writers of the age of the Principate. In the wealthy families of Rome, in which a wife, married very young, had to manage a large household with an abundance of personal and economic problems, it was not infrequently the case that her steward, 'the *procurator* with the crimped locks', became her confidant and lover. Her attendance at dinner parties and plays could be the occasion of numerous encounters and temptations. Since the days of Augustus' daughter Julia – and Ovid – it was especially the *jeunesse dorée* of Rome who again and again rebelled against the puritanical revivals of ancient Roman ways and lived the good life without inhibitions. *Principes* like Caligula, Nero and Otho took the lead in such movements, while the Flavians and Antonines sought to dam the torrents and attempted again and again, at least outwardly, to restore the old standards and curb promiscuity.

EDUCATION

Traditionalist critics like Tacitus idealised the ancient principles of upbringing which mothers had once followed:

'Once upon a time every man's son, born of a chaste mother, was reared not by a bought nurse in her den but at his mother's breast and on her lap. And for her the highest merit was to keep house and look after the children. Moreover, they also chose out an older female relative to whose tried and proven character all the children of a single family could be entrusted. In her presence nobody dared to say what it was not nice to say, or do what it was wrong to do. And she governed not only the lessons and tasks but also the recreation and play of the children with a certain sanctity and reverence. Thus Cornelia, so we are told, governed the upbringing of the Gracchi, Aurelia that of Julius Caesar, and Atia that of Augustus, all as children destined for high rank. Such discipline and severity had the effect that the nature of each child, sincerely and whole-heartedly and undistracted by any faults of character, at once grasped at the honourable arts, and whether they were drawn to military pursuits or the science of law or the study of eloquence, they could concentrate on that alone and absorb it wholly.

'But now the new-born baby is handed over to some little Greek nursemaid, with a man slave for assistant, just picked out of the house mob and often the lowest of the low, fit for no serious duties. From that moment the raw and tender minds are soaked in their fables and superstitions. And not a member of the household minds a bit what he or she says or does in front of the infant master. On the contrary the parents themselves, far from imbuing the little ones with habits of honour and modesty, encourage them in skittishness and frivolity, so that they become gradually filled with impudence and a contempt for themselves and others. The peculiar, special vices of this city, it seems to me, are conceived almost in the mother's womb – the enthusiasm for the stage and the passion for gladiators and horses. How much room is left for decent arts in a mind thus occupied and obsessed, how few you will find who at home talk of anything else? What other conversation shall we hear among the young men when we enter the classroom? Even the teachers have nothing better to talk about with their students. And they collect students not by the seriousness of their own teaching or the exercise of the students' intelligence but by the fulsomeness of their own greetings and the enticing flattery of their manners.' (Tacitus, *Dialogus de Oratoribus*, 28–9)

In the life of the Roman ladies under the Principate the bringing up of children played a smaller and smaller part. The reasons were twofold. First, the average number of children was decreasing, especially in the wealthier families; and secondly, infant mortality even among these classes was extraordinarily high. This can be explained by medical ignorance and the lack of the most primitive antiseptic methods, and also by the change in the general mentality. Here, however, there was a fundamental difference between life in Rome and life in the colonies and municipalities of the provinces, with their simpler and more rugged patterns of living.

Against that, we can rarely form an exact impression of the Roman woman in occupational life. No doubt there were more fisher women (*piscatrix*) and women greengrocers (*negotiatrix leguminaria*), more milliners (*vestifica*) and wool or silk drapers (*lanipenda, sericaria*) than the frequency of the inscriptions with trade designations would suggest. Even so, the list is dominated by the typical 'womanly occupations', nurse (*nutrix*) and midwife (*obstetrix*) on the one hand, and dressmaker (*sarcinatrix*) and hairdresser (*tonstrix*) on the other. These were all functions which in many great houses were performed by slaves and freedwomen. Professional women like doctors (*medica*), governesses (*paedagoga*), clerks (*amanuensis*), stenographers (*notaria*) or secretaries (*libraria*) seem to have been much rarer.

As I have pointed out, in the age of the Principate the education of children was widely delegated to nurses and slaves, and after that to a system of schooling generally divided into three phases. From the age of seven onward, girls and boys together went to the elementary schools (*ludi litterarii*), private institutions in which the children were taught 'the three r's' – 'reading, writing and arithmetic' – for small fees and often by very stupid methods, with continual shouting and caning by the schoolmaster. This phase of schooling was attended by most children, which was by no means the case with the next, in which the *grammaticus* or 'grammarian' provided the educational core, and which a large proportion of children did not attend. To begin with, only the Greek language and literature figured extensively in the syllabus, but from the Augustan period onward, this was enlarged to include the Latin classics, especially Ennius, Terence and Virgil.

The last phase was played out in the schools of rhetoric, which were supposed to instil the knowledge required for all careers of state and politics and the law. Here too the education was bilingual; the aim was to 'imitate' the great Greek and Latin orators, and training was predominantly formal. While in the *controversiae* the students were required to learn the art of dialectic on historical themes, which were often fictitious and on richly imaginative legal cases, in the *suasoriae* argumentation played the main part. Tacitus thus stigmatised this 'school of impudence', as Cicero first called it:

'So questions like the reward for tyrant slaying, or whether the raped girl should choose death or marriage for her attacker, or the recourse to human sacrifice in a plague epidemic, or maternal incest or all the other nonsense daily performed in the schools but rarely if ever in the Forum, all this is set out at length in outrageous language . . .' (Tacitus, *Dialogus de Oratoribus*, 35)

From the late Republic onward, for young gentlemen of the governing class it became usual after this to do a 'grand tour' to Athens, Asia Minor, Rhodes or other intellectual centres of the Hellenistic East, a journey which did as a rule enable them to become better acquainted with Greek philosophy.

Thus there was no comprehensive system of state schooling. Not until the Principate did some individual cities start to pay salaries to teachers on an official basis. Pliny the Younger, for instance, endeavoured to found in Como a kind of council of elders which took on the organisation of a city school of their own. No figures can be estimated for the number of illiterates in the *imperium Romanum*, but it is certain that the figures varied considerably from one part of the empire to another. In any case, no very optimistic assumptions about the prevalence of literacy would be justified.

HOUSING

No matter how great the variety of sites and settings for living accommodation throughout the extent of the *imperium Romanum*, the characteristic types of residential unit, at any rate within the Roman–Italian heartland, may be reduced to two. There were the individual dwelling house, generally identical with the so-called 'atrium house' (*domus*), and the complexes of tenements in the tall apartment blocks (*insulae*). According to the regional registers in the fourth century AD, there were 1797 villa type housing complexes of the rich in Rome, against 46,602 *insulae* each with numerous dwelling units for the poorer population. (Besides these are listed 254 mills, 190 grain silos, 8 bridges, 8 great squares, 11 forums, 36 triumphal arches, 1152 fountains, 28 public libraries, 2 circuses, 2 amphitheatres, 3 theatres, 11 large hot spring baths and 856 smaller private bath houses.) In Pompeii, a *domus* could cover an area of 800 to 900 square metres (about 9000 square feet), while the ground plan of an *insula* was of course more modest. According to some land registry fragments preserved from the Severan age, in Rome they averaged only some 300 to 400 square metres (about 4000 square feet). They were quite frequently five to six storeys high, and the existence of three-storey houses in Rome is attested by literary sources as early as the end of the third century BC.

The city villas of the *atrium* house type are relatively well known, especially from the Vesuvius cities, Pompeii and Herculaneum, but also from Rome itself. They represent the typical city house of the *haute bourgeoisie* and wealthier classes. They mostly have two standard features, about which the various rooms were grouped. One was the open courtyard of the *atrium*, and the other the peristyle section, a garden area at the back of the house surrounded by a portico, around which generally the dining-room (*triclinium*), the bedrooms (*cubicula*), also the kitchen, and in individual cases a small private bath were grouped. Thus the peristyle section had a decidedly more intimate character than the *atrium* section near the house entrance.

Originally the *atrium*, functionally speaking, was the core of the house. It contained the hearth, the women worked there, and at first it was where the household ate. The extension of the old back yard into the peristyle section, and the change of emphasis which resulted, was a later development, which can still be made out clearly in Pompeii, where *atria* in some cases reached an area of 12 metres by 17 (about 40

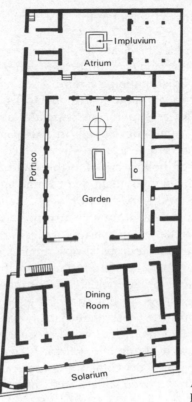

7 The House of the
Atrium with a Mosaic,
Herculaneum

feet by 55) and yet merely served representational purposes. Slaves and
service staff in dwellings of this size generally lived on the upper floor.

While the *domus* was closed to the exterior and, with its simple façade,
might give only a modest impression, the *atrium* was flooded with light,
and the peristyle section, with works of art and varied garden effects,
was worked up into an attractive living area. The living rooms,
moreover, were decorated with impressive and colourful wall paintings
(see p. 152), and from the second century onwards floor mosaics
spread rapidly.

In most cities of the *imperium* the problems of water supply and
sewerage, considering the technical possibilities of the age, were solved
in quite exemplary fashion. In Rome, fourteen monumental aqueducts
delivered pure spring water from the Apennines into the city, about a
billion litres a day (220 million gallons), according to modern estimates.
There were 247 reservoirs (*castella*) to regulate the supply. Arches of
some five metres (over 16 feet) in diameter survive to this day in
evidence of the monumental dimensions of the *cloaca maxima*, the
tremendous drainage canal system constructed in early republican

times from the Forum to the foot of the Aventine, where it discharged into the Tiber.

Since the water needs of a *domus* for cooking, pools and baths were exceptionally large, these housing units were connected by lead piping directly to the city distribution system. Such comforts were not, however, for the occupants of the apartment blocks, which as a rule had neither their own water supply nor separate latrines. The heating systems too were highly developed in the *domus*. The so-called 'hypocaust' system of central heating was actuated by warm air under the floors and through hollow bricks in the walls.

But the mass of the city populations of Rome and Italy lived in the wretched tenements of the apartment blocks, the *insulae*, which have become known in more detail through excavations and reconstructions, especially at Ostia. In the rented apartment blocks of Ostia, the ground floors were frequently taken up by shop premises, specially high and connected to workshops and store-rooms. On the first floors were dwelling units of three to five rooms each, of modest size, while the garrets on the upper floors became increasingly small and dark. The total height of an apartment block under Trajan was limited to about 18 metres (60 feet). Living in them was not only wretched but also dangerous on account of the frequent fires. It could perhaps only be endured because the warm, dry climate allowed poorer people to spend much of their lives in the open streets and squares and at the games.

CLOTHING

The characteristic garment of Roman men was the toga, a large white woollen cloth cut into a semicircle. Its quantity of material kept increasing under the Principate till in the end it became more and more unshapely and inconvenient. Putting on the toga allowed and called for a rather complicated folding process and abundant draping. It was therefore natural that this old official 'gown of state', *the* male national costume, should in the course of time be increasingly displaced by a more convenient garment. Thus under the Severi the *dalmatica* came into fashion, a topcoat with wide long sleeves, often of silk or half-silk. Very popular too was the *paenula*, a simple funnel-shaped, sleeveless garment which could also serve as a cloak when it was made of wool. But the traditional undergarment, which was not taken off even at night, was the *tunica*, a short-sleeved shirt-like garment made of two pieces sewn together.

The Romans in general did not cover their heads. Only at prayer and sacrifice was the toga lifted over the back of the head, a custom known from portraits, where the *capite velato*, i.e. 'with covered head', is a demonstrative expression of the piety of the subject. The footwear for peasants and soldiers was a sturdy, hardwearing leather shoe, generally with nailed soles, and uppers slit into strips, the *caliga*. But the normal enclosed Roman boot was the *calceus*, with uppers of soft leather in front and a gaiter-like leg over the anklebone. The *calceus* of patricians and senators was distinguished at first by a red colour and later by black.

The dress of Roman women for a long time remained very simple. Over a long tunic reaching to the ankles they originally wore the *stola*, a gown belted at the waist. Later the *palla*, a broad mantle, was worn over the shoulders. The ensemble could be completed by leather sandals or shoes, veil, bonnet and of course jewellery, more or less valuable according to means, consisting of earrings, bracelets, brooches and rings with pearls and precious or semi-precious stones. Prostitutes wore the toga with transparent materials from Cos. Hair styles changed rapidly, with the fashions often set by the ladies of the *domus principis*.

Men were shaved clean, in rather cruel fashion, the face being merely rubbed with water before shaving. It was Hadrian who introduced the full beard, and under the Severi the changes were rung between luxuriant and shorter beards. The care of hair and beard made frequent visits to the barber (*tonsor*) obligatory. The barber's shop (*tonstrina*) was already in those days a place for the exchange of news and social intercourse in the broadest sense. For the Roman lady, too, every day began with the morning toilet, mostly behind closed doors and sometimes elaborate. Here it was the *ornatrix*, or woman hairdresser, who played the main part. In all the wealthier houses, functions like these would as a matter of course have been performed by slaves.

Although the everyday clothing of the Romans often showed very little difference between slaves, freed men or women and free citizens, it was none the less not a purely private matter, especially among the governing class. From the very beginning Roman costume, quite unlike that of the Greeks, was strictly differentiated according to rank. First of all the patricians distinguished themselves from all plebeians, however rich, by the purple stripe on their tunics, the *latus clavus*, their short mantle (*trabea*), also purple-striped, the special patrician boot (*calceus*), the gold ring (*anulus aureus*), the horse of state (*equus publicus*) and their horse's silver ornaments (*phalerae*). Then, when the Roman aristocracy was transformed from a hereditary aristocracy to a senatorial nobility of office, these 'status symbols' were extended to all senators, except for the striking patrician boot, which continued to be reserved solely for the members of the patrician clans.

Then, when in the second century AD the senators were separated out of the group of the *equites*, there were further changes in their clothing. The senators were now distinguished by the broad stripe, and the *equites*

by a narrow stripe (*angustus clavus*). More important than the detail of
these distinctions of clothing was the fact that in course of time they
hardened into a rigid state system. From the third century A D onward
especially, any usurpation of symbols was ruthlessly put down, and
such distinctions of clothing acquired even greater importance in the
context of a rigidly aligned society.

FOOD AND MEALS

The Roman day, generally speaking, was divided up by three main
meals – so far as they really deserved the name. Immediately after
getting up, there was breakfast (*ientaculum*), which consisted as a rule
only of bread and cheese. Then there was lunch (*prandium*), somewhat
more varied but still very frugal, of bread, cold meat, fruit, a little wine.
Finally there was dinner (*cena*), the main meal, taken late in the
afternoon or at evening. This too was originally very simple, like Roman
meals in general. The chief food of the Romans was originally *puls*, a
kind of porridge of spelt, with an accompaniment of vegetables, onions,
garlic, cheese and fruit, but only rarely meat. Then baked bread came in
as an additional food. Bakeries in Rome are attested in the literature
from the second century B C onward.

About the same time, however, there also began that luxury of the
rich man's table so often described, and already criticised by Varro.
Aulus Gellius thus quotes him:

'I will limit myself to an approximate account, so far as I can remember them,
of the sorts and names and places of origin of the delicacies for which land and
sea were scoured with tireless gluttony, as enumerated with such strong
disapproval by Varro. Here is the list: peacock (*pavus*) from Samos, hazel hens
(*attagena*) from Phrygia, cranes (*grues*) from Media, young kid (*haedus*) from
Ambracia, tunnyfish (*pelamis*) from Chalcedon (in Bithynia), lampreys (*murena*)
from Tartesus (in Spain), whitefish (*aselli*) from Pessinus (in Phrygia), oysters
(*ostrea*) from Tarentum, scallops (*pectunculus*) from Chios, swordfish (*helops*)
from Rhodes, parrot fish (*scari*) from Cilicia, nuts (*nuces*) from Thasos, dates
(*palma*) from Egypt, acorns (*glans*) from Iberia. Such greed of a palate which looks
everywhere for rare delicacies brought from far countries, such a hunt for tidbits
will be found the more disgusting the more we think of some verses of Euripides
often quoted by Chrysippus, that certain dainties are only concocted, not
because they are necessary to sustain life but for sensual overindulgence
disdaining anything easy to prepare and from exaggerated luxury.' (Aulus
Gellius, *Noctes Atticae* VI, 16, 4ff.)

Thus from the first century B C onwards the refinements of luxury at
the upper class table took on more and more sophisticated forms. All the
same, the principal evening meal of the Roman citizen remained modest
on the whole. As a rule it had three courses. The first (*gustum*)

comprised a series of small hors d'œuvres, egg dishes, vegetables, salads, salt fish, shellfish or the favourite dormice. With this was drunk *mulsum*, wine mixed with honey, or some sort of fruit juice. The main course which followed consisted of roast or boiled meat or poultry, with which wine was served, and usually mixed with water before drinking. The third and final course (*mensae secundae*) originally also included spiced and salted dishes or shellfish, but at a later period it became usual to serve only fruit and sweets. Often with these an extended wine-drinking session would begin. Especial favourites were the Caccuban wines from Gaeta and the Falernian from Campania. As implements for eating, only knife and spoon were laid, no forks. As the eaters also reclined at table, they ate with their fingers, so that they frequently had to wash their hands.

In Rome itself, however, many of the poorer families living in the *insulae* had no kitchens of their own at all. Some of them could cook on small stoves or charcoal braziers in front of their houses, while the rest had to fetch their warm dishes from one of the numerous cookshops, the *popinae*. It is well established, however, that the art of cooking in the wealthier Roman families became increasingly refined. A cookery book containing a few recipes has been handed down under the name of Marcus Gavius Apicius, a famous gourmet of the early first century A D, but in the form in which we have it today it probably dates from no earlier than the end of the fourth century A D.

For the upper classes and governing élite, the great banquets were a focal point of social life, as they were also, among hosts, for anyone who could afford to give such a dinner, or among guests for any client who could procure an invitation. The ludicrous ostentation of these occasions among the new rich and freedmen is satirised in the famous *cena Trimalchionis* of Petronius, with its total of sixty-two different dishes and drinks. The dinners were more than just meals in common or drinking sessions. Varro's idea of what was needed is thus quoted by Aulus Gellius:

'Four things are required for a good dinner: pleasant guests, well-chosen time and place, and good preparation. Guests should be neither too talkative nor too dumb. Eloquence may be all right in the Forum or the courts, while long silences are more suited to the bedroom than the table. And conversation at table, so Varro thinks, should not deal with tiresome or complicated matters but be intriguing and agreeable, calculated to improve our minds and cheer our spirits. But this end can really be attained only if the subjects of conversation are confined to matters of everyday life, such as we have no time to think about when in court or in the press of public affairs. Moreover, the host must aim not so much at extravagance in his dinner as at an absence of meanness.' (Aulus Gellius, *Noctes Atticae* XIII, 11,3ff.)

THE GAMES

Panem – et circenses! Bread and games: 'circus games' of the most various kinds occupied a more and more important place in Roman civilisation. They became its most obvious expression. At first they were primarily religious occasions, and for some time retained their solemn opening processions of gods, but in the later republican period and during the Principate it was entirely their political significance which predominated. At the beginning their purpose was to thank the gods for their help, but later, beginning especially with Sulla and Julius Caesar, they came to celebrate the great military successes, the thanksgiving days and the achievements of the *principes* and their house. The gigantic expenditure involved was the price paid by the politicians and generals for their ambitions and prestige, their conspicuous tribute to the Roman people. At first they consisted only of theatrical performances and especially chariot races, but soon the wild beast shows, gladiatorial combats, more and more outlandish competitions and extravagant stagings, even on water, were added. Their further evolution was marked by the accumulation of effects, the titillation of the emotions, and the employment of every technical device. At the same time their content became more and more inhuman.

Under the Principate especially, the games were for a long time the only vital mass assemblies of the Roman population. In them public opinion found unbridled expression; they offered hours of direct communion with the *princeps* and his family and with the leading families of the state. The attitude of leading politicians and the *principes* to these occasions was always two-edged. On the one hand, there was here a possibility of winning new sympathies by direct action on public opinion; on the other, they were not infrequently compelled against their will to fall in with the wishes of the masses, and at least to pardon and set free the heroes of the hour.

This did not always happen from conviction, as in the touching story of Androcles and the lion. (The slave Androcles had run away from his master and was therefore condemned to death by wild beasts – *ad bestias*. But the lion to whom he was cast in the arena recognised in Androcles the very man who had once taken a thorn out of his paw and therefore spared him. The spectators on learning the circumstances thereupon loudly demanded the release of Androcles, lion and all, and this was granted by the Emperor Claudius.)

Under the Principate, the games, as I have said, were the price paid for neutralisation of the emotions of the Roman population and also an expression of it. This observation is not just an outcome of modern analysis but was already known to contemporaries, as we may gather from the oft-quoted remark of the mime Pylades to Augustus: 'It is to your advantage, Caesar, that we keep the public occupied.' And the public did occupy itself more and more frequently and intensively with the games. In one year of Augustus there was a total of sixty-five days of games of the most varied kinds. But by the middle of the fourth century AD the total in one year had reached ten days of fighting sports, sixty-four days of chariot races, wild-beast baitings and races of other kinds in the circus, on 102 days play performances in the theatre – though these of course were much less popular.

At a very early date, in the valley between the Aventine and the Palatine, there were horse races and chariot races, and for these under Julius Caesar and Augustus the monumental Circus Maximus was built up and developed with successive enlargements till it could finally accommodate 150,000–180,000 spectators. From then on it formed a splendid setting for the relatively infrequent horse races, which were often accompanied by acrobatic shows; for athletic competitions, and especially for the highly popular chariot races. These last were run not only with two horses drawing the small chariot, the *bigae*, but as a rule with four. And indeed the number was constantly increased. Nero at Olympia tried his hand at a ten-horse team. The course was seven rounds of the circus and the total distance 8.4 kilometres (just under $5\frac{1}{4}$ miles). Each race lasted about a quarter of an hour. There were on average twenty-four different races on a racing day.

The races were a contest between companies (*factiones*), of which there were four, each with its own colour, white, red, green and blue. Under the early Principate, the Greens and the Blues began to absorb the other two. Each of the *factiones* commanded great resources: its own stables, equipment stores, training centres – its own 'outfit' in fact. The fans of each company formed a permanent body, and completely identified themselves with the charioteers and horses of their colour. These *factiones* were undoubtedly the largest and most lively mass organisations of the Roman population in the age of the Principate, although in the Rome of the first two centuries AD they never achieved the political importance of the similarly constituted circus companies in the Constantinople of Late Antiquity. The last chariot races of ancient Rome were held in the year 549 AD by the Ostrogoth king Totila.

The centrepoint of the gladiatorial contests and wild-beast shows under the Principate was the Flavian Amphitheatre (the 'Colosseum'), with its four storeys, eighty great arches, a height of over 48 metres (160 feet), and a capacity of some 50,000 spectators. Over the area where once Nero's gigantomania ran riot in the lavish complexities of his 'Golden House' there now rose great buildings in the service of the whole Roman people. The Flavian amphitheatre itself was only part of a monumental construction programme.

8 Imperial Rome

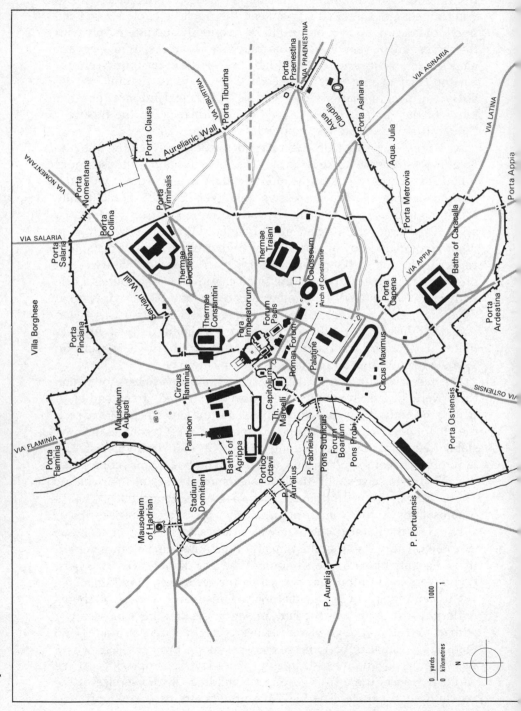

'Here where the Sun Colossus has his near view of the stars,
Here where the theatre engines tower
The hated palace of the cruel despot once stood,
A single house in the space of a whole city.
Here where the huge bulk of the splendid amphitheatre
Now rears its majestic head, once Nero had his lake.
Here where we admire the hot baths so quickly built,
A splendid park had robbed the poor of their homes.
Where the Claudian colonnade spreads wide its shade,
The outer extremities of the palace once ended.
Rome is restored to itself, and under your government, Caesar,
What once served only the despot now serves the people's pleasure.'

(Martial, *Epigrams* I, 2)

In the *Book of Shows* here quoted, the first of his great collection of epigrams, Martial never tired of extolling the Colosseum. In the very first poem, he compared it with the 'wonders of the world' – to their disadvantage:

'Every building is eclipsed by Caesar's Amphitheatre,
One work alone will monopolise the fame once shared by all.'

He described the influx from all over the world – Thracians, Sarmatians, Egyptians, Sabaean Arabs, Cilicians, Sugambrians, Ethiopians, all streamed together to Rome to attend the great games. Martial described some of the exciting events which so fascinated the spectators in the Flavian Amphitheatre: fights between rhinoceros and bull, tiger and lion, bull and elephant, between two gazelles. He told of the pregnant wild sow which in its death struggle farrowed a young one; of the gazelle which in apparent supplication came to a standstill before the emperor's box; of the gladiator Carpophorus, a hero of the arena who killed one after the other a bear, a lion and a panther. He tells of the cruel, implacable duels of the gladiators, the colourful and resplendent water pageants and sea fights mounted by Domitian.

The first recorded wild-beast baiting took place in Rome as early as 186 BC, under M. Fulvius Nobilior. The shows at first were often held in the Circus Maximus. Rare and exotic animals were not only exhibited at them but made to fight one another in all kinds of pairings, and frequently too against human beings. Besides a selection of Italian animals (roe deer, red deer, wild boar, bears and bulls), from the second century BC onward there were already lions, panthers, leopards and ostriches being shown, and by late republican times demands and expectations were raised to a higher and higher pitch. In 58 BC Aemilius Scaurus showed crocodile and hippopotamus; in 55 BC Pompey the rhinoceros, rare African apes and Gallic lynxes; Caesar in 47 BC giraffes. At the same time the numbers of animals and the duration and form of the massacres steadily increased. Already in Pompey's and Caesar's games hundreds of lions were slaughtered; in the total of 26 wild-beast baitings staged by Augustus some 3500 African animals were killed; in Trajan's games in the year 107 BC some 11,000 wild animals were slaughtered. The morbid peak was reached by the wild-beast baitings under the sick emperor Commodus, who on a single afternoon killed five crocodiles by his own hand, on others again two elephants, several rhinoceroses and a giraffe. On a much smaller scale, *venationes* of this kind were held in many smaller cities of the *imperium*.

The gladiatorial games had a very modest beginning. In the year 264 BC, the sons of D. Iunius Brutus Pera, on the occasion of their father's burial, engaged three pairs of gladiators to fight one another on the Roman ox market. In accordance with a custom prevalent in Etruria and Campania, these were originally always 'games' in honour of a dead man who would in ancient thinking consume the blood thus shed. The Christian rhetorician Tertullian later described the whole development:

'Anything sacrificed was regarded as a service to the dead . . . and it was called office for the dead (*munus*). . . . But the ancients continued to regard it as a service to the dead when they had softened its character by a milder form of cruelty. Previously prisoners of war or bad slaves were bought and sacrificed at the funerals because it was believed that the spirits of the dead could be appeased by human blood. Later men delighted in turning this wickedness into an entertainment. And thus people who had been procured just to learn how to be killed were instructed in the use of arms as well as they then could be and then on the day fixed for the sacrifice to the dead were made to perform by the grave mounds. Thus people sought consolation for bereavement in murder.' (Tertullian, *De Spectaculis*, 12)

Here too the number of particular participants and the duration of the fights continually increased. Their religious associations were lost, and the fights finally became entertainment in its most brutal form, the apotheosis of sadism and perversion. As early as the year 174 BC, the philhellene T. Quinctius Flamininus put on seventy-four gladiators at the games in honour of his father. It was in 105 BC that Roman consuls for the first time mounted gladiatorial shows at state expense; in 65 BC Caesar as aedile put on 320 pairs; Titus for the opening of the *Amphitheatrum Flavium* in AD 80 several thousands; and Trajan between AD 106 and 114, it is said, some 23,000 men. And despite all the efforts of Christianity, the gladiator fights in Rome continued up to the end of the fourth century AD.

Not only slaves and prisoners of war fought as gladiators, but often criminals condemned to the arena for a great variety of offences, and, as is well known, a large number of Christians. There were even free citizens among them, men who were failures, or an occasional member

of the governing class who preferred the wild excitement of such a form
of existence to the monotony of his own. The volunteer gladiators swore
an oath to let themselves be beaten with rods, burned with fire and
killed with iron'.

The whole gladiatorial business was thoroughly organised. Special
managers (the *lanistae*) maintained gladiator families, arranged for
replacements, looked after their training, rented them out or sold them.
In the smaller cities of the *imperium* especially, they undertook the
organisation of the games as agents of the magistrates. The training and
exercise of gladiators took place in special schools, of which those in
Capua became widely known through the Spartacus rebellion. Under
the Principate in Rome itself, where the *princeps* had a monopoly in the
keeping of gladiators (after Nero's death 2000 gladiators here changed
masters), there were three gladiator schools, the greatest of which (*ludus
magnus*), adjacent to the Colosseum in the neighbourhood of the Via
Labicana, has been partly excavated. The schools were not only
technically well equipped and provided with experienced sword
masters but they also had good masseurs and qualified doctors.

There were different types of gladiators, defined by their arms and
style of combat, and these to some extent originated in typically
'national' weapons among former prisoners of war. The 'Samnites', for
instance, were armed with huge rectangular shields, short swords,
greaves and visor helmets with a high crest and tuft of feathers. The
'Thracians' had small round shields and curved swords. The *retiarii* had
a trident, net and dagger, the *secutores* a shield, sword and helmet with
visor. Then there were the *andabatae*, riders in armour who fought with
closed visors, and the *essedarii*, who fought from the typical British war
chariots. The merest sketch of these different types shows how much
agility was needed to master the use of different weapons. Only
specialists could judge the technique and quality of the strokes and
parries, yet it was easy to become a connoisseur by long watching of the
best fighters.

The gladiator fights themselves, which often lasted all day, were
usually introduced by mimic fighters (*paegniarii*) and mock fighters
(*lusorii*), who engaged one another merely with wooden weapons. Only
after these did the gladiators fight in earnest in the most varied
combinations. They fought often with frenzied encouragement from
the mob, a real mass hysteria. The fight continued until one of the
contestants was killed or so severely wounded that he could not carry
on. Then the crowd by waving handkerchiefs or raised thumbs would
demand a pardon, or, not infrequently, by thumbs down, death. The
decision, however, was always given by the president of the games, the
magistrate who had organised them, or the *princeps*. It was he, too, who

presented the victors with golden bowls, crowns and gold pieces, as well as the usual palm leaf.

The mob of spectators was worked up into a frenzy of blood lust. Seneca describes the scenes he witnessed in the 'quiet' time of the midday interval between the main fights, which it was merely a question of bridging, and when only a part of the spectators were present:

'By chance I arrived at a midday interval, expecting fun and jokes, some relief and relaxation after the sight of human blood. Quite the opposite! All previous fights were compassionate by comparison – no trifling now, just sheer murder! No protection for the fighters, their whole bodies exposed to every thrust, they themselves striking home with every thrust. And this the crowd enjoys more than the pairings of real gladiators, whether ordinary or even those by special request. Of course they do! Not a helmet or shield to parry the sword. What need of protection? What need of skill? They only delay the death. In the morning, men are thrown to the lions and bears; at noon, to the spectators. They call for the killers to be thrown to other killers, the victor to be saved for new slaughter; for these fighters the end is always death. Fire and sword rule the day. So it goes on, till the arena is "empty". "But", you say, "he was a robber, wasn't he, he killed a man?" Well and good, he's a murderer and has got his deserts. But you, you miserable wretch, what gives you the right to enjoy the spectacle? "Kill him, beat him, burn him!" "Why does he run on the sword so timidly?" "Why doesn't he hit back?" "Why doesn't he want to die?" "Flog them into fighting!" "Breast to naked breast, that's how they should strike and meet the sword!" But it's an interval! "Well, can't they cut a few throats then, just to pass the time?" (Seneca, *Letters to Lucilius* VII, 3ff.)

In the end the very massing of the fights dulled the public appetite. Even Julius Caesar and Augustus were already changing over to the organisation of 'naval battles' in which huge troops of gladiators fought at sea, usually with historical trappings, as for instance a naval fight of Greek ships against Persians. The ultimate in this respect was the *naumachia* staged by Claudius in A D 52 on the Fucine Lake between two fleets of 19,000 men each. Domitian too presented games of this kind.

There were amphitheatres for gladiatorial contests and wild-beast fights throughout the Roman world. The earliest known (80 B C) is that at Pompeii. After enlargements, it finally contained 20,000 seats, probably more than the city had inhabitants. More than seventy such theatres are known from all parts of the *imperium*, the most famous among them including those at Verona, Pola, Corinth, Pergamum, Antioch, Berytos, Alexandria, Lambaesis, Caesarea in Mauretania, Arles, Nîmes and Trier. To begin with, private people too put up wooden temporary structures, sometimes with catastrophic results, as under Tiberius in Fidenae, where a structure of this kind collapsed and is said to have buried 50,000 people under it. The spread of gladiatorial games to the provinces, and the pressure on magistrates by popular opinion, finally had the result that these *munera* could hardly be financed any more. Thus a special *senatus consultum* (senatorial decree) of A D 177/178 fixed the pay of gladiators, who were grouped into five classes by rank and were to receive fees graduated from 1000 to 15,000 sesterces for each appearance.

Finally, there were still theatre performances. But these could not compete with chariot races, wild-beast baitings and gladiatorial contests. Their appeal was much more restricted. Of the three Roman theatres, that of Balbus could accommodate some 6,000 to 7,000 people, that of Pompey some 12,000, that of Marcellus some 10,000, so that all three together had no more than half the seats in the *Amphitheatrum Flavium*. The most important genres performed there were the *Atellana* and the *mimus*. The *Atellana* was originally a Campanian style of comedy or farce with constant type characters – the old man (*pappus*), the hunchback (*dossennus*), the glutton (*bucco*) and the fool (*maccus*). Originally it was rooted entirely in situations of rustic artisan life but later took up other types of milieu. The *mimus* was a clown burlesque without standard type-masks, cluttered with numerous inserted song-sequences and buffoonery of the crudest kind, jokes about gods, mountebank insets, broad love-and-adultery sketches. In the theatre too the magnificence of the scenery was more important than the artistic substance. The writers of comedies and tragedies wrote new plays not for staging but for recitation. Recitation became an epidemic.

Readings of any kind, to small or large audiences, had long been the rage. In heightened tones, with grand 'artistic' gestures, any and every piece was read aloud – historical writings, stories, poetry, plays, speeches, would-be 'literary' prose of every kind, for hours at a time. In one kind of performance, it was true, the Principate did still experience great artistic achievements, and that was in 'pantomime'. These performers had once been singers and dancers together in one person, like the elder Pylades under Augustus, but in the age of Domitian and Trajan they combined only dance and mime, conveying the most varied effects by the dumb language of their movements.

BATHS

There were other buildings which acquired an importance as centres of social life similar to that of the Circus Maximus and the Amphitheatre, and in this case on a permanent basis. These were the monumental public baths put up in quick succession from Agrippa to Constantine. The architectural remains of the baths of Caracalla and Diocletian, with ground plans of 11 to 13 hectares (27 to 32 acres) and a bewildering agglomeration of rooms and courtyards, still impress every visitor to

Rome. Each of them made up what was not only a varied system of all imaginable kinds of baths – cold, warm, hot, steam, air and sun baths – but also a centre of leisure pursuits and communication, of exercise and games, gymnastics and massage facilities, gardens and parks, even libraries and museums. The relatively small admittance charges and the cost of oil for body care did none the less restrain a considerable part of the population from all too frequent use. Even so, it is remarkable that the number of smaller bathing establishments (*balnea*) in the capital increased from about 170 under Augustus to over 900 in Late Antiquity.

LIFE-STYLES

A verse frequently scribbled on walls of the period gives us an insight into the mentality of the simple citizens of Rome under the Principate:

> 'Baths, wine and love-making destroy our bodies,
> Yet love-making, wine and baths make life worth living.'
> (*Balnea, vina, Venus corrumpunt corpora nostra,*
> *At vitam faciunt balnea, vina, Venus.*)

The philosophy of life encountered in this *graffito* is rather different from that reflected by those eulogies of the Roman nobility with their striving after *virtus, honos* and *gloria*, but also after wealth, large families and constant increase in social prestige. Of course under the Principate there were thousands of ambitious Romans obsessed by social climbing, activists by all means and in every respect. They included above all the social climbers from country towns and colonies, the provincial élite, but also freedmen and ordinary provincials. And besides these, though in ever smaller number, there were also, inside the governing class, the sticklers for tradition, who made a parade of their adherence to the old standards and the old way of life.

Yet there were other more important developments. The new structure of political power led to what Jacob Burckhardt called the 'withdrawal of the best people from politics'. By this he meant the reaction to a state of affairs where anyone in an exposed position – officials, dignitaries, the rich in general – could, at least under some regimes, on the denunciation of a single informer or the personal displeasure of the *princeps*, from one day to the next lose all his possessions. To this constant insecurity was added the unending increase in the burdens borne by richer citizens. It gave ever stronger conviction to a new ideal of living:

> 'What makes life enjoyable,
> my dearest Martial, is this:
> A fortune, inherited, not won with effort,

productive land, a hearth that keeps burning,
no lawsuits, formal dress but rarely, peace of mind,
good health, strength of a gentleman not a navvy,
frankness with tact, congenial friends,
pleasant company, simple food,
nights free of drink but also of care,
a bedmate willing but never wanton,
sleep which shortens the time of darkness,
to want to be none but yourself, no other,
neither to fear the end nor to desire it.'

(Martial, *Epigrams* X, 47)

The Greek ideal of observing moderation in all things came to have a greater and greater appeal. The violent excesses of unbridled force committed by individual *principes*, such as Caligula, Nero, Commodus, Caracalla, spread among the broad masses of the population a conscious longing for the modest enjoyment of small-scale happiness. Hectic fever and gigantomania at the centres of power produced understandable counterforces and reactions throughout the whole.

DISPOSAL AND REMEMBRANCE OF THE DEAD

So far as any general inferences can be made from the analysis of inscriptions, the life expectancy of the Romans was rather low. Values calculated from Ostia are not in every respect representative, but it is certainly remarkable that more than 80 per cent of all burial inscriptions known there are for persons less than thirty years old. This fact, and the extraordinarily high infant mortality rate, meant that every Roman family all the time, not just during the great wars and civil wars, was confronted with death and lived in its near presence. This gave rise not only to the *carpe diem* philosophy but also to the concern for suitable disposal of the dead and the concern of everyone for his or her own grave. It is true that initially for a great part of the poorer population of Rome mass graves predominated, like those shaft-like graves discovered on the Esquiline. But later it was for this very section of the population that the *collegia funeraticia* came into existence. These were club-like associations, of which the members by small monthly payments assured themselves of a place of their own in one of the great funeral institutions, the *columbaria* ('dovecots') for cremation or the catacombs for burial.

Anyone who could afford it had himself commemorated by a gravestone with full name, and, often enough, all the essential information about offices or public rank held or, in the case of freedmen especially, about their professional qualifications and successes. For a long time burial and cremation co-existed, but from the second century A D

onward burial began to predominate. In either case, however, the
Romans tried to preserve and keep alive the memory of every dead
person in the fullest individuality and in the artistically most expressive
form. Grave reliefs, urn ornaments and, from the Principate onwards,
increasingly also sarcophagus sculptures unfolded around the dead the
world of myth, or also, but less often, the occupational world. Goethe,
who thought very deeply about the Roman memorials to the dead in
Italy and Germany, described them thus:

> 'Sarcophagus and urn the heathen decked with life.
> Fauns dance around them, with the Bacchant crew
> in colourful formation. The goat-foot, chubby-cheeked,
> forces the glad wild tones from shattering horn.
> Cymbals, drums resound. We see and hear the marble.
> Fluttering birds! How glorious the taste of fruit to beak!
> No noise startles you, no noise the god of love,
> not him, in the bright throng gladdened by torches.
> So plenty conquers death, and the ashes inside there
> in that still place seem yet to live in joy.'
> (*Venetian Epigrams*, No. 1 'Sarcophagus')

But the Romans also honoured their dead with sayings in verse and
prose, and not just with strings of titles and career notes, and it may be
that these utterances, often so direct and simple, will move a modern
reader more deeply than the grand luxury memorials which in some
cases, on the evidence of account sheets, must have swallowed up a
year's salary. Although many of these inscriptions to the dead use set
formulas with traditional metaphors, the human destinies which they
reflect and the expectations to which they testify, whether pessimistic
and materialistic or also naively hopeful and credulous, do remain
documents of human experience:

> 'Here is eternal dwelling-place,
> here is an end of trouble,
> here is some remembrance.'

> 'Friends who read this, I pray you mix some wine,
> then drink it far from here, your heads wreathed with flowers,
> then with beautiful women share the delights of love.
> What remains after death let fire and earth consume.'

> 'He who walking upon it the peaceful waves of the lake
> tamed, who had the power to loosen the bonds of death,
> who after the dark of night on the third day from the dead
> rose, who restored to the light and to Martha her brother alive,
> he'll wake Damasus too – I believe in eternal life.'

(*Carmina Latina Epigraphica*, 225, 856 ['Grave inscriptions from Lamasba,
Numidia, and from Rome']; *Inscriptiones Latinae Christianae Veteres*, 969 ['Grave
Inscription of Pope Damasus'].)

ROMAN LAW

The concept of 'Roman law' arouses a general idea of abstractions. We think of a comprehensive code of law such as we find in the XII Tables, in the *edictum perpetuum* under Hadrian, and in the famous codifications of Late Antiquity, the *Codex Theodosianus* and the *Codex Iustinianus*. Last but not least, we think of the diffusion of Roman legal standards over the whole Mediterranean, with effects operative right into modern times. However much truth there may be in these common notions, there are many special aspects and manifestations of Roman law to which they fail to do justice. It has been left to modern scholarly research to bring out some of these. The interaction between case law and statute law gave the Roman system an evolutionary character, built up in course of time from layers of very different elements. And in its best period it was neither rigidly formalistic on the one hand nor reduced to mere juggling with words or platform histrionics on the other. The close interweaving of law, society and politics penetrates and determines every phase of Roman history. Today, after a long period in which Roman law has been studied mainly as a codified system, the emphasis is on interpreting it in terms of history.

The XII Tables, dated to the year 451/450 BC, were for Livy still 'the source of the entire public and private law' of the Romans (Livy, *History* III 34, 6). It was the first binding written record of a course of procedure by which justice might be done. Its individual provisions were either already in force or in process of being fixed by a compromise. With its establishment of the textual rules of criminal and civil law, it began a new epoch in the administration of justice. Right in the middle of the Struggle of the Orders, a ten-man commission with extraordinary powers, the *decemviri legibus scribundis*, laid the foundations of law for all Roman citizens, the complete *ius civile*.

The demand that the law in force should be written down is known from many class struggles in the ancient world. Its justification becomes clear when we consider the state of Roman law before the middle of the fifth century BC. For however important the sphere of purely private law, there were numerous cases concerned with sacral law, over which the *pontifices* presided. Their college alone was in possession of the correct decisions and formulae constituting this law. Only they could deliberate and give opinions. Thus the suspicion of class justice was often aroused, and the distrust of their uncontrollable activities not easy to appease. It was therefore a political gain of the first importance when the plebeians secured the writing down of the law.

A few sentences of the XII Tables give us a better idea than any description of the world with which they were dealing. For example, an article of the VIIIth Table, which was specially concerned with penal clauses, states: 'If anyone mutilates another's limb, he should suffer the same, unless he comes to a friendly understanding with the wounded one.' For Rome the talion principle we encounter here, the rule of an eye for an eye, became a fixed rule. Incendiaries must themselves be killed by fire; those who plunge their fellow citizens into ruin by bearing false witness against them must themselves be thrown into an abyss. At the same time it must be remembered that in all these cases the lawsuit was a private one brought by a private citizen. Even a case of murder consisted of a procedure designed to regulate the principles of private lawsuits and private indemnity. It was not in the first instance the Roman state which prosecuted and punished but the agnates, the next of kin in the male line. The judicial function of the state thus at first consisted solely in supervising the private pursuit of justice.

The characteristic institution of the age of the XII Tables is the *nexum*, the 'fettering', by which the debtor so far surrendered himself to his creditor as to become his slave if he did not pay the debt within the prescribed term. This institution remained in force until in 326 BC the *lex Poetelia Papiria de nexis*, one of the most important laws of the Roman Struggle of the Orders, put an end to debt slavery in this form.

Although the XII Tables had considerably strengthened the position of the plebeians, its interpretation and the supervision of the obligatory formulae remained within the competence of the *pontifices*, and therefore of the patricians. At the same time, as is clear from the case of the *nexum* just referred to, both private and procedural law were further developed also by statutes (*leges*) passed by the people's assembly on the motion of the consuls or of a tribune of the people. From the period between the XII Tables and the collapse of the Roman Republic some thirty such statutes, making new law or developing the old, are known at least by name and subject matter. Among the areas encompassed by them were procedure, damage to property, inheritance, gifts, guardianship and citizenship. The *repetundae* legislation from the time of the

Gracchi dealt with the abuse of office by Roman pro-magistrates in the provinces, while problems of settlement policy were legally regulated by a number of agrarian statutes. Every time the passage of one or other of these new laws was disputed, there was a renewal of the same passionate political conflicts.

But Roman law was also developed administratively by the legal decisions of particular magistrates (*ius honorarium*), especially the praetors and governors. The Roman law-dispensing magistrates, at the beginning of their term of office, published a statement of principles and formulae of their judicial practice in the form of an edict which in theory could be altered and elaborated by every office-holder in turn but in practice remained basically the same. It was not until the reign of Hadrian, however, that this codification of praetorian law was definitively edited by the great jurist Salvius Julianus. His published text of the so-called *edictum perpetuum* was then given legislative force by a resolution of the Senate. From then on, it could not be altered except by the *princeps*, and the making of law administratively by the praetors was thus brought to an end. Finally, the evolution of Roman law was also affected by the jurisprudence and manifold legal initiatives and decisions of the *principes*. It was thus compounded of legal ingredients from very different levels, which were not formally integrated until Late Antiquity, and even then could never disguise their varied historical origin.

The concentration of great masses of impoverished citizens in Rome during the period after the Punic wars clearly led to a large increase of crime, particularly crimes of violence. The Roman authorities reacted with an often brutal intensification of police justice, with deterrence as the object. Besides the *praetor urbanus*, special responsibility for police power and the execution of sentences lay with the *tresviri capitales*. The death penalty was imposed not only for straightforward crimes of violence, incendiarism, poisoning and theft but even for merely carrying weapons with criminal intent, as well as for the possession, purchase and sale of poison. If the criminal was caught red-handed or confessed punishment was inflicted without trial. If the accused denied the deed, there was a trial before the *praetor* or a deputy in charge of proceedings appointed by him if it was a reputable citizen. Otherwise the case was decided by the *triumvir* who was handling it, but in either case the question of guilt was discussed by the advisory commission (*consilium*) of the magistrate or deputy concerned.

In this *consilium* we encounter an institution, both political and legal, which was to become characteristic of those in an exposed position in Rome – magistrates, governors, army commanders and presiding judges – right up to the period of the Principate, and finally of the *princeps* himself. The presence and advice of an advisory commission became a regular rule. Even under the Principate it was more than a matter of personal style whether a *princeps* pronounced judgements alone or was supported by the advice and legal expertise of a *consilium*. Professional jurists of course acquired ever-increasing importance on such commissions.

Public criminal justice in Rome at first evolved in varied forms, which as a rule were completely determined by the peculiarities of the case. Cases of political crime in which the accused was liable to the death penalty were initially conducted within the system of the *comitia centuriata*. In the later republican period it became usual to set up extraordinary courts of justice (*quaestiones extraordinariae*) for cases of abuse of office or dereliction of duty by magistrates, mass crimes, or conspiracies against public order and the existence of the state. In all these cases consuls or praetors could be assigned to conduct the examinations and court proceedings.

It was only with the introduction of permanent courts of justice, the *quaestiones perpetuae*, that a stricter regulation of criminal procedure was effected. These in their turn made it necessary to enlarge the panel of candidates available for each *consilium* to include the *equites*. The *lex Sempronia iudiciaria*, a reform measure of the People's Tribune C. Gracchus of the year 122 BC, did do this, but the first comprehensive reorganisation took place under Sulla's dictatorship, when *quaestiones* were set up for the most varied categories of crime. From then on there was a special court for high treason (*maiestas*), embezzlement of public funds (*peculatus*), electoral corruption (*ambitus*), extortion in the provinces (*repetundae*), murder and poisoning (*de sicariis et veneficis*), forgery of wills and false coining (*de falsis*), violence to the person and breach of domestic peace (*de iniuriis*). Further special courts were set up later, as for instance one to deal with crimes of violence, another with adultery.

We have noted that public prosecuting authorities in the modern sense were unknown to Roman practice. Prosecutions were initiated by private indictment. In the time of the XII Tables this right was reserved to the party directly aggrieved, or his or her relations, but later almost every citizen of good repute had the right to bring in an indictment (*nominis delatio*) and conduct a prosecution, and was required to prove his own case. Material incentives, such as the defined fraction of the accused's property to which the accuser was entitled in the case of a death penalty, soon completely corrupted this institution. Its greatest excesses occurred in the time of the early Principate. The possibility of a suit of slander against false accusers (*calumnia*) did not eliminate the abuse of the indictment procedure.

The course of the proceedings before a *quaestio* depended to an important extent on whether the presiding magistrate even accepted the indictment, and this point would generally be decided at the outset after consultation with the members of his *consilium*. This commission or 'jury' would also have had some of the more critical decisions to take during the trial itself. Consisting often of several dozen members, in individual cases up to seventy-five, it was chosen for each case separately by lot from the corresponding panel of 'jurymen' or judges. The parties in the case each had the right to reject individuals, because of course the composition of the *consilium* was often decisive for the outcome of the case. Against that, all it could do during the actual proceedings was to listen, and all the presiding magistrate did was to supervise their orderly progress. It was the accuser and accused who dominated the scene, with their advocates and witnesses engaged in what were often very rancorous cross-examinations. Here the accused stood in a particularly strong position. Not only was he entitled to several advocates, but he was allowed one and a half times the total speaking time of the prosecution. The jury then gave a secret vote on the guilt or innocence of the accused. If the verdict was guilty, the penalty prescribed by law was carried out by the presiding magistrate. Only in the case of a fine the *consilium* might sometimes meet once more to fix the exact amount. In republican times, there was no penalty of imprisonment in the Roman penal system, so that the death penalty was rather frequent. But it was usually inflicted only on slaves and persons of the lower class, other citizens being very frequently enabled to escape into exile.

While the Roman *quaestiones* on the whole guaranteed an intensive and well-balanced handling of criminal cases, the proceedings were expensive, time-consuming and laborious. Since cases not infrequently had to be heard more than once, trials frequently dragged on. (Under Septimius Severus, the *de adulteriis* court alone had over 3000 undecided cases.) The ordinary criminal procedure was undoubtedly cumbersome, with the result that under the Principate the so-called *extra*-ordinary criminal procedure, the *cognitio extra ordinem*, became more and more important, while the jury courts, though still attested in the second century A D, practically speaking faded into the background. With Sulla's judicial reforms, the administration of civil justice had been put in charge of the urban praetor or the peregrine praetor (for foreigners), according to the circumstances. In this field too the presiding magistrate merely directed and supervised the proceedings, the verdicts being brought in by juries. In exceptional cases, especially those relating to private transactions of great value such as legacies, the grand jury of the court of the *centumviri* was invoked, but generally speaking civil suits under the late Republic were heard either by an individual judge (*sub uno iudice*) or before small arbitrating commissions, the *arbitri* or *recuperatores*. Here the proceedings were in two parts. First, before the presiding magistrate (*in iure*), the admissibility of the petition was decided, originally in highly formalised language, and the responsible juror or jurors were appointed. The case at issue was then heard by the latter (*apud iudicem*). Its subject matter was precisely laid down by the presiding magistrate's ruling but also confined to the procedural formula. Gradually a more elastic style of procedure, not so rigid in its formulation, became established, especially for the cases where the old formulae no longer applied, as for instance in the unformalised contracts of labour, works, hire or purchase.

Augustus at first held himself aloof from jurisdiction, although he had the necessary powers. These were given him for the army and the provinces by his *imperium proconsulare*, as we know from the Edicts of Cyrene, and applied to the whole empire, not only to the so-called imperial provinces. For the domain of the city of Rome he had his consular powers. Yet however much an individual *princeps* might try to avoid actually giving judgment in the courts, he was more and more inevitably drawn into it, as formerly the people's tribunes had been, by appeals against the court decisions, and by all the various petitions for justice. Then too, juristically inclined *principes* like Claudius were always extending the radius of competence of the so-called imperial court. In practice, after all, the *princeps* could bring any legal dispute into the imperial court and decide it there in final instance. Its special characteristics were that the *princeps* was not governed by any law of procedure or confined to a particular place of judgement and, moreover, had complete freedom in the composition of his *consilium*. He also had a free hand in the definition of offences, the choice of penalty, the mode of punishment and the degree of its severity. The decisions of the imperial court (*decreta*) quickly acquired the status and force of laws. Therefore the *princeps* was the most important *iudex* too.

The juridical authority of the *princeps*, however, was not exhausted by the *extraordinaria cognitio* of the imperial penal court. By virtue of his tribunician power, the *princeps* could have laws passed, such as the various *leges Iuliae* under Augustus, and from 19 B C onward the edicts of the *princeps* had the force of law. Besides the *decreta*, the instructions of the *princeps* to the magistrates and to his legates, the *mandata*, acquired legal force, as did his decisions in the form of the rescripts or *epistulae* on petitions and individual questions. The clearest example of law-making by the *princeps* can undoubtedly be seen in the *constitutiones*, the legally binding enactments derived from the *lex de imperio*. In all these ways the jurisdiction of the *princeps* was further and further extended. Problems arising from the dispensation of justice came in the end to absorb most of the working day of a responsible *princeps*.

In Rome itself, the urban prefect (*praefectus urbi*), a consular appointed by the *princeps*, came to be in general charge of the police courts. This too was a form of the *cognitio extra ordinem* marked by stricter and at the same time more elastic rules of procedure. The urban prefect was not bound by the limitations of competence of the *quaestiones*. In conjunction with a *consilium* composed of senators, he could deal at short notice with any infringement of public security and order. The impact of the *princeps* on the administration of justice, here seen indirectly, was even more marked in the case of the so-called Senate Court. In the late Republic, the Senate had originally concerned itself solely with cases of high treason, but under Augustus crimes against *maiestas* and, from 4 BC onwards, cases of alleged abuse of power by Roman magistrates in the provinces (*repetundae*) came before the Senate. But the Senate Court was no 'court of peers'. Under Augustus, *equites* too like Cornelius Gallus, or client kings like Antiochus II of Commagene, were prosecuted before the Senate. This extension of the judicial authority of the Senate was all to the advantage of the new political system. It offered the Roman aristocracy some partial compensation for the loss of its political privileges, gave it something to do, and at the same time associated it with the new order.

It would be a complete misunderstanding of the facts to regard the Senate Court as an independent senatorial court of justice. In fact the influence of the *princeps* was no less dominant in the Senate Court than in a normal session of the Senate. The *princeps* could not only assume the role of presiding judge but, as *primus inter pares*, could himself at any time intervene in the proceedings and, in case of need, use his *intercessio* to have them broken off. He could also bring in an indictment on his own account, or support or quash the indictments of others. Indeed, the Senate made such zealous efforts to fall in with the interests and ideas of the *princeps* that 'too much' would be a more appropriate comment than 'too little'. Much the same applied in the sphere of legislation. A resolution of the Senate, *senatus consultum*, had already acquired the force of law in practice during the late Republic. While the Assembly of the People was no longer involved in legislation after Claudius, a great range of new laws were promulgated in the form of *senatus consulta*. Their subjects concerned the law of succession and testamentary law, the laws of debt, and private law. But here too, as with the definition of new criminal offences, the *senatus consulta* were always vehicles of the *princeps*' will.

The Roman understanding of law and jurisprudence was thus defined by the jurist Ulpian in some famous sentences: 'Justice is the ldfast and unchanging will to give every man his due. The commandments of the law are these: to live honourably, not to injure one's fellow men, to give every man his due. Jurisprudence is the knowledge of things divine and human, the science of what is right and wrong' (Ulpian, *Regulae* I, *Digesta* I, 1, 10).

The law in Roman society commanded the highest respect. The republican governing class had the same intense devotion to law as the *principes*. The prosecution and defence of the great trials of republican times had offered similar prospects of winning personal prestige similar to those afforded under the Principate by the giving of learned opinions or membership of the *consilium principis*.

From its beginnings, Roman law had a reciprocal relationship with the law of other states. There were already probable connections between the XII Tables and Greek law. Later we find traces of Hellenistic ingredients in taxation and business law. Awareness of the tensions set up by the overlap with foreign law also affected the private domain. It followed that international law had a broad private law basis and, from 242 BC onward, had been in charge of its own judicial magistrate, the *praetor peregrinus*. So little is known about his activities, however, that the exact extent of foreign influences on Roman law is hard to estimate. Taken as a whole, though, it is obvious that genuinely Roman ideas and traditions of law retained their ascendancy.

The special character of Roman law, with its constant absorption of new insights and experiences, cannot be reduced to a few thematic notions and abstractions. In its beginnings, it clearly reflected the values which set the standard for Roman politics and society which, often provocatively, were claimed for itself by Rome. First place was occupied by the concept of *fides*, the recognition in the widest sense of mutual obligations. From this may be derived on the one hand the fullest juridical recognition of the *word*, spoken or written, as legally binding, and on the other the notably strong force at law of all pledges, promises and declarations of intent. To balance these, we note also how scrupulously the idea of *bona fides* was used to prevent obstinate or one-sided pressing of impermissible claims.

The Roman conception of law has perhaps never been more tellingly formulated than in the saying, already proverbial by Cicero's time but in fact very much older, which sought to discredit the extravagant use of legal titles and formulae – 'extreme justice is extreme injustice' (*summum ius summa iniuria*). Generally speaking, the magistrates and *principes* responsible for the preservation and further development of Roman law performed their tasks very effectively – and yet with striking restraint in this particular case of private law. According to the impressive account of the great legal historian Fritz Schulz, it was here above all that the Roman preference was most clearly felt for 'as little justice as possible' and 'as little community as possible'.

What are quite alien to modern sensibilities are the infringements of the principle of equality before the law. We have to realise that Roman social thinking did not start from a democratically moulded pattern of equal rights and duties. Its model was an internally differentiated society which gave its wealthier citizens an array of privileges, with special status marked by special dress, and in return demanded from them greater duties and services to the whole society. This division had definite consequences at law. The penalty for injuring a slave was less than that for injuring a free man. Death penalties on reputable free citizens, though pronounced, were very seldom enforced. In many big trials the defence advocates went into laborious detail to portray the accused, because they wanted to fix his social standing. It is probable that right from the very beginning there had been a different treatment, in court and in execution of sentence, of the privileged members of the governing class (*honestiores*) from that of other population groups (*humiliores*), and that this gap increased considerably under the Principate and was later institutionalised.

Roman jurisprudence originated with the priestly college of the *pontifices*. In the third century B C their formulae for all kinds of causes were collected and published, and many members of the governing class then took up jurisprudence. The main focus of their activities was the giving of legal opinions, unpaid, for magistrates of lawcourts and parties at law. They could also bring their special knowledge into the *consilia*. Apart from this, the jurisconsults of the Republic were principally engaged in drafting forms of contract and editing collections of them, one example being the work of Manius Manilius (consul 149 B C), 'Terms of Business for the Sale of Marketable Goods' (*venalium vendendorum leges*).

Although Roman jurisprudence too was influenced by Greek thought, yet it remained 'in its total development something specifically Roman. It may well be seen as the most important achievement of the Roman mind and as Rome's most significant contribution to the development of European civilisation' (W. Kunkel, *Römische Rechtsgeschichte*, Cologne 1972, 66, 94).

The classic peak of Roman jurisprudence was not reached, it is true, until the second century A D. One good reason for this was that the *principes* took the greatest conceivable interest in it. Augustus himself granted a small number of specially qualified jurists of the senatorial order the privilege of giving legal opinions on his own *auctoritas* – or, according to a more far-reaching interpretation of the passage, appointed them, so to speak, licensed public jurisconsults for the giving

...l opinions in court (*ius publice respondendi*). In this way the decisive ...f consultant on legal questions was confined to a relatively small ... of specially qualified experts of high social standing. Clearly this particular group of jurists must have had the greatest imaginable significance for the further development of the law. But elsewhere too, in the *consilium principis* and in the many branches of the administrative organisation of the Principate, competence in the law was valued. Jurists found a good range of posts open to them, in the equestrian sector right up to the prefecture of the Praetorian Guard.

From the long gallery of famous Roman jurists I mention only a few of the great figures. As early as the first century BC, there was Q. Mucius Scaevola (consul 95 BC) whose handbook on the *ius civile* was for a long time the standard work. Servius Sulpicius Rufus (consul 51 BC), a friend of Cicero's, is credited with having introduced the dialectic method into jurisprudence. From the Augustan age, M. Antistius Labeo, a decided opponent of the Principate, and C. Ateius Capito, both well-known, were credited with having each founded his own school of law. Under Hadrian finally, P. Iuventius Celsus (2nd consulate AD 129) and P. Salvius Iulianus (consul AD 148) were prominent. Celsus' main work is 39 books of *digesta* (classified legal decisions). He is credited with having originated quite a number of famous definitions and pungent maxims, as for instance the well-known formula *impossibilium nulla obligatio* (*Digesta*, 50, 17, 185) – 'there can be no legal obligation to do the impossible'. Salvius Iulianus became famous not only for his edition of the *edictum perpetuum* already referred to, but also for a considerable literary output, in which 90 books of *digesta* are prominent.

In jurisprudence, as elsewhere, some authors owed their fame rather to fortune than to intellectual eminence. Sextus Pomponius and Gaius were not outstanding jurists but their commentaries, especially Gaius' elementary primer, the four books of *institutiones*, had far-reaching repercussions and kept alive the names of two authors otherwise unknown. In the third century AD, Roman jurisprudence had a 'late classical' revival. Although the great jurists now no longer came from the senatorial order, as they had once done, but were men from the provinces, especially the east, and often enough had embarked on equestrian careers, in the top post of *praefectus praetorio*, with its steadily increasing judicial functions, they obtained great influence on the rulers of the Severan house and the following Soldier Emperors. Aemilius Papinianus is perhaps the best-known figure of this group. As praetorian prefect for the ten years AD 203–213, he won renown not only for his great compendia (*quaestiones, responsa*) but also for his bold denunciation of the murder of Geta, which cost him his own life. The members of the next generation of jurists too, Iulius Paulus and

Domitius Ulpianus, reached the top post of *praefectus praetorio*, and they too paid their tribute to the literature of commentaries and collections. Also among the better-known writers of this age was Ulpian's pupil, Herennius Modestinus, who held the post of *praefectus vigilum* between AD 226 and 244.

Roman law followed everywhere in the train of Roman colonisation, as a consequence of Roman citizenship policies and as an ingredient of the romanisation process. But in the western provinces of the *imperium*, with native legal traditions which over large areas must have been weaker and more restricted than in the Hellenistic East, Roman law spread correspondingly more quickly and with greater permanence. It was not, however, imposed by force within the area of Roman power. On the contrary, it was characteristic that obligations at private law to non-Roman legal communities were all recognised, and existing citizen rights inside the *imperium* were as a rule not touched. Ludwig Mitteis in a pioneering study *Reichsrecht und Volksrecht in den östlichen Provinzen des römischen Kaiserreichs* (1891) proved in addition that, especially in the eastern part of the *imperium*, the 'international' statutes of the Hellenistic world were valid right into imperial times, while the Roman law introduced principally by the governors' courts and the Roman law schools (Berytos), the 'imperial law', established itself only slowly. It was not until the great citizenship levelling statute of AD 212/213, the *Constitutio Antoniniana*, that the whole pattern was completely changed.

The development of law in Late Antiquity was marked by a characteristic dichotomy. On the one hand, the making of law in the totalitarian state of that period became more and more strongly centralised, with fewer and fewer loopholes. The emperor and his administration were increasingly taken up with legal problems. Great efforts were put in hand by the emperors to bring some order into the almost unsortable layers upon layers of lawmaking, and these eventually issued in the great codifications of Theodosius II and Justinian. All this time, however, living Roman jurisprudence, which was in essence the giving of legal opinions, was itself being annihilated at its source by the very flood of new imperial decisions, especially the rescripts. In the age of the 'citation laws', mere classification of legal authorities, at a time when constitutions and law codes were collected and new codifications made, but also the period of the so-called 'Vulgar Law', when Roman law itself declined and regressed to more primitive forms and content, this once lively discipline withered away. Yet the fundamental standards of Roman law continued to determine law-giving in the Germanic kingdoms of the western half of the empire just as much as in Byzantium.

Then, around AD 1100, a new order of jurists came to be formed, in

Bologna. They put the *Corpus Iuris* at the centre of legal teaching theory, and from the fifteenth century onward, especially in Germany, such a widespread adoption of Roman law occurred as to retain canonical force until the modern statute books came into being. 'The modern science of private law, the core of all jurisprudence, in the countries of the continent of Europe and the regions settled by them in other parts of the world rests on the common Roman foundation' (Max Kaser, *Das römische Privatrecht*, Munich 1971, I², 1).

LITERATURE, ART, SCIENCE AND TECHNOLOGY, RELIGION

For a long time Roman public life accorded only a low priority to the arts and sciences. In these, and in intellectual pursuits generally, the Romans themselves were quite conscious that other peoples were superior to them, as Virgil in some famous lines expressed it:

'Others, I can well believe, will more delicately beat the bronze into breathing likenesses, or carve living faces out of marble, or plead cases better, or plot with their rod the motions of the sky and name the rising of the constellations. But your arts it will be, Roman, remember, to guide the peoples with your authority, to impose the ways of peace, to spare the conquered and subdue the proud with war.' (Virgil, *Aeneid* VI, 847ff.)

Yet however far the Romans may have been from matching Greek creativity in art and literature, their works are not mere copies of Greek models but have a status entirely of their own. Their importance is exceptional, moreover, for the very reason that Europe for so long knew of antiquity only in its Roman forms.

BEGINNINGS OF ROMAN LITERATURE

From the beginnings of intellectual self-expression only a few fragments have come down to us and few sure facts are known. What is obvious is that the obligatory formulae in the religious, as in the legal, sphere became stereotyped very early, and that this probably occurred also in other branches of life and usage. Cult texts were repeated unchanged, even when their sense was no longer understood, and the compulsory nature of legal rules of procedure has already been mentioned. It seems characteristic of the tight involvement of Roman society with its religion that the *collegium* of *pontifices* was the keeper of the legal as well as the cult formulae, of the calendar as well as the chronicles (*annales*) of state, and thus regulated the passage of public events, present and past.

Alongside this strongly stereotyping tendency, however, which may also have dominated the early funeral orations of the aristocracy, there was another just as powerful. In harvest songs and mocking verses, improvisations at all kinds of festivals, and also in the popular buffoonery of the so-called *fabula Atellana* which was later to blossom out so vigorously in a new guise, the unbridled vitality of feeling often burst out in extreme forms. No doubt the tradition owed something to foreign sources – the burlesque itself derived from the Oscan town of Atella, the mocking verses from the Faliscan town of Fescennia. No doubt too, in some way which can no longer be clarified, there were layers of old Italic and of Etruscan inspiration, but the decisive transformation later on was under Greek influence.

Roman literature in the narrower sense began characteristically with the work of a former Greek prisoner of war from Tarentum, who in the year 240 BC for the first time in Rome staged Latin translations of Greek tragedy and of a Greek comedy during the *ludi Romani*. This Livius Andronicus inaugurated the literature of translation, a wide field which holds the centre of the Roman 'pre-classical' age (*c.* 240–102 BC). He translated the *Odyssey* into the old Italic Saturnian metre, and then also composed new cult songs for state religious ceremonies. From his time onward, the field was dominated by translations and adaptations of Greek tragedies and comedies, one good reason being that the religious demand for plays for the *ludi scaenici* required a constant succession of new works. Indeed the social need for such early theatre is just as obvious as the religious. The authors were protected by leading members of the aristocracy, often enough in their plays they celebrated the deeds of their patrons' *gens*, and also found themselves not infrequently drawn into the rivalries and internal political squabbles of their patrons.

This was the context in which the works of Naevius (died 202 BC) and Ennius (*c.* 239–169 BC) came into being, followed a generation or so later by Caecilius, Pacuvius, L. Accius, and above all Plautus and Terence. These two, each in a quite distinct, very personal style, domesticated Hellenistic comedy in Rome; Plautus with generous irresistible vitality, Terence with artistic stylised formality; Plautus often uninhibited, loud and uncouth, Terence sensitive and reflective. The very opposition between these two writers shows the breadth of spectrum which this literature of translation ran through, combining, often recklessly, parts of quite different Greek originals.

At the same time, Roman education became increasingly bilingual. The adoption of Greek literary forms and verse meters, and subjects as well, especially from Greek mythology, occurred quite spontaneously. And yet the copying and translation gave rise to an intellectual dialogue with the originals, a growing consciousness of native ways and native values, the shaping and working out of what was Roman against the indispensable background of Greek culture. Simultaneously the Latin language achieved a more and more varied and delicate power of expression of its own. The severity and constraint of the beginnings, which often seemed so monolithic, made way for more elastic forms of expression, though these again retained some basis of the old monumental effect. With the political supremacy of Rome, the dialectical process between Roman and Greek became a mutually rewarding encounter. Greeks wrote Roman history in Greek (Polybius, Dionysius of Halicarnassus, Appian, Dio Cassius), imparted Greek philosophy (Posidonius, Epictetus, Plutarch), described the Roman world (Strabo) and the monuments of Greece (Pausanias), and celebrated Rome in poetry and panegyric (Melinno, Dio Chrysostom, Aelius Aristides).

ROMAN HISTORIANS

The development of Roman intellectual life, especially literature and the arts, cannot be imagined without the Greek language. It was symptomatic of its start that even the writing of Roman history began in the Greek language (Q. Fabius Pictor), a fact which provoked a passionate protest from Cato the Censor, who in his seven books of *Origines*, in impressive Latin prose, described the beginnings of Rome together with those of the other Italian cities and their historical development up to his own time.

What was largely typical of the historians of the Roman Republic was their limited urban outlook and their annalistic form. Their writings had evolved out of the annual chronicles of the *pontifices*. The yearly rhythm of magistrate changes, with its regular breaks in political continuity, went on governing their arrangement of events long after the narrow limits of summer campaigns in neighbouring Italy had ceased to be relevant. When the new range of long-term politics and warfare had made these annual 'tree rings' into fetters falsifying every account, they still kept the city of Rome at the centre of historical thought and as a point of reference for all history. Even the non-Roman historians of the Principate drew up their schemes and periods in such a way that the history of foreign states and peoples was projected on Rome. The military, economic and administrative centres of gravity of the *imperium Romanum* might move to its provinces and frontier regions, but for Roman historians it remained unthinkable that they should change their outlook. It was they as much as anyone who prepared the soil for the 'Rome' myth.

Its immediate social benefit, especially for the Roman governing class, was to furnish a decisive criterion of value for all cultural activities. The writing of history became for them a preferred form of political engagement. Even under the influence of the schools of rhetoric it remained an instrument of political training and political teaching. The senator-historian was a characteristic Roman type (Fabius Pictor, Cato, Sallust, Asinius Pollio, Tacitus – to name only the most important names in a long line).

Moral judgments are a mark of the Roman historian. His writing was never free from a censorious undercurrent; it approved and disapproved; he was always seeking to form and preserve a collective morality. And this for him, both in the beginning and for a long time after that, meant almost exclusively the generalised morality of the *res publica* as determined by the governing class. Tacitus still saw it as the 'prime task' of his history to ensure that 'virtues are not passed over in silence and that evil doers and evil speakers have some fear of posterity and ill fame' (Tacitus, *Annals* III, 65). Alongside oratory, especially state and funeral orations, it was the historian in particular who inculcated the idealised 'customs of our forefathers', whether he was diagnosing symptoms of crisis or indeed communicating that special note of fundamental pessimism which distinguished the Roman understanding of history and came out in so many of its phases. The defection from the pagan gods, the abandonment of the old religion, old morality and old values were often enough seen as deeper causes of a process of' decline with which historians of the most different epochs, Cato like Sallust, Livy like Tacitus, identified their respective presents.

But history writing was also a means of legitimation. For the aristocracy, the 'deeds of our forefathers' were the historical basis of their claims to leadership, even though they sometimes found expression in annalistic distortions of the exploits of particular noble clans. The *Res Gestae Divi Augusti*, the great record of the deeds and achievements of the first *princeps*, is among other things a legitimation of his new political *status*. But the Roman historian above all supplied a total and fundamental legitimation of Roman rule. This was the case with Cicero no less than Tacitus, the critical analyst of the phenomenology of the Principate.

The Roman historian is moreover the source and expression of a systematic process of personalisation. The subject of Cato's history was still the collectivity of the Roman people, but later annalists started from its dominant units, the aristocratic clans, who supplied what was primarily Claudian, Valerian or Licinian history. Then, in the period of the late Republic, individualisation reached its first peak in works of contemporary history (*historiae*) by leading politicians – memoirs, biographies and campaign reports by the great field commanders. In keeping with the partial chaos of those times, we still find a plurality of contributors to the historical record; but in the period which followed, the interest was almost entirely concentrated on the *principes*. (What is probably the most important of all Roman biographies, Tacitus' *Agricola*, which in a very personal way exploded the whole genre, was one of the great exceptions.)

By contrast, Suetonius' collection of lives of the emperors from Julius Caesar to Domitian finally established a historiographical structure which was to dominate the field until Late Antiquity, and beyond that had the greatest imaginable influence on the writing of history in the Middle Ages. Older Hellenistic models of biography were transposed, almost like mechanical copies, to the person of the *princeps*, with spicy details of his private life, in a fashion which no doubt pleased a large public. Such 'emperor stories' were probably so popular because the almost limitless power of this individual in the eyes of the inhabitants of the *imperium Romanum* could at any time seal the fate of any one of them. Although collections of the lives of philosophers or saints might come to join them, the emperor biographies maintained their priority.

The membership of a historical structure of such unusually long duration, such apparently organic growth and such amazing extent that it seemed to encompass all the important parts of the known world, at the same expanded and deepened the experiences of human existence. Roman historical writing elaborated this historical consciousness and made it available to broad sections of people. It showed the dependence not only of its content and values but of the whole of life on the political system at a particular time, and to this the writing itself in part fell victim. For its privileges under the Principate, Roman historiography had a particular price to pay in the political outlawry of ill-timed works and the silencing of critical writers.

ROMAN POETRY

The periods into which Roman literature can be divided do not match those of the general course of politics. Lucilius (died 102 BC), for instance, is reckoned as still pre-classical, and yet in his satires we already encounter that decidedly subjective character which was also to mark the later development of Roman poetry.

> 'No, to become state contractor for Asia, to collect grazing rents,
> instead of being Lucilius, not for all the money in the world!'
> (*Lucili Carminum Reliquiae*, 671–2 [Marx])

Roman poetry reached its first peak with Lucretius (died 55 BC) and Catullus. Lucretius' great didactic poem *De Rerum Natura* gave an account of the philosophy of Epicurus, with the object of freeing human beings from fear by insight into the laws of nature. He sought to show them their limits, yet make them, as knowing and understanding beings, independent. His teaching of rational emancipation in poetic form was unexampled. Also unexampled in Roman eyes was the open expression of extreme feelings in Catullus. Love and hate, grief and joy, forced their way out in the most concentrated couplet form no less than in the artificial grand compositions. These were modelled on Hellenistic examples no less than many of the miniature forms worked out by the so-called *neoteroi*, or 'moderns', the circle of poets before and around Catullus. Never before and never again in the Latin language after Catullus were the heights and depths of a love so concentrated as in the two lines of his *Odi et amo*:

> I hate and love. Perhaps you ask me why.
> I do not know but feel – in agony.
> (Catullus, *Poems* 85)

But it was in Augustan times that Roman poetry reached its summit. There we find formal perfection in the most varied categories, with precise expression, harmony between metrical elements and poetic rhythm, a rich musicality of language, in short, perfect congruence of form and content. The poems of the Augustan age are as a rule concentrated and polished, mostly spare in their range, not dashed off with a careless hand (except by Ovid) but achieved with great intellectual labour.

Virgil and Horace were the foremost contributors to the atmosphere in which the political system of Augustus became stabilised. Their uniqueness was in no small measure due to the very aloofness and discretion they were able to maintain: Virgil in his magnificent didactic poem about agriculture, the *Georgics,* and in the most famous of Latin epics, the *Aeneid*; Horace especially in his 'Roman' odes and his *Secular Hymn*. Yet neither of them was primarily an official propagandist or a 'court poet'. Only a generation later, with Ovid, and then for very personal reasons, do we find the explosion of exaggerated personal veneration of the *princeps* which became customary.

In the *Aeneid, the* Roman epic, myth and history are again interwoven in masterly fashion. I quote as an example the famous 'shield description' from the eighth book, with its picture of the Battle of Actium (31 BC):

'In the centre could be seen the bronze-plated fleets engaged at Actium, all Leucate in a turmoil of battle lines, the waves brilliant with gold. On one side Augustus Caesar, with Senate and people, with household gods and great gods, leading Italy into war. High on the poop he stood, gaily from his temples flashed twin fires, and from the crown of his helmet blazed his father's Julian star. At another point Agrippa, wind and fortune favouring, from on high commanded a column of ships and on his brow, proud distinction, shone the ship-beaks of the naval crown. Opposing them was Antony, with all the wealth of strange lands and arms of a varied kind. As conqueror from the people of the sunrise he comes and from the Erythraean coast, on board with him he brings an Egyptian army, the strength of the Orient and furthest Bactria, and is followed (the shame of it!) by his Egyptian wife. All together they are closing in, and the whole sea is stirred into foam by the back-drawn oars and the three-pronged ship beaks. They head for open water. You would think the Cyclades Islands had been torn out and set afloat, or that one high mountain was ramming another, so massive are the turreted poops on which the men are standing. Bolts of blazing tow are scattered by hand, and points of iron carried flying by their wooden shafts till the fields of Neptune run red with fresh blood. The queen in the centre calls up her troops with the Isis-rattle of her homeland. She has yet no thought of the two snakes awaiting her in the rear. And her monstrous rabble of gods of every shape with barking Anubis bear arms against Neptune and Venus and Minerva. Mars in the thick of the fighting moulded in iron, and the grim Furies out of the sky, and Discord with her torn cloak stride joyfully, followed by Bellona with her blood-soaked scourge. But now, from high above, Actian Apollo sees it all, and bends his bow. At the terror of it, the men of Egypt and the Indies, all the Arabs, all the Sabaeans, are ready to turn in rout. The queen herself is seen to be calling the winds and setting sail. She is pictured at the very moment of letting out the sheets. So Vulcan showed her, amid the slaughter, pale with her death soon to be, carried off by wave and north-west wind, while awaiting her sadly throughout his length is Father Nile, spreading his robe to receive her, calling the defeated to his sky-blue lap and his tributaries with their shaded recesses. But Caesar now drives through the walls of Rome in triple triumph and consecrates his immortal vow to the Italian gods to build three hundred great shrines all over the city.' (Virgil, *Aeneid* VIII, 675ff.)

But the poetry of this age too, so to speak on a new, higher level, starts out from an independent dialogue with Greek models. This was now joined, however, by the conviction of a Roman-Italic tradition, a new self-awareness after the profound convulsions of the civil wars, a consciousness of the high quality of their own achievements:

> I have raised a monument more lasting
> than bronze, higher than Pharaoh's pyramids,
> such that neither devouring rain nor angry north wind,
> nor the countless chain of years nor flight of seasons
> can destroy. I shall not wholly die,
> a good part of me will escape mortality.
> My fame will grow so long as the high priest climbs
> with the silent Vestal the Capitoline Hill.
> It will be said of me where torrential
> Aufidus roars and Daunus once reigned king
> over a dry land and rustic people
> that I, though humbly born, first had the skill

to adapt Greek lyric to Italian measures.
Take pride in my ˙deserts, Melpomene,
and willingly garland my head with Apollo's bay.
(Horace, *Odes* III, 30)

Horace, the son of a freedman, had originally fought in the ranks of
Octavian's opponents but was then no less proud to be a recipient of
Maecenas' favour, which had procured him a livelihood. Again and
again he put his own experiences into poetry, controlled his passions
and preserved his independence, even of Maecenas, Agrippa and
Augustus. However close the mutual relations of poetry, society and
politics were for him, at the same time he made strong efforts to free his
own existence and his own work from them. Even Augustan elegiac
poetry was governed by the pull of *apoliteia*, a life above politics. The
Roman *eques* Tibullus in his love elegies, full of sentiment and an
occasional dreamy melancholy, gives himself over entirely to his loves
for Delia and Nemesis, and to the disappointments they occasion.
Maecenas' client Propertius, a proud, wilful Umbrian, expressed his
love for Cynthia in lines that were often obscure and learned, then again
in passionate outbursts. Ovid finally, who at first had the easiest time of
all, in every respect, but was later exiled to Tomi (Constanza), an
irreverent chatterbox, playful at love and being loved, always put love
and sex at the centre of human life. His challenging provocative poem
Militat omnis amans ('Every lover is a soldier'), for instance, reduced the
often cramped and pathetic boasts about Roman *virtus* to an absurdity:

'Every lover is a soldier, and Cupid has his encampments,
it's true, Atticus, every lover is a soldier.
The age for warfare is also the age for love –
an old lover is no more use than an old soldier.
The qualities a general looks for in a good soldier
are those a girl looks for in her fellow.
Both can sit up all night, both can sleep on the ground,
the one guards his mistress's door, the other his general's.
Soldiering is a long road – send the girl away,
a staunch lover will follow her to the end,
climb mountains in his path, cross rivers flooded by rain,
cleave the snow drifts, put to sea without excuses
about strong east winds, nor search the stars, not he,
for good weather before manning the oars.
Who but a soldier, or a lover, will stoutly
face the cold and sleet of a bad night?'
(Ovid, *Amores* I, 9, 1ff.)

It had to be Ovid of all people who became a victim of the new regime.
Try as he might to adapt himself with the writing of 'unobjectionable'

long major poems such as the *Fasti* ('festival calendar'), and the *Metamorphoses*, or mythological transformation fables, he was unable to change his destiny.

PEAKS OF LATIN PROSE

Roman prose, by contrast, had already reached its peak with Cicero, outstanding orator and very productive writer. His extensive correspondence and his great political and lawcourt speeches are an incomparable source for any student of the crisis of the late Republic, while his rhetorical writings (*De Oratore, Brutus, Orator*) provide us with the theoretical foundations of Roman oratory. The later political and philosophical works (such as *De Re Publica, De Officiis, De Legibus*) were an attempt to domesticate important elements of Greek philosophy in Rome, and to renovate the ideology of the Roman governing class. We should not over-estimate Cicero's originality. His political line in broad terms makes a constantly naive or at best utopian impression, though his unswerving fight against Antony did in the end show an impressive logic. What cannot be denied, however, are his services to the development of the Latin language and to the enlargement of Rome's spiritual horizons.

The Augustan age showed itself in the most different branches of literature as a time of collecting and sifting, of conscious ordering and mastering of tradition with a view to orientation and reassurance. The first great world history in Latin, by the romanised Celt from Narbonne, Pompeius Trogus, is as much a part of this context as Livy's history *From the Foundation of the City*, Varro's once voluminous essays on antiquities, the Latin language and literature, and agriculture, Agrippa's world map with its important commentary, Vitruvius' famous treatise *De Architectura*, a wide-ranging collection of technical knowledge which for centuries afterwards remained in use as a handbook. This same trend was followed in Greek too by such large-scale works as Strabo's *Geography* and Diodorus Siculus' world history.

At the same time, the writers of the Augustan age – Virgil, Horace, Tibullus, Propertius, Ovid in poetry, Livy in prose – embody the core of that Latin humanistic tradition which remained fundamental for the literature and intellectual life of Europe until early modern times. Neither the austerity of the monasteries nor the emotionalism of the humanists nor the eternal pedantry of the Schools could obliterate these intellectual forces, without which the Latin middle ages of Europe would have been just as unthinkable as the variants of humanism all over the world.

POST-AUGUSTAN LITERATURE

During the Tibero–Claudian period, Latin history-writing became more and more infected with rhetoric. This applies to the widely read history of Alexander the Great by Curtius Rufus just as much as to the famous collection of *exempla* by Valerius Maximus, who supplied the needs both of rhetoric and moral teaching with examples of Roman and also foreign history arranged in subject groups. It applies also to the *Historia Romana* of Velleius Paterculus, which is important particularly for its section of contemporary history, his account of the Roman campaigns in Germany.

Nero's age was the beginning of a second flowering of Roman literature known as the Silver period of Latin. The authors concerned were now able to attach themselves to Roman examples, the epic poets Lucan and Silius Italicus to Virgil, the satirist Persius to Horace, or else they could take up a markedly individual line and pioneer entirely new territory, like Seneca and Petronius.

Lucan's *Pharsalia* is a re-telling and revaluation of history in epic form. In this great work, the civil war between Caesar and Pompey is treated in a manner very revealing of the political and intellectual tensions of its own day. Although Lucan may have been taken in at first by the Neronian propaganda and put great hopes in this new principate, he was more and more strongly repelled by the reality. In consequence, it was Cato's morality and tragic figure which triumphed in his work over the victorious Caesar. This existential trait was absent from the later flowering of epic in Flavian times, as the subject matter alone shows. In the *Punica*, Silius Italicus (consul 69) offered merely an antiquarian history of the Second Punic War, while the *Thebaïs* of Statius (*c.* 96) on the expedition of the *Seven against Thebes* and the fighting for the city, his *Achilleïs*, the story of Achilles up to the Trojan expedition, and Valerius Flaccus' *Argonautica*, an account of the voyage of the Argonauts after Apollonius Rhodius and, as literature, perhaps the best of the group, were entirely given over to mythology.

The six satires of Persius, who was only 28 when he died, offer, in an often precious and artificial style, what are probably among the most difficult pieces of Latin we know. They testify to a set of attitudes, demands and values already voiced by Horace:

> Souls bent to earth with nothing heavenly in you,
> what's the good of giving our temples the modern touch
> or guessing what the gods like from this sinful flesh,
> which for its use ruins good oil by dissolving spices in it,
> or boils up white Calabrian wool with spoiling purple
> or makes us tear the pearl from its shell
> and separate the veins of glowing metal from crude ore?

It too sins, it sins yet gains by sinning – but you,
tell me, priests, what good is gold in a holy place?
No more than what maidens dedicate to Venus – dolls!
Why don't we give the gods what great Messalla's
blear-eyed son could not give from his abundance,
justice and right blended in the soul,
purity in the shrine of the intellect
and a heart steeped in generous honesty?
Grant me to bring these to the temples,
and a pinch of meal will do the rest.
(Persius, *Satires* II, 61ff.)

The younger Seneca (4 BC–AD 65) is one of the most disputed literary and political figures of the Neronian age. As Nero's tutor and adviser, the educated man of letters was drawn into the power maze at the highest level. His tract for princes *De Clementia* worked out an idealised form of the ideology of the Principate, while his malicious satire *Apocolocyntosis* ('pumpkinification') made fun of the *princeps* Claudius deified after his death. As one of the regents of the *imperium* after Nero's accession, he amassed an immense fortune, but in AD 62 he turned his back on politics and in AD 65, in connection with the Pisonian conspiracy, was forced to commit suicide. He was not one who was able to put his philosophically based principles into practice. He was not only brazen enough to defend the murder of the Empress Mother Agrippina before the Senate, but covered up also for other excesses of Nero's.

In his instructional dialogues and letters Seneca was first and foremost an important Roman teacher of the Stoic philosophy. It was characteristic of him, as of Roman philosophy generally, that questions of ethics were central to his writings. With considerable emotion and stylised rhetoric, he sought to bring matters round to the internal independence of the individual, with particular reference to death and its importance as a fact of human life. His rigorously rational attempts to discipline his own character were accompanied by a remarkably cosmopolitan outlook and a fundamental humanity, as in his insistence that the slave was human.

Apart from the works mentioned, nine tragedies under Seneca's name have come down to us. They are unmistakably plays for reading and deal with subjects of classical mythology. Besides them, we have under his name a *praetexta* ('Roman' tragedy) *Octavia*, an exciting piece about the unfortunate daughter of Claudius and wife of Nero. Seneca's fundamental moral attitudes were already quite acceptable for the Church Fathers. He thus became one of those Latin authors whose works had very great influence right into the beginning of the modern period, and put him among the strongest spiritual forces of ancient Rome.

C. Petronius Arbiter (died A D 66), a man who in his senatorial career had reached the consulate and who combined a wide education with extreme refinement and luxury in his life-style, keen powers of observation and cool disillusion, wrote a work of entertainment without parallel. His *Satiricon,* a picaresque novel of adventure and social satire, revolved around an entirely new section of society, the world of rich freedmen, slaves and parasites. Numerous insets, like the famous *Feast of Trimalchio,* but also rhetorical and epic elements, coarsely impudent and erotic scenes, and outbursts of bubbling vitality, are carried along by a fundamental tone of parody. His scenes are broadly painted, and he explores the most varied layers of language.

The literature of the Flavian age (A D 69–96) is as lacking in uniformity as its *principes* themselves. Besides the epic revival already mentioned, there were great compilations and also the beginnings of a 'court' poetry with tendencies to panegyric. Pliny the Elder's great *Naturalis Historia* has no parallel as an example of encyclopaedic labour, even though it consists largely of excerpts from older specialist works. It contains a description of the earth and another of man, with accounts of animals, plants, medicinal herbs, minerals, even of the arts, and is in fact a storehouse of the knowledge of a whole epoch. The great *Institutio Oratoria* of Quintilian is similarly comprehensive. Right in the middle of the decline of the great art of public oratory in Rome, it gives once more a systematic account of the complete literary training of an orator and the practice of the art of public speaking. The work was conceived on so broad a scale that in his tenth book Quintilian gives nothing less than a history of ancient literature. Often his assessments are still valid today. Another writer whose works served purposes primarily practical was Frontinus. His *Strategemata* gave details of cunning moves in military tactics, for repeated use. While his work on land surveying has been preserved only in fragments, his *De Aquis Urbis Romae,* a treatise on the history, technique and organisation of the water supply of Rome, won great authority if only because Frontinus, as *curator aquarum* under Nerva, had himself reorganised the supply.

The 'courtly' streak I have mentioned – quite apart from private and often poetic elements – is discernible in the occasional poems of Statius' *Silvae* no less than in the *Epigrams* of Martial (*c.* A D 40–104), which I have already quoted more than once. They give a colourful, iridescent picture of life and manners in the Rome of this period. Yet Martial, who had often so exuberantly presented himself as a supporter of Domitian, could not help recording the change of style in Trajan's reign, and the bounds thus set to his former excesses:

> Flatteries, no use springing to my lips now,
> pathetically rubbing them sore.

> Now I have none to address as lord and god,
> and you have no more place in this city.
> Go far away to the bonneted Parthians
> and in vile crawling abasement kiss the soles
> of their bright-clothed ruler's feet!
> Here is no lord now but a commander,
> a senator justice itself,
> who from her Stygian home brought back
> rustic truth with her unperfumed hair.
> If you're clever, under this princeps, Rome,
> take care not to speak as once you did!
> (Martial, *Epigrams* X, 72)

In his sixteen satires, Juvenal (A D *c.* 60–*c.* 130) brought this genre to new heights of bitterness:

> 'When the mincing eunuch takes to matrimony,
> when Mevia goes pigsticking in Tuscany
> and bare-breasted wields her hunting spear,
> when the one-time barber who shaved me in my youth
> now risen to riches challenges all the patricians,
> when the guttersnipe from the Nile, Crispinus,
> slave-born in Canopus, now with a toss of his purple
> cloak brandishes the thin gold ring on sweaty fingers
> and can't bear the weight of a heavier gem –
> well, then it's difficult not to write satire.'
> (Juvenal, *Satires* I, 22ff.)

In biting words and an imitation of Cato's style, Juvenal stigmatised the whole spectrum of moral decadence exhibited by the Roman governing class and also by the *domus principis*, the general lack of scruples, the revolting sides of life in the great city. In the rapid scene changes of the savage satire on women (VI), he passionately denounced both woman and her notion of wedlock. By the traditional standards of Roman society, it was unprecedented that in his completely aristocratic woman it should actually be her pride of ancestry that Juvenal reviled. For the modern social analyst it is perhaps disappointing, and yet entirely characteristic of the Roman attitude, that he should still be falling back on the notions of 'moral decadence':

> 'You ask the why and wherefore of all these horrors?
> What once kept the Latin woman chaste was the modesty of her means.
> Hard work under a humble roof, little sleep,
> hands rough and calloused from spinning Tuscan wool,
> Hannibal at the gates, husband on guard at the Colline Tower,
> all these kept vice away. But now we suffer
> the evils of a long peace, now wanton excess
> ravages us more fiercely than war, and revenges

the conquest of the world. No crime, no deed of lust
is missing since Rome lost her poverty.
All Sybaris, all Rhodes, all Miletus flock to Rome's hills
with wreathed, impudent, drunken Tarentum.
It was vile wealth which first brought us
foreign manners, and enervating riches with base luxury broke
the strength of centuries.'
(Juvenal, *Satires* VI, 288ff.)

The correspondence and the *Panegyricus* of Pliny the Younger, the
nephew of the older, are of great historical interest for their content but
not exactly impressive as literature. The same may be said of Florus'
Epitome, an outline of the history of the wars of the Roman people, based
on the idea of periods of growth. It is, however, true that, as
characteristic literary forms, both the panegyric and the epitome were to
have influence.

From the literary point of view, the age of the adoptive emperors (AD
96–192) was characterised on the one hand by the fullest development of
Greek literature and literary forms within the *imperium Romanum*.
Leading names were those of Herodes Atticus, Aelius Aristides,
Appian, Arrian, Plutarch, Pausanias, Lucian and Galen. On the other
hand, Latin literature at the same time became completely penetrated by
rhetoric. It was dominated too by Spanish and African writers, and
there was a tendency to use archaisms and popular forms of expression
of a simple or playful character. An obvious example was the exchange
of verses between Florus and Hadrian which has come down to us in the
Historia Augusta (*Vita Hadriani*, 16):

I'm glad I'm not Caesar
ranging through Britain,
hiding in forests,
freezing to death in Scythia!

I'm glad I'm not Florus,
ranging through taverns,
hiding in kitchens,
bitten to death by mosquitoes!

A noteworthy example of the close contact between literature,
rhetoricians and *principes* was Fronto, one of the most gifted authors of
the period, who was the tutor of Marcus Aurelius and Lucius Verus. His
pupil Aulus Gellius, with his *Noctes Atticae*, a colourful collection of
stylised readings from literature, became one of the most important
sources for our knowledge of antiquity. Another rhetorician of this
period, as celebrated as Gellius, was Apuleius of Madaurus in Numidia.
His novel *The Golden Ass* or *Metamorphoses* relates the adventures of a

young man transformed into a donkey and subsequently restored to human shape by Isis. The main story is punctuated with many inserted tales, including the delightful *Cupid and Psyche*. In this work elements of popular story-telling are interwoven with striking religious texts in a colourful fabric which can still enchant the modern reader.

EVOLUTION OF ROMAN ART

In the visual arts as in literature, genuinely and unquestionably Roman products are encountered rather late. It is no doubt the case that early Rome had already taken over forms of artistic expression from the Etruscans and Greeks, and for some time now the beginnings of artistic production from the region of Old Latium and the neighbouring Italic areas have been systematically explored. But it was to be a very long road before an independent Roman art began, after the appropriation of foreign art treasures which was still going on in the Second Punic War and in the second century BC amounted to massive looting.

It was characteristic of the needs and priorities of Roman society on the one hand, and of the evolution of artistic forms on the other, that architecture, town planning and public buildings of the most varied kind were already the main focus of Roman interest during the early and the classical Republic. In this respect, Rome very soon demonstrated its will to produce. The Roman effort was fully absorbed at first by the Forum, as the political and social centre of the city; by temples, as the expression of the close relations between the community and its gods; by market halls (*basilicae*) and places of assembly; victory memorials and arches of triumph; above all by the utility buildings which were so unusually splendid for their period (aqueducts, fountains, drainage systems, bridges and main roads); and finally by the monumental fortification of the city.

Hand in hand with these went the mastering of new techniques and the use of more and more costly materials. Mortar work, cast concrete walling and arched vaulting were the necessary basis for bolder and bolder construction. Later, in large buildings the ceilings were broken up by coffering; then came cross-vaulting and the use of domes; and finally, the revetting of domes with mosaic. Not until after the middle of the second century BC was the first marble temple built in Rome, an indication of the 'retarded' development of the city by comparison with the centres of the Greek world. It was then Augustus who, after the beginnings of an imperial architecture under Sulla, Pompey and Caesar, caused a city of marble to rise from the old brick.

The geographer Strabo writing in the time of Tiberius thus described the specific element in the evolution of Roman planning:

'While the Greeks when they founded cities were specially concerned with beauty, permanence, harbours and productive land, and saw their end as achieved with these, the Romans paid most attention to things the Greeks cared little about – the surfacing of the streets, the water supply, underground drains to wash the city's sewage into the Tiber. They also paved the country roads, levelling the rises and filling up the hollows, so that ship cargoes could be transported onward by cart. Their underground sewers, with vaults of jointed stones, would in many places allow entire hay wagons to drive through them. The quantities of water brought into the city by the aqueducts are so large that whole rivers stream through the city and its underground drains, and that almost every house has water cisterns and piped water and abundantly spouting fountains. M. Agrippa, who had also adorned the city with many magnificent sacred buildings as his own gift, none the less considered his practical public installations the more important. While the ancients so to speak attached less importance to the beauty of Rome, being concerned with other greater and more necessary tasks, later Romans, especially those living in our own day, have not been backward in this either but have filled the city with numerous splendid sanctuaries. Pompey, the divine Caesar, Augustus and his sons, his friends, his wife and sisters have surpassed all earlier enthusiasm and munificence in public building. Most of these are in the Campus Martius, the natural advantages of which have been increased with planned adornments by the hand of man. . . . If we then return to the old Forum and see how one forum after another is ranged alongside it, and then the royal basilicas and temples, and added to that the Capitol with its buildings and those on the Palatine . . . one could easily forget what lies outside.' (Strabo, 5, 3, 8ff.)

Then, under the Principate, Rome as the political power centre became also a centre of the ancient world's art and architecture. The forums of the *principes* became larger and larger. Finally the Forum of Trajan, by Apollodorus of Damascus, with a length of some 300 metres (1000 feet), put all the others in the shade. Axial symmetry, fixed directions and regular boundaries were as characteristic of the Roman forums as they were of city installations and legionary camps. The ordered planning and parcelling of space was clearly a characteristic feature of the Roman mind. The high standard of Roman surveying is evidence of that. At the same time the works of imperial architecture towered higher and higher. The Colosseum and Hadrian's Mausoleum were over 40 metres (130 feet) high; the obelisks brought from Egypt, and the monumental imperial pillars with their long spiral friezes, were further dominant features of the scene.

At the same time, the Roman builder's art became a vehicle and symbol of the political programme-building of the new kind of state. While the mausoleum of Augustus had demonstrated artistically his city roots and attachment to Roman–Italian traditions, the buildings in the *Forum Romanum* bore even stronger witness to various political tendencies:

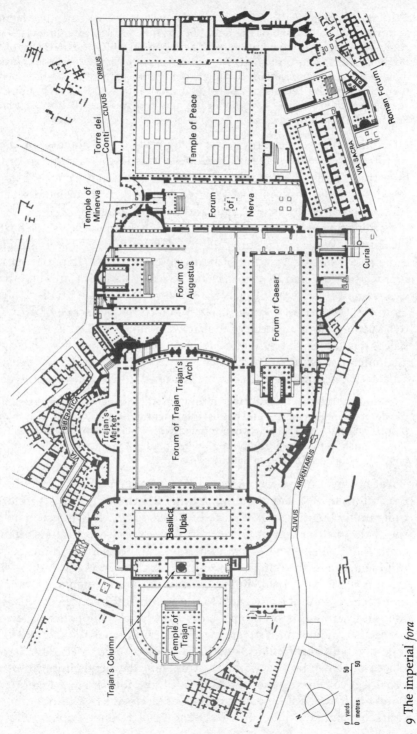

9 The imperial *fora*

'With the buildings dedicated in 29 BC, Octavian took possession, as the new autocrat, of the old stage of the Republic. In the Parthian Monument (19 BC) Augustus appears as the inaugurator of a new age in which the traditions of the Republic are to be incorporated. The buildings of the last two decades BC turn the spotlight on the successors designate of the *princeps*. First Gaius and Lucius, then Tiberius. The Temple of Concord concludes the building programme. It stands over the Forum as a symbol of the new body politic.' (P. Zanker, *Forum Romanum*, Tübingen, 1972, 23)

Of course the political programme figured in the themes of other monuments, in the reliefs of the *Ara Pacis* as in the decoration of the breastplate in the Primaporta statue of Augustus, in the colossal statue of Nero as in the decoration of Trajan's Arch at Beneventum or the relief friezes on the columns of Trajan and Marcus Aurelius.

Architecture was a special beneficiary of the new tasks set by the Principate. While Augustus still lived in a house of very modest dimensions on the Palatine, Tiberius built the first 'imperial palace' there in the so-called *Domus Tiberiana*. On the island of Capri he put up extravagant clusters of villas. Nero set new standards with his 'Golden House' (*Domus Aurea*), an artificial architectural landscape of provocative vastness in the middle of the city. Domitian set his no less typical palace on the Palatine, while Hadrian planted his wilful, extensive agglomeration of architectural styles and units, the *Villa Hadriana*, in Tivoli. At the same time, luxury overflowed in the homes of the élite:

'We think ourselves poor and mean if the Alexandrian marble is not varied with panels of Numidian marble and in turn inlaid with a decoration artfully imitating painting, if the vaulted ceiling is not faced with a glass mosaic, if marble from Thasos such as was once rarely seen even in a temple does not surround our bath. . . .' (Seneca, *Letters to Lucilius*, 86)

Yet however many foreign ingredients Rome might entertain for its own adornment, it did at the same time export the elements and forms of its utility buildings to all parts of the *imperium*. It is not so much in the wider distribution of Greek temples, Greek sculpture and handicrafts that Roman rule has left its strongest impression as in the Roman utility buildings, the remains of which are still so impressive today. The monumental city installations, with all the elements of Roman architecture, from the city gates to the forum or the concealed porticos, the underground storerooms and workshops, aqueducts, sewers, harbours, bridges and streets, water supply installations and wells, together with the military buildings, victory memorials, tombs and places of remembrance visible to this very day, constitute in all the provinces of Rome the signatures of its former presence. Jacob Burckhardt, when still a young man, was fascinated by the monumental character and the quite unusual solidity of Roman public buildings even on the fringes of the *imperium*: 'There is in these Roman buildings a power of control over the material which fascinates and fills us with quiet astonishment. They have nothing mean or botched. The masses make their effect even when the dimensions are small' (*Werke* I, 286). At the same time, this architecture is the purest expression of the Roman will to power.

The Roman art of portraiture and the Roman relief, especially the historical and mythological relief, also had its flowering from the first century onward. As Bernhard Schweitzer aptly put it, Greek art ends with the portrait while Roman art only begins with the need for portraiture. The desire to capture an individual's features truthfully for posterity had already been aroused by the specific forms of ancestor worship among the Roman aristocracy. Thus a keen *verismo* is often characteristic of Roman portraiture. The portraits of great ancestors, the death masks, statues and busts, do not idealise them or make them heroic. They show the individual with his peculiarities, in the historical costume of a magistrate, in the toga or in armour. But the historical relief, like the historical paintings which are so largely lost, attempts to capture the achievements of an ancestor; in political or military successes, it documents the social status of the individual and his family, influences public opinion, strengthens authority. Nor do these busts or statues seek to palliate anything. Despite the stylisation of Augustan classicism, portraits under the Principate were generally of remarkable power and fidelity to life.

What may be considered as one of the earliest Roman reliefs is a frieze commissioned by L. Aemilius Paullus Macedonicus for the pillar supporting a rider statue in Delphi after the battle of Pydna. Victory monuments, altars, temple decorations, and also sarcophagi, tombs and memorials of the most different kinds produced a considerable development in such arts, though not every work of the kind had the perfection of the *Ara Pacis Augustae*. Here the great relief panels, like Virgil, combine the Roman myth with the Augustan present. The illustration of the great sacrificial procession for the dedication of the altar shows the family and staff of the *princeps* united with magistrates and state functionaries – huge richly ornamented pictures of the earth and fertility goddess Tellus, the sacrifice by Aeneas, the twins Romulus and Remus, and other panels decorated with scrolls and festoons slung from bulls' heads, yet all combine to enclose the whole subject in a framework of religion.

In the long spiral friezes of historical scenes on the Trajan and Marcus Aurelius columns (the frieze on Trajan's column is about 200 metres, or 650 feet, long with no fewer than 155 individual scenes) the historical subject matter is of more documentary than artistic value. But undoubtedly we have here the external triumph of the Roman art of relief sculpture so far as composition and size are concerned. It is true, too, that in many of its details we already have some beginnings of the typology and style of Late Antiquity.

The adoption of Greek models is specially clear in sculpture. In late republican times it became more and more difficult to procure Greek and Hellenistic originals, and at the same time the demand of the Roman governing class for sculpture and other representational adornments for their luxurious city houses, gardens and country villas steadily increased. So local copying studios started up in Rome itself. Quite a number of Greek masterpieces have survived only in this form. Quite as numerous, however, are the sculptures based on Greek originals and yet incorporating Roman ideas. There was thus a fruitful symbiosis of Greek and Roman art. One of the best-known examples of this type is the famous statue of Augustus in armour from Livia's villa near Primaporta. In its proportions it is modelled on the *Doryphorus* of Polyclitus, and it shows Augustus as general (in the field), in the attitude of *adlocutio*, with the gesture commanding silence before he addresses the troops.

Clearly in Roman sculpture, as in architecture and the other arts, again and again the personal ideas and values of the Roman *principes* impressed themselves, and in any case they used all the arts as media of their policies and their specific shaping of the principate ideology. This appears in the alternation of Italianate and Hellenistic tendencies just as much as in the idiosyncrasies of Augustan classicism; in the emotionalism of Neronic art, the stylised grandeur of Domitian's reign, the earnest utilitarianism of the age of Trajan, or the philhellenic classicism of Hadrian. Then, towards the end of the second century, new forms of expression began to appear, especially in Roman sculpture. The classic rules are overthrown. Hair masses, facial folds, the treatment of the eyes now express lively arousal and disturbance. However great the risk of reading historical circumstances into works of art, the onset of new stylistic tendencies and new ideas remains unmistakable.

Of Roman painting, whole categories can only be guessed at, or have come down to us in very few examples. We have definite evidence of history-painting, panel pictures, paintings on canvas, and portrait-painting. Our total impression today derives chiefly from the wall-paintings of the wealthier private homes, the palaces and also the tomb-paintings. The most important of these, in terms of our being able to view them, are in the two Vesuvius cities, Pompeii and Herculaneum. At first the walls were simply partitioned by painting, but after the time of Sulla there were *trompe-l'œil* architecture, garden landscape and mythological scenes. We see a stronger and stronger attempt to extend by illusionist means the space enclosed by the walls, or else to deepen it with distant 'views'. The theatrical effect of *trompe-l'œil* architecture was at first the main feature, but soon the landscape and architectural scenery was enhanced with mythological accessories. The large figure paintings and serial storytelling, like the famous 'mystery frieze' from Pompeii, were the latest summits of this development, in which the vigour of the colours was often just as fascinating as the rhythm and accuracy of the drawing.

Mosaic was another category of Greek art which the Romans adopted. The small stones cut into dice shapes (*tessellae*) had been in use in the Greek world since the fifth century BC, at first for simple ornamental floor-coverings, later for more and more artistic compositions, including small subjects from life. From the second century BC onward, it began to take hold in Italy. It is probable that the models for the floor mosaics, which at that time began to establish themselves by way of Campania in the closer environs of Rome, were originally to be seen in Hellenistic palaces and the richly furnished houses of Delos. Through all the many changes undergone by this art form, what always remained character-istic of Roman mosaic, as of Roman sculpture, was its functional incorporation into the total architecture of the building concerned.

At first, bold black outlines on a white ground predominated, as can be seen especially in the mosaics of Pompeii and Ostia. The subjects in these were predominantly seascapes and mythological scenes but also everyday vignettes. Mosaics in many colours, like the landscapes in the *Villa Hadriana*, are an exception. There was a specially wide distribution and an unusually artistic quality of mosaic in the villas and houses of the governing class in the North African provinces. Although the scenes were at first mostly mythological, soon their subjects became lively farming and hunting episodes. Syria, another key area of mosaic art, with a leading production centre in Antioch, followed its own rules of style. There the Hellenistic tradition was still influential, with a preference also for naturalistic ideas. In the end, mosaic reached almost every Roman province, right over to Britain.

Mosaics spread from the floors and well-heads over the walls of buildings, to high ceiling-vaults. Their peak of monumental splendour was only reached in its most imposing, large-scale form with the Christian picture cycles of Late Antiquity, especially in Ravenna and Constantinople.

Only a few hints can be given here concerning the wide field of handicrafts. Glyptic, the art of cut stones, reached a high level under the Principate. Carved gems and cameos combined history and mythology and became, like the *Gemma Augustea* in Vienna or the great Paris Cameo, splendid representations of the Principate ideology. Like the portraits, pictures and legends on coins, they propagated political programmes in concentrated form. This was above all a field in which the stylistic relationships bridged the differences of individual art forms. There were, for instance, close connections between the relief ornaments of the *Ara Pacis* and the forms of the jewels in the Hildesheim Silver Hoard, as there were also between the chasing of metal objects and the themes of the red-glazed clay vessels of Arretine *terra sigillata*.

In the various categories of art I have outlined above, it would of course be wrong to assume that stylistic tendencies were uniform, and that developments were likewise uniform and without peaks. It is true that great city art under the Principate, that is to say the official state art or imperial art as it is called, again and again launched or promoted or influenced in part by the *principes* themselves, set the example for the whole *imperium*. Yet side by side with it, even in Rome and Italy, there survived a 'people's art', maintained by craftwork and determined by the interests, needs, means and possibilities of the broad lower classes, while above all in the provinces there was 'provincial art' to bear the stamp of the powerful regional traditions. Nor must we forget that the everyday relationship of the Roman to art, if we pass over the impressions made by public buildings, installations and works of art, was overwhelmingly determined by his social position. While the members of the aristocracy were often surrounded by masterpieces or copies of Greek and Hellenistic art, living in ingeniously painted rooms and eating from expensive silver plate, the simple artisan had nothing but a few modest images in his *lararium*, mass-produced pottery utensils and cheap eating-implements. The often fascinating showcase pieces of the great museums, the small bronzes, candelabra, terracottas, glasses, ivory and jewelled objects of all shapes and materials were often to be found only in the possession of the more wealthy bourgeoisie.

SCIENCE AND TECHNOLOGY

Research in natural science as understood by the pre-Socratics or even the Hellenistic schools was completely alien to Roman thought. They were interested neither in fundamental questions of philosophy nor in the systematics of science for their own sake, nor were they ever seized with the passion for investigating theoretical problems. What was always decisive for them about scientific or technical knowledge was whether it could be applied. Which philosophic school was to be preferred to which was a question just as secondary for them as which was the appropriate school of medicine. What was characteristic of the Romans in both cases was their eclecticism. Their ends were wholly practical. This in no way belies the fact that great compilations like Pliny the Elder's *Naturalis Historia,* translations like that of Celsus in the first century A D, and broadly planned systematic studies like that of Galen, stored up the discoveries of Greek natural science and medicine, and continued their influence until well into the Middle Ages. Original Roman researches bore fruit only in relatively limited fields, determined entirely by practice and involved with it.

Only recently has it been pointed out that a whole series of technical inventions and improvements date from Roman times: the so-called hydraulic cement of lime and pozzolana, a building material like concrete which made possible the great public buildings of the Principate, especially their new vaulting techniques; the development of dome and vault construction with the help of retaining walls, ribbed vaults and cross vaults; the systematic perfecting of hypocaust house-heating systems through the use of hard-baked bricks; the improvement of the screw press, which was introduced in large numbers (rope, winch and cranked screw presses); extensive use of wooden and metal screws; wide diffusion of blown, colourless glass, but also the refinement of luxury glass techniques (grinding techniques, snake-trailed glasses, gilding of glass, *diatreta* glasses).

One can certainly put forward a different case, by maintaining that inventions already achieved, like the water-mill or the Gallic 'harvesting machine', were not properly exploited; that in shipping they clung to the single mast, and on land made as little progress in developing the windmill and the steam turbine as a rational harness for draught animals; that even their military engineering was stagnant. Clearly they were content more or less with the equipment at their disposal for tackling the work on hand.

Roman civilisation had some remarkable appliances at its command. The abacus, the calculating board with lines for units, tens, hundreds, and so on, was further developed into the hand abacus in the style of a modern pocket reckoner. The chorobates, a levelling instrument based on the principle of the spirit-level, functioned in much the same way as modern theodolites. Quite a number of handworking tools had already attained the forms still standard in the early modern period. In the larger workshops simple hoists, building cranes, and tackle blocks were already in use, occasionally even machines as complicated as the treadwheel crane used by Lucceius Peculiaris in his column workshop in Capua. The army used an arrow-gun consisting of two tension arms joined by a string and capable of great accuracy. Its 1.20-metre (4-feet) long arrow, after a flight of 340 metres (370 yards), could still strike right through a hardwood shield 2 cm ($\frac{3}{4}$ inch) thick to a depth of 30 cm (1 foot) beyond. There was also a single armed siege gun capable of shooting stone balls a distance of 300 metres (330 yards).

In the interplay between traditional inertia and encounters with foreign achievement, the individual sciences were exposed to a variety of influences. These can be illustrated by examples from the medical field. In early Rome both public and private medicine were a matter largely for the *pater familias*. Wool and cabbage seem to have been fundamental ingredients of his treatment, quite often accompanied by archaic magical formulae:

'When something is dislocated it can be healed by the following spell: Take a green reed four to five feet long, split it down the middle and let two men hold it to their hips. Begin to recite the spell: *moetas uaeta daries dardaries astataries dissunapiter,* until they come together. Lay a knife upon it. When both parts have come together and touch one another, take them in your hand, cut them off to the right and to the left, bind it to the dislocation or break and it will heal. But you must recite daily: *huat huat huat ista sistas sistardannabou dannaustra.*' (Cato, *De Agricultura,* 160)

We cannot tell how strong an influence was exerted by Etruscan medicine on the Roman. In any case, that of Greek medicine was stronger. The building of a temple of Asclepius on the Tiber Island early in the third century BC marked the beginning there of a contact which lasted for centuries and was by no means confined to a grateful acceptance of Greek discoveries and practices. Cato himself was deeply distrustful of Greek doctors. Rome's first Greek doctor known by name was Archagathus from the Peloponnese, who settled in Rome in 219 BC. Later there were such men as Asklepiades of Prusa (*c.* 120–40 BC), who had tried his hand first as a rhetorician and who despised anatomical studies, yet through self-confidence, psychological skill and hastily acquired medical lore won a respected position. More typical still, perhaps, were the careers of the dozens of Greek slaves who, after what was often only a brief apprenticeship in the retinue of a doctor, were themselves bold enough to set up in independent practice.

Thus at first the social standing of doctors working in Rome was very low, many being discredited as butchers, burners, and quacks. Yet gradually specialists established themselves, in particular surgeons and oculists. Fees reached astronomic heights. Under Caesar and Augustus, the medical men enjoyed official recognition; under Hadrian, privileges. The 'personal physicians' of the *principes*, such as Antonius Musa under Augustus, Xenophon of Cos under Claudius, Galen under Marcus Aurelius, attained great influence. The position of doctors was fully secured when Antoninus Pius appointed state doctors for universal medical care to each of the fourteen regions of Rome, and when other cities of the *imperium* also created similar institutions. The range of medical instrumentation, moreover, was highly developed, and from Pompeii alone some 200 medical implements are known.

Evidently under the Republic the level of medical provision and care of the wounded in the Roman army were not very impressive, but under the Principate there were fundamental changes. There were large military hospitals (*valetudinaria*), as for instance at Inchtuthil in Scotland, Xanten and Neuss in Germany and Windisch in Switzerland. The *medici* functioning in the legions and cohorts were no doubt comparable in their qualifications more with the field surgeons or sanitary orderlies of early modern armies than with the army doctors of today. However unsatisfactory the medical services for the new population may appear by our standards, it must be remembered that the provision of fresh water, baths and drainage on a scale which we must often regard as downright luxurious must have given protection against many possible health risks.

We have seen how systematically the Romans rejected all merely theoretical speculations, and this had the consequence that they were unwilling to come down in favour of any particular Hellenistic medical 'school'. The 'dogmatists' who wanted a strictly logical system of relationships between body and ailment were in the Roman view no more entitled to exclusive consideration than the 'empiricists' who based themselves on their own observations, the history of an illness, and inferences by analogy, or the 'method men' who wanted a return to elementary opposites and treated extremes by extremes, or the '*pneuma* men' who took Stoic conceptions of the *pneuma* ('breath' or 'spirit') as a universal principle for the starting-point of their medical teaching. Thus an eclecticism based on practice dominated the field and reached its peak in the work of the Greek Galen.

The Romans themselves made no contributions worth mentioning to the development of medicine, apart from the compilation of Pliny the Elder, translations (Celsus), and a few late practical handbooks. All they did was to promote a certain late flowering of Greek medicine within the framework of the *imperium*, which however was very far from reaching the level of its really creative phases (Hippocrates, Schools of Cos and Cnidos, Aristotle, Theophrastus, Alexandrine research).

ROMAN RELIGION

So far as the beginnings of Roman religion can be recognised, it emerged as a typical farmer's religion. Sacrifices, processions to bless the fields, and aversion ceremonies were characteristic forms of expression. The Roman peasantry believed themselves surrounded, protected, or threatened by numerous non-material powers, and these had to be kept at bay by well-defined rites. It is noticeable how strict was the formalism which from the very beginning governed the performance of any sacramental act or the utterance of any prayer.

'It is thought that sacrifices or petitions to the gods are ineffectual without prayer. The text for invoking a happy omen is different from that for averting an ill or that for making a request. The highest officials pray in fixed forms of words, and to make sure that not a word is omitted or spoken in the wrong place, a prompter reads the text before them, another person is appointed to watch over it, yet another to command silence, and the flute-player plays to mask all other sounds. There are well-known examples of both kinds of mishap, either where the effectiveness of the prayer was spoiled by a chance expletive or where there was a slip in the recitation of the prayer.' (Pliny the Elder, *Natural History* XXIII, 10f.)

This was the manner in which ancient prayers and religious chants were preserved, like the powerful chant of the Arval brothers, handed down in an inscription of AD 218:

> Come hither, you Lares, help,
> let no plague, disaster, Mars break in upon the throng.
> Wild Mars, take your fill, jump on to the threshold and stay there.
> All the Semunes shall he invoke in turn.
> Let Mars come to our aid.
> Triumph, triumph, triumph, triumph, triumph.

The most powerful peasant deity was Jupiter, lord of heaven's vault who cast the thunderbolts, who soon became the Roman state deity. With Juno, the protectress of women, and Minerva, the goddess of craftsmen, he was united in a powerful triad on the Capitol. Beside him Mars stood out not only as a god of war but as god of hard labour in the fields. There was Saturn too, also an ancient god of agriculture, and Vesta, guardian of the fire entrusted to the care of the Vestal Virgins. The fertility goddess Ceres became the specific deity of the Roman *plebs*; Mercury was worshipped as the protector of shopkeepers; Vulcan as god of fire and smiths; Neptune as deity of all the waters and seas. The old Latian goddess Diana became the patron goddess of women and slaves. Fortuna, the mistress of good luck, was worshipped from an early date, whereas Venus, the goddess of love, came later on the scene.

These great deities were joined by dozens of other gods and goddesses, Etruscan and Old Italian divinities for special kinds of farm work and animal husbandry, others for particular quarters of the city, then too the family divinities or *di parentes*, later the *di manes*, or spirits of the dead of each particular family, which also received religious worship, and the *lares*, or good spirits associated with a locality, which were worshipped especially at crossroads, and again the family and household deities such as the *penates*, to name only the most important. From the very beginning, too, foreign deities were readily accepted by the Romans. More than that, they made anxious efforts to appease foreign sources of supernatural power. They worshipped the city god of the conquered Veii as eagerly as the numerous Greek deities who took up residence in Rome. Characteristically, however, they were just as ready, in parallel with the emergence of the nobility from the third century B C onwards, to accord cult and worship to such key concepts as *virtus, honos, fides, victoria, pietas, libertas,* and other abstractions by which the aristocratic ethic was defined.

The fundamental religious attitude of the Romans was dictated in the first instance by a sober, deeply rooted recognition of the power of the gods. The obligations to the gods were acknowledged and affirmed. It was necessary to pay attention to omens as an expression of their good will, to put them in a favourable mood by sacrifices and prayers, and thus to bring about and maintain the *pax deum,* the harmony with the gods. Roman *pietas* is more than just 'piety'. It is the virtue of unqualified acceptance of obligations. Octavian's revenge on the murderers of Caesar, his adoptive father, was in the Roman view an act of *pietas.* Yet the Roman's relationship with the gods, like the relationship of *cliens* to *patronus,* was one of mutual obligations. The duties of either side were governed by the prosaic principle *do ut des.* In this relationship too, *fides* was dominant.

The continual close contact with the gods was for the Romans not only a private matter but likewise a political affair of state. Before an important political occasion, like the opening of the popular assembly, or important military acts, like the marching out of the army or its entry into battle, the will of the gods was ascertained by observations of the sky, analysis of the flight of birds, or examination of entrails. To question the gods, pray to them, procure their favour, and also to thank them, were supreme duties of state discharged by sacrifice, games, and the building of temples, but also by the fact that it was not the victorious general who triumphed but Jupiter in him. For an author as traditional in his beliefs as Livy, the whole of Roman history was still, in the time of Augustus, a proof that Roman world domination was due to Roman observance of the will of the gods, the *sequi deos.* 'You will find that those who followed the gods had every success, while those who disregarded them were visited with misfortune' (Livy, *History* V, 51, 5).

It was a further characteristic of Roman religion that the individual's links with deity were not primarily direct but through an intermediary. In the early social cells, the *familia,* the *gens* and the state, communication with the gods so to speak, was the task of the *pater familias,* or head of the family, and the state priests, or *pontifices.* Owing to the close interconnections between religion and politics, the sacral domain could not be separated from one which was profane but also political. The aristocracy as members of the great ancient priesthoods, especially the *pontifices*, the *augures* and the *XVviri sacris faciundis*, exerted an additional influence, just as the occupation of a priestly office was advantageous for a political career. Of sixty-six *pontifices* known by name under the Republic, fifty-one reached the consulate and nine the praetorship; and of fifty-four augurs known by name, thirty-nine reached the consulate and five the praetorship.

From the third century BC onward, there were changes in Roman religion. The violent shocks of the Punic Wars led in 249 BC to the introduction of Secular Games, a combined feast of atonement and new beginning; and in 205 BC the cult stone of the great mother-goddess Cybele was brought to Rome from Pessinus in Phrygia, and the cult with its ecstatic and orgiastic features was thereafter celebrated in Rome. Even before this, new forms of worship had been introduced, so as to provide for direct encounters with the gods. In the banquet of the gods (*lectisternium*) the images of the gods were brought from the temples to a square and there honoured with a festive meal in common. In the *pompa circensis*, they were carried through the circus before games and races. In the *supplicationes*, the citizens of Rome in a sort of procession visited all the Roman temples to pray or give thanks.

In all this we see on the one hand the wish for immediate religious contacts, and on the other dissatisfaction with traditional obligations. The cult of the Great Mother and almost at the same time the Dionysus cult, with their enraptured celebrants roused by music and dancing to throw off all restraints, attracted thousands of followers. The so-called Bacchanalian conspiracy of the year 186 BC is evidence that the Roman Senate thought the social order was endangered when at the nightly gatherings of the Dionysus cult the barriers between the ranks and sexes were blurred, and the cult was discredited by such excesses. The continuing tolerance of the Roman state towards foreign cults was only matched by its defensive hostility towards any suspected threat to morality, tradition and public order. Behind secret meetings and cult vows they suspected political conspiracy; proselytising suggested political propaganda, and magical practices were misinterpreted as witchcraft. Christianity was yet to suffer from such prejudices.

In the time of the late Republic, the rigid framework of the old Roman religion had more or less disintegrated. While among large sections of the country folk the old faith was still as lively as ever, and even persisted in original forms such as the worship of male potency, and while splendid new temples and images of the gods adorned the cities, among the governing and educated classes, and also among the Roman bourgeoisie philosophical scepticism and rationalism, but above all faith in astrology were spreading more and more. The governing class clung to the state religion for opportunistic reasons and yet could not prevent priestly offices from falling vacant for lack of a successor, while cults and religious rites ceased to be observed or were forgotten. The election to *pontifex maximus* became a political one, as is shown by the examples of Julius Caesar, Lepidus and Augustus.

Then the disasters of the civil wars led to a renewal of buried religious feelings. There was a widespread conviction that all the sufferings and deprivations of the age were a punishment from the gods:

> Roman, you shall pay the penalty
> for crimes you did not commit –
> until you have restored the temples
> and crumbling homes of the gods
> and their images foul with the black smoke.
> (Horace, *Odes* III, 6)

This is the point at which the work of systematic religious restoration by Augustus began. In Rome alone he ordered the restoration of eighty-two ruined temples, the re-editing of the Sibylline books, the revival of half-forgotten rites and festivals, the refilling of vacant priestly offices, the holding of the Secular Games. Above all he himself set the example of active participation in the tasks of the old priesthoods: 'I was *pontifex maximus, augur, XVvir sacris faciundis, VIIvir epulonum, frater arvalis, sodalis Titius, fetialis' (Res Gestae Divi Augusti* VII). Yet these varied activities could not restore belief in the old Roman gods. It was an illusion to suppose they could. While the old forms persisted, the old Roman convictions disappeared in wide sections of the population. This discrepancy was fundamental to the whole period of the Principate, and profoundly affected its development.

At the same time, the systematic merger of politics and religion was characteristic of the new political system. The cult worship of the *princeps* became an act of political loyalty. At the same time it was characteristic of Augustus' cautious manoeuvring that he attached himself wherever possible to beginnings already made. He never, as it were, issued a uniform decree applying to the whole empire and enforcing a uniform state cult of his person, but encouraged or tolerated for different sections of the population and different parts of the empire different forms of religious veneration. Especially in the east of the *imperium*, where the cult worship of the ruler had long been usual, private individuals, cities and provinces competed in the demonstrative religious worship of the man to whom they were indebted, after the excesses of the civil wars, for peace, well-being and security. For this too must be realised: the cult worship of the *princeps* was by no means a result uniquely of state pressure from above.

In Rome itself Augustus combined a reform of the so-called *compitalia* cult with the organisation of the religious worship of his own person. The *compitalia* were originally a country feast of sacrifice among those who resided near a crossroads. It was thus a cult deeply rooted in a particular locality among the lower social groups, and in its celebrations, at least in certain areas, slaves and freedmen predominated. The subdivision of the city of Rome into 265 *vici* or neighbourhood precincts offered an occasion for a systematic reorganisation. The cult centres remained, as before, the respective crossroad chapels of the *lares* at a crossroads (*compita*) but the cult itself was now combined, between 14 and 7 BC, with that of the *genius Augusti*, the divine life force of Augustus personified. Augustus himself provided for the material equipment of the cult concerned in the case of the poorer sections by presenting the *vicomagistri*, or subdistrict presidents, with the *lar* statuettes for the chapels. At the same time, the cult was associated with the *domus principis* by the participation of young male members of the family of the *princeps* bearing *lar* and *genius* statuettes in the processions, as we learn from archaeological evidence.

The worship of the *genius* of Augustus with the *lares* was central to the forms of cult permitted by Augustus throughout the whole area of citizenship. There was thus set up a conscious parallel with the connection which had long been usual in the private sphere between the *lares* sacrifices and those to the *pater familias*. This was even more fully emphasised when Augustus, in 2 BC, was named *pater patriae*. In the cities of the *imperium*, it was particularly the municipal aristocracy and the *Augustales* or the *seviri Augustales* who assumed responsibility for the *princeps* cult. These were associations in which the wealthier freedmen especially found opportunities of distinguishing themselves socially by their activities and donations.

For the provinces again other forms were chosen. 'Although it was already known to him that even proconsuls often had temples erected in their honour, he never allowed this to be done in his own case unless the name of the goddess Roma was added to his' (Suetonius, *Divus Augustus* LII). The first temples for 'Roma and Augustus' were built in Pergamum and Nicomedia in 29 BC, and this was the beginning of the 'emperor cult' or 'provincial cult'. It spread gradually in the western provinces also, and Lugdunum (Lyons) became a special cult centre of the Gallic provinces. There, in the altar quarter near the mouth of the Saône, representatives of the tribal aristocracy of all sixty tribes assembled to choose the 'provincial high priest'. He conducted not only the sacrifices and games but also the *concilium* (*koinon* in the eastern provinces), an assembly which besides its representational cult function had some rights of tendering grievances and recommending distinctions to the governor but never had the authority of a modern 'state parliament' or 'diet'. Similar provincial cults and councils are known from almost every province of the *imperium*. For Germany in Augustan times there was already an appropriate altar with its corresponding priest in Cologne. Later, after the failure of Roman attempts to occupy north-west Germany and the transfer of Roman activities to the south-west, it is clear that the functions were taken over by the *arae Flaviae*.

The religious worship of Augustus thus ran through a considerable variety of forms and intensities. In the Greek East he already received cult worship from individuals during his lifetime, as a god or together with gods such as Asklepios, Hygieia, Zeus – and the characteristic epithets of the Hellenistic ruler cult, the 'Saviour', 'Benefactor', 'Redeemer', were applied to him. But in the West, and in Rome itself, there was greater detachment, though even there provincial groups, the municipal aristocracy and *Augustales*, joined in. In certain cities, the *ordo decurionum* appointed its own *sacerdotes* or *flamines* (priests); in Narbonne, three *equites e plebe* (*equites* from the *plebs*) and three freedmen were required to sacrifice animals, incense and wine to the divine efficacy of Augustus, and to supply the same sacrificial materials to the city *plebs*; in some Italian cities, the worship of the *princeps* was added to an already existing cult and thus established itself. In all these varied ways the *princeps* cult was introduced and established itself, becoming more and more strongly institutionalised.

The idea that they met with their own deities under other names among foreigners was one which the Romans had in common with the Greeks. Thus in the west of the *imperium*, for instance, there was the so-called *interpretatio Romana* ('Roman translation') of the many Celtic deities. An old Celtic god would have his name coupled with a Latin equivalent, like Lenus Mars in Trier or Apollo Grannus in Baden-Baden. As we learn from Caesar's account of the Gallic gods or Tacitus' of the German, it was the function of the god concerned which determined the equivalence. In many cases the 'translation' of the god's name into Latin might offer alternatives. The British Cocidius occurs as Mars or Silvanus Cocidius, the Ligurian Vintius as Mars Vintius or Vintius Pollux.

The worship of a polytheist world of gods, the growing dissatisfaction with traditional cults, the readiness to welcome strange new divinities, and the corresponding readiness of the oriental cults to adapt themselves to Roman ideas and procedures, account for the widespread blurrring of once-distinctive ancient forms which was so characteristic of the *imperium Romanum*. There was a merging of opposites, the mutual transfer and interpenetration of divine images by the phenomenon known as syncretism. This was by no means confined to the Romans.

The Phrygian Sabazius was identified with Sabaoth, as was Isis with Demeter, Venus and a whole series of other goddesses. The abundance of religious encounters, superimpositions and at least partial identifications was bound in the end, even in the orthodox Graeco-Roman tradition, to give rise to monotheistic ideas not only on the highest philosophical level but also on the broader levels of popular belief.

The most lively cults under the Principate were first and foremost undoubtedly the mystery religions, the cults of Isis, of the Great Mother, of Mithras, and of two other oriental goddesses: Isis in the course of syncretism had been transformed into the mother of all civilisation and the redeemer goddess of all humanity; Cybele the Great Mother, who in manic guise mourned her dead lover Attis, was a focus of ecstatic ceremonies. Finally, in the Mithras cult a variety of oriental religious ideas, especially of Iranian origin, had come together.

The most important stations in the life-story of Mithras are illustrated on his altars: born of a rock, worshipped by shepherds, his meeting with the sun god, the killing of the world bull from whose blood all life is generated – usually the central scene on the altars – finally the god's ascent to heaven. Mithras was again and again the go-between for men, their great helper in the fight with evil which he will finally destroy at his second coming. Other auxiliary gods such as Herakles were associated with the cult. Typical too, however, is the importance of astrological elements. The zodiac plays a big part on the monuments, and there were seven different grades of initiates corresponding to the traditional number of planets. Initiation was by baptism, and the cult also had a fixed liturgy with the dedication of bread and water. The worship of Mithras mostly took place in small communities in cave-like sanctuaries. The contrast between light and darkness was an important feature. Its believers were at first above all soldiers, who felt specially drawn to this decidedly forceful god, but later also officials, small tradesmen and slaves. It spread particularly in the garrisons, mostly on the *limes* and in the northern frontier regions of the *imperium*. *Mithraea*, the sanctuaries, are known not only from Ostia and Rome but also, for example, from Carnuntum (7), Friedberg (3) and Heddernheim (4).

The mystery religions have a whole series of common features. They addressed themselves particularly to weak, suffering, insecure humanity, promised cleansing and purification, salvation and eternal bliss. In specially intensive cult performances, exciting religious services which worked strongly on the senses, in the security and exclusiveness of small communities, they procured for every individual direct encounters and communion with the deity whose death and resurrection were again and again experienced. The parallels with early Christianity are obvious. At all events, it was 'Mithraism' and not the ancient

Graeco-Roman pantheon or the emperor cult which became the most
important antithesis to Christianity. It was unable to stand up to the
monotheistic faith of Christianity not only because of the interventions
of history in the development of religions in Late Antiquity but just as
much because of its specifically masculine basis.

IMPERIUM ROMANUM AND CHRISTIANITY

Within the frontiers of the Roman empire, only two religions
represented a system of belief which was monotheistic without
compromise: Judaism and Christianity. For a long time the Jewish
religion was able to conduct a very successful mission of its own. The
Jews indeed profited from the liberality of belief, they set up points of
contact by the thousand. In Egypt alone, with about a million Jewish
citizens, they made up a good 10–15 per cent of the whole population.
One crippling aspect of the Jewish religion, however, apart from its
unusually strong ethnic ties and traditions, was its fragmentation into
sects.

First there were the two great groups – Pharisees, vigorous upholders
of the religious law as received and practised, and the Sadducees,
extreme adherents of a restricted code of written law. Then there were
smaller groups, secluded communities like the Essenes, or fanatical
activists like the Zealots. But the repeated Jewish insurrections, above
all that of Bar Kochba, led to a far-reaching isolation of the Jews in the
imperium. From then on they concentrated their mission especially in the
east. After the drastic political destruction of the Jews in their homeland,
which was far from the original intentions of Julius Caesar and
Augustus with their decided good will for the Jews, there could no
longer be any question of fully integrating Jewry in the Roman state.

The advent of Jesus Christ and his teaching were also rooted in late
Judaism and in many details of its idea of God – the immediate contact
between man and God, the consciousness of being called, the
eschatological expectations and messianic hopes. This explains why
Christianity was so slow to detach itself from Judaism. Yet this process
had to be completed before Christianity could achieve world efficacy, as
it did first inside the *imperium Romanum*. The words of Luke's gospel
gave impressively concrete expression to this historical context: 'And it
happened in those days that an order went out from Caesar Augustus
that all the world was to be registered. This first registration took place
when Cyrenius was governor of Syria' (Luke 2,1f.). There are still many
problems of dating about this account. P. Sulpicius Quirinius was sent
to Syria as governor in AD 6, with orders to occupy Judaea and
incorporate it in Syria. The holding of a Roman census would then have

been automatic. But Luke's wording became received truth, and established what was in a Christian view that providential link between the Roman empire and Christianity which was later invoked by so many Christian apologists.

It was through the missionary activities of St Paul especially that Christianity spread so rapidly in the eastern provinces of the *imperium*. Strong Christian centres were established in the regions of Syria, Greek Asia Minor, and Egypt. Antioch, Ephesus and Alexandria became capitals of the new religion, with Jerusalem. The city of Rome was for a long time of secondary importance among believing Christians. Probably a community of Jewish Christians was established there soon after the death of Christ, and Suetonius has it that Jews who, under the incitement of a certain Chrestus, were always provoking disorders had already been expelled from Rome under Claudius. The Christian community, which later formed round St Paul under Nero, was then annihilated after the great fire of Rome.

Tacitus' account of these events not only reveals the circumstances of this first confrontation of a Roman *princeps* with Christendom, but also gives us the picture which a thoroughly open-minded member of the Roman upper class might have of Christianity:

'But the terrible rumour that Nero himself had ordered the burning of Rome could not be quelled by charitable distributions or donations by the *princeps* or ceremonies of atonement. Therefore Nero sought to put down the rumour by providing culprits and visited with outrageous punishments a group called Christians by the mob and hated for their misdeeds. They took their name from a certain Christus who had been punished with death by the procurator Pontius Pilate in the reign of Tiberius. And though suppressed for the time being this destructive superstition broke out again, not only in Judaea where the evil had its origin but also in the city where every horror and outrage from anywhere finds its way and is practised. So they first arrested professing Christians, then on their evidence a huge multitude who were convicted not so much on the charge of incendiarism as of hatred of the human race. And they made sport of the condemned, wrapping some in animals' skins and having them torn to pieces by dogs, crucifying others or setting them on fire as living torches after nightfall. Nero lent his own gardens for the spectacle, staging a mock circus, mixing with the crowd in charioteer's uniform or himself driving a chariot. Thus, however guilty they might be and deserving of extreme penalties, pity was aroused, with a feeling that not the public good but the savagery of an individual was the cause of their destruction.' (Tacitus, *Annals* XV, 44)

Domitian's authoritative style of government and his enforcement of the emperor cult then led, especially in Asia Minor, to a conflict of principle between the excessive religious exaltation of the Principate and the Christian religion. The most important source for the attitude of the Roman state to Christianity during the Principate is Pliny the

Younger's correspondence with Trajan (*Letters* X, 96f.). In A D 111 Pliny as *legatus* of the *princeps* with consular powers had assumed control of Roman administration in Bithynia and Pontus to put right a number of abuses. Finding Christianity widespread in the province, he felt he needed a fundamental ruling about it.

Pliny was uncertain whether the mere membership of the sect ought to be punishable, especially in those cases where the accused had renounced the Christian faith. Then again he was not clear whether young and old alike were all to receive the same punishment. Pliny himself saw the public confession of Christianity before the governor and the consequent refusal to sacrifice to the state gods as behaviour plainly punishable with death. Equally, he released prisoners who did perform the sacrifice. His researches into the Christian cult, on which he also reported to Trajan and which in his eyes was a crude superstition, constitute a priceless source on the early Christian liturgy and the reality of early Christian community life.

Trajan's reply on critical points confirmed Pliny's findings and action. In addition he declared roundly that there were to be no state searches for adherents of the Christian faith (*conquirendi non sunt*). In particular there was to be no following up of anonymous denunciations. That would set the worst possible example and be contrary to the spirit of the age (*nam et pessimi exempli nec nostri saeculi est*).

Trajan's reply demonstrates the curious inconsequence of the Roman state attitude to Christianity. Its importance is due to the fact that, by its publication, the exchange of letters acquired the force of law for the whole *imperium*. Confession of Christianity was therewith a crime punishable by death on denunciation if confirmed by examination of the facts. Against that, there was to be no active persecution of these criminals, who by a single act of sacrifice could purge themselves of the offence. Christian apologetics never tired of pointing out these contradictions. Yet Trajan's line was at first followed by his successors. Hadrian even gave it more precision by ruling that there must be no yielding to formless general accusations made in tumultuous fashion, and that proceedings against anyone suspected of Christianity could only be instituted if the complainant brought an accusation in correct form before a court. In the event of false accusations, the complainant was to be punished.

Hadrian's rescript shows the part often played by spontaneous outbursts of the pagan masses in proceedings against Christians. After all, even Pontius Pilate in the end was only giving way to Jewish-orthodox importunity, and like him later Roman governors again and again found themselves under massive and tumultuous pressures. For the pagans Christianity was suspect in the highest degree because of the exclusiveness of its communities, its unintelligible services and its creed. In part, too, the Christian cult was suspected of secret orgies and excesses, but above all every disaster was put down to their account: 'If the Tiber bursts its banks, if the Nile fails to water the fields, if the storm will not pass over, if the earth quakes, if there is a famine or a plague, at once you hear the cry, "Christians to the lions!"' (Tertullian, *Apologeticus* XL).

These developments reached their culmination under Marcus Aurelius. The adherents of the Christian faith were ready to endure every persecution, however, and they were prepared for it. They knew the sentences of Luke's gospel: 'Blessed are you when men shall hate you and throw you out and revile you and reject your name as evil, all for the son of man's sake' (6,22); or of Matthew's, 'And you will be hated by everyone because of my name, and he that stands fast to the end will be saved' (10,22). In this expectation, and in the certainty of eternal salvation, the Christians indeed often provoked the persecutions and thwarted all the attempts of individual officials to overlook denunciations. This was especially the case with such sects as the Montanists.

The more menacing the Crisis of Empire became from the second century A D onward, the greater the number of Christians. It was not only because people were ready to die for this religion, and because Christians in their systematic reverence for the martyrs soon everywhere found 'classical soil under their feet' (Jacob Burckhardt), but because this religion of love, forgiveness and hope, which modified all earthly relations and in graphic fashion opened up a new dimension of human existence, was also lived. It was lived in cells, havens of a new assurance, for which rank, status, legal rights, property, place of residence and level of education were irrelevant. Christianity was the first faith actually to embrace that universality which had all along been implied by the *imperium Romanum*. And for all its recognition of earthly power, Christianity too was the first faith to set itself above this and every other empire.

THE EMPIRE OF LATE
ANTIQUITY

THE AGE OF THE SEVERANS AND
THE CRISIS OF EMPIRE

The first symptoms of crisis in the society and economy of the *imperium Romanum* had already shown themselves in the 'great calm' of the second century A D. There was the stagnation of output, particularly by slave labour, the necessary introduction of poor relief (the *alimentatio*), the crushing public load on the municipal aristocracy, and the decline of the currency. But the germs of the crisis did not become really virulent until the last few decades of the second century, under the pressure of the Parthian wars and the German invasions, while the very system itself was eroded by usurpations, plague and inflation. That was when the ideological trappings of the Principate began to fall, when the military monarchy emerged in all its brutality. Now the army – characteristically, however, not the army as a compact body but the different frontier armies, each with its particular interests – took the stage as the decisive power factor.

The developments and changes of the third century A D cannot be reduced to a struggle between town and country or a 'social revolution' or a crisis of property relations. But neither were they to be attributed solely to innovations in weaponry or military practice; to the increasing importance of cavalry, for instance, or to the fact that, in order to increase the military potential of the *imperium*, recruitment was now being extended to new vigorous marginal groups, to Germans and Moors, Arabs and Sarmatians, even semi-nomads and nomads from the eastern and southern frontier zones. But all these and other developments interacted to intensify and spread the crisis.

In a series of constantly renewed initiatives, the rulers of the Severan dynasty and the Syrian empresses (A D 193–235), and after them the so-called 'Soldier Emperors' (A D 235–284), tried to increase the power of the emperor's position and, with it, their own as well, and thus to preserve the unity of the *imperium*, threatened as it was from inside and out. It is remarkable that during decades of strife the idea of a single Roman empire, the primacy of the city of Rome and the prestige of the Roman Senate was steadily maintained, although whole sections of the empire were making themselves independent, although the capital cities of the frontier regions were developing into military and political centres rivalling Rome as the 'seat of government', and although the Roman Senate often enough played a passive representational role while the decisive political impulses came from the army and its representatives.

Septimius Severus (AD 193–211) came to power in a new, bloody civil war. With him and his wife Julia Domna, a daughter of the sun priest of Emesa, a romanised Punic-Syrian family came to the imperial throne, and energetic personalities from the frontier zones joined the governing class. Under mobilisation of all available military force, Septimius Severus launched great offensives against the Parthian empire and against the Caledonians of northern Britain, with the aim of securing these endangered frontier zones. The military character of the Principate was pushed to an extreme, and its frontier defences systematically extended. State intervention was carried out with ruthless severity. The police apparatus was inflated, and opponents of the regime physically annihilated.

Developments which were to characterise the epoch were already apparent at many points. There was the militarisation of the state and bureaucracy, the breaking up of large blocks of administration into smaller units, the first compulsory measures against cities and trades, the confinement of frontier troops to their defence zones, the military mobilisation of population groups not yet properly romanised, the decline of Italy to the level of a province. Yet neither Severus nor his son Caracalla (died AD 218) nor their weaker successors achieved a lasting consolidation, and in the 'age of the Soldier Emperors' there was no end either to usurpations of the throne or to invasions of the empire.

With the third century AD a new phase began. Roman history now became closely involved with that of central and eastern Europe on the north, and of western Asia on the east. And here the initiative was no longer with Rome. In place of the weakened Parthian kingdom, from AD 226 onward there was a revival of the ancient Iranian civilisation with its Zoroastrian religion. A new dynasty, the Sassanids, founded an empire with expansive tendencies. Roman domination of the east was profoundly shaken, and a chain of Roman disasters culminated, in AD 260, in the capture of the Roman emperor Valerian by Shapur.

But also in the whole Danube area, in Greece and Asia Minor, on the Rhine approaches and even in Italy and Gaul, aggressive Germanic and Sarmatian tribes were pressing in, Goths and Hermunduri, Vandals and Alans, Alamanni and Franks. The defeat of the Emperor Decius in a battle against the Goths in the Dobrudja (AD 251), the abandonment of the Upper Germano-Rhaetian frontier after deep incursions by the Alamanni (AD 233, 254, 259/260), the withdrawal from Dacia and the invasion of northern and central Italy by Alamanni and Iuthungi (AD 271) were characteristic effects of the new situation. The temporary detachment of splinter states (AD 259–273 Gaul, 262–272 Palmyra, 288–296 Britain), in which regional defence forces cut themselves off from the main empire, was a further result of the impotence of the central authorities in face of setbacks on every frontier.

The invasions by the new enemies had devastating effects. Old Roman territories long interior to the *imperium* were plundered, the populations and their economies severely damaged. Rome answered by massing fortifications in the frontier zones. Turrets, watchtowers and small fortresses took the place of the great encampments. The decisive criterion for the establishment and enclosure of settlements was now whether their situation was favourable to defence. The open type of settlement could no longer be maintained in endangered territories. City fortifications were the rule of the day. The vast Aurelian city wall of Rome, begun in AD 271, with a circumference of 18.8 kilometres (11.7 miles), a height of 6 metres (20 feet), a width of 3.6 metres (12 feet), 18 gates and 381 salient fortress towers, was so to speak the architectural symbol of the changed situation, and at the same time proof that not even the capital city of the *imperium* was safe.

In the age of the Soldier Emperors, the Roman empire thus found itself ringed by a raging sea of hostile forces. Against the offensives of the Sassanids and the beginnings of the migration of peoples, every Roman success again and again melted away. Victories which once would have been enough to stabilise the situation on a section of front for years and decades now lost their value after a few weeks either because the frontier peoples opposite were themselves pushed forward from behind or because their leaders, even after being defeated, renewed their plundering forays in order to keep their followers together.

The imperial title in those years was itself a very dubious acquisition. The generals raised to the throne usually found themselves pushed from one crisis to another. Whether they failed or, by drastic measures, succeeded, they were almost equally certain to provoke an attack or their own overthrow by usurpation. Of the 26 emperors really deserving the name during the period AD 235–285, only one died a natural death, so that to be proclaimed emperor was equivalent to a sentence of death *sine die*.

The Soldier Emperors were no doubt in many cases narrow-minded and limited, rigid and ruthless. But it was no longer possible for them to hold on to their power or restore unity and preserve the *imperium* by traditional methods or in the old forms. The old privileges were swept away. The *Constitutio Antoniniana*, a decree of Caracalla's of the year A D 212/213, accorded full Roman citizenship to all free citizens of the Roman empire except for the relatively small group of the so-called *dediticii* (according to Gaius' definition, those foreigners who had once fought against the Roman people, been defeated and surrendered). The old pyramid of civil rights was thus levelled. But neither could the self-government of cities or the free movement of citizens be any longer guaranteed. The urgent problems could only be solved by the intensification, tightening and consolidation of state controls, with the help of an all-powerful army, the beginnings of taxation in kind (or by services) and a managed economy, and the reserving of certain occupations, offices and duties so that individuals could not leave them. By such emergency measures the Soldier Emperors laid the foundations of the new social structures of Late Antiquity.

The complexities of the Crisis of Empire affected all social classes and all economic sectors. The imperial governing class was systematically militarised. Military staffs dominated entirely by motives of power, for whom only obedience, loyalty and efficiency counted, replaced the *familia Caesaris*. Where once the central governing élite had included a corps of specialists who in their particular capacities would survive what were in any case infrequent changes of government, under the Soldier Emperors there was a succession of short-term governments by private officer cliques. In the senatorial order, the percentage of Italian senators was still further reduced, and that of African and oriental senators considerably increased. At the same time, many social climbers of this period were simply no longer attracted by a seat in the Senate. For men whose main concern was with power, influence and material advantages, the posts of the equestrian order or a purely military career (frequently the two were identical) offered better prospects.

Meanwhile the economic basis of senatorial rank did not decline. The senators profited from the fact that, despite all the tendencies for the *latifundia* to grow in size, large landed estates with a decentralised administration often survived the periods of destruction and plunder better than the agricultural villa units closely associated with cities. It was particularly in the large landed estate that the colonate tenant-farming system spread more and more. Not only did it give the proprietor a safer return than industrial farming with slaves but also at this particular period there were considerable numbers of landless poor available for employment.

The leasehold contracts between large landowners and their *coloni* as a rule had a term of five years, and there was also a quite frequent form of tenancy for life (*perpetua conductio*). Of course the obligations of a *colonus* were exactly fixed. They included not only a money rent, which was rapidly eroded by the steep inflation of the third century AD, and payments in kind but also services. However burdensome his obligations, the *colonus* was above all tied to the soil he cultivated, and was thus not tempted like a slave to run away, for he would then lose his labour investment. The institution of the colonate thus had a static effect, and served the interest of the state as well as the proprietor. It constituted the real basis for the privileged economic position of the aristocracy of large landowners.

According to the conclusions of modern research in economic history, the third century AD brought the expansion of the *latifundia* overseas and the decline of the villa agriculture which depended on the coordination and specialisation of slave labour. The villa industrial farms were being ruined not only because there were fewer and fewer qualified slaves, or because slaves were running away in greater numbers, or because farms in the immediate neighbourhood of the cities were more frequently plundered or destroyed during invasions, usurpations and civil wars, but above all because their owners, as members of the municipal aristocracy, were being ruthlessly exploited on all sides.

It was only the equestrian order and the army which profited from the new developments. As military and law officers, the *equites* were the indispensable official élite of the system. To damage their interests would have been suicide for any emperor. There was a steady increase in their numbers and in their duties in the imperial service. While under Augustus there had been 25 equestrian procurators, under Antoninus Pius in the middle of the second century AD the number was already 109, and under Philippus Arabs (AD 244–249), 182. From the time of Gallienus (AD 253–268), even the command of a legion was an equestrian post and not one reserved for senators as previously. Yet while the senior military ranks and administrative officers of the military dictatorships rose to the top of the social tree, the groups of the same equestrian order engaged in industry, trade or farming often enough declined into poverty.

A further economic and social tendency of importance in the third century lay in the changing relation of city and countryside. While the cities, the goal of all invaders and usurpers, were objects both of plunder and of state impositions, and thus suffered more and more damage in their economic life, and while their one-time organs of independent administration had long since declined to executive instruments of central control, the great estates in the country which had so to speak developed into autarchic structures were able to survive. While city property was ruined by long-continuing inflation, property in the country as a rule kept its value, and could quite often be successfully defended against marauders,looters and bandits. The partial return of a barter economy in this case had the advantage that agricultural products would be exchanged for goods rather than for worthless currency.

Altogether, both the state and society of the *imperium Romanum* in the third century AD were characterised by new social and ethnic groupings. It was no longer the old Roman noble families which called the tune, nor the families of the Italian and romanised provincial élite which had joined the governing class, but principally the groups of professional soldiers from the Danube area and the Balkans, from Illyricum, and even from the frontier regions of the *imperium*. The romanised Berber Macrinus, the 'Thracian' Maximinus, Philip the 'Arab' from the Hauran, the Illyrian and Pannonian Soldier Emperors right on to Diocletian and Constantine, were the men of the hour.

The most important factor, however, as has already been stressed, was now the army. 'Be united, enrich the soldiers, mind nothing else' is said to have been the motto which Septimius Severus had already impressed upon his sons Geta and Caracalla. And he too acted on the same principle, at least as far as the army was concerned. Tradition had credited him with the saying, 'Nobody but me needs money, and I need it to give to the soldiers.' In fact, the corruption of the troops sometimes went to extravagant lengths, and an emperor who failed to observe the rule, like Postumus who forbade his army to plunder Mainz, was murdered out of hand.

In the crisis of the third century AD, in which power was again and again exercised without hope of continuity, it was natural to use pressure, force and terror not only physically but also mentally and ideologically in order at least to give the appearance of political determination. The various spasmodic attempts at restoring and reviving Roman intellectual life and religion, especially under Decius and Gallienus, were just as much part of the story as the systematic persecution of the Christians. It is not at all certain that those rulers who took the most unremitting measures against Christianity, such as Maximinus Thrax, Decius or Valerian, were filled with anti-Christian feelings. Yet Christianity must necessarily have been the most provocative object of attack for an intolerant religious policy which rigidly dogmatised pagan traditions and chose victims from those under official supervision. Thus it is not a mere matter of chance that the only systematic persecutions of Christianity by the *imperium* did not occur until the third century.

But Christianity by then could not be destroyed. All attempts to do so still further increased the internal fragmentation of a population already under excessive strain and inclined to apathy. Temporary compromises like those under Gallienus already pointed the way to the political alternative, a full incorporation of the Christians in the empire. But the Roman state was not yet ready for this as a matter of public policy.

The age of the Soldier Emperors can thus be identified with a complex and far-reaching crisis and the beginnings of its solution. What is important here is not only that the crisis *was* ultimately brought to an end, with great losses, but also how. From the point of view of pagan Rome, the question we have to answer is whether the upshot was really worth the price. Obviously in the brutalisation and violence of state interventions, in the destruction of social classes like the municipal aristocracy and parts of the middle classes, in religious coercion and occupational constraints, the very values and advantages which had once characterised the *imperium* were threatened. Toleration and liberal values were all at stake, so was the chance of social mobility for all, however limited, so was the hope of confining state regimentation to a few critical areas, of putting a stop to bureaucratic overgrowth, and setting limits to the militarisation of the state and the deification of its ruler.

On the whole, the Soldier Emperors showed not the slightest desire to bring about a different state or a different order of society, and this was particularly the case with their most impressive representatives, Decius (AD 249–251), Claudius Gothicus (AD 268–270), Aurelian (AD 270–275) and Probus (AD 276–282). All they were determined on was the ruthless application of every means for the defence of the empire. Yet the more logically they laboured, the more certainly they prepared the systematic changes of structure which were not in fact to mature until Diocletian's tetrarchic reorganisation of the empire and the following new empire of Constantine the Great. But in both cases a period of continuous exercise of power lasting for decades was necessary before the permanent reforms which eluded the Soldier Emperors could be achieved. We may call it an irony of history that those who fought most vigorously for the ancient order were the very ones who thereby laid the foundations of a new state, a new society and a new religion.

LATE ANTIQUITY AND ITS EPOCHS

Despite sustained attempts at dividing its history into periods, modern historians have not succeeded in setting an agreed term to the age known as Late Antiquity. It is true that its start, in the narrower sense that disregards earlier beginnings, is usually dated to the accession of Diocletian (A D 284). But many alternatives, each based on plausible arguments, have been chosen for its closing date. There is A D 476, for instance, the collapse of the western Roman empire; or A D 568, the invasion of Italy by the Langobardi; or A D 610, the beginning of the reign of the East Roman emperor Heraclius and the renewed consolidation of the Byzantine empire; or finally A D 622, the Hijra (the flight of Mohammed from Mecca to Medina and the great divide of Arabian history). These dates show clearly how many sectors of history and cultural areas overlap one another. The final phase of the history of the *imperium Romanum* has to include the Germanic migrations and the Arab expansion, while out of it emerged a separate Byzantine empire. Thus alongside a 'late Roman' we have an 'early Byzantine' line of development. The history of the Huns is just as much part of Late Antiquity as that of the migration of peoples.

Late Antiquity is thus not intelligible from ancient Roman ideas and potentialities alone. The ancient Roman tradition, it is true, was never more strongly and passionately asserted than when it was being formalised and transmuted. But the contradiction between ideology and reality was also never greater than in the centuries when the *Romaioi* of the East felt themselves the true heirs of Rome, and Constantinople became a 'second Rome' while, in the west, German warlords defended *Roma aeterna*. From the fifth century A D onward, the primacy of the eastern half of the *imperium Romanum* was unmistakable. There it was that the stronger forces were assembled; there that the theological wrestling over questions of faith, the main preoccupation of the day, was more concentrated; there that the intellectually and artistically greater talents were at work. It is moreover symptomatic that the only major attempt to restore the *imperium Romanum* to its ancient bounds, under Justinian (A D 527–565), which was moreover briefly successful, came from the East and not from the West.

It is thus not only Antiquity and the Middle Ages which we find bracketed together in the notion of Late Antiquity. It also covers a number of special developments, regional in kind and often very different from one another, which were set in train by new historical causes. In the Roman view which gave rise to this notion, the decisive point was the growing antagonism between the eastern and western halves of the *imperium*. In the East, with the foundation of Constantinople (A D 330), the 'Byzantine millennium' (H. G. Beck) began its course. Byzantium, it is true, originated in the old *imperium Romanum* and always ostentatiously professed loyalty to the Roman tradition, yet it was a completely new thing, in its form and in its content. The fate of the West by contrast was a long tale of political and military erosion, a process in which the western Roman empire came gradually to an end. On its territories various Germanic states emerged adopting individual elements of the Roman tradition and carrying it on, even if in a debased form.

Late Antiquity may be said to have begun with a systematic transformation of the Roman state and the Roman constitution. Under pressure of military, fiscal and administrative needs, in the necessity of effectively coordinating state power, Diocletian and Constantine the Great created for the autocratic regime of Late Antiquity a constitution which may be said to have given permanent form to a state of emergency. They set up a close-meshed network of state involvement and supervision of the individual, an inflation of bureaucracy and police control, an organisation of small administrative and legal units commanded in their turn by new intermediate authorities, and a hitherto unknown degree of state planning and managerial intervention in every sphere.

At the same time, there was a break with traditional Roman policy on religion. Under Diocletian and Galerius, Maxentius and Maximinus Daia, Julian and Eugenius, the last attempts at restoring and reviving paganism failed. Constantine the Great, on the contrary, began the attempt to unite the Christian religion and its Church with the *imperium*, as stabilising factors. But the religious pluralism under which paganism and Christianity stood side by side, as at first under Constantine, could not last. Instead, by Constantine's decision, the Roman state was plunged into the dogmatic disputes which shook the Christian Church at that period. From then on, Roman internal policies were dominated by questions of religious controversy. These were at length only disposed of by the forcible suppression of pagan cults and by the intolerance of orthodox Christianity, now become 'imperial religion', in its disputes with a great variety of heresies.

Although in the Roman *imperium* of Late Antiquity the army had already increased considerably under Diocletian, the available troops were soon inadequate to deal with the defence problems posed by the unceasing series of invasions along the whole northern front. More and more, therefore, 'barbarians', that is to say Germanic and other foreign formations, were taken into Roman service and settled on the Roman side of the frontier, or else forced occupations of imperial territory were simply legalised in retrospect. In contrast with earlier examples of this policy, however, the integration of the new forces was no longer successful. Although individual German warlords and formations of auxiliary troops on the most various legal footings might remain quite loyal to Rome, the risky experiment failed in general for the very reason that their relative strengths and the whole military situation had changed since the Principate. Hatred, betrayal and mistrust became chronic on both sides, and so no genuine symbiosis between Roman and Barbarian could any longer occur.

Edward Gibbon, in his *History of the Decline and Fall of the Roman Empire*, took the classic view of Late Antiquity. His assessment of it was governed primarily by the standards and received wisdom of the ancient pagan world, and this for a long time hindered any proper understanding of the forms of expression, content and cultural achievement of Late Antiquity. It was only at the beginning of the twentieth century that scholars began to see in its art no longer mere barbaric decline and decadence but the shaping of an entirely new 'will to art' (A. Riegl). Then it was particularly in the realm of archaeology, through the researches of R. Delbrück, G. Rodenwaldt, A. Alföldi, B. Schweitzer and many others, that an understanding of the artistic and intellectual peculiarities of that age began to make headway. Of course there was an impoverishment in Late Antiquity of the classic forms of the arts and sciences and of law. Of course there were tendencies to provincialism and vulgarism, but the age was characterised also by a new range of emotion in state and ecclesiastical art, the flowering of mosaic and ivory-carving, the full development of ancient Christian intellectual life not only in an abundant theological literature but also in lyric poetry, in church hymns and in the philosophy of history. Also characteristic of Late Antiquity were the great codifications of law and the revival of pagan literature in the Symmachus circle, with its conscious preservation and editing of classical texts and its last attempts to rival their great *exempla*.

In the documents of Late Antiquity we have considerable evidence that human life at that time was characterised by a high degree of state pressure and state violence, repeated invasions and devastations by foreign peoples, and the depressing experience of an obvious decline in ancient Roman power. There were historic disasters such as the fall of Rome in AD 410, or the battle of Adrianople in AD 378, when the Emperor Valens, in command of the Roman army of the East, was defeated and killed by the Visigoths. The looting of territories which had enjoyed centuries of peace under the Principate soon became as much of an everyday experience as the confrontation with Huns and Germans. A sullen fatalism was one reaction; another, the hope of an 'eternal Rome'. While the Christians logically insisted on the relativity of all earthly power, the pagans with just as much logic maintained that all their catastrophes and sufferings were a consequence of turning away from the old gods.

But the central concern for pagans as well as Christians, apart from the elementary provision for their own security and livelihood in the emergencies of the time, was the question of the true faith. This included both 'the parsonical tendencies' (J. Burckhardt) of individual Christian rulers and the importunate pagan fanaticism of Julian the Apostate, both the theological hair-splitting in the battle of dogma and the simple inwardness of an Ambrosian hymn. What was at stake in either case was the transcendence of human existence, an other-worldly orientation of life, and a lack of compromise strange to earlier centuries. New attitudes and forms of life were being worked out, and held thousands in their grip. Hermits, monks and monasteries testified to an estrangement from the ancient city culture no less than the pagans with their withdrawal into the fortress of classical education. The autonomy of human existence, to quote Fritz Taeger, had been replaced by a 'theonomous' conception of self.

GOVERNMENT AND ORGANISATION

Diocletian's tetrarchic system

Under Diocletian, too, the old centres of crisis at first persisted as before. There were usurpations in Britain and Egypt, risings of peasants and shepherds – the *Bacaudae* – in Gaul, German invasions on the lower Rhine and the upper and lower Danube, new hostilities with the Sassanids. At the same time, the inadequacy of the imperial administration, especially in the collection of taxes, became more and more obvious. Diocletian's answer was the systematic reorganisation of the army and the administration, the new system of the 'Tetrarchy'.

He had already appointed his old comrade in arms Maximianus as *Caesar* in the summer of AD 285. In AD 286 he promoted him to *Augustus*, and in AD 293 he appointed two *Caesares*, each assigned to an *Augustus*. For the East, where Diocletian himself resided, the *Caesar* was Galerius; for the West, Constantius Chlorus. At the same time, the *Caesares* were not only adopted by their *Augusti* in a dynastic relation to themselves, but they also received surnames corresponding to the religious genealogy constructed by Diocletian. The *Caesar* of the East, like Diocletian himself, became a *Iovius*; that of the West, a *Herculius*.

Out of the necessity for sharing out the military and administrative duties there thus grew a graduated, quadripartite, collective imperial summit which was yet in all essentials dominated by Diocletian. At the same time, the rank and authority of the rulers were not limited to their own regions: all four were recognised throughout the whole empire. Laws and decrees were always promulgated in the names of all four, coins were minted by all in common, imperial sacrifice and other ceremonies of homage were performed before the busts of all four. The emperorship had thus become a self-reproducing organism, because when an *Augustus* died it was to be assumed that his *Caesar* would succeed him. Such a proliferation of the imperial summit was calculated to make attempts at usurpations seem pointless. Of course the really sensitive point of this artificial system was concord among the four, who consequently hastened to demonstrate their mutual amity by all possible means. Its most impressive artistic demonstration was probably the porphyry group of the four rulers in Venice, in which the individuality of each is completely subordinated to the tight compactness of the whole.

The imperial dignity was at the same time systematically enhanced by ceremonial, display and worship, by giving the imperial ideology new form and content. The Soldier Emperors had had themselves portrayed as generals, in armour, with spear and radiant crown, and placed special emphasis on their military qualifications and successes. But now the most various properties, including those of oriental and Hellenistic origin, were used to elevate the emperor above the ordinary human level. The nimbus, the gleaming disc of light about the ruler's head, the globe and sceptre, an imperial robe sewn all over with pearls, now became characteristic attributes of the emperor's person. The emperor himself in his palace, the *sacrum palatium*, was set apart by a framework of complicated ceremonial, and subjects were required to kneel and kiss the hem of the emperor's robe at audiences and meetings. This arduous court etiquette was combined with tremendous pomp. The most precious metals and stones served to exalt the emperor: porphyry became usual for imperial busts; the capital and new cities of residence (Trier, Milan, Thessalonica, Nicomedia) were adorned with palaces, memorials and striking new monuments, like the monument of the tetrarchs in the Roman Forum. The new stylised emperorship of Late Antiquity, however, was above all rooted in religion and charismatically determined. The protégés of Jupiter and Hercules saw themselves as members of a hierarchy encompassing gods and emperors; they had approached closer to the divine realm than any Roman *princeps* before them. The emperorship of Late Antiquity, also called the dominate, has thus been rightly described as a 'theocracy of Roman stamp' (J. Vogt).

The imperial household too (*sacer comitatus*) was radically reformed at this time. The privy council (*sacrum consistorium*) now had merely advisory functions. The bulk of the administrative work was done in the various departments of the great imperial chancellery, which were called, after the document containers, *scrinia*. The heads of the different offices were called *magistri*. The *magister epistolarum* was in charge of correspondence, the *magister libellorum*, of petitions; the *magister cognitionum* headed the department of justice; and the *magister rationalis*, that of finance. To some extent this reflected the need for continuity with previous arrangements; but the specialisation and multiplication of the court servants, the *castrensiani*, speaks for itself. These included the servants of the imperial bedchamber, the *cubicularii*, and the *velarii*, whose job it was to raise and lower the curtains in the hall of audience.

Diocletian made radical changes in the army. He considerably increased the size in numbers to a total strength of about half a million. In this, the 60 or so legions no longer had a regular strength of more than 1000–2000 men each. The rest of the armed forces consisted of auxiliary formations, in which the Germanic elements were increasingly prominent from the time of Constantine the Great onwards. As a rule, there were in every frontier province two legions under the command of an officer (*dux*) of equestrian status. These legions were to a large extent recruited from soldiers' families, whose children had priority of acceptance. But there was conscription also among all the non-specialists of the population; that is, citizens who did not belong to any guild. In theory, even peasants and *coloni* were exempt from military service; but in practice, they could not be dispensed with, so that the estate owners were constantly being required to furnish recruits.

The military situation had already, from the time of Gallienus onward, required the formation of a strong mobile field army, the *comitatus*, the only means by which the emperors could secure the strongpoints of their defences and achieve rapid massing of troops. In this regard, it was Diocletian who carried through the final organisational separation between the primarily mobile field army and the primarily stationary frontier troops, a measure which in the long run, it is true, had unwelcome consequences. For the more the striking power and prestige of the *comitatus* increased, the more unmistakably the quality of the frontier troops (*limitanei, ripenses*) sank to the level of a shabby frontier militia.

Diocletian's reorganisation of the provincial administration was particularly impressive and durable. At the beginning of his reign, the *imperium* comprised some fifty provinces. By a lengthy process Diocletian partitioned these into smaller administrative units, so that by AD 297 the number of new provinces totalled about 100. Thus the last relics of the old senatorial provincial administration were swept away, together with the special position of Italy. The central function of the governor from then on was the administration of justice and general public administration. For that reason, governors were often called *iudices* (judges). For governors from the senatorial order, the designation *consularis* or *corrector* became usual; and for those from the equestrian order, the title *praeses*. But in all the provinces in which there were standing troops, these were no longer commanded by the governor himself but by the *dux*. Thus the traditional, specifically Roman, union of civil and military government inside the provincial administration was dissolved.

But the greatly increased number of provincial administrative offices could no longer be controlled by the central authorities on their own. Diocletian therefore created a new administrative level superior to the provinces, the twelve dioceses (*dioeceses*), as follows:

Oriens: the whole Syro-Palestinian area south of the Taurus mountains with Isauria to the west.
Pontus: the eastern and northern regions of Asia Minor.
Asiana: the western regions of Asia Minor.
Thraciae: the east of the Balkan peninsula.
Moesiae: the west of the Balkan peninsula.
Pannoniae: the regions of the middle Danube with Dalmatia in the south and Noricum in the north-west.
Italia: the Italian peninsula with Sicily, Sardinia and Corsica, and Raetia in the north.
Viennensis: southern and western France as far as the Loire, with its capital at Vienne (*Vienna*).
Gallia: the rest of Gaul with the Rhineland.
Hispaniae: Spain with *Mauretania Tingitana* (western Morocco).
Britanniae: Britain.
Africa: northern Africa from *Mauretania Caesariensis* in the west to the Greater Syrtis in the east.

These twelve were soon increased to thirteen by the separation of Egypt and Libya from *Oriens*, to form with Cyrenaica the diocese of *Aegyptus*, and later again to fifteen by further subdivisions in Italy and Greece. As units of administration which remained in existence throughout Late Antiquity, the dioceses were governed by deputies of the praetorian prefects, the *vicarii*. Besides controlling the provincial administration, the *vicarii* functioned in particular as courts of appeal in judicial proceedings, and their creation supplied a new series of senior posts for members of the equestrian order.

Diocletian's reorganisation of the tax system was also to prove of lasting importance. The system was at first quite inadequate to meet the financial needs which rose steeply under the Tetrarchy. Neither Aurelian nor Diocletian succeeded in stabilising the currency, which had been completely disrupted by decades of inflation. Thus the only forms of tax which were still effective were the *annona*, a tax in kind levied according to need on the basis of land holdings, and the *capitatio*, a *per capita* tax in cash. Starting from these completely irregular and variously rated forms of taxation, Diocletian set up the comprehensive system of the *capitatio-iugatio*. In fully developed form, however, this is not attested until AD 311.

The basis of the *capitatio-iugatio* in its final detail was the *iugum*, that is, a plot of land of an area which could furnish a living for one person, a *caput* (literally, 'head'), and be farmed by that one person alone. Plot and labour thus provided a unit of taxation assessment which varied according to the quality and use of soils, vineyards, pasturage and so on. A general imperial census, the *indictio*, held every fifteen years from AD 312 onward, fixed the appropriate tax units. Its painful significance for the life of every individual is best indicated by the fact that the Middle Ages still recognised the word *indictio* as a unit of time. The aim of the *capitatio-iugatio* was to spread the requirements of the administration of the empire, and more especially of its armed forces, evenly and justly over all the provinces. For in contrast with modern principles, the management of state finances in Late Antiquity did not begin with tax receipts but with a quantified calculation of state requirements at the centre, which was subsequently converted into tax demands.

In contrast to the reorganisation of the tax system, attempts to reform the currency were unsuccessful. The one measure which proved of lasting effect was the change in the production of the coins themselves, the abolition of the old local and provincial issues and the construction of a decentralised but strictly supervised system of large imperial mints. The London mint, for instance, became important, as did the mints at Trier, Arles, Lyons and of course in Rome itself. But public distrust of the monetary system was merely increased by the assignment of new face values to the coins, and their purchasing power declined still further. The soldiers' wages and 'donatives' (or supplements) ran like water through their fingers as the shopkeepers kept putting up their prices. The countermeasure by the tetrarchs, their 'maximum prices edict' of AD 301, was the most systematic attempt at a price regulation by the state, and thus also at state planning in the economic sector, known to the ancients. The greater part of this *edictum de pretiis* has come down to us through numerous inscribed fragments. In a tone of great moral fervour and pedantic exhortation, it announced fixed prices for nearly a thousand articles and labour units which were not to be exceeded on pain of death. It was supposed to apply to the whole *imperium* but soon misfired completely, since all that happened was the disappearance of the most important goods from the market. Yet this edict remains the most characteristic symptom of the planning bias of the new system.

The list gives, almost without omissions, maximum prices for meat, fish, fruit, wine, labour rates in various occupations and trades, the prices for hides, boots and shoes, goat and camel hair, wood, woven articles, carts, textiles of all sorts, and transport fees. To name only a few concrete examples, the day wage of a landworker, apart from his food, was set at 25 *denarii*, the same sum as a scribe could earn for 100 lines of the best script. For one Roman pound (327.5 grams, or 11½ ounces) of pork up to 12 *denarii* must be paid, for half a litre (just under a pint) of Falernian wine 30 *denarii*. Half a litre of beer cost 4 *denarii*, the same as five lettuces, or 4 pounds (1.8 kg) of dessert grapes or the hire per mile (1.6 km) of a loaded donkey. For luxury materials, however, prices became astronomic – some 12,000 *denarii* for a pound (450 grams) of white silk, and even 150,000 *denarii* for a pound of genuine purple silk.

The unit coin, one *denarius*, at the base of these calculations was so to speak an abstract quantity, since it soon lapsed. The most widespread coin of reckoning from then on became the *follis*, of copper washed with a decoction of silver, which however again did not retain its value in the price-fixing of the Diocletian period but became worth less and less. The *folles* were distributed in large numbers in all the frontier zones and are constantly being found today in every Roman province. They are the last pathetic manifestations of the late Roman system of coinage.

There were many other economic initiatives which showed the Tetrarchy's liking for state control. Among them was the construction of arms factories in the east of the *imperium* for the supply of the armed forces, and the setting up of weaving and purple-dyeing plant for large state contracts.

The empire of Constantine the Great

Constantine's reorganisation of the Roman empire grew out of Diocletian's system and cannot be separated from it. But it was Constantine's solutions which finally established the developing structures of Late Antiquity in all spheres of state and society, and fixed its enduring characteristics. At the summit of the *imperium*, in place of the *collegium* of the *Augusti* and *Caesares*, there was a new sole ruler of the entire empire, and with him a new dynasty. Except for some relatively short breaks, the series of emperors of Late Antiquty was once more provided by a succession of dynasties. The house of Constantine (A D 306–363) was followed by that of Valentinian (A D 364–392), and that by the house of Theodosius the Great (A D 379–455). The devotion to the dynastic principle was so strong in that period that again and again 'child emperors' were tolerated in order to secure the dynastic continuity of succession. The weakness and practical unfitness to govern of not a few of these rulers may also explain the great influence of the strong men of the imperial administration, the heads of army departments and courtiers.

The aggrandisement of the emperor's position was still further exaggerated by Constantine. His personal craze for pomp and splendour, for brilliance and formality, dictated the majesty of his projection of his own person. From A D 325 onward, the emperor wore the diadem, the head fillet derived from oriental priests and kings which since the Hellenistic age had become the most conspicuous symbol of the absolute monarch, and was still specially provocative in ancient Roman eyes. The imperial robe, with its rich adornment of pearls and other jewellery, the ceremonial regalia, the use of the nimbus, the renewed incorporation of the emperor in the ancient Roman *aeternitas* symbolism of the coin portraits, the raising of his victory attributes to the universal level, the ideological extension of his ruling power over the whole globe, coupled with the global degradation of all non-Romans, and above all the sanctification of the ruler's position by Christianity, were the striking characteristics of Constantine's ideology of emperor-ship.

The *tricennalia* speech, the ceremonial address by Bishop Eusebius of Caesarea on the occasion of Constantine's thirtieth anniversary, is an example of the extravagant terms in which the Roman emperor was now associated in the Christian world with the heavenly rule of God. The transcendence of earthly power has seldom been so directly proclaimed as in Eusebius' conception, in which the cooperation of Logos and Ruler determined the function of the emperor in the world and was derived from God himself. The Roman emperor was thereby now become the 'Holy Speaker of God's Word', he proclaimed 'with a loud voice to all people on earth the true laws of righteousness'. 'In his demand for improvement' he purifies 'his earthly kingdom from the filth of godless error and summons hosts of pious and holy men into his palace in his efforts to save the whole host of his subjects man for man.' The charismatic exaltation of the Roman emperor made him ruler 'by the grace of God'. It sanctified his position and secured it by the force of religion. Against that, the emperor was now confronted with tasks of a primarily religious nature which he had never before been called on to deal with on such a scale.

Just as under Augustus and in the age of the Julio–Claudian house the emperor's family had been involved in affairs of state, so Constantine's family and relations were affected by the new extreme aggrandisement of the emperor's person. Indeed their exposure could be dangerous also for themselves. Constantine gave his mother Helena the titles of *Augusta* and *nobilissima femina*, and her influence was considerable. On her famous pilgrimage to the Holy Land she made use of her privilege of freely disposing of the imperial treasury. She founded churches in Bethlehem and on the Mount of Olives, and distributed quantities of alms to the poor. The alleged finding of the True Cross at that time gave excessive encouragement to the worship of holy relics.

After the Empress Fausta and her stepson Crispus had been put to death in AD 326 on charges of adultery, Fausta's sons Constantine II,

Constantius II and Constans, with her daughters Helena and Constantia, had become the most important younger members of the imperial house. But Constantine's notion of a dynasty had a wider range. It included step-brothers and other relations, down to the nephews. Even at the expense of the unity of empire, his ramifying dynasty must rule on after his death.

The connéctions between the administrative systems of Constantine the Great and Diocletian are so close that it is still not always possible to decide which of the two emperors was responsible for a particular institution. For all the divergencies in the naming of offices and other details, in principle and in intention there was continuity. The most important group of imperial functionaries under Constantine were the *comites* (companions), trusted commissioners of the emperor who could be sent on special duty to control particular regions or be appointed to carry out particular policy decisions, while at the same time constituting the *sacrum consistorium* or supreme privy council. The heads of the most important offices of state also held this rank.

From AD 320 onward, a *magister officiorum* is attested, a sort of chancellor with an unusual combination of powers. He combined the function of head of the central administration with that of the old-time prefect of the Praetorian Guard. He had charge not only of the administrative departments which were subdivided into different *scholae,* that is, into militarily organised staffs of officials, but also the bodyguard, the *scholae palatinae,* and the entire staff of servants of the court. At the same time, he was a sort of court Lord Chamberlain, and yet he also had the secret agents, the *agentes in rebus,* subordinate to him. The second most powerful man at court was the *quaestor sacri palatii,* through whom the entire correspondence of the emperor passed. In the Finance Office the old divisions of duties were retained but the officials in charge received new titles. The Imperial Treasury, into which all taxes flowed, was headed by the *comes sacrarum largitionum,* while imperial private property and crown possessions were managed by the *comes rerum privatarum.*

In the dioceses and provinces, the system of Diocletian was only slightly modified. The office of Praetorian Prefect was converted from a central court post to the highest external office of the imperial administration, a measure which was probably due to some actual emergency. For when Constantine's son Crispus, in AD 317, was entrusted with the nominal supreme command on the Rhine front, it seemed sensible to assign a praetorian prefect to him as a second in command, and this officer then subsequently remained in charge of the whole administration in the western *imperium* with his residence in Trier. There is evidence later of another *praefectus praetorio* in Antioch, and finally, towards the end of Constantine's reign, corresponding to the intended division of the empire among the four *Caesares*, there were also four *praefecti praetorio*. It is significant that in the East, in the *praefectura Orientis*, this position was held for almost a decade by the Christian Ablabius. Under the *praefecti praetorio*, the *vicarii* continued to function as heads of dioceses, and governors of the provinces, that is to say, as purely civilian officials, in accordance with the Diocletianic reforms.

On the military side, the separation between the stationary frontier army and the mobile field army was maintained. The *palatini*, or guard regiments, were counted as part of the field army. Constantine also retained the institution of the *protectores*, general staff officers, of whom the group concentrated at court, the *protectores domestici*, had their own commander, a *comes domesticorum*. The rearrangement most momentous in the long run was that of the top military commands. Here there was a newly created rank of Army Master. At first there were two of them, the Master of Infantry and the Master of the Horse (*magister peditum, magister equitum*). Later the number of army masters was increased, and officers of this rank were put in command of groups of all arms. They were in fact the supreme commanders of the Roman army groups of Late Antiquity, and many of them were Germans, as for example Merobaudes and Stilicho.

This last fact was a result of the increasing part played by Germans and other non-Romans in the army of Late Antiquity, a development which Constantine the Great had accelerated. From the very first he found it necessary to levy British and German auxiliaries in his own cause. Above all, however, after his victory over Licinius, he had to accept the fact that large sections of the empire's population were tied to occupations, functions and offices which excluded them from military service. Thus the internal pressures of the imperial structure in Late Antiquity actually compelled the increasing mobilisation in the Roman army of the tribes which had invaded it or settled just beyond the frontier.

In his financial, taxation and monetary policies Constantine at first held fast to the Diocletianic system. The funds for the immense state expenses, often bordering on the extravagant, were rigorously collected. The *capitatio-iugatio* remained the most important form of tax. The senators were now burdened with a special tax, the *collatio glebalis*, graded according to their land-holdings. In the cities, the upper ranks were required to furnish every five years the *aurum coronarium*, a levy in the form of gold crowns or gold coins. Merchants and businessmen too, who had hitherto reaped the advantage of a tax system based on agriculture, now had to contribute every five years a property and turnover tax, the *auri lustralis collatio*.

Unlike Diocletian, Constantine did have some partial success with his reform of the currency. In AD 306 he introduced a new standard gold coin, the *solidus*, weighing 4.48 grams (1/6 oz) or 1/72 of a Roman pound. It established itself and remained for some seven centuries the basis of the currency, especially in the Byzantine zone. However, a new silver unit, the *siliqua*, valued at one twenty-fourth of the *solidus*, was minted only on a limited scale. The everyday copper coins, at first lightly washed with silver, were issued in large quantities. But the great opportunity presented on the one hand by the success of the *solidus* and on the other by the great confiscations of temple property and the Licinius booty was squandered. It is true that a brake was put on the regression to a barter economy, but the silver and copper coinage were not kept stable. The Roman currency was already facing a new crisis by the end of Constantine's reign.

Probably Constantine's most momentous decision, and the most far-reaching in its consequences, was of a different kind. Like Diocletian, he had not felt at home in Rome. When in AD 326 he celebrated the twentieth anniversary of his reign and then refused to take part in the solemn procession to the Capitol to thank the ancient gods of city and state, his behaviour was badly received by the Senate and people. According to Zosimus, it was then that Constantine decided to lay out a capital city of his own. On 11 May 330, the 'new city of Constantine', Constantinople, was consecrated, grown out of the old Byzantium and the city development there of Septimius Severus.

J. Burckhardt rightly described the creation of the new city as 'the most conscious and deliberate act' of Constantine's government. His explanation of the development was that the emperor 'was looking for a residence and city population which owed everything to him, referred only to him and could thus offer a centre and receptacle for so much that was new in the state and in society'. In judging this step, however, he did not go so far as Voltaire, whose impression was that Constantine in his city had 'sacrificed the West to the East' (*Essai sur les mœurs . . .*, ed. R. Pomeau, I, 1963, 299).

As often in Late Antiquity, neighbouring cities and provinces had to supply materials and constructional elements for the architectural and artistic elaboration of the new metropolis. For this purpose monuments were broken up and transported in the most brutal manner, temples and sanctuaries were plundered, metal melted down wherever it could be found. Out of such materials there grew up in Constantinople vast new constructions of imperial display: the emperor's palace by the Sea of Marmora; the circular Forum of Constantine in the west of the city, in the centre of which, on a high column of porphyry, stood a parcel-gilt bronze statue of Constantine with the nimbus and, enclosed in the column's foundation stone, Christian relics; and beside the Church of the Apostles, the Mausoleum of the Constantinian dynasty. Nor was it only Christianity which profited from Constantine's initiative. While the Church of Hagia Irene was enlarged and the building of Hagia Sophia begun, in the old architectural centre of the city (now renamed *Augusteion*) new temples were built for Rhea, the tutelary goddess, and for the Tyche, or Fortune, of Rome.

In external appearance, Constantinople was in many ways consciously planned as a copy of Rome. Here, too, seven hills could be distinguished, and fourteen regions marked out. Constantinople, too, was excluded from the standard provincial and diocesan organisation; its inhabitants also received the privilege of free distribution of grain; the city council under Constantine II was transformed into a senate; the highest official of the city was raised, in A D 359, to the rank of the Roman *praefectus urbi*. By favour and pressure, moreover, specially distinguished members of the governing class were enticed to Constantinople or, practically speaking, forced to take residence there. The leaseholders of imperial estates were required in future to furnish evidence that they owned a house in the city, which in addition was to be made attractive for educated people by a large library and the subsequent development of the university.

With the development of Constantinople, Rome soon lost its previous function as a permanent imperial residence and as the only centre of government for the whole *imperium*. Emperors in future only stopped in the city for short periods. When Constantius II, one of the Emperor's sons, visited Rome in A D 356, he came to what was for him a foreign city. Even the rulers of the western half of the empire later on did not choose Rome but Milan or, later still, Ravenna as their city of residence. The emperors effective throughout the empire, such as Constantius II (A D 337–361), Julian the Apostate (A D 361–363), Theodosius the Great (A D 379–395), Theodosius II (A D 408–450), Leo I (A D 457–474), Anastasius I (A D 491–518) and Justinian I (A D 527–565), had nothing more to do with Rome. Thus it was only with the development of Constantinople that the consequences of the reorganisation instituted by Diocletian and Constantine became visible for Rome. Rome became more and more the stronghold of a great political tradition, while in the East its opposite pole, the new capital, in the long term was bringing about the independence of the eastern half of the empire. And the *Romaioi* of the East wanted nothing more to do with the traditions of the ancient Roman Republic.

Social and economic structure

The social and economic development of the world of Late Antiquity as a whole is characterised by changes which began and took root during the crisis of the third century A D. The consolidation of the power of large landed property; the expansion of the senatorial aristocracy, which was once more absorbing the majority of the social climbers of the new system; the inflation of the imperial bureaucracy and the appointment of non-Romans to military commands at the expense of the old equestrian order; the continuing excessive demands on the members of the governing classes in the cities, now mostly known as *curiales*, and their ultimate extinction; the extension of the colonate over large areas; the impoverishment of that part of the population which was once juridically free but was now tied and dependent, owing to the continual imposition of fresh constraints; the continuing decline of slavery, and the growing proportion of non-Romans in the Roman armed forces; all these were early indications of the changed structure of society.

Purely from outside, a case can be made for viewing the *imperium* as still made up of three main social groups, if the *curiales* are inserted as a middle class. But such relics of the old structure were no longer decisive. What counted was the polarisation between the concentrated wealth and power of privileged dignitaries on the one hand and the impoverished masses on the other, the polarisation between the *potentes* (or *honestiores*) and the *tenuiores* (or *plebei*). It was now that a real dichotomy came about in imperial society. While large landed property became completely 'decommunalised' (Max Weber) into almost feudal forms, broad sections of the population were wholly alienated from this Roman totalitarian state of Late Antiquity.

Only in some sections of the governing class could the individual identify with this system. As we learn from numerous laws, the city councillors fled from their dignities and *munera* as frequently as the *coloni* from their obligations. The Roman state in desperation attempted to preserve the totalitarian order of society, and an economy which could only function in its own interest by remaining static. Thus it is one of the paradoxes of Late Antiquity that this state, which for long periods at a time was unable to perform its most elementary tasks, simultaneously kept increasing its demands, and exalted not only its emperor but his officials and dignitaries to unprecedented heights by a more and more artificial enhancement of the system's brilliant façade of display.

Inside the Roman governing class we note a striking shift of weight towards the Senate, while the rise of the military and the equestrian order, which was the mark of the third century A D, was in fact checked by Constantine the Great. Under him the *equites* in higher posts were moved into the senate, which was considerably increased in numbers. Nominally, the Roman Senate in the fourth century had 2000 members, but this was doubled by the creation of the Constantinople Senate with a similar number. In practice, however, only fifty senators need be present to make a quorum for resolutions, an indication of how slight the political and military competence of the body had become.

The old order of rank among senators, determined by their *cursus honorum* (*censorii, consulares, praetorii*), was replaced in AD 372 by Valentinian I, who finally established the new rank groups of *viri illustres, spectabiles* and *clarissimi*, which in Late Antiquity were announced as titles. At the same time, there were just a few positions of higher importance occupied by men of senatorial rank in the administration, the court bureaucracy and the military. In the administrative sector, these top positions included the urban prefects of Rome and Constantinople, the praetorian prefects, and the governors (proconsuls) of *Asia, Africa* and *Achaia*; in the service of the court, the offices of Chancellor (*magister officiorum*), Lord Chamberlain (*quaestor sacri palatii*), Chief Clerk of all the secretaries (*primicerius notariorum*), and the heads of the great treasuries (*comes sacrarum largitionum, comes rei privatae*); and in the army, the *magistri militum* or 'army masters'.

For Rome itself, we have seen that the sole senatorial post which was still influential was that of urban prefect, if only because the emperor was so seldom there that this official became the highest in the whole city. His responsibilities included the general keeping of the peace there, the provisioning of the population, and the administration of justice in the capital and its surroundings.

In the time of the Republic and Principate, there had existed a typical senatorial career which, with slight modifications, and irrespective of all distinctions of birth and origin, was as valid for the *homo novus* as for the patrician. The integration of new forces in the governing class had as a rule come about through a long graduated ascent. But in Late Antiquity there was a fundamental change. Now the new men often climbed in one jump from the lower levels, or even from foreign peoples, to the highest-ranking senatorial posts. Military competence or the command of military resources was here as decisive as proven ability and loyalty in administration or court service. So, to a surprising extent, was the qualification of education. In their mentality, interests and life-style, however, there might still often be very little in common between a member of the ancient city nobility of Rome and a courtier or Germanic army commander.

What was of primary importance for the senator in Late Antiquity was no longer his work in the Senate but above all the privileges associated with his adoption into the order. Senators were exempt from the general taxes but, against that, they were liable to a landed property tax (*collatio glebalis*), and repeated special contributions (*aurum oblaticium*). The costs of mounting the great games still had to be borne to a considerable extent by them. In return, they enjoyed legal privileges corresponding to their rank at law. As a rule, shameful and dishonourable punishments or torture were not employed against them.

The increase in the total number of senators led to a corresponding rise in the importance of a common provincial origin and connections. A first step towards the regionalisation of the senatorial order was that a senator could now be assigned to one of the two constituent bodies, Rome or Constantinople. The Constantinople Senate was now the one in which the emperor's favourites, officials and social climbers, even representatives of the city trades, were often numerous. In the Roman Senate, it was still the representatives of the ancient families, landed proprietors and also the highly educated senators who set the tone. Adherents of paganism were more numerous and longer represented in Rome than in Constantinople. Christianity, not merely as a religion of convenience but also as a matter of conviction, was very slow to penetrate the Roman aristocracy. A convinced Christian of wealth and senatorial family like the younger Melania made over to the Church a property spread widely over the whole western *imperium*.

Besides the distinction between West and East, there were further subdivisions. Senators with their homes in Spain or Gaul or North Africa made common cause with their respective colleagues. In certain cases, as for instance the Gallic senators, they successfully put up their own candidate for the throne. By contrast, the city of Rome group round Symmachus showed how deeply rooted the Roman tradition inside the governing class still was.

In the Roman Senate, it was still great landed proprietors who made up the economically most important group. Their steady income from the land enabled them to enlarge their estates and increase their wealth still further. An individual's land-holdings in general continued to be scattered over wide areas. The family of Q. Aurelius Symmachus, for instance, owned three city houses in Rome itself, twelve villas in Rome's closer and more distant neighbourhood from Latium to the Gulf of Naples, and beyond that larger estates in southern Italy, Sicily and North Africa. Alongside the medium-sized estates, there now existed in considerable numbers large estates, the *fundi*, and entire compact territories, the *massae*.

The intensively farmed estates returned immense yearly incomes for the wealthy families, such as 120,000 *solidi* for the family of the Valerii, and 4000 pounds of gold for other leading landowners. Of course, alongside these there were substantially smaller incomes. One very modest category of property-owners under Theodosius I had to pay only seven *solidi* yearly in land tax. And what was still decisive was the antagonism between the provocative wealth of the large landowners and the poverty rife everywhere in the cities and on the land.

The great fortunes were sometimes won by merciless exploitation of the tenant farmers, an exploitation which the Church Fathers among others repeatedly castigated:

'If we examine how they [the landlords] treat the poor miserable countryfolk, we must come to the conclusion that they are more inhuman than the barbarians. The people who go hungry all their lives and work their hands to the bone are continually burdened with prohibitive services, made to shoulder laborious tasks, and used like donkeys and mules, like stones rather; are not allowed the slightest respite and, no matter whether the soil bears a crop or not, are sucked dry and shown no mercy. Can there be anything more pitiable than these people when they have laboured the whole winter through, worn themselves out with cold, rain and wakeful nights and now stand empty-handed, and worse, are in debt as well, when they quake and shiver at the bailiff's harassments, worse than hunger and failure, the summonses, the incarcerations, the accounts, the extortion of the rent, the pitiless demands? . . . With their labour, with the sweat of their brows, barns and cellars are filled without their even being allowed to take a trifle home for themselves. No, their whole harvest is piled into the estate chests and a miserable pittance thrown to them in return. More than that, they invent new forms of interest such as are not even allowed by pagan law, and write out debt certificates which are a disgrace. They demand not just one per cent but fifty per cent, and that from people who have to support wives and children, who are after all human and fill the landlords' barns and cellars with the labour of their hands.' (St John Chrysostom, *Commentary on St Matthew*, 61st Homily, 3, Migne PG)

The non-senatorial groups of the upper class of Late Antiquity were even more heterogeneous than the Senate. It included the *equites*, a great part of the officer corps and the numerous group of senior imperial officials, the *officiales*. The old equestrian order had been considerably reduced by the Constantinian reforms. It now consisted only of the lower section of its former members, supplemented by the middle ranks of the imperial bureaucracy. The dynamism and lustre of the one-time *equites* was a thing of the past.

There was no decline, however, in the privileged status of the higher court and empire officialdom, which was split up into countless offices, with dignities and grades strictly observed. They were highly paid, enjoyed like the senators special treatment at law, and above all had the best possibilities of ascent to still higher rank. However rigid the hierarchy of officialdom and the higher corps of Late Antiquity may appear at first sight to have been, it was only in its ranks that a genuine social mobility was possible.

The most frequently observed discrepancy between social status and standard of living was among the members of the old municipal aristocracy, the *curiales*. Here it was usual to distinguish between a smaller group of the wealthiest and most influential city councillors, the *principales*, and the general ruck of *curiales*. Members of both groups were subject to excessive demands. In view of the all-inclusive burdens put upon city councillors by the state in Late Antiquity, it is not surprising that the *curiales* tried to escape them, nor that, for instance, in AD 429, according to an edict of the Emperors Theodosius II and Valentinian III, there was hardly a single suitable city councillor in the *curiae* of the province *Africa proconsularis*. What is astonishing is that relics of these groups persisted for so long.

The ruin of the city councils resulted above all from the fact that the councillors were personally responsible, with their own fortunes, for the city finances, all the city's debts, the levying of the *capitatio-iugatio* for the imperial government, and any special outlays. In addition, there were the old obligations customary under the Principate – the share in the financing of the games, public buildings, social services, public order, and the defence and provisioning of the city. While there was a *curator* as state commissioner to control the effectiveness of the city administration and the soundness of its finances and, from the reign of Valentinian I onward, there was in all cities a *defensor plebis* to safeguard, at least theoretically, the rights of the lower classes, the *curiales* were virtually defenceless.

They no longer even had freedom of movement. The *curiales* were not allowed either to leave their municipality or to sell their estates without the permission of the responsible provincial governor. Their required residence in the city was strictly controlled, and the property of a *curialis* who was absent for longer than five years was confiscated. And to be registered in the album of city councillors was sometimes quite openly decreed as a punishment. If a *curialis* wanted to disappear into the army, among the clergy or as a hermit, the legislation of Late Antiquity is full of decrees seeking to hinder such a flight or bring about his return. As Max Weber trenchantly put it, the muncipalities of Late Antiquity chased after 'their runaway city councillors as if they were chasing a parish bull' (*Soziologie, Weltgeschichtliche Analysen, Politik*, ed. J. Winckelmann, 1968, 16f.). Usually in vain – of 100 city councillors who had fled from Antioch towards the end of the fourth century AD only three were caught.

Ancient historical tradition always neglected the lower strata of the population, and, in the Roman case, concentrated overwhelmingly on the governing class and the *principes* and their families. This becomes even more marked in Late Antiquity. Moreover, the evidence of archaeology and inscriptions, which did throw some light on the lives of ordinary people in earlier centuries, now becomes scarce or has not yet been properly evaluated. Both historians and Church Fathers of Late

Antiquity agree, however, in painting a gloomy picture of the situation of the ordinary man in that period, and even when allowance has been made for rhetorical or religious special pleading, there can be no doubt that there was widespread impoverishment and deprivation among the broad masses of the population. It was simply not the case, for instance, that in the areas free from German or Hun invasions islands of security and modest well-being continued intact. Rather, it was such areas in particular that were all the more heavily burdened with taxation and pressure for contributions the smaller the territory actually controlled by the Roman central authority became.

It is surprising that the permanent burden of state obligations which, wherever possible, was passed on by the landowners, *curiales* and proprietors of the smaller craft undertakings to the lowest groups of society did not lead to a complete levelling of their legal and social position. It did have some effect, however. Although there was a polarisation of society into *honestiores* and *humiliores*, the lower class still had its distinctions. As before, it included free craftworkers, small farmers with some land of their own, free landworkers, the *coloni* who were now more and more tied to the soil (*glebae adscripti*), a relatively small proportion of freedmen and still some slaves in numbers varying greatly from region to region. On one large estate near Rome belonging to Melania the younger, the slaves were grouped together in over twenty establishments of about 400 persons each, but against that, there were quite a number of eastern provinces in which we no longer have any evidence of slaves in agriculture in Late Antiquity. In the city public services and craftwork, however, rather more slaves were still working.

But all these were now joined by new groups: the monks and hermits, a way of life which tens of thousands had already taken up in the East; displaced persons and fugitives, who had lost their means of existence in the invasions or under state compulsion, groups mostly of German war prisoners who had been assigned as *tributarii*, with a slave-like legal status, to the great landlords as labourers, and finally other 'barbarians' who had settled as allies on imperial territory (*foederati, laeti*) with a form of treaty and legal status which varied a great deal according to their original numbers and military situation. However slight the recognition given by this last group to Roman authority and sovereignty might often be, the fiction of their independence was never abandoned on the Roman side.

Thus the lower classes in late Roman society were at least as strongly differentiated as the governing classes, and they remained so until the collapse of the western Roman empire, even though Roman judicial practice conceded that elementary barriers of status at private law, like that between the *colonus* and slave, had in reality disappeared. The traditional distinction between the *plebs urbana* and the *plebs rustica* was generally maintained in Late Antiquity, but the differences in their forms of livelihood over large areas of the *imperium* had almost faded into one another.

The decline of the cities in Late Antiquity had both external and internal causes. Besides warlike destruction due to invasion or usurpation, and besides fiscal pressures, there was the loss of their former market function owing to the movement towards self-sufficiency on the great estates. This was a far more potent factor in the long term than the establishment of state factories for weapons, uniforms and ceremonial equipment, the *fabricae* in which forcibly recruited free workers were employed alongside slaves. Of these production centres, after all, there were no more than twenty in the West and fifteen in the East. Besides the continual decline in sales to the landowners and countryfolk, there was at the same time a contraction of demand in the inner cities. The very notion of purchasing power among the impoverished masses of city dwellers was now almost meaningless.

In principle, the traditional forms of production in craftwork remained intact. But what was now characteristic of demand, as it was of social structure, was the quality gap in production. There was an 'up-market' demand for purposes of state ceremonial and the requirements of the governing class which could still only be met by work of the highest quality from specialist craftsmen (mosaic makers, sculptors, painters, gold and silversmiths, weavers and textile workers). But the level of quality for general use, as for instance in pottery, visibly declined. It means very little that in the great urban centres like Antioch strongly specialised small craft businesses still kept going. Taken as a whole, the deterioration of city producton and city trade was plain to see.

It is true that while this decline was in progress there were, especially in the fourth century A D in the time of Constantine the Great and Valentinian I (364–375), phases of recovery and stabilisation. But even in that period the state was forced to intervene in defence of these essential trades. At first only bakers and mariners were bound to their occupations and organised in guilds. But the more important it became to the state that they should function properly, the more widely such control was extended to other professions. Membership of the bakers' and mariners' trades actually became hereditary, so that they were not allowed even to join the army or enter the Church.

It was of little importance in practice that the members of the *plebs urbana* were exempt from the *capitatio* and, in its place, if their property was large enough, had to pay a property tax at intervals of five years. Since they could at any time be conscripted for forced services, they were never free from state pressure. State, private and church social services could mitigate the general impoverishment but never remove it. The fact that there were 'hunger risings' in Rome, and the apathy and resignation with which a large part of the population viewed the approach of the 'barbarians', are both evidence of the decline of the city of Rome.

The pressures of state taxation in everyday life, and the corruption of state officials and judges, were described in the fourth century by Gregory of Nazianzus for the eastern empire, but conditions in the West can scarcely have been different:

> 'To keep your small fortune, what torment!
> You must bear the emperor's burden on sore shoulders,
> listen unmoved to the tax-collector's cries.
> Truly today the tax makes slaves of the free,
> It adheres to property, relentless as revenge,
> pursues it without respite, gags its utterance.
> Then we must push through the noisy market,
> force our way to the high seat of the earthly judge,
> flapping like fishes in the net of much-entangled rights.
> There always the bad gets the better of the good.
> True the keepers of the law can be bought by either side,
> but the rascal wins his case by offering more.
> In such a world an upright man must perish
> unless God's help to the righteous pulls him from the swamp.
> Flee head over heels, throw the Devil his plunder,
> otherwise you must make common cause with the pack.'
> (Gregory of Nazianzus, 98off.)

On the land, the change to self-sufficiency by the great estates and the further spread of the colonate (in *Illyricum* and Palestine not till the second half of the fourth century) were the most important developments in the socio-economic field. Here too there was increasing loss of independence, in which, among all groups of the *plebs rustica*, the situation of the *coloni* worsened most clearly. There were decades of insurrection by the *Circumcelliones* of North Africa, migrant seasonal workers employed at harvest time on the great Numidian *latifundia*, or in Gaul and northern Spain by the *Bacaudae* (or *Bagaudae*). Under this last-named movement various peasant and shepherd groups were active, occasionally achieving a sort of warlike independence, at the end of the third century AD, then at the beginning and throughout the middle of the fourth. It is clear that the lower rural elements were no longer to be pacified even by violent repression.

Yet none of these insurrections led to a social revolution. Late Antiquity was to see neither a class war between slaves and slaveholders nor a united front of slaves, *coloni* and barbarians against the Roman state and its governing class. This is to contradict views which have long been current in Marxist scholarship since a casual remark of Stalin's in 1933. Against them, Friedrich Engels very emphatically stresses the connection between socio-economic developments and military events. It was 'the Germans', as he calls the Germanic peoples, who according to him first rejuvenated 'a world labouring under a moribund civilisation'. In other words, it was only the invading Germanic armies and the impact of their social organisation on conditions of production in the territories they settled which brought about the feudal system.

Yet the real heart of the process was the peculiarity of large-scale farming methods in Late Antiquity:

'For it is obvious that in this late imperial landlord rule and the existence side-by-side of two categories of adscriptive peasants, unfree (*servi*) without fixed labour quotas and personally free (*coloni, tributarii*) with rigidly fixed money dues, offerings in kind and later more and more actual quotas in kind, and in addition – not always but regularly – fixed socage duties, we are already confronted with the type of mediaeval feudal manor' (Max Weber, *op. cit.*, 17).

The expansion of the great estates to largely self-sufficient economic units in which all the necessary workshops were concentrated, as expressly recommended by the agricultural writer Palladius in the fourth century A D, was a development hardly to be over-estimated in its effects. While, all round, the waste lands were growing, in these a relatively high standard of production could be maintained. The proprietors had long since transferred their residence to their villas on the land, and there remained as a permanency. Their social rank was maintained or increased still further, while the state's authority was diminishing. The fact that only the great landed proprietors, who had not only arrogated to themselves the jurisdiction of their territories but also collected the taxes for their domains on behalf of the state, supplied recruits for the army or labour for public works, the fact that only they could still guarantee effective protection, is most clearly reflected in the spread of the relation called *patrocinium*.

As early as the fourth century A D, especially in Syria and Egypt, a threatened or endangered freeman, a peasant or craftworker, could put himself under the protection of a neighbouring large landowner or influential official. By regular payments in kind or in money, he set up an obligation to protect or help him in return. As with the Roman *clientela*, there was here a recognition of mutual obligations, except that in Late Antiquity the institution was directed unambiguously against the state. It spread quickly in Illyria and in the Roman West, and all attempts to suppress it by means of the law were unsuccessful. In A D 415 it had to be recognised by law, and thus the elimination of enclosed landed estates from the direct range of state influence was acquiesced in and sanctioned.

Thus the momentous social and political consequences in town and country of the 'barbarian' invasions, coupled with the effects of the totalitarian state of Late Antiquity, become visible. Together they led to a complex process of disintegration, brought about by the formation of separate Germanic kingdoms on Roman territory no less than by the spread of self-sufficiency in large landed estates or the institution of *patrocinium*. Simultaneously, and this was rooted in the structure of the state in Late Antiquity, there came about an isolation of the state from society. It was a state which, it is true, still made obeisance to Roman tradition but in essentials had long ceased to be Roman. The consequent 'absolutisation' of state demands, with the isolation of the emperor and the administration, led the citizens to refuse to identify themselves with this state. The torrent of forced measures and impositions was answered with retreat into religious isolation as a way of life, with political indifference, or with actual escape over to barbarian rule outside the empire:

'Meanwhile the poor are ravaged, the widows groan, the orphans are oppressed, so much that many of them, people who are by no means of lowly origin and who are well educated, escape to the enemy rather than remain to suffer or die from persecution by the state, and as it were seek Roman humanity among the Barbarians because they can no longer endure the Barbarian inhumanity among the Romans.' (Salvianus, *De Gubernatione Dei* V, 21; *Corpus Scriptorum Ecclesiasticorum Latinorum* 8)

STATE AND RELIGION

From the beginnings of the Roman Republic, the connections between religion and the state were close and varied. In the Roman provinces, too, political loyalty could be demonstrated in the form of a cult worship of the goddess Roma, of Roman governors or generals, and ultimately also of the *princeps* and his house. But participation in such cult ceremonies was never compulsory during the period of the Principate. The toleration of foreign religions by the *imperium*, or also of citizens without religion, was for a long time a dominant principle.

It was not until the Crisis of Empire in the third century AD that a turning-point in state religious policy was reached. An intensified religious restoration now became part of the internal political reaction to the crisis. Convinced adherents of paganism began forcibly imposing religious activity in traditional Roman forms. They regarded this as a test of political conviction and identification with the menaced *imperium*. They bracketed the state and its religion together more closely than ever before, and did not hesitate to organise systematically the active cult of the state gods, or to use force against any who refrained. These attempts to revive pagan religious observance and public acts of loyalty deepened the gulf between the state and the monotheistic religion of Christianity, which meanwhile had spread throughout the whole empire. But systematic persecution only strengthened Christianity as a whole, guaranteed its unity, and roused the forces of resistance among individual Christians and in the Christian communities.

For Diocletian law, morality, belief in the state and religion represented an inseparable whole. Whether in his marriage law of AD 295, his edict on high prices, or in his fight against the Manichaeans, he acted in the conviction that the care of the old religion, the worship of the pagan gods, and respect for the old laws and customs were fundamental to the maintenance of the *imperium*. Thus a new conflict with Christianity had become inevitable. In AD 299 a radical onslaught on this religion was announced, and in AD 303 a systematic persecution began, in which Galerius, Diocletian's *Caesar*, played a leading part. Clergy and, ultimately, all Christians who did not sacrifice to the old gods could expect the death penalty or forced labour; Christian members of the governing class lost rank and honours; and many martyrdoms, such as that of the Theban legion, marked the brutality of the violent repression. But although Christian churches were pulled down, manuscripts destroyed, divine service forbidden, the wave of persecution did not achieve its goal.

Constantine's climb to the sole rulership of the whole Roman empire, his explosion of the tetrarchic system, his overthrow first of Maxentius in the West (AD 312), then of Licinius in the East (AD 324), was from the standpoint of religious politics the way both to the final recognition of Christianity in the *imperium Romanum* and ultimately to a position of privilege for the Church there. Personal decisions of Constantine in matters of faith, his opinion of Christianity not only as a religion but also in matters of social politics, and more especially his view of the Church thus unquestionably took on world historical dimensions.

It was particularly under the impact of Diocletian's system that Constantine, when still very young, became aware of the political importance of religion. He had never fully submitted to the edifice of Jovian and Herculean relationships but very soon branched out into something of his own. On his coins at first Mars was put ostentatiously in the foreground, but from AD 310 it was *Sol invictus*. This personal choice of a tutelary sun-god could cover a lot of different ideas, the Apollo so widespread in Gaul, or Aurelian's divinity of empire, or the sun-god so intensively worshipped in the Balkans. In any case, by adopting this god Constantine ostentatiously set himself apart from the tetrarchic divine hierarchy and at the same time made universal claims.

But even before Constantine's historical acceptance of Christianity on the eve of the battle against Maxentius at the Milvian Bridge (AD 312), the official religious policy of the Roman empire towards Christianity had completely changed. Galerius, seriously ill but still the key figure in the political events of the time, both the most uncompromising supporter of Diocletian's ideas and his arch-persecutor of Christians, confessed in an edict of toleration of April, AD 311, that the persecutions had failed.

Galerius himself in this edict acknowledged the failure of recent policy. Many of the persecuted, he admitted, would now no longer worship either their own god or the old gods of the state. That, he said, was why he was openly declaring toleration of the Christian religion, always on condition that the Christians themselves did nothing against public order. At the same time he called on those hitherto persecuted to pray to their own god for the welfare of the emperor, the state and themselves. After a decade of systematic persecution, carried out in Galerius' own name with special fanaticism, the edict brought about a diametric reversal of the Roman state's attitude to Christianity. It brought about much more than the suspension of active state repression, more than passivity or indifference; it brought the recognition of Christianity as *religio licita*, and thus prepared the soil for further development.

The decisive religious turning-point for Constantine himself was associated with his vision of the cross on the eve of the battle of the Milvian Bridge against Maxentius. The sources are self-contradictory, giving glimpses of events at different times. We do learn, however, that Constantine believed he had had a vision of a Christian symbol, was claiming the help of Christ as that of an all-powerful god, and made practical use of the symbol revealed in his vision either by having it inscribed on the shields of his troops or by having a field standard adorned with it. Whatever the details of the occurrence, the legend 'By this sign thou shalt conquer' (*touto nika*) took on historic force.

Constantine did then ascribe his victory over Maxentius to the help of Christ. This can be most clearly inferred from the fact that he had a statue erected in his own honour in the forum in Rome marked with a cross, with the inscription: 'Through this beneficial sign, the proof of true force, I liberated your city from the tyrant's yoke and restored senate and people of Rome to their ancient glory.' Otherwise there was no precipitate or comprehensive propagation of Christian symbols and pictures but a very cautious avoidance of provocation. The dedicatory inscription on the Arch of Constantine referred not to the help of Christ but to the 'inspiration of the divinity and greatness of mind' of the ruler (*instinctu divinitatis mentis magnitudine*). In a ceremonial address to Constantine at Trier in A D 313, the emperor's guiding deity was not named; there was a reference merely to *mens divina* and *divinitas*.

Still more important is the evidence from coins. The earliest unquestionably Christian symbol is of A D 315, on a silver medal struck in Ticinum. It has a Christ monogram on the plume ridge of the emperor's helmet. In A D 317/8 the monogram appears similarly on the helmets of coin portraits from the Siscia mint; from A D 320 onward the Christian battle ensign is shown; from A D 321/2 the pagan portraits of gods, including Sol who for so long was given precedence, disappear from Constantine's coins. Thus the year 312 brought no radical change; on the contrary, the portraits of the pagan gods at first continued in evidence, and Christian symbols occurred only singly. The representation of old and new ideas side by side was characteristic of the first half of Constantine's reign.

To the degree that Constantine tried to unite the Christian religion and the Roman empire, so he himself was drawn into the internal conflicts of the Christian communities. For when persecutions were ended, Constantine had to deal not with a united church but with a communion of the faithful divided among themselves, who in those very decades were torn by great disputes. Constantine intervened repeatedly and with lasting effect not only in the Donatist controversy but also in the dogmatic controversies associated with the names of Arius and Athanasius.

In the Donatist quarrel, the issue was the treatment of those North African Christians who had compromised themselves during the persecutions. This developed into a personal rivalry between Caecilianus, the Bishop of Carthage, and a rival bishop, Donatus, who took up a severe and intolerant stand. The church quarrel was very soon enlivened by ethnic and social differences. The party of Donatus had its strongest support among the native African population of Numidia, a rural, Berber or Punic section of the population who were at that time stirred up against the great Roman landowners and could not for a long time be pacified.

Constantine from the beginning took a decided stand with the supporters of Caecilianus. He applied to their case the conception of a 'catholic' Church, which had long been current but now took on the special meaning of 'anti-sectarian'. He awarded them the privileges and financial support which he had intended for the whole Christian Church of Africa. Mediation attempts, arbitration awards, even the resolutions of the Synod of Arles in A D 314 were unavailing. Even by force Constantine was unable to bring about the unification of the North African Church. The more he and his successors intervened in the dispute, the more profound was the rejection of the state by the Donatists. It turned on Donatus' famous question, 'What has the emperor to do with the Church?' The so-called *Circumcelliones*, a social-revolutionary group which took up the Donatist demands, kept the conflict going for decades.

The Arian controversy was to prove even more serious in its consequences for empire and Church. It turned on the *Logos* problem, with special regard to the question of the relation between God the Father and God the Son. While according to Alexandrian theology God the Father and God the Son were in practical terms to be distinguished only by the fact that the Son was begotten by the Father, Arius held the view that God the Father was an all-encompassing infinitely superior god, whereas the Son was primarily his instrument for the salvation of the world and thus, in the ultimate extreme, a god derived or only just come into existence. The dispute quickly took hold of the whole eastern half of the *imperium*, and Constantine was confronted with it after his victory over Licinius.

Constantine's behaviour in the great church disputes may be said to have had something touchingly simplistic about it. It soon became evident that he was simply not equal to the tasks he had undertaken as arbitrator in theological questions. The compromises which his authority brought about and enforced, such as the solution by the Council of Nicaea, quite often proved disastrous. At the beginning of the dogmatic dispute he outlined his own intentions in a letter to the two adversaries, Arius and Alexander:

'My purpose in the matters on account of which I assumed my office was twofold, and for that I may justly call to witness the god of all things, the helper in my acts and my saviour. First, I wanted to unify the religious striving of all peoples, and secondly, to revive and unite the body of the globe common to us all, which was suffering, we may say, from serious wounds. These were the objects I had in view. The first I meditated in the secret light of knowledge, the second I sought to bring about with the might of the armed forces. With it all I knew that if I should succeed according to my prayers in restoring general harmony among all the servants of God, the body politic too would change for the better through the pious attitude of all.' (*Letters*, Migne PG 8)

Constantine's goal was the unity of the Christian Church, and we may say its unity at any cost. Only if this Church was united, in Constantine's opinion, would it be capable of guaranteeing the salvation of the empire and God's help for it on earth. This goal also to some extent explains the emperor's lack of consistency in the theological disputes; it explains too how he changed sides, one day promoting and the next dropping leading men of the Church. Because for him the unity of the Church and a common basis for its faith took precedence of all else, he was able temporarily to treat Donatus as he did Caecilianus, Arius as he did Alexander and Athanasius.

This fundamental attitude is more important than the number of individual measures he took for the advancement of the Christian Church, such as the ennoblement of the bishops, the restoration of Church property, the recognition of the clergy as a corporation, the official legalisation of the arbitral jurisdiction of the bishops, the munificent gifts and material assistance. It has its tragic aspect in that the Roman state was again and again compelled to use force in achieving the unity of the faith, and that the unity and unanimity of state and Church aimed at by Constantine could not be realised in his lifetime but only later, in another form, in the Byzantine empire.

The Arian dispute was to preoccupy generations. The compromise formula adopted under Constantine's decisive influence at the First Ecumenical Council, at Nicaea (A D 325), for the relation between Father and Son, 'of one essence' or 'substance' (*homoousios* = *consubstantialis*), was not accepted everywhere. Under Constantius II the parties diverged even more widely. The radical wing of the Arians hardened its position to the conception 'of unlike essence' (*anomoios*), the moderate wing to the formula 'of like essence' (*homoiousios*), while a third party decided on the term *homoios*, which could be interpreted either as 'of like essence' or as 'similar'. This last was the one Constantius II adopted, and at the Council of Constantinople in A D 360 he used the strongest possible pressure to have it made compulsory. Twenty years later, however, the conflict took a new turn when Theodosius the Great returned to the formula of the Nicene Creed, which was then given universal validity by the Second Ecumenical Council, at Constantinople (A D 381), though in the form that the Holy Spirit was now included in the dogma of the Trinity, which was entirely in the Nicene tradition.

The controversy over dogma and the arguments about the formulation of Christian belief were not the affair of a few philosophically minded theologians but something that excited the broad masses of the population in a way that is scarcely conceivable to the modern mind. A sermon of Gregory of Nyssa gives a lively picture of the impact of the debates in Constantinople:

'For all the quarters of the city are filled with such people, the narrow alleys, the markets, the squares and crossroads – clothes traders, money changers, owners of provision stalls. If you ask one of them how many obols something costs he starts preaching at you something about 'begotten' and 'unbegotten'. If you ask the price of bread, he answers, 'The Father is greater and the Son stands below the Father'. If you ask whether the bath is ready, he offers you a proof that the Son of God is created out of non-existence. I do not know what to call this abominable nonsense, an inflammation of the brain or a madness or similar affliction current among the people which turns all sensible thinking on its head.' (*On the Divinity of the Son and the Holy Spirit*, Migne, PG 46, 557)

The Arian controversy had its centre in the area between Alexandria and Constantinople, but quite early on had already drawn the West of the *imperium* under its spell. But there it never reached the heights of fine-spun theological dialectics which characterised the dispute in the East. Moreover, the massive state interventions in questions of faith were unknown to the West. On the contrary, it provoked a passionate protest by many bishops which in the end culminated in the staunch and authoritative action of Bishop Ambrose of Milan against Valentinian II and Theodosius the Great. While in the West the Roman emperors had been compelled by the end of the fourth century to acknowledge the unquestionable authority of the bishops in all questions of faith, in the East state and Church grew more and more strongly together into a Caesaro-Papist system.

But the real focus of theological life remained as always in the East. There the so-called christological controversy was already stirring up new passionate struggles almost before the echoes of the Arian controversy had died away. In this new conflict the special point at issue was the nature and person of Christ. The 'Dyophysites', who had their headquarters at Antioch, held the view that in Christ two natures were united unmixed, while the 'Monophysites', centred once more on Alexandria, maintained that not only the human Christ but the God-*Logos* himself had sacrificed himself for the salvation of the world. This question too was the subject of long, bitter conflicts, in the course of which the Nestorians seceded from the Catholic Church, until in AD 451 the Council of Chalcedon pronounced in favour of Dyophysitism. But the division of Eastern Christianity continued. For many Eastern Christians, the dogmatic concept of two natures in Christ was unintelligible. Much as in the case of Donatism, here too the religious opposition became entangled with ethnic feelings. It was the Copts and Syrians especially who clung to the Monophysite way of thinking.

After the end of the persecutions and the recruitment to Christianity of new masses who were often only superficially converted and who imported many pagan convictions into their new faith, the multitude of small Christian communities grew into the more and more hierarchically structured Christian Church. In this process, gradually at first but quite systematically, the bishops of Rome succeeded in strengthening their own position. The confirmation of the succession of St Peter, the assumption of the supreme spiritual jurisdiction for the whole empire, the establishment of a privileged status by the Council of Constantinople (AD 381) and the development of the decretal epistles were important formative stages in the evolution of the papacy, which also received a decisive cast from the personalities of the great Roman bishops such as Damasus (AD 366–384) and Leo the Great (AD 440–461).

Thus the growth of Christianity in Late Antiquity was characterised by the development of a Church organisation, the building of basilicas and many smaller churches in all parts of the empire, the working out of liturgy and Church life, and the standardisation of a universal form of creed. But perhaps no less important for the evolution of the new faith was the establishment of the Church as the most important social institution of the *imperium*. The fact that the Church now to an ever greater extent attracted legacies, gifts and donations was above all because it, and not the Roman state, supported and looked after widows and orphans, the ill and the old, travellers and the displaced; in short, needy persons of every kind. While the few locally circumscribed beginnings of an active state welfare organisation had proved completely inadequate and, moreover, as the example of the *alimentatio* shows, were no longer being expanded, the Christian Church stepped more and more strongly into the breach. But even to do a makeshift job it needed more and more money and resources. Only a wealthy Church could mitigate poverty.

While individual bishops already held offices as 'court bishops', while Church and state were growing into a closer and closer union, the radical opposition to all forms of secularisation of the Christian faith was forming in the shape of hermits, monks and the first monastic foundations. This was another movement that came from the East; here too the area from Egypt to Asia Minor became the base of a systematic and existential religious decision which showed itself in an entirely new way of life. St Antony (died c. AD 356) became the prototype of a hermit, while Pachomius (about 292–346) was the first founder of a monastic type of community. Athanasius' *Life of St Antony* made this ideal of a way of life known in the West as well. But it was the island monastery of Lérins (off Cannes), the monastery of Marseilles, the monasteries of St Martin (Ligugé, Marmoutiers) and finally the monastery founded on Monte Cassino by St Benedict of Nursia which established in the West the new cells of determined and isolated religious life, and prepared the soil for the rise of mediaeval monasticism. The measured and self-sufficient harmony of the *ora et labora* of the Benedictine rule founded an ideal of living which survived the ancient world.

Parallel with the involvement of the Roman state in the problems of the Christian Church was the more and more systematic suppression of all the pagan cults. In the world of paganism, it is astonishing how quickly large sections of the population were ready to give up their previous religious views and, at the same time, how long and obstinately the pagan cults were kept alive in the countryside. It soon became evident that the old faith could only hope to be preserved by a political upheaval. One such occasion did occur with Julian the Apostate (A D 361–3), but Julian's enforced 'Hellenism', an artificially constructed product of eclecticism, was not capable of reviving the old cults. Intolerance, limitations on the freedom of teaching, and inquisitorial methods began to assert themselves under the badge of paganism. But there was a deep gulf between the undoubted idealism of Julian, personally rather a crabbed individual, and any real restoration of the old religion. It is moreover interesting that Julian took over elements of the Christian liturgy, church organisation and social assistance, and copied them in order to make it attractive once more.

All that Julian succeeded in doing was to mobilise certain groups of people, especially circles which had formed around rhetoricians, philosophers and magicians, and also opportunists and fellow travellers, while large parts of the population remained passive or played a waiting game. There could thus be no thought of a genuine regeneration of the old faith even in future. In the dispute about the Victory altar in the Roman Senate, a group of pagan Roman senators led by the urban prefect Q. Aurelius Symmachus openly took up the cause of paganism, but here too the overthrow of the usurper Eugenius in the battle of the Frigidus sealed the fate of this small opposition group, whose steadfastness of belief, level of education and pagan enthusiasm were so much more impressive than the future prospects of their cause.

Julian's restoration and the connection between the pagan senators and a usurper's cause led on the opposing side to an escalation of oppressive measures. Constantine's sons Constans and Constantius II had already proceeded more rigorously against the pagan cults than their father. Decrees had already been passed in their day forbidding sacrifice, closing temples, punishing magical practices and every form of soothsaying, but for a long time they had proved ineffective. Even the stopping of subsidies to the still existing pagan priesthoods and the abolition of the privileges of the Vestal Virgins had not had much effect. It was the new strictly supervised decrees of Theodosius the Great, who no longer bore the title of *pontifex maximus*, which put an end to all forms of paganism. Once again, in A D 391/2, all sacrifices were forbidden, the cult places of paganism confiscated, the inspection of entrails brought into disrepute as high treason. In A D 393, for the same religious motives, the Olympic Games were discontinued, and in A D 396 the Eleusinian Mysteries were abolished. All the catastrophes befalling Christian emperors in this and the following centuries, even the fall of Rome, could well have confirmed the remaining adherents of the pagan cults in their views, but they could not change their fate.

LITERATURE AND ART

Introductory

The intellectual and artistic works of the third century and Late Antiquity are not only very varied in subject but often contradictory in intention. The contradictions can often be found side by side. The effort to maintain some sort of continuity with the old subjects and treatments, and to retain a certain fundamental character of classicism, is as evident in every sphere as the straining after novel forms. The new works achieve their effects not only in the abstract and on a reduced scale but also in grand stylised monuments.

The commitment to a long-term common heritage of ideas either in art and style or in standards and ideals had largely disappeared. Only for a few short periods, in the Severan Age, in the time of the 'Gallienic Renaissance', under the Tetrarchies, Constantine the Great, Theodosius the Great and Justinian I, were there the beginnings of a self-contained world of internally consistent forms. The dialectics of this development were determined not only by the antagonism between representational and abstract art, between classical and oriental tendencies of style, between national and imperial traditions, between pagan and Christian ideas and values, but at the same time by the redirection of intellectual and artistic energies to a few dominant branches of art which received their priority from the representational needs of the state or from religious convictions and church requirements just as much as from the enduring influence of pagan education.

Literature

In a period when many exacting branches of literature were withering away – history, philosophy and science, epic, drama, comedy – it is symptomatic that such elementary forms of communication as letters and speeches, being used to exhort, justify or influence people, remained at a respectable level. Both Constantine the Great and Julian the Apostate were among the great letter-writers of the age. The more than 1500 letters of the pagan rhetorician Libanius are as fundamental for our understanding of social and intellectual life in Antioch during the fourth century as those of Basil of Caesarea and Gregory of Nazianzus are for the contemporary ecclesiastical and political problems of Constantinople and Asia Minor. The Neoplatonist Synesius of Cyrene, who became Bishop in Libya, is another important letter-writer of Late Antiquity. So were Aurelius Symmachus, Apollinaris Sidonius (c. 430–479) and Pope Gregory the Great (540–604). Many of these letters, with their pedantic devotion to models like the younger Pliny, strike us as artificial, and the social outlook of writers like

Symmachus or Apollinaris Sidonius often seems limited. But in their efforts to rise above the disasters of the times, to preserve some private life and be true to themselves, or to live like Christians, they do reflect the great issues of their age.

While any possibility of free political speech-making had vanished with the early Principate, the great ceremonial oration pronounced at court or in the Senate on such occasions as the assumption of office, the New Year, anniversaries, victory celebrations, state visits and so on, became a central feature of imperial self-advertisement and propaganda. In the tradition of Pliny the Younger's *Panegyricus* on Trajan (A D 100), or the orations of Dio of Prusa (also from Trajan's time), the display-speech flourished in Late Antiquity. The surviving speeches of the Tetrarchic and Constantinian period, some of them anonymous, were followed by the great speeches of Themistius in the second half of the fourth century, the speech of Drepanius on Theodosius the Great (389), and the speech on kingship (about 400) by Synesius of Cyrene, a particularly stirring appeal for action in a desperate situation. This form of composition persisted right into the time of the migration of peoples, though there were changes in those addressed. Instead of Roman emperors we find German warlords, Stilicho, Theodoric or Lupus the Frank. The writers of panegyric always expressed the current ideal of a ruler; they celebrated every success of domestic or foreign policy, however small, in the most brilliant colours; they expressed hopes and, often indirectly, their own wishes and anxieties. Above all, however, they reproduced the stereotyped formulae of the official emperor and empire ideal, and, like the coin inscriptions, they celebrated a time of relentless, almost uninterrupted disaster in emotional stock phrases.

Even under the Roman Republic dramatic incantations of religious feeling in rhetorical form had not been unknown. Then, with the coming of the loyalty cult under the Principate, they had degenerated into mere academic declamation. The dialogue with Christianity and its demands then gave new life to the speech of primarily religious content, or concerning the politics of religion. The great speeches of Eusebius of Caesarea are of this kind. So is the speech-like *relatio* (petition) of Symmachus on the dispute about the preservation or removal of the Victory altar in the Roman Senate House. The speech as art of argument and means of influence and persuasion was thus once more raised to its highest level.

It was especially in the Greek East, however, that pagan rhetoric persisted as the highest stage of all education, and as its main vehicle, through such impressive masters as Libanius and Themistius. Libanius (*c.* 314–393) came from Antioch. After teaching in many cities of the Greek East, and after repeated lecturing visits to Constantinople, he retired to his home city. The great Church Fathers of the East were among his pupils. So was Julian the Apostate. In Libanius we meet the image of a highly educated, tolerant pagan who, even after the death of Julian, continued for thirty years to practise quite openly the pagan rhetorical system of education in the classical sense, who really knew almost all the Greek authors and took them, especially Demosthenes and Aristides, as stylistic models. Yet the formal mastery which he achieved and taught his pupils was not for him an end in itself or a mere classical pastime. Libanius, on the contrary, believed that the old rhetorical education was superior even to the specialised studies of his own day, not least because a comprehensive rhetorical education, in his opinion, still qualified the student for an exemplary moral life no less than for an exemplary political career.

Themistius (317–388), who came from Bithynia, was almost his exact contemporary. Both a philosopher in the Platonic and Aristotelian tradition and a great rhetorician, he taught with success in Constantinople from about 345 onward. Like many other pagans, he managed to achieve a compromise with the Christian emperors. Like Dio of Prusa before him, in public orations before the emperors of his time he worked out a philosophically based ideal of emperorship. Thus it was Theodosius the Great himself who finally appointed him urban prefect of Constantinople and tutor of Arcadius.

One consequence of the changed political and social conditions was the decline of Roman historiography. In the time of the Severans, it was the two Greeks, Dio Cassius and Herodian, who so to speak marked the transition. Dio Cassius, who came from Nicaea in Bithynia and reached his second consulate under Severus Alexander in 229, used the ancient Roman annalistic form to write a very detailed, complete and comprehensive history of Rome in the Greek language. Large sections of this have been preserved, and the rest is known in its essential outlines from Byzantine excerpts. Another thoroughly serious work of history, despite the many rhetorical insertions and anachronistic reflections of the views of his own time on to Rome in the most flourishing period of the Principate, was the monograph of the Syrian Herodian. It dealt with the period AD 180–238 in an unpretentious, colourful and sometimes moralising narrative.

The writing of Roman history began in the Greek language and, during both Republic and Principate, was again and again the work of Greeks. It is among the many paradoxes of Late Antiquity that a Greek staff officer from Antioch, Ammianus Marcellinus, ventured on a Latin continuation of the historian Tacitus and, in his *XXXI Libri Rerum Gestarum*, gave an account of the period AD 96–378, once more using annalistic form. This pagan writer, with his rhetoric and digressions,

also played up to the expectations of his readership. He was at his best in
retailing his own observations, whether of the life-style of the Roman
city aristocracy or of events on the eastern Roman frontier in which he
himself had been involved.

The great political histories of the Republic and the Principate
undoubtedly had their dignity, their *gravitas* and *auctoritas*. It is true they
were not free of rhetorical components either, but these were blended
with narrative and comment. The degenerate forms of this kind of
history-writing were simple stories striving after effect, historical light
literature, history dissolved into biographies and biographical miscella-
nies, and finally the form specific to Late Antiquity in which history was
reduced to collections of elementary information in potted form, like the
anthologies and collections of historic portraits in miniature. These tiny
volumes exactly met the modest needs of the new governing class. Sex.
Aurelius Victor, for instance, in 360 published a collection of 'brief lives'
of the Caesars, while Eutropius, on an initiative of the emperor Valens,
went one better with a concentrated *Breviarium Ab Urbe Condita*, in
which the whole of Roman history up to A D 364 was soberly set forth.
Only a few years later, there followed the similarly compiled *Breviarium
Rerum Gestarum Populi Romani* and, towards the end of the century, a
new *Epitome De Caesaribus* by an author whose name is not known.

Biographical assortments from Graeco-Roman history had been
originally pioneered by Suetonius and Plutarch. There was a direct
sequel to Suetonius, in work now lost, by Marius Maximus (second
consulate A D 223) with 'lives' from Nerva to Elagabalus. The next
collection, by the *Scriptores Historiae Augustae*, allegedly six different
authors of the time of Diocletian and Constantine, with relatively short
'lives of the emperors' from Hadrian to Numerian, is anything but a
serious historical work. It does contain some reliable elements of the
historical and antiquarian tradition, but far more characteristic is the
often shameless play with forged documents, names and persons,
the acrobatics among the 'time zones', as, for instance, when the
'biography' of Severus Alexander is found to contain an idealisation of
Julian the Apostate.

Christian historians in the Latin language in Late Antiquity are
represented first of all by Lactantius and Orosius. Lactantius, who also
became tutor to Constantine's son Crispus, in his monograph *De
Mortibus Persecutorum* ('How the Persecutors Died') transferred the Old
Testament notion of God's judgment in history on those who persecute
the just to the persecutions of Christians in the Roman empire. The
Spanish priest Orosius, in seven books of *Historiarum Adversum Paganos*,
was the first Christian chronicler to deal with the migration of peoples.
In this he was bold enough to write a history of the world from Adam to

AD 417, in which on the one hand he stressed the providential connection of the establishment of the Roman empire with the spread of the Christian faith, but on the other, in a manner often provocative in Roman eyes, associated the troubles of his own day with the historic role of the *imperium Romanum*.

While Orosius was still hesitant in allowing a positive role to the German invaders in the divine plan of salvation, the priest Salvianus, who may have come from Trier but later lived in the area of Marseilles and Lérins (*c.* 400–470), was already taking a step further. In his *De Gubernatione Dei* he gave an exciting account of the German invasions of Gaul and the living conditions in the occupied and plundered territories, the corruption of the administration, the encroachments of the great landowners, the hardness of heart of those who once again had got off scot free, and the general decadence on the Roman side. In a logical continuation of the old Tacitean idea in his *Germania*, the German barbarian was here confronted as the morally superior human being with the moral collapse of Late Antiquity, and emerged as the instrument of God's judgment:

After the principal city of Gaul [Trier] had three times sunk into the dust through continued destruction and the whole city was a living tomb, despite such disaster the vices again increased. The fall of one city brought the destruction of others. Everywhere, as I myself have seen and endured, were lying naked corpses of both sexes, torn to pieces, disfiguring the view of the city, half devoured by birds and dogs. Death breathed death into the air. What happened then? What followed after all that? Some people of rank who had survived the holocaust demanded from the emperor, as the best means of assistance for the devastated city, public games! . . . . Thus we are being punished by God, by a judgment of God executed here and now, and that is why, to our disgrace and destruction, a people has arisen which moves from town to town, from city to city, ravaging everything.' (Salvianus, *De Gubernatione Dei* VI, 15; VII, 12)

What Salvianus means for Gaul, Victor of Vita means for North Africa, although his *Historia Persecutionis Africae Provinciae Temporibus Vandalorum* ('History of the Persecution of the Province of Africa in the times of the Vandals') does not achieve the radicalism and completeness of Salvianus' conception. The most momentous Christian interpretation of history from that period had already been given by St Augustine in his great work *De Civitate Dei*, written between 410 and 426 and the most influential book of theological history in the Latin language ever published. This work too was conceived as a counter to pagan attacks which saw the abandonment of the old gods as the cause of the fall of the *imperium Romanum*. It was consequently with special reference to the fall of Rome in AD 410 that St Augustine, in the earlier part of his work, sought to prove that, on the contrary, the faith in the old Roman gods and goddesses was the ultimate root of all Rome's ills, and that the immorality of Rome was the cause of its internal and external degradation. The Roman empire, it is true, like all the world's kingdoms, had come about by the will of God, but it was for man to recognise and reject them for what they were , mere edifices of power.

The formation of the Roman empire was interpreted by Augustine as God's reward to the Romans for what were at any rate relative virtues. But he by no means gave automatic approval to the Christian rulers of Rome. In his *Mirror for Christian Rulers* we read:

'We call them happy if they rule justly, if despite all the flattering, idolising and grovelling speeches they do not become arrogant and forget that they are human, if they put their power at the service of God's majesty and spread the worship of God as far as they can, if they fear, love and worship God themselves, if they best love that empire in which they need fear no co-regent, if they are slow to punish and glad to overlook, if they impose punishment only because the guidance and protection of the state demand it, not to satisfy their revenge, if they practise mercy not so that crimes may go unpunished but in the hope of reforming the criminal, if the harsh measures they are often compelled to take are balanced by compassionate mildness and kindly generosity, when they refrain from excesses all the more readily the less they are hindered from practising them, when they would rather rule their evil passions than foreign peoples, and when they do all this not out of greed for vain reputation but out of a longing for eternal bliss, and when also they do not neglect for their sins to make their true God the sacrifice of humility, lament and prayer. Such Christian emperors we call happy, at first only in hope but in future fully and entirely if what we look for has come about.' (*De Civitate Dei* V, 24)

As the deciding formative principle of history, however, Augustine set up the dialectic between the two great *civitates*, the commonwealth of God, *civitas Dei*, and the commonwealth of this world, *civitas terrena*. The main part of his work was devoted to their origins, developments and a historical process ruled by God. *Civitas Dei* and *civitas terrena* were essentially metaphysical definitions which, in the material world, remained mixed and would be separated only on the day of judgment. Both contained angels as well as men. The decisive dividing line between the two communities was always the direction of their will, the *civitas Dei* being governed by the love of God, the *civitas terrena* by the love of self. Augustine put it thus:

'I have divided humanity into two sorts, those who live by men and those who live by God. These in a mystical way I have called two cities, that is, two human communities, one of which is destined eternally to reign with God, the other with the Devil to suffer eternal punishment.' (*De Civitate Dei* XV,1)

In this way, and this is the decisive consequence of Augustine's view of history, the importance of the history of humanity in the world becomes altogether relative; the precedence of the history of redemption over all human history is newly emphasised. The history of the Christians, however, is elevated above its partial contact with the historical formation of Rome, which in turn is lowered in its proper value. The detachment of Christianity from the Crisis of Empire and the fall of the *imperium Romanum* was the inevitable consequence of this idea. By raising the Christians above all earthly empires and above time, Augustine raised them all the more above the mundane crisis which had prompted his work. In it he gave them an indestructible support.

The work of historians in the Greek language on the subject of Rome in the third century A D and in Late Antiquity has reached us largely in fragments. This is the case with the history of the Gothic wars and the chronicle of the world up to A D 270 by the Athenian sophist P. Herennius Dexippus, as also with the continuation of this by Eunapius of Sardis and many other works of early Byzantine history. Only the works of Zosimus and Procopius are fully represented. The *New History* of Zosimus, written at the beginning of the sixth century, begins with a brief sketch of the Principate and proceeds with a fuller account of developments between 270 and 410. This writer's convictions are consistently pagan. Once more, the turning away from the old religion and the old gods is given as the main cause of Rome's fall.

Procopius reached the post of urban prefect in Constantinople. He became the great historian of the age of Justinian I, and gave accounts of his wars (*Historikon*) and buildings (*Peri Ktismaton*). But besides these, in his *Anekdota* he gave a critical, well-informed, sometimes racy, secret history of the court and society. The Byzantine Greek world chronicles of the two Antioch writers, Ioannes Malalas (sixth century) and Ioannes Antiochenus (seventh century), mark the end of historical writing in Greek in Late Antiquity, at least from the Roman point of view.

Latin poetry broke off completely in the age of the Soldier Emperors. Then, in the time of Constantine, Optatianus Porfyrius made a name for himself with his portrait poems, the most obvious expression of worthy court literature. Their lack of any real content was disguised by his acrostic skill, which greatly impressed Constantine. It was not until the turn of the fourth to fifth centuries that impressive poems in the Latin language were again produced, by Claudian, born in Alexandria but living in Rome and Milan. Even when he tackled mythological or courtly themes, as in his *Rape of Proserpine*, or epithalamia or epic such as that on the Gothic War of 402, his work showed an unusually varied and vigorous poetic feeling. On occasion, he could achieve magnificent pictures of lasting impact, as in his eulogy of *Roma aeterna*, embedded, of all places, in a poem to celebrate Stilicho's consulate:

'Very near to the gods, consul, you have charge of this great city, the loftiest
thing enfolded by the aether upon earth. No view can take in her entirety, no
heart can encompass her loveliness, no voice can utter all her praise. Eagerly
with golden sparkle she reaches to tangle her roof tops with the stars. With her
seven hills she matches the seven orbits of heaven. Rome, mother of arms,
mother of laws, who spreads her authority far and wide, who gave us the first
judicial code, Rome it is who, sprung from narrow bounds, has expanded to the
two poles, and starting from a small abode, spread her arms wide as the sun to
embrace the world. She has faced disaster, fought battles without number all at
once . . .

Rome alone it is who took the conquered on her lap and cherished the human
race with a common name, like a mother not a ruler, and called fellow citizens
those whom she had subdued, and joined with the bond of love those wide
apart. Her peace-bringing ways have we to thank that the stranger feels at home,
that anyone can change his residence, that it is child's play to see distant Thule
and penetrate once grim fastnesses, that we can drink from Rhône or Orontes at
our choice, that we are all a single people. And there is neither frontier nor end to
Roman power. For other empires has indulgence ruined through vice and pride
toppled through hate.' (Claudius Claudianus, *Opera* XXIV, 130ff.)

It is characteristic that the very decades in which the fame of eternal
Rome was most often sung were those in which the city's military
situation was most desperate. Thus Honorius' court official Rutilius
Namatianus, in the very couplets describing his return to his home in
southern Gaul, written on leaving Rome to inspect his looted estates,
inserted a song of praise about Rome. Although here and in similar
cases there was a repetition and variation of formulae already
stereotyped, the ideal picture of an eternal Rome became more and
more strongly emphasised towards the end of Late Antiquity. The
ancient Roman mythology was still being constantly revived in artificial
forms of allegorical poetry. An example was the 'Menippean satire' of
the African Maritanus Capella, *De Nuptiis Mercurii et Philologiae*, at the
beginning of the fifth century, celebrating the 'seven free arts' in
alternating prose and verse.

Education became a bastion of the pagan aristocracy and the pagan
intelligentsia. The editing of the ancient texts, and their elucidation with
commentaries and interpretations, was already characteristic of Q.
Aurelius Symmachus and Nicomachus Flavianus and their circle in the
last decades of the fourth century. They consciously adhered to the old
verse and prose forms, stylised their own letters, official memoranda
and speeches in accordance with these and thus, it is true, often gave
mastery of form preference over quality of content. The study of
language and literature gained from these tendencies, and in any case
showed a preference for pagan revivals. The great Terence commentary
of Aelius Donatus and his grammar which long remained in use, the

important commentary on Virgil by Servius and the rediscovery of Juvenal, were a result of these efforts. This backward-looking movement culminated in the *Saturnalia* of Macrobius, written about AD 400, which, in dialogue form and entirely in the Ciceronian tradition, attempted to promote the correct understanding and appreciation of Virgil.

Characteristically, this was how education in Late Antiquity recovered some of its old importance. The Christian emperors themselves fully recognised the need, and even in Gaul, for instance, schools such as that at Autun experienced a marked revival. Symmachus commented that the path to the magistracies was frequently smoothed by education. Ausonius, after all, climbed from being tutor of princes to the posts of praetorian prefect and consul (in 379). The stronger the influence in the Roman empire of uneducated professional soldiers, blinkered officials and courtiers and finally barbarian warlords, the more closely the adherents of paganism and especially the old aristocracy clung to the educational tradition which was still theirs. The tradition itself had become increasingly private in the course of time, because even the knowledge of Greek had become very rare in the west of the *imperium*. Yet the old aristocracy persisted in it, as they did also in their own life-style. This did not necessarily mean, however, that they became intellectual. We are expressly told by Ammianus Marcellinus that not a few of the aristocrats kept their libraries firmly closed, and were quite capable of taking the name of a classical author for that of a fish dish.

In philosophy, the most significant achievements of the third century AD and of Late Antiquity, as of earlier periods, were due to the Greeks. The most important philosopher of the whole period was Plotinus (*c.* 204–269). At first he attached himself to the Platonist Ammonius Saccas, who lived in Egypt in complete seclusion; then he took part in the Persian campaign of Gordian III as a means of becoming acquainted with Persian and Indian philosophy; and finally he settled in Rome. There he soon became the respected counsellor of the governing class, whom he impressed both by the seriousness of his work and by the occult powers he was credited with. Above all, he won the favour of Gallienus and his Empress Salonina, and he is said to have formed a plan of founding with the emperor's help a Platonic philosophers' settlement, a *Platonopolis*, on the site of an abandoned Pythagorean centre in Campania.

Plotinus himself wrote nothing but papers for the pupils whom he had assembled about him. Among them a Syrian called Porphyrius was probably the most important. It was he, at any rate, who published six groups of nine essays, each by Plotinus, the *Enneads*. The collection was not systematically planned but covered almost the whole area of philosophy, from ethics to physics and psychology to logic. Fundamentally, Plotinus was thinking as a Platonist in a completely changed world for which Plato's whole philosophy of the state and the law had become irrelevant. Body, soul and mind are for Plotinus stages in the content of existence. While body and soul merely participate in existence, mind is existence itself. Parallel with this progression is that of the multiplicity of bodies and souls, and even the relative multiplicity of mind, relative, that is, to the ultimate supreme power of the One. This unutterable One is at the same time identical with the highest Deity. Thus we are presented with a magnificent and complete picture of the world of mind achieved by a radical rejection of the orders, criteria, needs and problems of its time. In the midst of internal confusion and war Plotinus called for inner purification and liberation, for the attainment of a higher world. He taught the priority of mind and the comprehensive supreme power of the divine One, and at the same time also the way to one's own self.

As the founder of the philosophical system called Neoplatonism, Plotinus created the last great philosophical system of Late Antiquity which appealed to acquiescent pagans as much as to doubting Christians. For many independent minds of the age, this system was at least a formative stage of their intellectual development, for Synesius as it was for Augustine.

I cannot here offer a complete survey of the riches of ancient Christian literature. It is in fact the very core of the literature of Late Antiquity. All I can do is to give a bare sketch of those authors who were of outstanding importance for the development of the social, political and religious life of the time, with their intellectual achievements. Even of these I can only offer a much condensed choice. First of all, the Greek half of the empire undoubtedly took precedence in the intellectual interaction of Christianity with the world around it. In Alexandria, towards the end of the second century, a Christian catechist school had emerged, of which T. Flavius Clemens became head in about 200. There was hardly a teacher before him who had paid such tribute to the achievements of Greek philosophy as Clement of Alexandria, or given it such credit for the development of the Christian faith. He was also the first to demand that this faith should be recognised as a form of knowledge.

Clement's successor, Origen, who met his death in the Decian persecution, wrote extensively. His special concern was to produce a reliable text of the Bible, and also to interpret the scriptures. In his *Hexapla* he brought together for comparison six different Old Testament texts. His essay *Contra Celsum* is perhaps the greatest of all defences of Christianity. He was positive that the *imperium* had been providential for it but was no more ready for compromise than Clement. He categorically rejected the official gods of the Roman state; Christians were to pray only for good emperors and Roman soldiers engaged in just wars.

From the second century onward, Christian chronographers concerned themselves with the orientation of Christians in time and the necessary coordination of Jewish, Christian and profane world history. About A D 220, Sex. Iulius Africanus, who probably came from Jerusalem, compiled the first fundamental work of this kind. It began with a figure of 6000 years for the entire duration of human history, and estimated the interval between the creation of the world and the birth of Christ as 5500 years. At the middle of the third century A D, therefore, there were still two and a half centuries to go before the return of the Lord. Thus the Christians of this period lived in an entirely different eschatological climate from the members of the primitive community, who had expected the end of the world to come very soon.

Outstanding among works of this kind was the two-volume chronicle of Eusebius of Caesarea, who began with Abraham (dated 2016/5 B C) and ended at the year A D 325. Apart from the Armenian version in which the work has come down to us, it was disseminated above all in the Latin of St Jerome, who additionally completed it up to A D 378. Although other successors worked more superficially and less precisely, the whole of mediaeval chronicle literature grew from these roots.

In just the same way, Eusebius set the example with his history of the Church. In this he was the first to base himself on the unity of a new historical structure, the Christian community, its fate, sufferings, persecutions, heresies. Through him the once widely scattered, partially isolated Christian groups, in the moment of attaining a position of privilege in the Roman empire, also received a common history of their own, a fact the importance of which can hardly be over-estimated in the development of Christian self-awareness and a Christian Church. From the point of view of method, too, this was an unusual work. While it had been usual in ancient history-writing to amplify, loosen up and deepen the narrative by inserted speeches, Eusebius instead inserted abundant historical documentation. Letters, decrees, records were incorporated in large numbers, so that the writing of church history from these beginnings onward acquired both in the form and content a new, characteristic profile. This work, too, was translated into Latin by Rufinus, and continuations right up to the end of the sixth century were later supplied by Sozomenus, Socrates and Evagrius.

Eusebius' *Vita Constantini*, which was published after the emperor's death, is by contrast so exaggerated in its panegyric that it has often been characterised as blasphemy. Yet the fact is that Eusebius did see in Constantine God's instrument, the fulfiller of Holy Writ, the emperor who had conjured up the time of salvation. For Eusebius the great axis of history ran from Abraham through Christ to Constantine. According to his understanding of history, God's promise to Abraham was fulfilled, after Jesus Christ's act of redemption, in the Christian empire of Constantine.

During the fourth century in the Greek East of the empire, the territory of Cappadocia formed the leading spiritual province, since it was here that 'the three great Cappadocians' worked side by side – Basil of Caesarea, Gregory of Nazianzus and Gregory of Nyssa. Basil the Great had studied in Athens, beginning as a rhetorician, then founding his own monastery and in 370 being appointed Bishop of Caesarea. In this office he distinguished himself not only by his rivalry with the Bishop of Tyana but especially by a successful church social policy. Around his episcopal church, for instance, he set up a complete centre of handicraft workshops. It was through his writings, however, that Basil exerted a far-reaching influence. In the books of observance of both his monasteries, he sketched a comprehensive scheme of organisation in which the aim was not fanatical asceticism but the spiritual schooling of the monks by a clearly organised and balanced rule of life. In his tract *To the Young*, on the reading of pagan literature, he even within certain limits accepted classical literature as school reading, and that prepared the way for Christian humanism.

Basil's close friend Gregory of Nazianzus was always a more philosophically reflective person, though he himself in A D 380 rose to be Bishop of Constantinople. Disappointed and embittered, however, he resigned this office, publishing numerous speeches, over 240 letters and his poems. The poems were emotional and strongly personal, a direct outpouring of his often turbulent spirit. Finally Gregory of Nyssa, Basil's brother, in a variety of dogmatic and exegetic tracts, worked out a solidly based Christian theology which, in its whole scheme of assumptions, was far superior to Augustine's efforts.

Beside these three great Cappadocians, only John Chrysostom reached the same level. He first worked in Antioch as a preacher, then from 398 to 404 served as Bishop of Constantinople but was banished and died at Comana, Pontus, in 407. A fascinating speaker, he based his style on the Second Sophistic movement but subordinated it entirely to the interpretation of the Old and New Testament, with special regard, however, to the moral, ethical and religious guidance of his listeners. His theological essays served the same purpose, while his many short letters from exile sought to comfort his old friends and adherents.

In the Latin-language areas, it was first of all North Africa which produced the most considerable achievements of Christian literature.

This whole field begins with Tertullian (c. 160–225) who, in his passionate eloquence, combined legal argument with impressive rhetoric. The very subjects of his tracts testify to the rigour of his attitude, the unbending insistence of his demands, and the fascinating vitality of this enthusiast. With a truly rhetorical gesture, he laid down the toga of a Roman citizen and instead put on the cloak of a philosopher. The tract *De Pallio* gave his reasons for this gesture. His subsequent works dealt not only with questions of faith, such as the rejection of pagan cults, not only with prayer and baptism, but took up quite concrete questions of ethics, from attendance at the games to women's dress. The most important historically is his defence of Christianity, the *Apologeticus* (A D 197), cast in the form of a great speech before the governors in defence of Christianity:

'But keep at it, you good governors, people will think you all the better if you give them a Christian sacrifice. Crucify, torture, wipe us out – your injustice only proves our innocence. . . . And yet all your refinements of cruelty will not avail you. They are only a bait for our community. The more you mow us down, the more our numbers increase. The blood of Christians is like seed.' (*Apologeticus* L, 12)

The white-hot glow of Tertullian's *Apologeticus* can only be fully appreciated if the near-contemporary dialogue *Octavius* by Minucius Felix is compared with it. This takes place in relaxed holiday mood on the beach of Ostia, and in it the Christian Octavius refutes his pagan interlocutor Caecilius with Ciceronian elegance so successfully that Caecilius is converted to Christianity.

Cyprian, who was Bishop of Carthage between 248 and 258, like Tertullian had a rhetorical training, and it is probable that for a time also he occupied some senior public office. In him we meet for the first time with a new type of bishop, who organised the Church and its governors fully according to Roman law. He quite categorically expressed the view that the bishop was responsible only to God for his decisions, which were binding on the community. In his writings, a voluminous correspondence and various tracts, he continued with calm and confidence Tertullian's ethical and apologetic work, and at the same time contrived to give an impressive picture of the crisis of state and society in his time.

It is of great importance for the history of ideas that during the fourth century in the Latin West there began that fusion of Christian faith with classical education, which had long been normal in the Greek East. In the West, a similar synthesis under the sign of the cross first came about through the efforts of Hilary of Poitiers, Ambrose, Jerome and Augustine. Yet even then, despite such continued influence as pagan rhetoric, for instance, might have on the ceremonial sermons of the bishops, the plain, immediate forms of address and prayer held their own. And this was clearly due to the congregations, who insisted on a direct and simple dialogue with God or his spokesmen.

Representative, too, for the intellectual development of western Christianity was Ambrose of Milan. He was born in Trier, the son of a *praefectus praetorio*, studied in Rome and pursued an administrative career, his last post being that of governor of the province of Liguria. At this point he was elected bishop by the Milan clergy. Ambrose was highly educated, and deeply read in Virgil and Cicero who specially influenced his style. His command of Greek was also impressive, and he frequently made translations of Christian literature from Greek into Latin. However, it was Ambrose's firm conviction that the saints had no need to bother with philosophical problems. So the great Bishop of Milan did not function primarily as a theologian or theoretician but as a preacher and practiser of the religious life. Ambrose himself was the one who most regretted having to teach at the same time as learning, and it was characteristic that most of his writings started as sermons. It was not least through his biblical exegesis that Ambrose so strongly influenced the Church of his day, its peculiarity being that he interpreted Holy Writ first as literature, then morally, and finally, with a wide sweep of allegory and mysticism.

Concerning the relationship between Church and state, Ambrose in an aristocratic and authoritarian manner always championed three principles. First, he was unconditionally opposed to any influence of the state on the concerns of the Catholic Church, and in one of his letters roundly declared that in questions of faith the bishops were judges of Christian emperors, not the emperors of the bishops. Secondly, he demanded that the state should always and in all circumstances respect the Christian moral law. Thus he compelled Theodosius the Great to do penance in church for having put down a rebellion in Thessalonika with particular cruelty. Thirdly, Ambrose sought to achieve very close ties between Church and state, because he thought this would be a great advantage for the Church. He was a prince of the Church in whom humanity and clemency were combined with unbending strength of will and unconditional insistence on his own claims. For him there could be no doubt that Rome and the empire, and again and again the emperor too, were in the service of Christ. This was expressed by his oft-quoted words: 'The head of the peoples is chosen to occupy the teacher's chair' (*electa gentium caput sedes magistri gentium*).

Nothing could deter Ambrose from fighting for the authority and power of the Church. Thus it was he, fundamentally, who led the opposition to Symmachus in the battle of the Victory altar. And he proceeded in just as uncompromising a fashion as in his fight against the pagans and the heretics, whom he called brothers of the heathen. Besides that, it was Ambrose in particular who pressed for the veneration of relics, and who was at the same time an initiator in the West of the veneration of Mary. He also promoted church music, and eighteen early Christian hymns are attributed to him. One of the most famous is his matins hymn 'At Cock-crow' (*Ad Gallicinium*, Migne PL) composed in 388, in which, in a manner typical of early Christianity, the memory of the bird of light which scatters the demons of night is associated with that which punctuated Peter's denial of Christ:

> Eternal maker of the world,
> ruling both night and day,
> dispensing time in lesser times,
> to ease our weary road –
>
> But listen, now day's herald calls,
> who keeps the watch all night,
> nocturnal lamp for voyagers,
> marking off night from night.
>
> By this song roused, the star of day
> lifts darkness from the Pole,
> by this the night's marauding bands
> are warned from paths of crime.
>
> From this the sailor gathers strength,
> straits of the sea grow calm,
> at this, the Church's very Rock
> washes his fault with tears.
>
> With vigour therefore let us rise,
> the cock awakes the prone
> and loudly chides the slug-abed
> and crows the no-sayer down.
>
> Health is poured back upon the sick
> at cockcrow, hope returns,
> the robber's sword is sheathed again,
> lapsed faith revives anew.
>
> Jesus, but look on those who slip,
> a glance to put us right,
> one look, and all our errors fall,
> our faults dissolve in tears.
>
> O light, shine down upon our sense,
> shake out the sleep of mind,
> and let our voice but call you first,
> our mouths unclose to you.

It would be superfluous to analyse more closely the content and effect of such a hymn on the world of Late Antiquity with the rhetorical glitter of its normal means of self-expression. As Emil Auerbach showed, it was just this so-called *sermo humilis* that was the special characteristic of the Christian style in Late Antiquity and the Middle Ages. It was an emphatically simple, realistically gripping language, distinguished by a personal tone and strong metaphors, a language which alongside all the rhetorical influences always held its own in the Christian world.

Spain, too, in those decades produced another great Christian writer, Prudentius (*c.* 348–410). He was a member of the Spanish aristocracy who became a governor, but, from the turn of the century onwards, lived for his writing. In two books of hexameters, *Contra Symmachum*, he sang the praises of the *imperium Romanum* and especially of Theodosius the Great, then disputed the pagan views of Symmachus and celebrated the new Christian Rome. In his *Psychomachia*, an allegorical poem of over 900 hexameter lines, he described the battle for the soul, the struggle of Christian virtues against heathen vices. This work enjoyed great popularity in the Middle Ages. The form of Christian didactic poem was again chosen by Prudentius for other subjects, such as his *Apotheosis* which defended the doctrine of the Trinity against heresies, or his *Hamartigenia* which expounded the genesis of the sins. His hymns too were widely used, hymns to martyrs, hymns for feasts and for the twelve hours.

An even more consistent path than Prudentius was that trodden by Paulinus of Nola, only slightly younger than he. An aristocrat of Aquitania, he quickly rose to be governor of Campania, then in 393 determined to adopt a thoroughly Christian way of life. He broke up his property in his homeland, gave away most of it and, having been ordained to the priesthood, founded a monastery at Nola in Campania, with a hospice attached to it in which Paulinus himself tended the sick. In about 409 he was elected bishop. In impressive letters he gave his old teacher Ausonius his reasons for preferring God and the Saints to the Muses. The conclusion of his last letter became the anthem of an unforgettable friendship:

> The spirit lives on even when the body melts,
> strong as a denizen of heaven,
> preserves the senses and the heart's tenderness
> as breath of life eternal.
> The spirit can neither die nor forget
> that lives for ever and faithfully remembers.
> (Paulinus, *Corpus Scriptorum Ecclesiasticorum Latinorum* XXIX–XXX)

In similar mood, Paulinus also composed an epic poem on John the

Baptist, and a whole series of poems for the remembrance day of his local saint, St Felix, whose grave in Nola he piously tended.

Jerome (Eusebius Hieronymus, c. 335–420), who came from northern Bosnia, was destined to become the very prototype of Christian erudition. In long journeys, he got to know the West of the *imperium* as well as the East, and he had an unusually sound knowledge of the Greek language and Greek theology. In a number of years devoted to strict asceticism in the desert of Chalcis, he also learnt Hebrew. Between 382 and 385 Jerome lived in Rome in close contact with Pope Damasus, and after that as a hermit in the middle of a great library near Bethlehem. His main ecclesiastical work was his translation of the Bible, the so-called *Vulgate* of the Middle Ages. His *Chronicle* has already been mentioned. Alongside it is a collection of short notices of 135 Christian authors, an immense collection of writings on technical matters of theology, and hundreds of letters revealing the legendary scholar, so to speak 'warts and all'. His name thus became proverbial in a sense of which Albrecht Dürer's 'Jerome in his Hovel' gives a lively reflection.

Augustine (354–430) was the greatest figure of all the Church Fathers of the Latin West. He was born in Tagaste, Numidia, and to a large extent moulded by his mother St Monica. The great autodidact absorbed all the important intellectual and spiritual influences of his time: the ancient culture concentrated in Cicero, the teachings of the Persian philosopher Mani, Neoplatonism and Christianity. Even after his removal to Rome (383) and baptism by Ambrose (387), Augustine remained in a state of constant spiritual unrest, but after decades of straying in an uncertainty which his own powers never quite enabled him to resolve, he found his ultimate answer in the full spiritual acknowledgement of God, the goal which he described in the famous sentence, 'Thou hast created us for thee, and unquiet is our heart until it rests in thee' (*Fecisti nos ad te, et inquietum est cor nostrum, donec requiescat in te*).

In 388 he returned to Africa and, in his home city, founded a small community with which he lived in monastic fashion, philosophising and praying. Some time about 395 he was elected Bishop of Hippo Regius (Bône). There too he lived, in a community formed according to his ideas close to his episcopal church, a life of quiet asceticism and poverty. (The canonical communities of the Middle Ages modelled themselves on this tradition.) Preaching, teaching, caring for the poor and giving legal judgments, with all his writing work, kept the bishop fully occupied. His influence soon spread far outside the borders of his see. In still later years, the revered speaker and rhetorician preached in Carthage and undertook great journeys. When he died in 430, the Vandals already stood at the gates of his episcopal city.

Augustine's critical catalogue of works, the *Retractationes*, lists hundreds of titles, of sermons alone over five hundred. At the centre of his theological creativity stood his exegesis of the Bible. He was particularly attracted by Genesis, the Gospel of St John and the interpretation of the Psalms. In the realm of dogma, Augustine's *De Trinitate* gave a systematic answer to the theological problems which had agitated the Church during the fourth century. But he dealt also with questions of ethics, morals, education and culture in a number of smaller notes, many of which were written to meet the practical needs of a 'cure of souls'. Among these is an introduction to Christianity (*De Catechizandis Rudibus*), a Christian approach to higher studies (*De Doctrina Christiana*), and notes on marriage and fasting.

Beyond this, a good deal of room is taken up in Augustine's writings by his handling of the contemporary questions of doctrine and the threat to Christian unity of belief, particularly by the Donatists and Pelagians. But in a spirit of self-criticism, Augustine also analysed his own development. His *Confessions*, written about 400, is a work of a unique kind. They are reflections on Augustine's life up to the death of his mother, their most important individual ingredients being the great conversation with the Manichaean Faustus, an analysis of consciousness, an interpretation of Genesis, and the famous account of the phenomenon of time, but they are constantly interrupted by a conversation with God and with the praise of God. This objectivisation of a man's own ego in such a manner has no parallel in the ancient world. In the passionate questions by the seeker, in its richness of sentiment, and in its open profession of belief in God, the work thus opens a phase of emphatic Christian subjectivity.

Augustine was an extremely sensitive person, and he had only increased this sensitivity by his intensive spiritual labours and asceticism. Always pondering, shy and aware of the difficulties of human communication, he knew, as hardly anyone else has known, the abysses of the soul. The hundreds of painters who during the Middle Ages attempted their imagined likeness of this great father of the Church portrayed him with the book, the Holy Scripture as the pledge of salvation or symbol of wisdom, and with a flaming heart, the symbol of love. For it was always this Christian love in which he declared his belief, and to which he again and again attached the highest value, as he himself expressed it rhetorically in words: 'Let them all mark themselves with the sign of the cross, let them all say Amen, sing Hallelujah, let them all be baptised, go to church and build basilicas – there is nothing which distinguishes the children of God from the children of the devil but only love.'

Art

During the third century A D and in the following period which we call
Late Antiquity, architecture received a new impetus. It was characteristically in Rome itself that both the Severans and the new dynasties of the
fourth century launched intensive building campaigns. It seems that
they wanted to demonstrate their attachment to the ancient capital in
the very moment that they were establishing new centres of power in
their own home provinces. An example of this ambivalence was
Septimius Severus himself. In Rome he built a new imperial palace and
began the monumental bathing establishment which Caracalla was to
finish. The so-called Baths of Caracalla were the great tribute of the new
Afro-Syrian dynasty to the Roman people. In its size and in its whole
arrangement of halls and rooms, with such bold architectural features as
the dome of the hot baths or the cross vault of the central hall, it
represented one of the most typical, artistically complete buildings of its
period. But at the same time, in Leptis Magna, Septimius Severus built
an equally impressive complex, a new forum with a series of arcades
connecting the columns of the market halls surrounding the old forum.
The Severan age was marked by other impressive public buildings in
cities of North Africa (e.g. Thugga) and Syria (e.g. Heliopolis, Palmyra),
which bore witness to the creativity and vigour of the dynasty, though
on a smaller scale than in Rome and Leptis Magna.

After the Severans, there was a long interruption of state architecture,
since the efforts of the *imperium* were entirely devoted to fortification of
the cities and necessary public buildings in the new residential capitals
of the separatist states and frontier zones. There were no more imperial
constructions in the grand manner until the time of the Tetrarchy and
the reign of Constantine the Great, though here too the main emphasis
was outside Rome. We cannot yet form much idea of the larger
buildings of the eastern centres of government at Nicomedia and
Thessalonica, but the palace of Diocletian at Split, with its impressive
plan combining defence, display and mausoleum, is fresh evidence of
the consistent logic of Diocletian's view of his position.

The imperial architecture of Late Antiquity on the grand scale is
evident also at Trier. Regardless of all the problems of dating presented
by the individual buildings, it is clear that Trier did not attain its
dominant position as residential city of the West until the reigns of
Constantius Chlorus and Constantine the Great, though its development had already begun at the time of the Gallic separatist state
(*imperium Galliarum*). Inside the city wall, 6½ kilometres (4 miles) long,
distinguished by massive towered gateways in the style of the *Porta
Nigra*, the most impressive features were a separate palace quarter
which received particular emphasis from the *Aula Palatina*, a tall

impressive brick building, Constantine's double church, and the new Imperial Baths.

The villa of Piazza Armerina in Sicily, which was perhaps imperial, was an example of public splendour in that age in a different context. Here was a centre for country life, recreation and hunting, in which the numerous rooms, with their artistic array of many-coloured mosaics, must have been, in their relaxed way, as full of the glitter of life as the painted ceiling of the Palace at Trier. One was for strict ceremony, the other for times of ease.

In Rome itself, Constantine's great opponent Maxentius, despite his short reign (306–312), was responsible for a great deal of new construction. There was a cult memorial for his son Romulus, the Circus on the Appian Way, the renovation of the temple of Venus and Roma, and above all, bordering the Forum, the monumental basilica which Constantine later altered and the extraordinary size of which can still be gauged by its remains. It is altogether symbolic that Maxentius' gigantic propaganda structure was altered by Constantine into one with a cruciform ground plan and surmounted with a colossal statue of himself. The ruthless incorporation of parts of older construction in new Constantinian buildings on the so-called 'spoilage system' is incidentally demonstrated also by the reliefs of the Arch of Constantine.

The really new forms of the builder's art under Constantine, however, were applied to the construction of churches. In the Lateran Basilica, begun in 313, the purposes of a community church are admirably served by the adoption of ideas from everyday market-hall construction. Ancient temples, so to speak, functioned outwards. In the basilica, however, while the exterior was emphatically simple, the interior was designed to frame, with suitable splendour, a Christian church service. The high nave and lower aisles united the congregation; a triumphal arch marked off this complex from the altar set in a transept and from the apse, where priests and bishop sat. Apse, triumphal arch, and walls of the nave were inlaid with precious mosaics, so that the whole splendour of Roman civilisation was fitted into the new sacral frame.

Other characteristic forms of Christian architecture, which were now vigorously promoted all over the empire, were the martyrs' memorial churches and the baptisteries. In parallel with the intensification of the cult of martyrs, great martyrs' memorial churches were now being built in the cemeteries outside the cities. These were also mostly in basilica form, with the altar over the martyr's grave wherever possible. But the baptisteries (baptisteria), were so to speak attached to all the larger churches. In buildings which were frequently octagonal, the most important feature was the font, bordered with marble steps, its walls richly ornamented with mosaic to give dignity to the rite of baptism.

It is surprising how many elements of profane and pagan provenance were combined together in the church buildings of Late Antiquity. The basilica itself was of pagan origin, so was the apse, with its mosaic decoration. The peal of bells and the belfry of the central bathing palaces were also ancient forerunners of the Christian bell-tower, as the peristyle court in Roman homes was of the monastic cloister.

Even in the last century of the western Roman empire, the building of great churches in Rome went on. St Paul's Outside the Walls with its five naves was followed by the Basilica of Santa Sabina on the Aventine with three, and finally the oldest Mary church in Rome, Santa Maria Maggiore, a basilica with huge bands of mosaic which are still in part preserved today. But the supreme example of the mosaic art of Late Antiquity is in Ravenna. When, in view of the Gothic invasions, the open city of Milan became no longer suitable as a residence, the emperor Honorius withdrew in 402 to Ravenna, protected by land and connected by sea with Constantinople. There, under him and especially under his successors Galla Placidia, Theodoric and Justinian I, a quick succession of churches and imperial buildings appeared. The mosaics of the so-called mausoleum of Galla Placidia and the court church Sant'Apollinare Nuovo proclaim in overwhelming terms the triumph of Christianity amid the fall of the Roman world.

The continuity with Roman tradition was preserved also in portrait sculpture and the art of relief. Originally, the persistent success of these art forms had been due to the increase in the emperor cult, the rapid change of emperor in the time of the Soldier Emperors, and their compulsion to demonstrate in monumental form their own achievements and the necessity of their own ascent to the throne. In this context the series of emperor portraits, whether sculpted in the large or engraved on coins in miniature, reflects an exciting succession of the most different forms of artistic expression, diametrically opposed to the monotony of the age of the Antonines. Where once was classicist idealisation, pathos, verism and the picturesque now rang the changes; traditional tricks of style were replaced by abstractions and new methods of steeping a portrait in spirituality. In the art of relief, as in the triumphal arches of Septimius Severus in Rome and Leptis Magna, there was similarly a foretaste of new principles of design and new forms of expression. The occasionally monotonous abundance of figures in the compositions was relieved by scenes in which the representation became majestically full-face, and the sculptural movement gave way to an abstract flattering mode of representation.

Free-standing sculpture, however, became increasingly rare. Under the Principate, whole avenues of columns adorned the forums and squares, but later the statues were pushed back into the recesses of buildings, and their subjects entirely confined to emperor groups or a few high dignitaries. Julian the Apostate, bearded, in philosopher's cloak, statues of Roman consuls in toga with roll, or the Colossus of Barletta, the monumental bronze statue of a ruler (Marcian?) adorned with the imperial insignia, all go to show that even in this field individual masterpieces were to be found. Theodosian art, however, with its stiff hieratic forms, belonged wholly to the Byzantine world, and this was assuming greater and greater importance in the West as well.

The art of relief in the third century was evolving not only on the old objects of state or imperial portraiture but also on the sarcophagi both of the pagan and the Christian upper class. The workshops of Asia Minor and Greece at first dominated this market but later in Rome and in the western provinces too there were centres of production of high quality. The abundance of sarcophagi in the museums of Provence today, and the sarcophagi stacked on top of one another at Les Alyscamps, still give us an idea how large and constant the demand for them was.

Besides a large number of stone containers decorated with simple pictures or ornaments, there are works of art with the most varied pictorial designs in the most varied styles, for example, the picturesque 'Ludovisi Battle Sarcophagus' which shows a victorious Roman general in the midst of a slaughter of barbarians; the idyllic 'Philosophers' Sarcophagus'; Christian sarcophagi showing the Good Shepherd; the *orans* with arms raised in prayer. Again and again, too, the great rescue scenes of the Old and New Testaments are depicted: Noah's Ark, Jonah and the Whale, Daniel in the Lions' Den, the Raising of Lazarus and many others – all obvious expressions of hope and faith that the buried person, too, may be saved and go to heaven. The same collection of themes is often encountered also in early Christian painting, once more showing how deeply the people of that age were affected by such ideas.

It was among the governing class that the sheer variety of Christian sarcophagus art was most marked. We find all sorts of styles side by side. Evidently for a long time there was still a demand for representational figures, and a sarcophagus of the Roman city prefect Iunius Bassus (359) shows that a series of Christian scenes could still be executed in a thoroughly classical manner.

There were undoubted revivals also of fine craftwork and representational art on a small scale. The table silver from the Augst Treasure, the huge silver dish which the emperor Theodosius dedicated to a high official, the ivory diptychs of consuls of Late Antiquity, 'gold-glasses' like those of Brescia (with decorations in gold leaf), magnificent cut gems like the Paris Cameo depicting the emperor Honorius with Stilicho's daughter Maria, splendid gold jewellery, medals of large size, 'contorniates' (New Year's mementoes in the form of medals) and gold coins, diadems sewn with pearls, richly jewelled ivory containers, and finally in an ecclesiastical context objects made of the most precious materials such as processional crosses, reliquaries, baldachins, paraments, vessels for mass and baptism and manuscript bindings – all these are examples of the brilliant art of objects for use which seems to concentrate the whole world of Late Antiquity at a few small points.

Seen as a whole, the art of Late Antiquity discarded the classical conception of the identity of natural and artistic form. The reason why so many figures and arrangements of the period make an inharmonious, even ugly or bizarre impression at first glance is that the traditional aesthetic was no longer operative, and artistic energies were entirely concentrated on reproducing the feelings of the soul, which was generally in an excited state. Of course the more ancient past was still influential. Older models, for instance, can be quoted for the way whole groups of figures are arranged symmetrically in the reliefs, with a frontal view emphasising the importance and scale of the central few, exalting and exaggerating Christ or emperor figures by the size alone. But even in such cases, the whole remains characteristic of the new world of style.

Bernhard Schweitzer once convincingly demonstrated that the art of Late Antiquity can only be adequately grasped if we consider that it was based on fundamentally different relationships and conditions from the ancient classical. The art of Late Antiquity was not simply addressing itself to a viewer who came to look but to somebody who saw in the work of art nothing less than the key to his edification, his instruction, his prayer and his praise to God.

FALL OF THE WESTERN ROMAN EMPIRE

The compulsion to arrange late Roman history in periods for a long while caused the significance of certain individual events to be over-estimated. The defeat of the eastern Roman army under the emperor Valens at the battle of Adrianople (378), the capture of Rome by Alaric (24 August 410), the plundering of the city by Gaiseric's Vandals (455) and finally the deposition of the western Roman emperor Romulus Augustulus by Odoacer (476) were undoubtedly exciting episodes in the last period of western Roman history, but it would probably be more correct to regard the fall of the western Roman empire primarily as a long-term process, punctuated with many dramatic events.

On the western Roman side, this process of decline was characterised by the structural changes described above in society and economy, state and religion. Its dramatic movement, however, came from the great invasions of the migration of peoples, the deep penetration of the central countryside of the western parts of the empire by Germanic, Sarmatian and Hun war bands, and by the consolidation of Germanic states inside the ancient *imperium*.

Even during the fourth century the Roman empire on the Rhine and on the Danube had to withstand continual attacks from across the frontier, and there the focus of defence moved more and more clearly to the lower Danube. While Constantine the Great, his son Constans, Julian the Apostate (357 battle at Strasbourg) and finally Valentinian I (364–375) had succeeded in stabilising the situation on the Rhine by the extension of frontier fortifications, counter-offensives and supervised settlement of Germans in the frontier areas, the developments on the lower Danube were heading for catastrophe.

The destruction of the entire eastern Roman army at Adrianople may be seen as the torch which lit the conflagration. Its consequences were devastating. In contrast with earlier disasters of the kind, the situation here was never restored, and the security of imperial territory could never again be guaranteed; the advancing Germans and Huns could in future only be diverted westward, the invaders no longer absorbed. The supremacy of the Germans, Huns and other tribes was the constant factor of the following decades; the victorious intruders after their plundering forays no longer returned to their places of departure, they merely exchanged one zone of occupation inside the empire for another. At the same time the preponderance of the German element inside the Roman army, both quantitatively and qualitatively, became more and more clear; the dependence of the *imperium* on the loyalty of non-Roman war bands and warlords was evident.

The individual factors and the circumstances of the changed situation were indeed not new in themselves. German *foederati* (allies) had earlier received support inside the Roman frontier zone and on the approaches to the *imperium*. Such arrangements were of strictly limited extent, however. What was decisive, as in the similar case of prisoner-of-war settlements (*laeti, gentiles*), was the tightness and efficiency of Roman control and the effectiveness of 'barbarian' help in return. But the treaty of peace made by Theodosius the Great in 382 with the Visigoths and many similar treaties after it were no more than legal affirmations of the *status quo* and Roman self-deceptions, since it was left to the sole decision of the signatories how far they adhered to such arrangements, which step by step dissolved the Roman administrative structure and frontier defence.

However high the tribute paid by Rome, whatever wages were paid to Germanic, Sarmatian or Hun war bands, whatever 'hospitality' arrangements were made for their upkeep as 'guests' on a third, sometimes a higher proportion, of the land of Roman landowners on whom they were compulsorily settled, Rome itself became the plaything of these forces. At the same time, the two halves of the empire were moving further and further apart. The separation of the two halves after the death of Theodosius the Great (395) was at first not by any means intended as a final division of the *imperium*, but from that moment onward the direction which had been taken with the building of Constantinople became irreversible. No doubt Rome and the Roman West tried again and again to lean on Constantinople for support. Its defensive possibilities were far better, its military potential much greater, and its financial resources incomparably stronger; but the eastern empire could give help only temporarily and within limits because it was preoccupied with its own problems.

The important stages in the process of erosion of Roman power can be listed: the crossing of the Danube by the Ostrogoths under Radagaisus, pushed from behind by the Huns; the invasion of Gaul (near Mainz, end of 406) by the Alans, Vandals, Quadi and other groups; the 'fall of Rome' (410); the settlement of the Visigoths in Aquitania (418); the formation of the kingdom of Burgundy on the Rhine (413–436) and on the Rhône (443–534); the conquest of Carthage by the Vandals (439) and the consolidation of their North African kingdom (429–533); the great defeat and repulse of the Huns in the battle of the Catalaunian Fields round Châlons (451); the Ostrogothic domination of Italy (493–553), and the stabilisation of the Visigothic kingdom in Spain (507–711).

The long duration of the agony and the complexity of its development are to be explained by the fact that the Germans in question were not always destructive in their effects but for a long time exerted their military strength on behalf of Roman interests. Stilicho, who rose to be the Roman supreme commander under Theodosius the Great, acknowledged the power of the Roman tradition no less than the Visigothic king Athaulf, who is said to have 'aimed at winning fame for himself by the complete re-establishment and elevation of the Roman name with the help of the Goths', or the Ostrogothic ruler Theodoric the Great (473–526).

Nevertheless, on the Roman side, from the battle of Adrianople onward, there was a growing 'anti-Germanism', to which in Constantinople as early as 399 the Germanic army master Gainas fell victim. Moreover, the German Christians being mostly Arians, there was a religious division between them and the main Catholic population of the empire which left no common ground for an amalgamation of Romans and Germans. There was, however, a demonstrative acknowledgement among the Germans of Roman forms. All that this

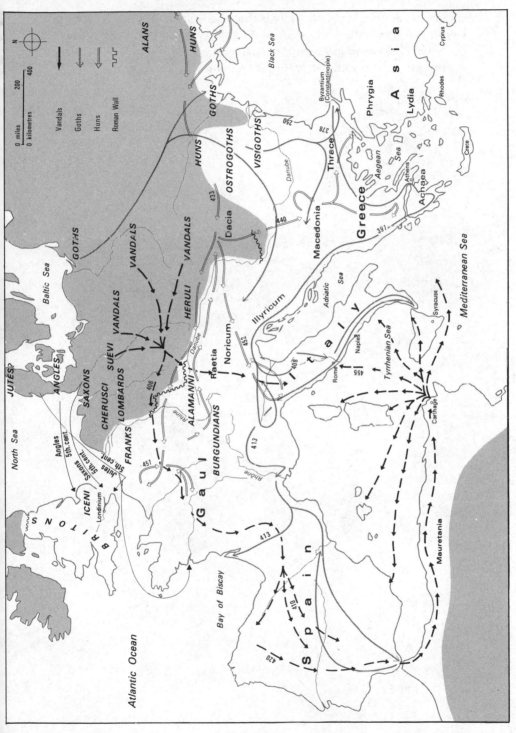

10 Invasions of the Germanic tribes and Huns

seems to have meant historically is that the Roman empire, which once under the Principate had begun with the stylisation of its own power, ended in Late Antiquity when the German warlords and kings adorned their own power with the trappings of the Roman *imperium*.

THE ROMAN TRADITION

Roman self-awareness in its national and its historical context is very clearly stated by the Augustan historian Livy in the introduction to his history. His desire, he tells us, was to demonstrate:

'the way of life, the customs, the sort of men, the domestic and military arts by which our empire was won and enlarged. . . , how with the gradual crumbling of discipline the state of morals so to speak gave way, then abruptly collapsed, until it finally reached such a pass in our own day that we could no longer endure either our own corruption or the means taken against it. This is the healing, fruitful thing we value about history. It gives us lessons of all kinds about good and evil in a form plain to see. From it we may take for ourselves and for the life of our own state examples to imitate and also, where what is badly begun comes to a bad end, to avoid.

'Moreover, if I have not been carried away by attachment to a work in progress, there really has been no state greater, nobler or richer in good examples. Nowhere did greed and self-indulgence make a later entry. Nowhere were poverty and frugality so long held in honour. For the smaller the possessions, the less the covetousness. Not until recent times did wealth bring greed in its train, and with excess of all enjoyments came the lust to ruin ourselves by extravagance and riotous living and by spreading ruin about us.' (Livy, *History, Praefatio*)

The view of Roman history as a collection of especially good or bad instances of moral behaviour, concentrated in the obligations of the *exempla maiorum*, with people and their doings stylised as examples – that is one side of Livy and it is a Roman side. But inseparably bound up with it is a conviction of the necessity of living and acting always in harmony with the will of the gods, and combined with that a consciousness of universal decadence. If we view Roman history as a completed process, it becomes quite natural for actions which in fact occurred only once to be made absolute, and lifted out of time as abstract examples to correct later conduct. But it is clear, too, that it deceived many members of the Roman governing class, including Cato Uticensis himself, into overlooking both the dependence of human existence and political standards on time, and the irreversible nature of the social and economic changes which had occurred in Rome after the fourth century B C. The rigid adherence to modes of behaviour and forms of thought which had long ceased to be practicable was a consequence of this static, backward-looking attitude.

The process of the enlightenment of the classical Roman Republic had already begun in the crisis of the second century B C. It was intensified by the phase of the Roman Republic's decline and in the opposition to the Principate. In the literary sphere, apart from Livy, it was especially Plutarch who made heroes out of the great Romans of the Republic. The free Roman citizen's canon of virtues thus launched a political tradition which was repeatedly realised. It was adopted later both in the Italian republics and in the free German cities of the Holy Roman Empire, then with special force in the French Revolution and in the founding and consolidation of the United States of America. The 'Roman virtues', love of freedom, independence, austerity, discipline, thrift, endurance, obedience and the rest were extolled as much by Corneille as by Bossuet, in the context of the philological history of ideas or in the educational policy of the 'Third Reich'; while the rejection of these values, ever since the time of Cato and Sallust, has been branded as 'moral decay'.

A different approach to the understanding of 'Roman-ness' had already been outlined by Polybius. He put the question, 'Where is there anyone so dull as not to want to know how and by what means of statesmanship almost the whole inhabited world was conquered in no more than 53 years and brought under the uniform rule of the Romans, a thing which has never happened before?' His search for an answer led him to a thorough analysis of the Roman constitution and an attempt to work out the lessons of universal political experience from that of Rome. The Romans thus became the great models of state-making and organisation and exercise of political power. From the days of Machiavelli onward, attempts to analyse and teach the development and possibilities of political power by reference to the history of Rome have never ceased.

Thus, intellectually, in many different ways, the Romans became the political tutors of statesmen, princes and rulers, in Reinhard Lorichius' *Wie iunge fursten und grosser herrn kind rechtschaffen instituirt und unterwisen/Auch in welchen stucken lant und leut zu gut sy fruchtbarlich unterricht mögen werden* (Marburg 1537) ('How young princes and children of great lords may be rightly taught and educated also in what matters they may be profitably instructed for the good of country and people') as in Montesquieu's famous *Considérations sur les causes de la grandeur des Romains et de leur décadence* (Amsterdam 1734) which, according to Frederick the Great, was the 'quintessence of everything that the human intellect can produce in the way of philosophical reflection about Roman politics'.

The maxims of Roman politics thus abstracted, whether actual or supposed, as for instance the *divide et impera* ('divide and rule') for which we have no ancient testimony, often ended up as a transfiguration of the *pax Romana*. The *imperium Romanum*, especially the empire of Augustus and the Caesars, became the model of an ancient order of government, the ideal of effective and correct state administration, a guarantee of justice and order, exchange and freedom of movement, toleration and humanity. Even Theodor Mommsen observed that

'the government of the Roman empire . . . in its sphere, which those who belonged to it were not far wrong in regarding as the world, fostered the peace and prosperity of the many nations united under its sway longer and more completely than any other leading power has ever succeeded in doing. . . . Even now there are various regions of the East, as of the West, as regards which the imperial period marks a climax of good government, very modest in itself, but never withal attained before or since; and, if an angel of the Lord were to strike the balance whether the domain ruled by Severus Antoninus was governed with the greater intelligence and the greater humanity at that time or in the present day, whether civilisation and national prosperity generally have since that time advanced or retrograded, it is very doubtful whether the decision would prove in favour of the present.' (*The Provinces of the Roman Empire*, 1908, I, p. 5)

A similar interpretation of Roman rule was appealed to in legitimation of its own power by the Holy Roman Empire, as also by the British Empire and the theorists of the *pax Americana*. Among historians, both Leopold von Ranke and Jacob Burckhardt celebrated the unifying force of the Roman empire and its mediating role for the civilisation of early Europe as one of their concepts of universal history. With that they gave due recognition to Christian Rome, the mutual interpenetration of political power with Christianity from the time of Constantine onward, and to Late Antiquity's new form of 'Romanness', a political and historical tradition derived from Rome which the 'new Romans' of the East, the Byzantine empire, had adopted as their own, and Moscow after them with its 'Third Rome'. In Italy itself, meanwhile, the lustre of the ancient political capitals had long since passed over to the city of the popes.

In opposition to all these overwhelmingly idealising notions, there were others which did not have quite the same success. Thus Johann Gottfried Herder in the 14th Book of his *Ideen zur Philosophie der Geschichte der Menschheit* (1784–91) ('Ideas on the Philosophy of the

History of Humankind') systematically stated the case against Roman world domination as a destructive phenomenon. He characterised Rome as a 'warrior state', denounced the destructiveness and arrogance of Roman power: 'There has never been a colder pride or ultimately more shameless arrogance in any military intruder than that of these Romans. They thought the world was theirs and, behold, it became so.' Whether in Latium or southern Italy, in Carthage or Greece, the Hellenistic East or the lands of the West, everywhere 'was sucked dry, enervated, depopulated'. 'Thus the Romans who claim to bring light to the world first everywhere make desolating night. Treasures of gold and works of art are extorted; whole regions of the world and whole ages of ancient thought sink into the abyss. The characters of peoples are extinguished, and the provinces under a series of the most detestable emperors are sucked dry, robbed, mishandled.' Rome for Herder was 'the robbers' cave', the acts of the Scipios and Caesar 'murderers' handiwork', Rome's collapse a form of retribution imposed by the laws of the eternal order of nature.

Determined critical judgments are found also in Hegel's *Vorlesungen über die Philosophie der Geschichte* ('Lectures on the Philosophy of History') (1822–1831). The Roman world, according to him, 'has been elected to put the moral individual in chains, while it absorbs all gods and spirits into the pantheon of world rule in order to make them into an abstract universal'. For Hegel too the Roman state rests 'both geographically and historically on the moments of violence'. The 'robber beginnings' of the state govern its whole later development: 'The Roman principle thus turns out to be the cold abstraction of domination and power, the purest self-seeking of will against the rest, with no moral fulfilment in itself but gaining content only through private interests.' That, according to Hegel, was why the Republic was overthrown, not by 'the contingency of Caesar . . . but by the necessity of the Republic. The Roman principle was entirely dependent on domination and military power. It had no intellectual centre in itself for the purposes of mind, its employment and enjoyment.'

Then, from the end of the nineteenth century onward, the critique of Roman social and economic structure became sharper and sharper. According to Max Weber, it was even an advantage of Roman history that 'economic and social class interests with all their consequences . . .' showed themselves 'in a shameless nakedness which had the same advantages for the ancient politician and the modern social historian as the similar unclothed condition of classical antiquity had for ancient art'. The exploitation of the *ager publicus* was for Weber 'the most uninhibited instance of capitalism in agriculture ever heard of in history' (*Die römische Agrargeschichte in ihrer Bedeutung für das Staats- und Privatrecht,*

1891, 129). The scathing criticisms of the Roman slave barracks also goes back to Max Weber, as do the attempts to elucidate the social reasons for the general decline of ancient civilisation.

And yet, taken as a whole, neither the later polemics against Roman 'imperialism' nor the attempts to evaluate Roman history in terms of the class war, nor the numerous modern studies of the role of slavery and the peculiarities of the Roman economy, have noticeably prejudiced the positive assessments of the Roman contribution. Herder's observation is as valid as ever: 'Roman history, because European culture depended on its language, has been enriched with both political and scholarly studies such as hardly any other department of world history can boast. The greatest minds ever to think about history have thought about it in connection with Roman principles and actions, and worked out their own thoughts accordingly.' And it is the ideas of these 'greatest minds' which determine the picture of the Romans and their history in the widest circles.

Edward Gibbon's *Decline and Fall* (1776–88) sought to explain away the virtues of the Roman Republic as a mere backcloth for its decline, just as he tried to make the collapse of the *imperium* a consequence of its excessive size, of the influences of wealth and luxury, the degeneration of the army and the effects of Christianity. For Barthold Georg Niebuhr's *Römische Geschichte* (1811–32) the centre of interest was the agrarian constitution of the free citizen community and the scholarly problem of recovering early Roman history with the help of a systematically applied critique of sources.

Not so Theodor Mommsen. In his *Römische Geschichte* (1854–56, 1885) the history of the Roman Republic was written by a liberal patriot as that of a nationalist unification movement. Mommsen's hatred of the *Junkers* of his time was matched by his hatred for the nobility of the late Republic. His apotheosis of Julius Caesar was so unusual that he had to defend it against misuse in justification of modern monarchy and Caesarism. The entanglement of historical assessment with political school preaching here was unmistakable.

Other more recent major interpretations of Roman history, such as M. I. Rostovtzeff's *Social and Economic History of the Roman Empire* (2nd ed. 1957) and R. Syme, *The Roman Revolution* (1939) show a similar combination of the author's contemporary experiences, political awareness, and historical judgement. The understanding of Roman history has thus become a gauge of the intellectual and political standards of successive periods of the modern age.

Rome as a historical unit lasted a thousand years, and was in its coherence, temporal duration and geographical extent the greatest known to European civilisation. Starting as a single city in a chain of successive disputes, it became nothing less than the whole world of classical antiquity. As an object of historical reflection and study it is so fascinating that, in future no doubt as hitherto, every generation will have to work out its own image of Roman civilisation. However interpreted and accounted for, whether as an area of exemplary moral modes of behaviour, as a model of political experience, or as an object of scholarly research, Rome remains a historical base of our own world.

THE PLATES

PLATE 1 *Top:* The Flavian Amphitheatre (Colosseum), Rome
Bottom: Residential street, Herculaneum. See notes on page 251

PLATE 2 Marble statue of a Roman senator with toga and ancestral images. See note on page 251

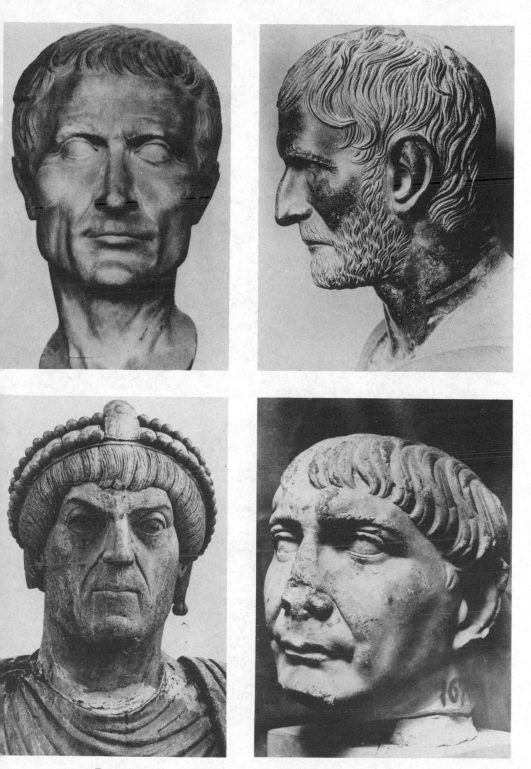

PLATE 3 Roman portraits: *Top left:* Caesar, *right* 'Brutus'
Bottom left: Marcian(?), *right* Trajan. See notes on page 252

PLATE 4 *Top: Haruspices* (diviners) examining the entrails of a sacrificial animal, Temple of Jupiter, Rome. *Bottom:* Trajan distributing *alimenta*, Trajan's Arch, Beneventum. See notes on pages 252–3

PLATE 5 *Top: Ara Pacis*, Rome. *Bottom:* decorative band on a *terra sigillata* bowl of the Augustan period. See notes on page 253

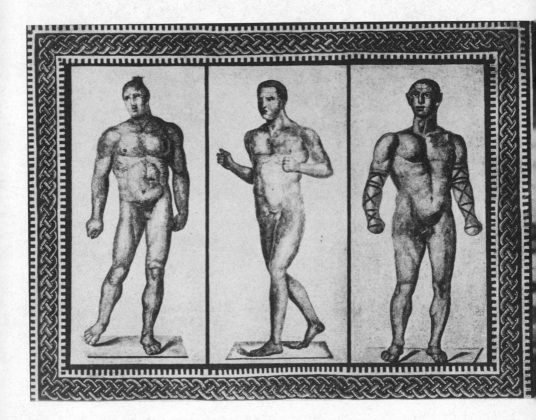

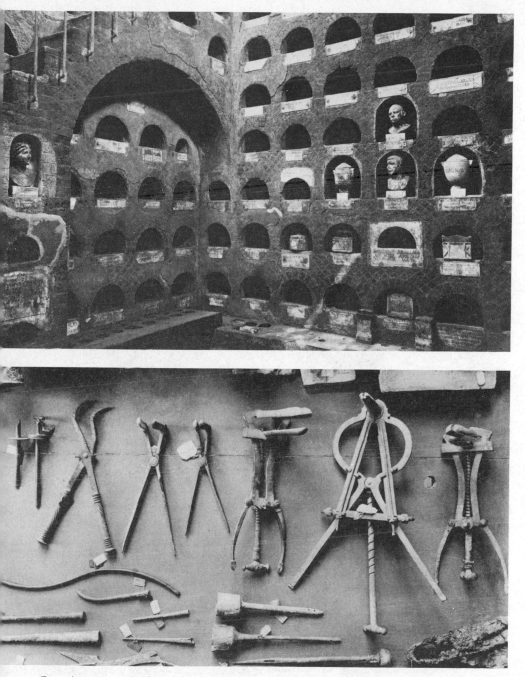

Opposite PLATE 6 *Above left:* gladiatorial contest, floor mosaic. *Above right:* gladiator's helmet. *Below:* athletes (wrestler, runner, boxer), floor mosaic. See notes on page 253
PLATE 7 *Top:* sepulchral chamber (*columbarium*), Via Codini, Rome
Bottom: medical appliances from Pompeii. See notes on pages 253–4

PLATE 8 *Top:* coin commemorating the consecration of Augustus (head of Augustus, obverse; square altar, reverse). *Middle:* silver medallion of Constantine the Great (obverse and reverse). *Bottom:* Roman ship transporting wine. See notes on pages 254–5

Notes on the plates

1a The Flavian Amphitheatre (Colosseum), A D 80. (*Foto Marburg*)

Begun under Vespasian (A D 69–79), the Colosseum was dedicated under Titus. The oldest stone amphitheatre in Rome, it measured 187 m × 155 m. Its four storeys, the three lower of which were arcaded, had seating for 45,000 and standing room for 5,000 spectators. An offering to the Roman *plebs* by the new Flavian dynasty, the building expressed in monumental form the divorcement of the old Roman citizenry from politics. Here instead, on many days every year, it could enjoy the combination of sport with public executions to which it had become addicted. See also pp. 111 ff. above.

1b Residential street, Herculaneum, first century A D. (*Mansell Collection*)

The eruption of Vesuvius in A D 79 largely destroyed Pompeii, first by the rain of pumice and ash, then through the rescue operations and looting. Herculaneum, however, under a sea of tuff, has been better preserved. The laval stream pouring through the streets turned everything to stone, as it were, a catastrophe which centuries later allowed a vivid picture of ancient Italian life to be uncovered.

The houses with their overhanging roofs and balconies gave on narrow but well-paved streets. The ground-floor rooms mostly had solid ashlar or brick walls, but the upper storeys were of flimsy latticework (*parietes craticii*) and often a fire risk (cf. pp. 104 ff. above).

2 Marble statue of a Roman senator wearing a toga and holding ancestral images. Height 1.65 m, Augustan period. Rome, Palazzo dei Conservatori. (*German Archaeological Institute, Rome*)

The close attachment to their ancestors cherished by members of the Roman governing class (see p. 24) is clearly brought out by this statue. We know from Horace (*Satires* I, 6, 16) that right into Augustan times the Roman public would feast its eyes on inscriptions and ancestral images establishing social eminence.

3 Roman portraits (*Foto Marburg*)

3a Caesar, Pisa, Campo Santo.

This type of Caesar portrait was distributed in several copies. It derives from an idealised representation in the early Augustan age, marked by its emphasis on the high brow, austere oval head and abundant growth of hair. Clearly the artist wanted to bring out the lofty intelligence and overwhelming determination of a dynamic personality.

3b 'Brutus'. Male head, bronze, middle of third century BC. 32 cm (12½ in) high. Rome, Palazzo dei Conservatori.

This head, which was found at the beginning of the sixteenth century, has repeatedly been identified as that of L. Iunius Brutus, the first consul of the Roman Republic, and sometimes as that of the Brutus who murdered Julius Caesar. The eyes are of ivory, with iris brown and pupil black. The strength of will, severity, self-confidence and self-control conceived as typical of the Roman governing class are impressively conveyed.

3c Head of a 'colossus' statue from Late Antiquity, Barletta, fifth century AD.

The bronze statue, originally five metres (over 16 feet) high, was probably of the Emperor Marcian (AD 450–457). Parts of the head above the diadem and also of the body have been restored. This tremendous fragment, which has been set up in Barletta, outside Sansepolcro, gives an idea of the stylisation to be seen in monuments of the period. See also page 229 above.

3d Portrait of Trajan (AD 98–117) from Carpentras (Vaucluse, France). Height 22 cm (8½ in), depth 19 cm (7½ in).

Despite the low brow and broad features, the sober simplicity of the *optimus princeps* comes clearly to life. Emperor portraits were important in the provinces as reminders of the personified idea of empire.

4a *Haruspices* examining entrails at the Temple of Jupiter on the Capitoline Hill, Rome. Beginning of second century AD. The left part of a marble relief, Louvre. (*Foto Marburg*)

The relief, by M. Ulpius Orestes, probably came from the Forum of Trajan in Rome. Under the Roman Republic the inspection of entrails was ordered by the magistrate invested with the *imperium*, and under the empire by the *princeps*, to ascertain the will of the gods before important occasions. The observation of the flight of birds and the examination of the entrails of sacrificial animals were among the most important acts of Roman state religion (see pages 159 and 207 above). The scene shows an assistant bending over the slaughtered bull to prise the liver from the intestine and show it to a priest standing on the left with a toga over his shoulder.

4b Arch of Trajan, Beneventum. Trajan distributes *alimenta*. Marble frieze, A D 114, height 2.40 m (7 ft 10 in). (*German Archaeological Institute, Rome*)

Trajan's scheme of assistance to needy children of free citizens (see p. 78 above) is symbolically depicted. On the left are the emperor and his suite; in the centre, the money table; on the right, inhabitants of Beneventum with children, among them four women crowned with walls, each personifying a wł le city.

5a Frieze from the *Ara Pacis Augustae*, Rome. Relief. 13–9 B C, height 1.55 m (5 ft), original length 8.60 m (28 ft). (*Foto Marburg*)

This south frieze shows in its left half the cult attendants surrounding Augustus in the procession. They are followed by the *domus principis*, the family and close entourage of the emperor, among whom M. Agrippa in priest's robes and Julia with C. Caesar and Livia stand out. See also page 151 above.

5b Decorative band on a *terra sigillata* bowl of the Augustan period. Workshop of Ateius. Found in the area of the Roman Camp at Mainz. (*Foto Marburg*) See also page 154 above.

6a Gladiatorial contest. Mosaic, third century A D. (*Foto Marburg*)

Part of a coloured floor mosaic from a Roman villa near Nennig, Rhineland. The central subject, a design of 10 × 15 m (32 × 49 ft), is a training fight between a fully armed *retiarius* (right) and a lightly armed *myrmillo* (left). In the background is a trainer watching the fight. See also pages 114–16 above.

6b Gladiator's helmet. (*Foto Marburg*)

The helmets worn by heavy-armed gladiators were often richly decorated and among their most valuable pieces of equipment. They varied in form but the designs were fairly constant. Their face-guards could be even more elaborate than this one.

6c Mosaic from the Baths of Caracalla, beginning of third century A D. (*Foto Marburg*)

The vast complex (see pages 117 and 226 above) was once adorned with numerous mosaics. Ours shows three characteristic types of athlete – wrestler, runner, boxer. Professionals of these sports who took part in public competitions were often high-bred slaves, mostly of Greek or 'barbarian' origin. The brutal-looking faces are no doubt merely a rendering of the popular expectation of the times.

7a *Columbarium* in the Via Codini, Rome. (*Anderson Collection*)

The sepulchral chambers with many rows of niches for urns containing ashes of the dead resembled Roman dovecots and so were named *columbaria*. Under the late Republic and early Empire, after the dead had been burned on a pyre their ashes were placed in a marble urn and stored in this way, each urn in its niche with an inscription and sometimes also a portrait bust. See also pages 119–20 above.

7b Medical appliances from Pompeii, first century A D. (*Foto Marburg*)

In Pompeii especially, but also in other cities of the *imperium*, a whole series of surgical and medical appliances have been found, often complete sets of many individual pieces. These have now all found their way into the great museums, such as the Museo Nazionale in Naples, the British Museum, and the Römisch-Germanisches Zentralmuseum in Mainz.

Under the group of cutting forceps (top left) may be seen a urethroscope, and (top right) vaginal specula for gynaecological use, which could be opened by a screw mechanism after insertion in the vagina. See also page 156 above.

8a and 8b Coin (*dupondius*), minted under Tiberius, after A D 22. (*Staatliche Münzsammlung, Munich*)

8a Obverse. Legend: DIVUS AUGUSTUS PATER. Head of Augustus radiate. Idealised portrait.
8b Reverse. Legend: PROVIDENT [ia] – S[enatus] C[onsulto]. Square altar.

The coin commemorates the consecration of Augustus, the official elevation of the founder of the Principate to the gods. The radiate head links him with eternity (*aeternitas*). The *providentia* (foresight, forethought) refers to his settlement of the succession to the Principate, to which the *princeps* of the day (Tiberius, A D 14–37) owed his position. The emphasis on the Senate's authority indicated by capital letters is to be interpreted not only as a reference to its minting authority (which was in any case limited) but also as an attempt by Tiberius to stress his close association as ruler with the Senate.

8c and 8d Silver medallion of Constantine the Great, from the Ticinum mint, A D 315, 6.4 g (108 grains), diameter 2.4 cm (1 in) (*Staatliche Münzsammlung, Munich*)

8c Obverse. Legend: IMP[erator] CONSTANTINUS P[ius] F[elix] AUG[ustus]. (The usual abbreviation of the imperial titles in Late Antiquity: the Emperor Constantine, the Pious, the Fortunate, the August.)

Full-face portrait of Constantine in armour, helmeted, leading a horse by the bridle with his right hand, a shield over his left arm adorned with the She-Wolf and Twins, behind it a sceptre with crosspiece and globe; the emperor's head surmounted by an imposing barred helmet adorned with rosettes, and, over his right eye, the crest attached by a round plate on which the chi-rho monogram of Christ can be read. See also page 202 above.

8d Reverse. Legend: SALUS REI PUBLICAE (The Salvation of the State).

The Emperor standing on a *podium* in the attitude of *adlocutio* (the address to cavalry units), wearing armour and field commander's cloak, his right hand raised, in the left, a trophy – sign of victory; on his right, Victory herself, standing, with palm branch; around the *podium*, a party of cavalrymen with round shields, helmets, lances and horses, the two rearmost riders holding each a standard.

8e Roman wine ship on the Moselle, second or third century A D, Trier, Landesmuseum.

Large sculpture from the tomb of a wine merchant, Neumagen. The ship's stem and stern post adorned with animal heads, the bow terminating in a ram of dolphin form, the chiselled eye hardly recognisable, the cargo four large wine barrels. On each side, port and starboard, six rowers with helmsman and coxswain, but actual total of oars 22 (whether for artistic reasons or to give a greater impression of speed).

APPENDICES

1. CHRONOLOGICAL TABLE

POLITICAL HISTORY
BC
1000
Early Iron Age, 'Proto-Villanovan'
Age in Etruria.
950
Evidence of settlement on the
Palatine, Esquiline, and later Roman
Forum.
800
753 Legendary year of Rome's
founding.
600
Rome under Etruscan domination.

509 (?) Expulsion of King Tarquinius
Superbus.
508/7 (?) First Roman–Carthaginian
trade treaty.
500
494 First secession of *plebs*.
493 Alliance between Rome and the
Latins (*foedus Cassianum*).

474 Defeat of Etruscans at Cumae.

LITERATURE, ART & ENTERTAINMENT,
PUBLIC WORKS, THOUGHT

600
Laying of *Cloaca Maxima*, paving of
Roman Forum.
575–550 Phase I of Regia.
550 Earliest of the XIII altars at
Lavinium.
540–530 Hercules–Athena terracotta
statue group from the Forum
Boarium.
520–500 'Lapis Niger' altar in Forum.
509 (?) Temple of *Iuppiter Capitolinus*
with sculpture by Vulca of Veii.

500

493 Temple of Ceres, Liber, Libera
Temple of Saturn.
484 Temple of Castor and Pollux.
*c.*480 Capitoline She-Wolf statue.

451/50 Law of the XII Tables.

433 Temple of Apollo in Campo. Works of monumental Etruscan bronze sculpture ('Chimera' of Arezzo, 'Mars' of Todi).

400

400
396 Capture of Veii.
387 Defeat by the Celts at the Allia river. Sack of Rome.

Fortification of the City ('Servian' Wall); rebuilding of Rome after sack. Concordia Temple.

367/6 *Leges Liciniae-Sextiae.*
343–341 First Samnite War.
340–338 Latin War. Earliest colonies.
327–304 Second Samnite War.
326 Alliance with Naples.
312 Censorship of Appius Claudius Caecus.

Via Appia: Rome–Capua; Aqua Appia.

300
298–290 Third Samnite War.

300
From 300: Rome begins to 'Hellenise' itself; beginnings of historical painting; sarcophagus of L. Cornelius Scipio Barbatus.
293 Cult of Aesculapius installed on the Tiber Island.

287 *Lex Hortensia*: Struggle of the Orders ends.
280–275 Warfare against Pyrrhus.

264–241 First Punic War.

272 Aqua Anio Vetus. Introduction of gladiatorial combats in Rome.
260 Column of C. Duilius.
240 Livius Andronicus: first stage play on the Greek model in Rome.
239 Poet Cn. Naevius active (*c.* 265–201); poet Q. Ennius born (died 169).

238 Occupation of Sardinia and Corsica.
229 First Illyrian War.
225–222 Warfare against the Celts.

220 Via Flaminia: Rome–Rimini.
220–140 Pacuvius, tragedies.

219 Second Illyrian War.
218–201 Second Punic War.
216 Battle of Cannae.

216 Fabius Pictor begins first annalistic history of Rome.

215–205 First Macedonian War against Philip V.

212 Plunder of Syracuse; works of art looted from conquered Greek cities (Tarentum, 209).

c.212 Minting of Roman *denarius*
begun.
c.212–184 Comedies of Plautus (born
c.250).
205/4 Stone of Cybele the Great
Mother brought to Rome.
204–169 Ennius in Rome.

200
200–197 Second Macedonian War.

200
c.200/150–78 Pompeii: wall painting,
First Style.

197 Provinces of *Hispania Citerior* and
Hispania Ulterior created.
196 Declaration of Freedom for
Greece by T. Quinctius Flamininus.

192 Temple of Veiovis.

191 Province of *Gallia Cisalpina*.
191–188 War against Antiochus III of
Syria.

191 Dedication of the Temple of
Cybele.

c.190–130 *Floruit* of tragic poet
Pacuvius.
188 Statue of Marsyas set up in
Forum as symbol of freedom of
trade.
186 'Bacchanalian riots'.
c.185–109 Panaetius of Rhodes, the
'Middle Stoa'.

184 Censorship of Cato.

184 Death of Plautus.
184 Building begins on *Basilica Porcia*,
Basilica Aemilia (179), *Basilica
Sempronia* (170); surfacing of main
streets of Rome; Roman architect M.
Cossutius working on the Olympeion
in Athens.

183 Death of Hannibal and Scipio
Africanus.
180 *Lex Villia annalis*.

c.180 Cato starts writing. Roman
prose reaches its first peak.
173 Expulsion of Epicurean
philosophers from Rome.

171–168 War against King Perseus of
Macedon.

168 Battle of Pydna.

c.170–85(?) Tragedies of L. Accius.
After 168 The historian Polybius in
Rome.
168/7 Delphi: reliefs on Victory
Memorial of Aemilius Paullus.
166–160 Terence, *Comedies*.
161 Greek rhetoricians and
philosophers expelled from Rome.

154–133 Warfare in Spain.

149–146 Third Punic War.
149 Institution of the Court for
extortion proceedings.
148 Province of *Macedonia*.
146 Destruction of Carthage and
Corinth.

136–132 First Slave War in
Sicily.
133 Tiberius Gracchus People's
Tribune; fall of Numantia; kingdom
of Pergamum falls to Rome by
bequest.
132–129 Insurrection of Aristonicus in
kingdom of Pergamum.
129 Province of *Asia*.

123–122 C. Gracchus People's
Tribune.
121 Province of *Gallia Narbonensis*.

113–101 Warfare against Cimbri and
Teutones.
112–105 Jugurthine War.

104–100 Second Slave War in Sicily.
100
100 Marius' sixth consulate.

156/55 Greek 'philosphers'
deputation' (Carneades, Critolaus,
Diogenes) in Rome.

c.150 Tomb of the Cornelii
remodelled.

146 Work of Neo-Attic architect
Hermodorus of Salamis begins in
Rome (Temple of Jupiter Stator).
144. Aqua Marcia.
142 Temple of Hercules Invictus (*Ara
maxima*).
c.140 Terracotta sculpted façade of
the 'Via S. Gregorio' temple.

c.133–107 Lucilius, *Satires*.

125 Aqua Tepula

c.120 Death of Polybius.
120/80 Temple of Fortuna at
Praeneste built in *opus caementicium*.
120/110 House of the Griffins on the
Palatine; early Second Style
painting.
116–27 M. Terentius Varro, politician
and leading antiquarian scholar.

106–43 M. Tullius Cicero.

100

c.100 *Fabula Atellana* at its height;
Tomb of Ser. Sulpicius Galba;
Temple of Vesta on the Forum
Boarium; bronze portrait statue of
the '*Arringatore*'.

96 Cyrene falls to Rome.
92 Sulla governor of Cilicia, contact with the Parthian kingdom.
91–89 Social War.
88 Sulla's first march on Rome.
88–64 Wars against Mithridates VI of Pontus.
87–84 Rule of Cinna.
86 Looting of Athens by Sulla's army.
83–81 Civil War between the adherents of Marius and Sulla.
82–79 Dictatorship of Sulla.

81 Cicero's first speech (*pro Quinctio*).
80–78 Tabularium; building of the Odeion and Amphitheatre in Pompeii.

78 Death of Sulla.
77–72 Warfare of Pompey against Sertorius.
74 Bithynia falls to Rome by bequest.
73–71 Slave rebellion of Spartacus.
70 Trial of Verres, prosecuted by Cicero.

*c.***70–60** Pompeii: painting in the 'Villa of the Mysteries'.

67 Pompey's war against the pirates.
66 Pompey's reorganisation of the East.
63 Consulate of Cicero; conspiracy of Catiline; Pompey in Judaea.
60 First Triumvirate (Pompey, Crassus, Caesar).

*c.***60** *Floruit* of Epicurean circle of Siro; *floruit* of poet Catullus (87/4–58/4), the Neoteric circle, and the Epicurean poet Lucretius (*c.*94–55).

59 Caesar's first consulate.
58–50 Caesar in Gaul.
55,54 Thrusts into Britain.
55,53 Crossings of the Rhine.
55–53 Crassus' unsuccessful Parthian campaign.

55–52 Cicero, *De Oratore, De Re Publica, De Legibus.*
Theatre of Pompey built.
Floruit of Neopythagorean philosopher-politician P. Nigidius Figulus (praetor 58).
54–46 *Basilica Iulia* built; Forum of Julius Caesar begun.

53 Defeat of Crassus at Carrhae.
52 Clodius murdered by Milo.

52–51 Caesar *De Bello Gallico.*
51 Death of philosopher Posidonius of Apamea.
*c.***50** 'Odyssey Landscapes' paintings (Second Style).
*c.***50** BC to AD **50** *Floruit* of Arretine ware.

49–48 Civil War between Caesar and Pompey.

48–44 Dictatorship of Caesar.

46 Death of Cato Uticensis.
44 Murder of Caesar (15 March).
43–33 Second Triumvirate (Antony,
Lepidus, Octavian).
43 Proscriptions, murder of Cicero.
42 Caesar's assassins defeated at the
battles of Philippi.

36 Antony's unsuccessful Parthian
campaign; sea victory of M. Agrippa
at Naulochus against Sex. Pompeius.

31 Battle of Actium (2 September).
30 Capture of Alexandria, death of
Antony and Cleopatra.
29 Triple triumph of Octavian.

27 Legalisation of the Augustan
Principate (13 January).

26–25 Augustus in Spain.

23 Augustus' legal position revised.
20 Return of the standards captured
by the Parthians.

18 Julian laws on marriage.

16–15 Subjugation of the Alpine
Tribes.
16/15–13 Augustus in Gaul.

48 Senate orders temples of Isis and
Sarapis to be destroyed.
47 Varro dedicates *Antiquities* to
Caesar.
46 Reform of the Calendar.
44 *Curia Iulia* (Senate House) built.

42 Octavian vows temple of Mars
Ultor.
42–38/35 Virgil, *Eclogues*.
c.40–31 Horace, *Epodes*; *Satires*.
39 First public library in Rome.
c.37–29 Virgil *Georgics*.

35 Death of historian Sallust.

c.30 Vitruvius writes *De Architectura*.

29 Dedication of temple to Divus
Iulius; Altar and Statue of Victory set
up in the Senate House; Arch of
Augustus in the Forum.
29–19 Virgil, *Aeneid*.
28 Dedication of Temple to Apollo;
restoration of 82 ruined temples;
Mausoleum of Augustus.
c.28–16 Propertius, *Elegies*.
27 Pantheon and Baths of Agrippa;
house of Augustus.
c.27–19 Tibullus, *Elegies*.
26 Suicide of poet-politician
Cornelius Gallus.
26 BC to AD 12/17 *Floruit* of historian
Livy (b. 64/59).
c.25 BC–AD 17 Ovid.

20 Building of Mars Ultor temple.
c.20–10 (?) Vienne: temple of
Augustus.
19 Death of Virgil; death of Tibullus.

17 Secular Games; Horace, *Carmen
Saeculare*.
c.15 Cameo of Livia, Gemma
Augustea.

*c.*13 Theatres of Marcellus and Balbus
dedicated.
Before 12 Cestius Pyramid built;
'Auditorium of Maecenas' (Third
Style painting).
13–9 *Ara Pacis.*

12–8 Thrusts into Germany.

12 Altar of Roma and Augustus in
Lyons.
11–4 Augustus restores the
aqueducts.
8 Death of Horace; death of
Maecenas.
7 Rome divided into XIV regions.
2 Dedication of Forum of Augustus

AD
4–6 New thrusts into Germany.
6/7 Census of Quirinius in Judaea,
now a Roman province.
6–9 Dalmatian–Pannonian rebellion.

8 Exile of Ovid to Tomis.

9 Roman defeat at the battle of the
Teutoburg Forest.

12 *Basilica Iulia* rebuilt after a fire.

14 Death of Augustus (19 August).
14–37 Tiberius *princeps.*
16 Recall of Germanicus (died 19),
suspension of great Roman
offensives against Germany.

*c.*20–30 *Floruit* of historian Velleius
Paterculus.
*c.*22 Building of *Domus Tiberiana,* the
first 'imperial palace'.

23 Construction of the Praetorian
Barracks in Rome.
26–36 Pontius Pilate procurator in
Judae.
27 Tiberius moves to Capri.
37–41 Caligula.

38–52 Aqua Claudia, Aqua Anio
Novus.
40 New port (*Portus*) built at Ostia.
*c.*40–50 'Underground Basilica' at the
Porta Maggiore.

41–54 Claudius.
43 Provinces of *Britannia, Lycia* and
Pamphylia.
46 Province of *Thracia.*

*c.*50 Baalbek: building of Jupiter Temple begins.
*c.*50–60 Sebasteion built at Aphrodisias.
*c.*50–100 Wall painting, Fourth Style.
52 Porta Maggiore built.

54–68 Nero.

55–68 Temple of the Divine Claudius.

58–63 Campaigns of Corbulo in Armenia.

*c.*60 Nero builds villas at Anzio and Subiaco, and palace (*Domus Transitoria*) in Rome.

61 Revolt of Boudicca in Britain.

62 Death of satirical poet Persius.
64 Nero's *Domus Aurea* (architects: Severus and Celer; paintings by Famulus or Fabullus).

64 Fire of Rome, persecution of Christians.

65 Pisonian conspiracy.

65 Death of Seneca; death of epic poet Lucan.
66 Death of novelist Petronius.
Mainz: Jupiter Column.

66 Tiridates crowned king of Armenia in Rome; Nero's Greek journey.
66–70 Jewish rebellion.
68–69 Galba, Otho, Vitellius.
69–79 Vespasian.

69 Quintilian the rhetorician given state support in Rome.

70 Capture of Jerusalem by Titus.

74 *Templum Pacis.*
Floruit of Flavius Josephus, Jewish historian.

77–84 Campaign of Agricola in Britain.
79–81 Titus.
79 Eruption of Vesuvius; Pompeii and Herculaneum destroyed.

79 Death of Pliny the Elder.

80 Dedication of the Colosseum; *floruit* of epigrammatist Martial.
After 81 Arch of Titus.
Baths of Titus built over part of *Domus Aurea.*

81–96 Domitian.

*c.*81–96 Flavian palace (architect Rabirius).
*c.*83 'Cancelleria' reliefs.
*c.*85 Restoration of temple of Isis (first built by Caligula?).
90 *Floruit* of the poets Statius (died 96) and Silius Italicus (died *c.* 101).
Nerva forum.

*c.*90 Provinces of *Germania Inferior* and *Germania Superior.*
96–98 Nerva; dynastic adoption revived.
98–117 Trajan.

98 Tacitus, *Agricola, Germania.*

100

100 Pliny the Younger, *Panegyricus*.
c.100–110 Rome: Trajan's markets;
Satires of Juvenal.
c.103 Death of Sex. Iulius Frontinus,
author of book on the aqueducts.

106 Province of *Arabia*.
107 Province of *Dacia*.

107–113 Rome: Forum of Trajan,
Trajan's Column; reconstruction of
the Forum of Julius Caesar (architect:
Apollodorus of Damascus).
109 Adamklissi: *Tropaeum Traiani*.

114–117 Parthian War.

114 Beneventum: Arch of Trajan.
Rome: 'Great Trajanic' frieze.

115–117 Jewish revolts in Egypt,
Cyrene, Cyprus.
117–138 Hadrian.

c.115–185 Pausanias, travel writer.

c.118–128 Rebuilding of the Pantheon.
c.118–134 Tivoli: *Villa Hadriana*.

120 Provinces of *Mesopotamia* and
Assyria abandoned; Hadrian's wall
built in Britain.

120 Death of philosopher Epictetus.
c.120 Appearance of sarcophagi for
inhumation.
125 Death of Plutarch, prolific writer
on philosophy and Graeco–Roman
antiquities.

130 Death of Antinous in Egypt.

130 Death of biographer Suetonius.
c.130–140 Ephesus: Temple of
Hadrian; Library of Celsus.
c.130–170 Antiquarian Aulus Gellius;
novelist Apuleius.

132–135 Insurrection of Bar Kochba.
138–161 Antoninus Pius.

139 Hadrian's Mausoleum (Castel
Sant' Angelo); Fronto, tutor of
Marcus Aurelius.
c.141 Temple of Antoninus and
Faustina.
145 Temple of the Divine Hadrian.
c.160–220 Tertullian, Church writer.
160 *Floruit* of Herodes Atticus (*c*.
101–177), sophist and benefactor.

161–180 Marcus Aurelius, and Lucius
Verus (161–169).
162/3–166 Parthian War.

c.161–180 Aspendos: theatre.
c.161 Column of Antoninus Pius.
162 Galen in Rome as court
physician.
c.165 Miletus: market gateway.

166 Plague.
167–175 Warfare against
Marcomanni, Quadi and other tribes.

*c.***173** Bronze equestrian statue of
Marcus Aurelius.

175 Revolt of Avidius Cassius in
East.
177 Commodus co-regent.
Martyrdom of Christians of Lyons
and Vienne.
180 Plague in Europe.
180–192 Commodus. Peace with
Marcomanni.
182 Conspiracy against Commodus.
Commodus worshipped as Hercules;
Rome renamed *Colonia Commodiana.*

180–193 Column of Marcus Aurelius.
180–215 *Floruit* of the Catechetical
School of Christian philosophy in
Alexandria (Pantaeus, Clement,
Origen).

*c.***190** Bust of Commodus as Hercules.

193 Commodus murdered (1 Jan.),
193–211 Septimius Severus.
195, 197–199 Parthian Wars.
198 Caracalla and Geta co-regents.
200

200
203 Arch of Severus in the Forum;
Septizodium. Leptis Magna: Severan
Forum, arch, basilica, colonnaded
street.

208–211 Britain campaign.

*c.***210** *Floruit* of literary circle of
empress Julia Domna.
Baths of Caracalla.

211–217 Caracalla and Geta; Geta
murdered in 212.
212/13 *Constitutio Antoniniana.*

215 Early Christian cemetery of St
Callixtus.

218–222 Elagabalus.
222–235 Severus Alexander.
226 Sassanids control Persia.

227 Baths of Severus Alexander.

235–284 Age of the Soldier Emperors.
235 Victory of Maximinus Thrax over
the Alamanni.

*c.***240** Synagogue, mythraeum, house
church at Dura Europos (destroyed
in *c.* 256).

243–244 Campaign of Gordian III
against the Sassanids.

*c.***245–270** Plotinus in Rome.
*c.***245** *Floruit* of Mani (216–77),
founder of Manichaeism.

248 Celebration of Rome's thousandth
birthday under Philip the Arabian.
249/50 Harsh persecution of
Christians under Traianus Decius.

249 Baths of Decius.

253–260 Valerian and Gallienus.

258 Death of Cyprian.

259–270 Separatist 'Empire of the Gauls'.
260 Valerian taken prisoner by Shapur I.
260–268 Gallienus, 'Time of the 30 Tyrants'.

'Gallienic Renaissance'.

267 Heruli sack Athens, Corinth, Argos, and Sparta.
269–272 Separatist empire of Palmyra.
270–275 Aurelian.

Aurelian's city wall in Rome.

271 Dacia abandoned.

273 Temple of the Sun.
283 Great fire in the Forum (damage repaired by Diocletian).

284–305 Diocletian.
288–296 Separatist empire of Britain.
12 Dioceses created.
297 Edict against the Manichaeans.

297–305 Thessalonica: Arch of Galerius.
298–306 Rome: Baths of Diocletian.

300

300
c.300 Trier: Imperial Baths.
Venice: Group of the Tetrarchs.
Split: Palace of Diocletian.

301 Maximum Prices Edict.
303 Persecution of Christians.

303 Floruit of Christian writers Lactantius and Arnobius.

306–337 Constantine the Great.

After 307
Rome: Basilica of Maxentius.

311 Galerius' Edict of Toleration.
312 Battle of the Milvian Bridge (28 October).

Villa at Piazza Armerina.

313 Edict of Milan.

313–315 Arch of Constantine; Baths of Constantine.
314–321 Basilicas of St John Lateran (313/14), St Peter (321), St Sebastian (320/50), Sts Marcellinus and Peter (320).

314 Council of Arles, Donatist Controversy.
314–324 Licinius and Constantine co-emperors.

c.315 Colossal statue of Constantine.
c.315–326 Trier: painted and coffered ceiling.

324 Defeat of Licinius; building of
Constantinople begun; reunification
of the empire under Constantine.
325 Council of Nicaea, Arianism
condemned.
330 Dedication of Constantinople (11
May).

320–350 Pagan-Christian catacomb of
the Via Latina.

c.330–385 Ammianus Marcellinus,
historian.
331 Basilica of Iunius Bassus.
335 Death of Arius.

337–340 Reign of sons of Constantine.
340–350 Reign of Constans in the
West, Constantius II in the East.

340 Death of Bishop Eusebius of
Caesarea.
c.340–420 Jerome.
341 Mission of Ulfila, translator of
the Bible, among the Visigoths.
c.345 Mausoleum of St Constantia.
348–405 Prudentius.

350–361 Constantius II sole emperor.

356 Visit of Constantius II to Rome.
357 Victory altar removed from
Senate.
359 Sarcophagus of Iunius Bassus.
360/63 Julian returns Victory altar to
Senate.

361–63 Julian the Apostate; attempt
to restore paganism.
364–375 Reign of Valentinian I in the
West.
364–378 Government of Valens in the
East.

367 Death of Hilary of Poitiers.
368 Constantinople: aqueduct of
Valens.
374–397 Ambrose, Bishop of Milan.

375 Advance of the Huns.
378 Battle of Adrianople, where
Valens fell to the Visigoths.
379–395 Theodosius the Great.

379 Death of Basil.
382 Removal of Victory altar from the
Senate House.
390 Death of Gregory of Nazianzus.
Constantinople: Obelisk of
Theodosius.

391 Pagan cults banned; destruction
of the Temple of Sarapis at
Alexandria.

393 Death of Ausonius.

394 Battle of the Frigidus; defeat of
the pagan opposition in the Senate.
395–408 Honorius emperor in West
(395–423); Arcadius emperor in East
(383–408); final division of empire.
400

End 4th century (?): *Historia Augusta*
composed.
400
c.400 Diptych of the *Symmachi*;
Macrobius, *Saturnalia*.

402 Ravenna becomes imperial
residence in the West.

404 Last gladiatorial games in the
Colosseum.
405 Rome: Arch of Arcadius and
Honorius.

406 Vandals, Alans and other groups
cross the Rhine.
406–437 Kingdom of Burgundy on
the Rhine.
408–450 Theodosius II ruler of East.
410 Alaric sacks Rome.

Augustine begins *De Civitate Dei*.
416 Rutilius Namatianus, *De Reditu
Suo; Basilica Iulia* restored.
421 Statues erected in Theatre of
Marcellus.

424–455 Valentinian III.
429–533 Kingdom of the Vandals in
North Africa.

430 Death of Augustine.

431 Council of Ephesus condemns
the Pelagian heresy.

432–440 Rome: building and mosaic
decoration of Sta Maria Maggiore.
438 *Codex Theodosianus*.

440–461 Pope Leo the Great.

442 Earthquake damages Forum and
Colosseum.
443 Baths of Constantine restored.

443–534 Kingdom of Burgundy on
the Rhône.
451 Attila the Hun defeated at the
battle of the Catalaunian Fields;
Council of Chalcedon.
455 Vandal king Gaiseric sacks
Rome.
457–474 Leo I rules East.

c.460 *Floruit* of pagan Platonic
philosopher Proclus (410/12–85).

476 Deposition of Romulus
Augustulus.
476–493 Odoacer king of Italy; end of
the empire in the West.

482–511 Clovis king of the Franks.
488 March of the Ostrogoths under Theodoric to Italy.
491–518 Anastasius I rules East.
493 'Battle of the Ravens' before Ravenna.
493–526 Reign of Theodoric the Great, king of Italy.

496 The Franks adopt the Catholic faith.

500

500

507–711 Kingdom of the Visigoths in Spain.

507–511 Theatre of Pompey restored.

518–527 Justinus, emperor of the East.

523 Last hunts in the Colosseum.
524 Execution of Boethius, consul and philosopher.
526 Temple of Romulus converted to church.

527–565 Justinian I.

528–534 *Corpus Iuris Civilis.*
529 Philosophical schools in Athens closed; Benedict founds monastery of Monte Cassino.

532 'Nika Riots' in Constantinople.
535–553 Warfare with the Ostrogoths in Italy.
568–774 Lombard kingdom in Italy.
570–632 Mohammed the Prophet.

589 Visigoths adopt Catholicism.

590–604 Pope Gregory the Great.

608 Column dedicated to Phocas in the Forum.
609 Pantheon dedicated as church of Sta Maria ad Martyres.

700
711 Visigoths defeated by the Moslems.

2. POPULATION FIGURES

A CENSUS FIGURES OF ROMAN CITIZENS

131/130 BC	318,823
86/85	463,000
28	4,063,000
AD 14	4,937,000
47	5,984,072

B POPULATION ANALYSIS FOR ITALY IN THE TIME OF AUGUSTUS (estimated by P. Brunt)

Free	4,500,000
Slave	3,000,000
Total inhabitants	7,500,000

C POPULATION FIGURES IN DIFFERENT PARTS OF THE EMPIRE ABOUT AD 14 (estimated by O. A. W. Dilke)

Italy, including Rome	13,000,000
Sicily, Sardinia, Corsica	1,100,000
Spain	6,000,000
Gaul	4,900,000
Danube provinces	2,000,000
Greece and Islands	3,000,000
Asia Minor	13,000,000
Syria, Palestine, Cyprus	6,500,000
Egypt, Cyrenaica	5,500,000
Rest of North Africa	6,000,000
Total	61,000,000

3. CURRENCY SYSTEM

A AUGUSTAN SYSTEM

1 *aureus* = 25 *denarii*
1 *denarius* = 4 *sestertii* ('sesterces')
1 *sestertius* = 2 *dupondii*
1 *dupondius* = 2 *asses*

B CONSTANTINIAN SYSTEM

1 *solidus* = 24 *siliquae* (silver)
1 *siliqua* = 3/4 *miliarense* (silver)

C DEPRECIATION OF CONSTANTINIAN COPPER COINAGE (according to B. Overbeck)

AD	Average weight of standard copper coin (*follis*) in grams (grains)
310	5.20 (88)
312	4.50 (76)
314	3.75 (63)
318	3.35 (57)
322	3.00 (51)
330	2.25 (38)
335	1.50 (25)

BIBLIOGRAPHY

SOURCE COLLECTIONS

E. Barker, *From Alexander to Constantine*, Oxford 1966
A. H. M. Jones, *A History of Rome through the Fifth Century*, London 1968–70
N. Lewis, *Greek Historical Documents: The Roman Principate, 27 BC – 285 AD*,
　　Toronto 1974
N. Lewis and M. Reinhold, *Roman Civilisation*, New York 1966[2]
J. Stevenson, *The New Eusebius*, London 1963

GENERAL AND REFERENCE WORKS

F. F. Abbott, *A History and Description of Roman Political Institutions*, Boston 1911[3]
P. Anderson, *Passages from Antiquity to Feudalism*, London 1974
Aufstieg und Niedergang der römischen Welt, ed. H. Temporini and W. Haase.
　　Berlin 1972– . (A multi-volume *Festschrift* for J. Vogt, with articles by
　　numerous authors in various languages on the state of research on issues of
　　Roman history and culture)
T. R. S. Broughton, The *Magistrates of the Roman Republic,* New York 1951–52.
Cambridge Ancient History, vols. 7–12, Cambridge 1928–39
M. Cary, *The Geographical Background of Greek and Roman History*, Oxford 1949
M. Cary and H. H. Scullard, *A History of Rome down to the Age of Constantine*, New
　　York 1975[3]
K. Christ (ed.), *Römische Geschichte: Eine Bibliographie*, Darmstadt 1976
Everyman's Classical Atlas, London 1961
M. I. Finley (ed.), *Atlas of Classical Archaeology*, London 1977
T. Mommsen, *The History of Rome*, London 1908, 1913[2]
The Oxford Classical Dictionary, Oxford 1970[2]
M. Rostovtzeff, *Rome*, New York 1967
A. N. Sherwin-White, *The Roman Citizenship*, Oxford 1973[2]

EARLY ROME AND THE ETRUSCANS

A. Alföldi, *Early Rome and the Latins*, Ann Arbor 1963
R. Bloch, *The Origins of Rome*, London 1960

E. Gjerstad, *Early Rome* (6 vols.), Lund 1953–66

W. V. Harris, *Rome in Etruria and Umbria*, Oxford 1971

J. Heurgon, *The Rise of Rome*, London 1973

R. M. Ogilvie, *Early Rome and the Etruscans*, London 1976

M. Pallottino, *The Etruscans*, London 1975

R. E. A. Palmer, *The Archaic Community of the Romans*, Cambridge 1970

J. Pinsent, *Military Tribunes and Plebeian Consuls: The Fasti from 444 to 342*, Wiesbaden 1975

E. H. Richardson, *The Etruscans: Their Art and Civilization*, Chicago 1964

E. T. Salmon, *The Making of Roman Italy*, London 1982

E. T. Salmon, *Roman Colonization under the Republic*, London 1969

E. T. Salmon, *Samnium and the Samnites*, Cambridge 1967

H. H. Scullard, *The Etruscan Cities and Rome*, London 1967

H. H. Scullard, *A History of the Roman World, 753 to 146* BC, London 1980[4]

J. H. Thiel, *A History of Roman Sea-power before the Second Punic War*, Amsterdam 1954

J. H. Thiel, *Studies in the History of Roman Sea-power in Republic Times*, Amsterdam 1946

CLASSICAL REPUBLIC

F. E. Adcock, *Marcus Crassus, Millionaire*, Cambridge 1966

F. E. Adcock, *The Roman Art of War under the Republic*, Cambridge 1940

A. E. Astin, *Cato the Censor*, Oxford 1978

A. E. Astin, *Scipio Aemilianus*, Oxford 1967

E. Badian, *Foreign Clientelae (264–70 BC)*, Oxford 1958

E. Badian, *L. Sulla: The Deadly Reformer*, Sydney 1970

E. Badian, *Publicans and Sinners*, Oxford 1972

E. Badian, *Roman Imperialism in the Late Republic*, Oxford 1968[2]

E. Badian, *Studies in Greek and Roman History*, Oxford 1964

A. Bernstein, *Tiberius Sempronius Gracchus: Tradition and Apostasy*, London 1978

P. A. Brunt, *Social Conflicts in the Roman Republic*, London 1971

T. F. Carney, *A Biography of C. Marius*, Chicago 1970[2]

M. Crawford, *The Roman Republic*, Sussex 1978

T. A. Dorey and D. R. Dudley, *Rome against Carthage*, London 1971

D. Earl, *The Moral and Political Tradition of Rome*, London 1967

R. M. Errington, *The Dawn of Empire*, London 1971

M. I. Finley, *Ancient Sicily to the Arab Conquest*, London 1979[2]

K. von Fritz, *The Theory of the Mixed Constitution in Antiquity*, New York 1954

E. Gabba, *Republican Rome, the Army and the Allies*, Oxford 1976

M. Gelzer, *Caesar*, Oxford 1968

M. Gelzer, *The Roman Nobility*, Oxford 1969

E. S. Gruen, *The Last Generation of the Roman Republic*, Berkeley 1974

E. S. Gruen, *Roman Politics and the Criminal Courts, 149–78 BC*, Cambridge, Mass. 1968

W. V. Harris, *War and Imperialism in Republican Rome, 327–70 BC*, Oxford 1979

J. F. Lazenby, *Hannibal's War*, Warminster 1978

A. W. Lintott, *Violence in Republican Rome*, Oxford 1968

D. Magie, *Roman Rule in Asia Minor*, Princeton 1950

T. Mitchell, *Cicero: The Ascending Years*, New Haven 1979

F. Münzer, *Römische Adelsparteien und Adelsfamilien*, Stuttgart 1920

C. Nicolet, *L'ordre équestre à l'époque républicaine (312–43 avant J.-C.)*, Paris 1964–74

C. Nicolet, *The World of the Citizen in Republican Rome*, London 1980

E. Rawson, *Cicero: A Portrait*, London 1975

J. Richardson, *Roman Provincial Administration, 227 BC to AD 117*, Basingstoke 1976

H. H. Scullard, *From the Gracchi to Nero*, London 1982[5]

H. H. Scullard, *Roman Politics, 220–150 BC*, Oxford 1973[2]

H. H. Scullard, *Scipio Africanus: Soldier and Politician*, London 1970

R. Seager (ed.), *The Crisis of the Roman Republic*, Cambridge 1969

R. Seager, *Pompey: A Political Biography*, Oxford 1979

D. R. Shackleton Baily, *Cicero*, London 1971

D. R. Shackleton Bailey, *Cicero: Epistulae ad familiares*, Cambridge 1977

D. R. Shackleton Bailey, *Cicero's Letters to Atticus*, Cambridge 1966

I. Shatzman, *Senatorial Wealth and Roman Politics*, Brussels 1975

R. E. Smith, *Service in the Post-Marian Army*, Manchester 1958

E. S. Stavely, *Greek and Roman Voting and Elections*, London 1972

D. Stockton, *Cicero: A Political Biography*, Oxford 1971

D. Stockton, *The Gracchi*, Oxford 1979

C. H. V. Sutherland, *The Romans in Spain, 217 BC–AD 117*, London 1939

R. Syme, *The Roman Revolution*, Oxford 1939

L. R. Taylor, *Party Politics in the Age of Caesar*, Berkeley 1966

L. R. Taylor, *Roman Voting Assemblies*, Ann Arbor 1966

L. R. Taylor, *The Voting Districts of the Roman Republic*, Rome 1960

A. J. Toynbee, *Hannibal's Legacy*, London 1965

F. W. Walbank, *Philip V of Macedon*, Cambridge 1940

B. H. Warmington, *Carthage*, London 1969[2]

S. Weinstock, *Divus Iulius*, Oxford 1971

C. Wirszubski, *Libertas as a Political Idea at Rome during the Late Republic and Early Principate*, Cambridge 1950

T. P. Wiseman, *New Men in the Roman Senate, 139 BC–AD 14*, London 1971

Z. Yavetz, *Julius Caesar and his Public Image*, Ithaca, N.Y. 1983

IMPERIUM ROMANUM

F. F. Abbott and A. C. Johnson, *Municipal Administration in the Roman Empire*, New York 1926

J. P. V. D. Balsdon, *The Emperor Gaius (Caligula)*, Oxford 1934

R. A. Bauman, *Impietas in principem: A Study of Treason against the Roman Emperor with Special Reference to the First Century AD*, Munich 1974

A. Birley, *Marcus Aurelius*, London 1966

E. Birley, *Roman Britain and the Roman Army*, Kendal 1953

G. W. Bowersock, *Augustus and the Greek World*, Oxford 1965

E. Champlin, *Fronto and Antonine Rome*, Cambridge, Mass. 1980

D. Earl, *The Age of Augustus*, London 1968

P. D. A. Garnsey and C. R. Whittaker (eds.), *Imperialism in the Ancient World*, Cambridge 1978.

A. Garzetti, *From Tiberius to the Antonines: A History of the Roman Empire, AD 14–192*, London 1974

P. Greenhalgh, *The Year of the Four Emperors*, London 1975

M. Hammond, *The Antonine Monarchy*, Rome 1959

M. Hammond, *The Augustan Principate in Theory and Practice*, New York 1968[2]

B. W. Henderson, *Five Roman Emperors (Vespasian to Trajan)*, New York 1927

B. W. Henderson, *The Life and Principate of the Emperor Hadrian, AD 76–138*, London 1923

A. H. M. Jones, *Augustus*, London 1970

A. H. M. Jones, *The Cities of the Eastern Roman Provinces*, Oxford 1971[2]

A. H. M. Jones, *Studies in Roman Government and Law*, Oxford 1960

B. Levick, *Tiberius the Politician*, London 1976

E. N. Luttwak, *The Grand Strategy of the Roman Empire from the First Century AD to the Third*, Baltimore 1976

F. Millar, *The Emperor in the Roman World*, London 1977

F. Millar, *The Roman Empire and her Neighbours*, London 1981[2]

A. Momigliano, *Claudius: The Emperor and his Achievement*, Cambridge 1961[2]

T. Mommsen, *The Provinces of the Roman Empire*, London 1886

J. Nicols, *Vespasian and the Partes Flavianae*, Wiesbaden 1978

H. M. D. Parker, *The Roman Legions*, Cambridge 1971

P. Petit, *Pax Romana*, London 1976

R. Seager, *Tiberius*, London 1972

C. G. Starr, *Civilization and the Caesars*, New York 1954

C. G. Starr, *The Roman Imperial Navy, 31 BC–AD 324*, Ithaca, N.Y. 1941

B. H. Warmington, *Nero: Reality and Legend*, London 1969

G. R. Watson, *The Roman Soldier*, London 1969

P. R. C. Weaver, *Familia Caesaris*, Cambridge 1972

G. Webster, *The Roman Imperial Army of the First and Second Centuries*, London 1969

C. Wells, *The German Policy of Augustus*, Oxford 1972

Z. Yavetz, *Plebs and Princeps*, Oxford 1969

SOCIETY AND ECONOMY

J. P. V. D. Balsdon, *Life and Leisure in Ancient Rome*, London 1974[2]

J. P. V. D. Balsdon, *Roman Women*, London 1977[5]

R. H. Barrow, *Slavery in the Roman Empire*, London 1928

S. F. Bonner, *Education in Ancient Rome*, London 1977

P. A. Brunt, *Italian Manpower, 225 BC–AD 14*, Oxford 1971

A. Burford, *Craftsmen in Greek and Roman Society*, London 1972

A. Cameron, *Circus Factions: Blues and Greens at Rome and Byzantium*, Oxford 1976

J. Carcopino, *Daily Life in Ancient Rome*, London 1941

J. H. D'Arms and E. C. Kopff (eds.), *Roman Seaborne Commerce*, Rome 1980

A. M. Duff, *Freedmen in the Early Roman Empire*, Oxford 1928

R. Duncan-Jones, *The Economy of the Roman Empire*, Cambridge 1982[2]

M. I. Finley, *The Ancient Economy*, London 1973

M. I. Finley, *Ancient Slavery and Modern Ideology*, London 1980

M. I. Finley (ed.), *Slavery in Classical Antiquity*, Cambridge 1960

M. I. Finley (ed.), *Studies in Ancient Society*, London 1974
M. I. Finley (ed.), *Studies in Roman Property*, Cambridge 1976
T. Frank, *Economic History of Rome*, London 1927[2]
T. Frank, *An Economic Survey of Ancient Rome*, Baltimore 1933–40
L. Friedlaender, *Roman Life and Manners under the Early Empire*, 4 vols., London 1908–28[2]
P. D. A. Garnsey (ed.), *Non-slave Labour in the Greco-Roman world*, Cambridge 1980
P. D. A. Garnsey, K. Hopkins, C. R. Whittaker (eds.), *Trade in the Ancient Economy*, London 1983
A. R. Hands, *Charities and Social Aid in Greece and Rome*, London 1968
F. M. Heichelheim, *An Ancient Economic History*, Leiden 1958–70
W. E. Heitland, *Agricola: A Study of Agriculture and Rustic Life in the Greco-Roman World from the Point of View of Labour*, Cambridge 1921
M. K. Hopkins, *Conquerors and Slaves*, Cambridge 1978
A. H. M. Jones, *The Roman Economy* (ed. P. A. Brunt), Oxford 1974
R. MacMullen, *Roman Social Relations, 50 BC to AD 284*, New Haven 1974
H.-I. Marrou, *A History of Education of Antiquity*, New York 1956
C. Mossé, *The Ancient World at Work*, London 1969
J. Percival, *The Roman Villa*, London 1976
S. Pomeroy, *Goddesses, Whores, Wives, and Slaves*, London 1975
M. Rostovtzeff, *Social and Economic History of the Roman Empire*, Oxford 1957[2]
R. P. Saller, *Personal Patronage under the Early Empire*, Cambridge 1982
S. Treggiari, *Roman Freedmen during the Late Republic*, London 1969
J. Vogt, *Ancient Slavery and the Ideal of Man*, Oxford 1974
W. L. Westermann, *The Slave System of Greek and Roman Antiquity*, Philadelphia 1955
K. D. White, *Roman Farming*, London 1970

LAW

W. W. Buckland, *Roman Law of Slavery*, Cambridge 1908
W. W. Buckland, *A Text-book of Roman Law* (3rd ed. rev. by P. Stein), Cambridge 1963
J. A. Crook, *Consilium principis*, Cambridge 1955
J. A. Crook, *Law and Life of Rome*, London 1967
P. D. A. Garnsey, *Social Status and Legal Privilege in the Roman Empire*, Oxford 1970
H. F. Jolowicz and B. Nicholas, *Historical Introduction to Roman Law*, Oxford 1973[2]
A. H. M. Jones, *The Criminal Courts of the Roman Republic and Principate*, Oxford 1972
J. M. Kelly, *Roman Litigation*, Oxford 1966
W. Kunkel, *An Introduction to Roman Legal and Constitutional History*, Oxford 1973[2]
T. Mommsen, *Römisches Staatsrecht*, Leipzig 1887[3]
B. Nicholas, *An Introduction to Roman Law*, Oxford 1962
F. Schulz, *Principles of Roman Law*, Oxford 1936
J. A. C. Thomas, *Textbook of Roman Law*, Amsterdam 1976
A. Watson, *Rome of the XII Tables*, Princeton 1975

HISTORIANS AND HISTORIOGRAPHY

T. A. Dorey (ed.), *Latin Historians*, London 1966
D. Earl, *The Political Thought of Sallust*, Cambridge 1961
M. L. W. Laistner, *The Greater Roman Historians*, Berkeley 1947
F. Millar, *A Study of Cassius Dio*, Oxford 1964
A. Momigliano, *Alien Wisdom*, Cambridge 1975
A. Momigliano, *Essays in Ancient and Modern Historiography*, Oxford 1977
A. Momigliano, *Studies in Historiography*, New York 1966
R. Syme, *Ammianus Marcellinus and the Historia Augusta*, Oxford 1968
R. Syme, *Emperors and Biography*, Oxford 1971
R. Syme, *Sallust*, Berkeley 1964
R. Syme, *Tacitus*, Oxford 1958
E. A. Thompson, *The Historical Work of Ammianus Marcellinus*, Cambridge 1947
F. Walbank, *Polybius*, Berkeley 1972
P. G. Walsh, *Livy*, Cambridge 1961

LITERATURE: GENERAL WORKS

Useful for students approaching the various Latin authors and literary periods for the first time are the critical anthologies published under the editorship of D. R. Dudley and T. A. Dorey; they are not included in the following bibliography. For more detailed scholarly bibliographies on Roman authors the student should consult J. H. Dee, 'A Survey of Recent Bibliographies of Classical Literature', *Classical World* 73 (1979–80), 275–90.

W. S. Anderson, *Essays on Roman Satire*, Princeton 1982
F. Cairns, *Generic Composition in Greek and Roman Poetry*, Edinburgh 1972
Cambridge History of Classical Literature II, Cambridge 1981
M. L. Clarke, *Rhetoric at Rome*, London 1953
M. Coffey, *Roman Satire*, London 1976
F. O. Copley, *Exclusus amator: A Study in Latin Love Poetry*, Baltimore 1956
F. O. Copley, *Latin Literature from the Beginnings to the Close of the Second Century AD*, Ann Arbor 1969
J. F. D'Alton, *Roman Literary Theory and Criticism*, New York 1962
G. E. Duckworth, *The Nature of Roman Comedy*, Princeton 1952
J. W. Duff, *A Literary History of Rome*, 2 vols., London 1960³
E. Fantham, *Comparative Studies in Republican Latin Imagery*, Toronto 1972
W. R. Johnson, *The Idea of Lyric*, Berkeley and Los Angeles 1982
D. Konstan, *Roman Comedy*, Ithaca, N.Y. 1983
G. Kennedy, *The Art of Rhetoric in the Roman World*, Princeton 1972
A. D. Leeman, *Orationis Ratio: The Stylistic Theories and Practice of the Roman Orators, Historians, and Philosophers*, 2 vols., Amsterdam 1963
J. Lembke, *Bronze and Iron: Old Latin Poetry from its Beginnings to 100 BC*, Berkeley 1973
J. K. Newman, *Augustus and the New Poetry*, Brussels 1967
J. K. Newman, *The Concept of Vates in Augustan Poetry*, Brussels 1967
R. M. Ogilvie, *Roman Literature and Society*, Harmondsworth 1980
M. Putnam, *Essays on Latin Lyric, Elegy, and Epic*, Princeton 1982

K. Quinn, *Latin Explorations: Critical Studies in Roman Literature*, London 1963

D. O. Ross, *Backgrounds to Augustan Poetry: Gallus, Elegy, and Rome*, Cambridge 1975

J. P. Sullivan (ed.), *Critical Essays on Roman Literature: Elegy and Lyric*, London 1962

J. P. Sullivan, *Satire*, London 1963

P. G. Walsh, *The Roman Novel*, Cambridge 1970

D. West and T. Woodman (eds.), *Creative Imitation and Latin Literature*. Cambridge 1979

D. West, *Quality and Pleasure in Latin Poetry*, Cambridge 1974

L. P. Wilkinson, *Golden Latin Artistry*, Cambridge 1963

G. W. Williams, *Tradition and Originality in Roman Poetry*, Oxford 1968

G. W. Williams, *Change and Decline: Roman Literature in the Early Empire*, Berkeley 1978

G. W. Williams, *Figures of Thought in Roman Poetry*, New Haven 1980

T. P. Wiseman, *Cinna the Poet and other Roman Essays*, Leicester 1974

J. Wright, *Dancing in Chains: The Stylistic Unity of the Comoedia Palliata*, Rome 1974

LITERATURE: INDIVIDUAL AUTHORS

CATULLUS

E. M. Havelock, *The Lyric Genius of Catullus*, Oxford 1939

D. Konstan, *Catullus' Indictment of Rome: The Meaning of Catullus 64*, Amsterdam 1977

K. Quinn, *Catullus: An Interpretation*, London 1972

K. Quinn (ed.), *Approaches to Catullus*, Cambridge and New York 1972

D. Ross, *Style and Tradition in Catullus*, Cambridge, Mass. 1965

A. L. Wheeler, *Catullus and the Traditions of Ancient Poetry*, Berkeley 1934

CICERO

D. R. Shackleton Bailey, *Cicero*, London 1971

K. A. Geffcken, *Comedy in the Pro Caelio*, Leiden 1973

E. Rawson, *Cicero: A Portrait*, London 1975

HORACE

S. Commager, *The Odes of Horace*, New Haven 1962

E. Fraenkel, *Horace*, Oxford 1957

N. Rudd, *The Satires of Horace*, Cambridge 1966

D. West, *Reading Horace*, Edinburgh 1967

L. P. Wilkinson, *Horace and his Lyric Poetry*, Cambridge 1968

LUCAN

F. M. Ahl, *Lucan: An Introduction*, Ithaca, N. Y. 1976

M. Morford, *The Poet Lucan*, Oxford 1967

LUCRETIUS

L. Holland, *Lucretius and the Transpadanes*, Princeton 1980

D. West, *The Imagery and Poetry of Lucretius*, Edinburgh 1969

OVID

H. Fränkel, *Ovid: A Poet between two Worlds*, Berkeley 1945
G. K. Galinsky, *Ovid's Metamorphoses*, Berkeley 1975
H. Jacobson, *Ovid's Heroides*, Princeton 1974
B. Otis, *Ovid's Heroides*, Princeton 1974
B. Otis, *Ovid as Epic Poet*, Cambridge 1970
C. P. Segal, *Landscape in Ovid's Metamorphoses*, Wiesbaden 1969
J. C. Thibault, *The Mystery of Ovid's Exile*, Berkeley 1964
L. P. Wilkinson, *Ovid Recalled*, Cambridge 1955

PETRONIUS

H. P. Rankin, *Petronius the Artist*, The Hague 1971
J. P. Sullivan, *The Satyricon of Petronius: A Literary Study*, London 1968

PLAUTUS

E. Segal, *Roman Laughter: The Comedy of Plautus*, Cambridge, Mass. 1968
N. Zagagi, *Tradition and Originality in Plautus*, Göttingen 1980

PROPERTIUS

M. Hubbard, *Propertius*, London 1974
J. P. Sullivan, *Propertius: A Critical Introduction*, Cambridge 1976

SENECA

M. T. Griffin, *Seneca: A Philosopher in Politics*, Oxford 1976
J.-A. Shelton, *Seneca's Hercules Furens: Theme, Structure, and Style*, Göttingen 1978

STATIUS

D. Vessey, *Statius and the Thebaid*, Cambridge 1973

TIBULLUS

D. Bright, Haec Mihi Fingebam: Tibullus in his World, Leiden 1978
F. Cairns, *Tibullus: A Hellenistic Poet at Rome*, Cambridge 1979

VIRGIL

W. S. Anderson, *The Art of the* Aeneid, Englewood Cliffs, N.J. 1969
W. Berg, *Early Virgil*, London 1974
S. Commager (ed.), *Virgil: A Collection of Critical Essays*, Englewood Cliffs, N.J. 1966
G. K. Galinsky, *Aeneas, Sicily, and Rome*, Princeton 1969
G. Highet, *The Speeches in Virgil's* Aeneid, Princeton 1972
R. A. Hornsby, *Patterns of Action in the* Aeneid, Iowa City 1970
W. R. Johnson, *Darkness Visible: A Study of Virgil's* Aeneid, Berkeley and Los Angeles 1976
P. A. Johnston, *Vergil's Agricultural Golden Age: A Study of the* Georgics, Leiden 1980
E. W. Leach, *Vergil's Eclogues: Landscapes of Experience*, Ithaca, N.Y. 1974
G. Miles, *The Georgics of Virgil*, Berkeley and Los Angeles 1980

R. C. Monti, *The Dido Episode and the* Aeneid: *Roman Social and Political Values in the Epic*, Leiden 1981

B. Otis, *Virgil: A Study in Civilized Poetry*, Oxford 1964

M. Putnam, *The Poetry of the* Aeneid, Cambridge, Mass. 1965

M. Putnam, *Virgil's Pastoral Art: Studies in the* Eclogues, Princeton 1970

M. Putnam, *Virgil's Poem of the Earth*, Princeton 1979

K. Quinn, *Vergil's* Aeneid: *A Critical Description*, Ann Arbor 1968

J. Van Sickle, *The Design of Virgil's* Bucolics, Rome 1978

L. P. Wilkinson, *The* Georgics *of Virgil: A Critical Survey*, Cambridge 1969

ART, ARCHITECTURE, AND TOPOGRAPHY

B. Andreae, *The Art of Rome*, New York 1977

T. Ashby, *The Aqueducts of Ancient Rome*, Oxford 1935

R. Bianchi Bandinelli, *Rome: The Late Empire*, London 1971

M. Bieber, *The History of the Greek and Roman Theater*, Princeton 1961²

M. E. Blake, *Ancient Roman Construction in Italy*, 3 vols., Washington, D.C. and Philadelphia 1947–73

A. Boëthius, *The Golden House of Nero*, Ann Arbor 1960

A. Boëthius and J. B. Ward-Perkins, *Etruscan and Roman Architecture*, Harmondsworth 1970

O. Brendel, *Prolegomena to the Study of Roman Art*, New Haven 1979

R. Brilliant, *Roman Art from the Republic to Constantine*, Newton Abbot 1974

R. Brilliant, *Gesture and Rank in Roman Art*, New Haven 1963

R. Brilliant, *The Arch of Septimius Severus in the Roman Forum*, Rome 1967

F. E. Brown, *Roman Architecture*, New York 1961

F. E. Brown, *Cosa: The Making of a Roman Town*, Ann Arbor 1980

J. H. D'Arms, *Romans on the Bay of Naples*, Cambridge, Mass. 1970

J. J. Deiss, *Herculaneum: Italy's Buried Treasure*, New York 1966

D. R. Dudley, *Urbs Roma*, London 1967

K. Einaudi (ed.), *Fototeca Unione: Photographic Archive of Roman Topography on Microfiche*, 2 vols., Chicago 1982³

A. De Franciscis, *The Pompeian Wall Paintings in the Roman Villa of Oplontis*, Recklinghausen 1975

G. M. A. Hanfmann, *Roman Art: A Modern Survey of the Art of Imperial Rome*, New York 1975

J. A. Hanson, *Roman Theater-Temples*, Princeton 1959

H. von Heintze, *Roman Art*, New York 1971

M. Henig, *A Handbook of Roman Art*, Ithaca, N.Y. 1983

H. Kähler, *The Art of Rome and her Empire*, New York 1963

P. W. Lehmann, *Roman Wall Paintings from Boscoreale in the Metropolitan Museum of Art*, Cambridge, Mass. 1953

K. De F. Licht, *The Rotunda in Rome*, Copenhagen 1968

H. P. L'Orange, *Likeness and Icon*, Odense 1973

W. L. MacDonald, *The Architecture of the Roman Empire*, I, New Haven 1965

W. L. MacDonald, *The Pantheon*, Cambridge, Mass. 1976

A. M. McCann, *The Portraits of Septimius Severus (AD 193–211)*, Rome 1968

A. G. McKay, *Houses, Villas, and Palaces in the Roman World*, London 1975

P. MacKendrick, *The Mute Stones Speak*, New York 1960

A. Mau, *Pompeii: Its Life and Art*, New York 1902

R. Meiggs, *Roman Ostia*, Oxford 1973[2]

E. Nash, *Pictorial Dictionary of Ancient Rome*, 2 vols., London 1968[2]

J. Packer, *The Insulae of Imperial Ostia*, Rome 1971

S. B. Platner and T. Ashby, *A Topographical Dictionary of Ancient Rome*, Oxford 1929

J. J. Pollitt, *The Art of Rome c. 753 BC–337 AD: Sources and Documents*, Englewood Cliffs, N.J. 1966

L. Richardson, Jr., *Pompeii: The Casa dei Dioscuri and its Painters*, Rome 1955

I. A. Richmond, *The City Wall of Imperial Rome*, Oxford 1930

G. M. A. Richter, *Ancient Italy*, Ann Arbor 1955

G. M. A. Richter, *The Engraved Gems of the Greeks, Etruscans, and Romans*, 2 vols., London 1968–71.

F. Sear, *Roman Architecture*, Ithaca, N.Y. 1983

D. E. Strong, *Roman Art*, Harmondsworth 1976

D. E. Strong, *Roman Imperial Sculpture*, London 1961

J. M. C. Toynbee, *Roman Historical Portraits*, Ithaca, N.Y. 1978

E. B. Van Deman, *The Building of the Roman Aqueducts*, Washington, D.C. 1934

E. L. Wadsworth, *Roman Stuccoes in and around Rome*, Rome 1924

J. B. Ward-Perkins, *Greek and Roman Cities*, New York 1975

RELIGION, SCIENCE AND TECHNOLOGY

F. Altheim, *A History of Roman Religion*, London 1938

J. Collins-Clinton, *A Late Antique Shrine of Liber Pater at Cosa*, Leiden 1977

F. Cumont, *Afterlife in Roman Paganism*, New Haven 1923

E. R. Dodds, *Pagan and Christian in an Age of Anxiety: Some Aspects of Religious Experience from Marcus Aurelius to Constantine*, Cambridge 1965

A. B. Drachmann, *Atheism in Pagan Antiquity*, London 1922

G. Dumézil, *Archaic Roman Religion*, 2 vols., Chicago 1970

R. Duthoy, *The Taurobolium: Its Evolution and Terminology*, Leiden 1969

E. J. and L. Edelstein, *Asclepius: A Collection and Interpretation of the Testimonies*, 2 vols., Baltimore 1945

E. C. Evans, *The Cults of the Sabine Territory*, Rome 1939

B. Farrington, *Science in Antiquity*, Oxford 1969[2]

J. R. Fears, *Princeps A Diis Electus: The Divine Election of the Emperor as a Political Concept at Rome*, Rome 1977

J. Ferguson, *The Religions of the Roman Empire*, London 1970

R. J. Forbes, *Studies in Ancient Technology*, 9 vols., Leiden 1964–72

W. Warde Fowler, *The Roman Festivals of the Period of the Republic*, London 1899

G. H. Halsberghe, *The Cult of Sol Invictus*, Leiden 1972

J. F. Healy, *Mining and Metallurgy in the Greek and Roman World*, London 1978

S. K. Heyob, *The Cult of Isis among Women in the Graeco-Roman World*, Leiden 1975

J. G. Landels, *Engineering in the Ancient World*, London 1978

R. Lattimore, *Themes in Greek and Latin Epitaphs*, Urbana, Ill. 1942

J. H. W. G. Liebeschuetz, *Continuity and Change in Roman Religion*, Oxford 1979

R. MacMullen, *Paganism in the Roman Empire*, New Haven 1981

R. Mellor, *ΘΕΑ ΡΩΜΗ: The Worship of the Goddess Roma in the Greek World*, Göttingen 1975

A. K. Michels, *The Calendar of the Roman republic*, Princeton 1967

R. M. Ogilvie, *The Romans and their Gods in the Age of Augustus*, London 1969

H. J. Rose, *Ancient Roman Religion*, London 1949

G. Sarton, *A History of Science, Vol. 2: Hellenistic Science and Culture in the Last Three Centuries BC*, Cambridge, Mass. 1959

J. Scarborough, *Roman Medicine*, London 1969

H. H. Scullard, *Festivals and Ceremonies of the Roman Republic*, London 1981

F. Solmsen, *Isis among the Greeks and Romans*, Cambridge, Mass. 1979

M. P. Speidel, *The Religion of Iuppiter Dolichenus in the Roman Army*, Leiden 1978

M. P. Speidel, *Mithras-Orion: Greek Hero and Roman Army God*, Leiden 1980

W. H. Stahl, *Roman Science: Origins, Development and Influence to the Later Middle Ages*, Madison 1962

R. Syme, *Some Arval Brethren*, Oxford 1980

L. R. Taylor, *The Divinity of the Roman Emperor*, Middletown 1931

J. Teixidor, *The Pagan God: Popular Religion in the Greco-Roman Near East*, Princeton 1977.

J. M. C. Toynbee, *Death and Burial in the Roman World*, Ithaca, N.Y. 1971

M. J. Vermaseren, *The Legend of Attis in Greek and Roman Art*, Leiden 1966

M. J. Vermaseren, *Mithriaca I-III*, Leiden 1971–82

M. J. Vermaseren, *Cybele and Attis: The Myth and the Cult*, London 1977

M. J. Vermaseren and C. C. van Essen, *The Excavations in the Mithraeum of the Church of Santa Prisca in Rome*, Leiden 1965

H. S. Versnel (ed.), *Faith, Hope and Worship: Aspects of Religious Mentality in the Ancient World*, Leiden 1981

H. S. Versnel, *Triumphus: An Inquiry into the Origin, Development, and Meaning of the Roman Triumph*, Leiden 1970.

H. Wagenvoort, *Pietas: Selected Studies in Roman Religion*, Leiden 1980

R. A. Wild, *Water in the Cultic Worship of Isis and Sarapis*, Leiden 1981

R. E. Witt, *Isis in the Graeco-Roman World*, London 1971

JUDAISM AND EARLY CHRISTIANITY

T. D. Barnes, *Tertullian*, Oxford 1971

F. F. Bruce, *New Testament History*, London 1971[2]

H. Chadwick, *The Early Church*, London 1968

J. Daniélou and H.-I. Marrou, *The First Six Hundred Years*, London 1964

J. D. G. Dunn, *Unity and Diversity in the New Testament*, London 1977

W. H. C. Frend, *Martyrdom and Persecution in the Early Church*, Oxford 1965

J. Gager, *Kingdom and Community: The Social World of Early Christianity*, Englewood Cliffs, N.J. 1975

E. Goodenough, *Jewish Symbols in the Greco-Roman Period*, 13 vols., New York 1953–65

L. Goppelt, *Apostolic and Post-apostolic Times*, London 1970

M. Grant, *The Jews in the Roman World*, London 1973

R. M. Grant, *Early Christianity and Society*, New York 1977

J. Jeremias, *Jerusalem in the Time of Jesus*, London 1974[3]

W. G. Kümmel, *Introduction to the New Testament*, London 1975

A. D. Nock, *Early Gentile Christianity and its Hellenistic Background*, New York 1964

S. Safrai and M. Stern (eds.), *The Jewish People in the First Century*, Assen 1974–76

E. Schürer, G. Vermes and F. Millar, *A History of the Jewish People in the Age of Jesus Christ*, Edinburgh 1973–79

M. Simon, *Jewish Sects at the Time of Jesus*, New York 1964

E. M. Smallwood, *The Jews under Roman Rule*, Leiden 1976

G. Theissen, *The Sociology of Early Palestinian Christianity*, Philadelphia 1978.

LATE ANTIQUITY

A. Alföldi, *A Conflict of Ideas in the Later Roman Empire*, Oxford 1952

A. Alföldi, *The Conversion of Constantine and Pagan Rome*. Oxford 1969²

T. D. Barnes, *Constantine and Eusebius*, Cambridge, Mass. 1981

N. H. Baynes, *Constantine the Great and the Christian Church*, Oxford 1969²

A. Birley, *Septimius Severus: The African Emperor*, London 1971

D. Bowder, *The Age of Constantine and Julian*, London 1978

G. W. Bowersock (ed.), *Gibbon and the Decline and Fall of the Roman Empire*, Cambridge, Mass. 1977

G. W. Bowersock, *Julian the Apostate*, London 1978

P. Brown, *The World of Late Antiquity*, London 1971

R. Browning, *The Emperor Julian*, London 1975

J. Burckhardt, *The Age of Constantine the Great*, London 1949

D. J. Chitty, *The Desert a City*, Oxford 1966

S. Dill, *Roman Society in the Last Century of the Western Empire*, London 1898.

W. H. C. Frend, *The Donatist Church*, Oxford 1952

E. Gibbon, *History of the Decline and Fall of the Roman Empire*, London 1776–88

W. Goffart, *Barbarians and Romans, AD 418–584*, Princeton 1980

K. G. Hollum, *Theodosian Empresses: Women and Imperial Dominion in Late Antiquity*, Berkeley and Los Angeles 1982

A. H. M. Jones, *Constantine and the Conversion of Europe*, London 1948

A. H. M. Jones, *The Later Roman Empire, 284–602*, Oxford 1964

A. H. M. Jones, J. R. Martindale and J. Morris, *The Prosopography of the Later Roman Empire*, Cambridge 1971–80

W. Kaegi, Jr., *Byzantium and the Decline of Rome*, Princeton 1968

N. Q. King, *The Emperor Theodosius and the Establishment of Christianity*, London 1961

J. H. W. G. Liebeschuetz, *Antioch: City and Imperial Administration in the Later Roman Empire*, Oxford 1972.

R. MacMullen, *Constantine*, London 1970

R. Macmullen, *Roman Government's Response to Crisis, AD 235–337*, New Haven 1976

R. MacMullen, *Soldier and Civilian in the Later Roman Empire*, Cambridge, Mass. 1963

J. Matthews, *Western Aristocracies and Imperial Court, AD 364–425*, Oxford 1975

S. Mazzarino, *The End of the Ancient World*, London 1966

A. Momigliano (ed.), *The Conflict between Paganism and Christianity in the Fourth Century*, Oxford 1963

H. M. D. Parker, *A History of the Roman World from AD 138 to 337*, London 1935
E. A. Thompson, *The Early Germans*, Oxford 1965
E. A. Thompson, *The Goths in Spain*, Oxford 1969
E. A. Thompson, *A History of Attila and the Huns*, Oxford 1948
E. A. Thompson, *The Visigoths in the Time of Ulfila*, Oxford 1966
J. Vogt, *The Decline of Rome*, New York 1967
F. W. Walbank, *The Awful Revolution*, Liverpool 1969

LATE ANTIQUE CULTURE

J. Bregman, *Synesius of Cyrene: Philosopher–Bishop*, Berkeley and Los Angeles 1982
P. Brown, *Augustine of Hippo*, London 1967
P. Brown, *The Cult of the Saints*, London 1981
P. Brown, *The Making of Late Antiquity*, Cambridge, Mass. 1978
P. Brown, *Religion and Society in the Age of Saint Augustine*, London 1972
P. Brown, *Society and the Holy in Late Antiquity*, London 1982
A. Cameron, *Claudian*, Oxford 1970
H. Chadwick, *Early Christian Thought and the Classical Tradition*, Oxford 1966
J. N. D. Kelly, *Jerome*, London 1975
R. Krautheimer, *Corpus Basilicarum Christianarum Romae: The Early Christian Basilicas of Rome (IV–IX cent.)*, 5 vols., Vatican City 1937–77
R. Krautheimer, *Early Christian and Byzantine Architecture*, Harmondsworth 1975[2]
R. Krautheimer, *Rome: Profile of a City, 312–1308 AD*, Princeton 1980
H. P. L'Orange, *Art Forms and Civil Life in the Late Roman Empire*, Princeton 1966
S. G. MacCormack, *Art and Ceremony in Late Antiquity*, Berkeley 1981
R. R. Ruether, *Gregory of Nazianzus*, Oxford 1969
D. S. Wallace-Hadrill, *Eusebius of Caesarea*, London 1960
K. Weitzmann, *Late Antique and Early Christian Book Illumination*, New York 1977
A. Wright and T. A. Sinclair, *A History of the Later Latin Literature from the Middle of the Fourth to the End of the Seventeenth Century*, London 1931

THE ROMAN TRADITION

C. Bailey, *The Legacy of Rome*, Oxford 1923
R. R. Bolgar, *The Classical Heritage and its Beneficiaries*, Cambridge 1940
K. Christ, *Römische Geschichte und deutsche Geschichtswissenschaft*, Munich 1982
K. Christ, *Römische Geschichte und Wissenschaftsgeschichte*, 3 vols., Darmstadt 1982–83
P. Kristeller, *The Classics and Renaissance Thought*, Cambridge 1955
J. J. Norwich (ed.), *The Italian World*, London 1983
H. T. Parker, *The Cult of Antiquity and the French Revolutionaries*, Chicago 1937
E. T. Salmon, *The Nemesis of Empire*, Oxford 1974
J. Seznec, *The Survival of the Pagan Gods*, New York 1953
R. Weiss, *The Renaissance Discovery of Classical Antiquity*, Oxford 1969

INDEX

Ablabius, 187
Accius, Lucius, 134
Achaean League, 36
Achaia, 57, 191
Achilleïs, 142
Actium, battle of, 48, 138–9
adoptive emperors, 54, 66, 146
Adrianople, battle of, 178, 230–2
aedile, 28, 73, 114
Aegyptus, see Egypt
Aeneas, 5, 151
Aeneid, 138
Africa, 68, 182, 191; proconsularis, 194
Africa, 57,88, 91, 224; Church of, 202; North, 34,
    41, 72, 74, 80, 86, 88, 90, 93, 153, 182, 192,
    197, 212, 219, 226, 232
African writers, 146, 215
Africanus, Sextus Iulius, 218
ager publicus, 39, 41, 238; see also land
ager Romanus, 17
agrarian measures, 38–9, 123
Agricola (Tacitus), 137
agriculture, 43, 44, 81, 91, 95, 141, 159, 187
Agrippa, Marcus Vipsanius, 117, 139–41, 253
Agrippina, Julia (the Younger), 52, 66, 71, 143
Agrippina, Vipsania (the Elder), 65
Alamanni, 171
Alans, 171, 232
Alaric, 230
Alba Longa, 5–6
Alexander the Great, 50, 59, 142, 204
Alexandria, 86, 89, 116, 166, 205, 214, 217
alimentatio, 78, 92, 169, 206, 253
Allia, river, 16
allies, 1, 17–22, 38, 41–2, 65, 85; see also foederati;
    socii
Alps, 57, 86
altar(s), 151, 163–4, 227; see also Ara Pacis
    Augustae; arae Flaviae; Victory altar
Alyscamps, Les, 229
Ambrose, Bishop of Milan, 179, 205, 220–2, 224
Ammianus Marcellinus, 210, 216
Ammonios Saccas, 216
amphitheatre, 73, 94, 111–14, 116–17, 251; see
    also Colosseum
Anastasius I, 189
ancestors, 24, 64, 151, 251
Ancus Martius, 6
Androcles, 108

annalists, 24, 135
annona, 59, 182
Anthony, St, 206
Antioch, 86, 116, 153, 166, 186, 194, 196, 205,
    208–9, 214, 219
Antiochenus, Ioannes, 214
Antiochus III, 35
Antiochus IV, 36
Antiochus II of Commagene, 127
Antonine emperors, 66, 101, 228
Antoninus Pius, 54, 62, 68, 81, 156, 173
Antony, Mark (Marcus Antonius), 48–51, 55,
    59, 139, 141
Apicius, Marcus Gavius, 109
Apocolocyntosis, 83, 143
Apollinaris Sidonius, Gaius Sollius, 208–9
Apollo, 139–40, 163, 200
Apollodorus of Damascus, 149
Apollonius Rhodius, 142
Apologeticus, 220; see also Tertullian
Appian, 135, 146
Appian Way, 99, 227
Apuleius, 146
Aquitania, 67, 94, 223, 232
Arabia, 54, 60, 90, 94
Arabs, 64, 113, 139, 169, 176
arae Flaviae, 163
Ara Pacis Augustae, 62, 150–1, 154, 247,
    253
Arcadius, Flavius, 210
arch(es), 105, 147, 201, 227
archaeology, 5–9, 90, 178, 194
archaic Rome, 3, 9–12
Architectura, De, 141
architecture, 51, 88, 95–6, 147, 151
Arezzo, 90, 93
Arians, 203–5, 232
Ariovistus, 42
Aristides, Aelius, 88, 135, 146, 210
aristocracy, 9–11, 25, 27, 29, 41, 97, 107, 127,
    134, 136, 151, 154, 160, 194, 216
aristocrat(ic), 45–6, 69, 72, 97–8, 223
Aristonicus, 45
Aristotle, 157
Arius, 202–4
Arles, 116, 183, 202
Arminius, 72
arms and armour, 32, 115–16, 155, 158, 180, 184,
    202, 253, 255

army, 10, 29, 32, 39, 55, 57, 63, 65, 74, 90, 123,
    157, 159, 169, 176–8, 181, 184, 187, 190, 196,
    198
Arrian, 146
art, 43, 90, 105, 132, 144, 147–54, 156, 178,
    180–1, 199, 230–2, 234
artisan, 11–12, 23, 44, 95, 98–9, 154
Arval brotherhood, 158
Asclepius, 163
Asia, 36, 57, 68, 170, 191
Asia Minor, 35–6, 42, 64, 86, 92, 103, 166, 170,
    182, 206, 208, 229
assembly, 6, 10, 13, 26–32, 38, 74, 86, 126–7,
    147, 159; see also comitia
astrology, 160, 164
Ateius, workshop of, 253
Atellana, 117, 134
Athanasius, 202, 204, 206
Athaulf, king, 232
Athens, 21, 42, 103, 219
Augst Treasure, 229
augur(y), 68, 72, 160
Augusta, 66, 185
augustales, 79, 162–3
Augustan age, 49, 138
Augustine (Aurelius Augustinus), Bishop of
    Hippo, 9, 212–14, 217, 219–20, 224–5
Augustus, Gaius Julius Caesar Octavianus, 3, 9,
    45, 48–50, 162, 237, 254
Aula Palatina (Trier), 226
Aurelian(us), Lucius Domitius, 171, 175, 201
Aurelius Antoninus, Marcus, 55, 68, 74, 80,
    146, 150–1, 156, 168
Aurelius Victor, Sextus, 211
Ausonius, Decimus Magnus, 216, 223
auxiliary troops, 1, 70, 82–3, 85, 90, 177, 181,
    187
Aventine, 6, 106, 111, 228

Bacaudae, 179, 197
Bacchanalian conspiracy, 160
Baetica, 57, 88, 91
baker(s), 93, 98, 108, 196
Balbus, theatre of, 117
Balkans, 86, 174, 182, 200
banker(s), banking, 29, 72, 94
barbarian(s), 63, 178, 193, 195, 197, 199, 253
Barcids, 35
Bar Kochba, 54, 165
Barletta 'colossus', 229, 252
basilica(e), 147, 150, 209, 231–2, 245
Basil of Caesarea, 208, 219
baths, 96, 98, 104, 106, 113, 117–18, 120, 157,
    228
Benedict of Nursia, St, 206
Beneventum, 92, 150, 253
Berber(s), 174, 202; see also Macrinus
Berytos, -us, 116, 131
Bethlehem, 185, 224
Bible, 217, 224–5
bishop(s), 204–6, 208, 220–1, 227
Bithynia, 88, 210
Bithynia et Pontus, 57, 167
blood lust, 114, 116
Bossuet, J. B., 236
bread, 98, 108, 110
Brescia, 229

brick, 92–3, 106, 147, 155, 251
bridge(s), 104, 147, 150; see also Milvian Bridge
Britain, Britannia(e), 59–60, 86, 94, 153, 163,
    170–1, 179, 182, 240
British, Briton, 83, 86, 237
Brunt, P. A., 44, 79, 270
Brutus, Marcus Iunius, 47, 49, 252
Brutus Pera, Decimus Iunius, 114
buildings, 42, 46, 73, 89, 147, 150, 194, 226
bull(s), 113, 164, 252
Burckhardt, Jacob, 54, 118, 150, 168, 179, 188,
    237
bureaucracy, 21, 28, 170, 177, 190, 193
Burgundy, kingdom of, 232
Burrus, Sextus Afranius, 52, 71
butcher(s), 95, 99, 156
Byzantine, 176, 188, 204, 214, 229, 237
Byzantium, 131, 176, 188; see also
    Constantinople

Caecilian(us), Bishop of Carthage, 202, 204
Caecillus, 220
Caecilius Statius, 134
Caere, 18
Caesar, Gaius, 150, 253
Caesar, Gaius Iulius, 9, 28, 45–6, 48–9, 51–2, 60,
    74, 82, 87, 99–100, 102, 111, 113–14, 116, 137,
    139, 142, 156, 161, 163, 165, 179–80, 200,
    238–40
Caesar, Lucius, 150
Caesar(es), 184, 187, 237
calendar, 46, 133
'Caligula' (Gaius Iulius Caesar Germanicus), 52,
    101, 119
Campania, 109, 114, 153, 216
Cannae, battle of, 34
capite censi, 31, 39
Capito, Gaius Ateius, 130
Capitol, 7, 158, 188
Capitoline Hill, 139
Cappadocia, 219
Capri, 150
Capua, 34, 115, 155
'Caracalla' (Aurelius Antonius, Marcus), 119,
    170, 172, 174
Caracalla, Baths of, 117, 226, 253
career, 103; equestrian, 71; military, 75; of
    office, 67; see also cursus honorum
Carnuntum, 164
Carthage, 23, 33–5, 37, 44, 86, 92, 202, 220, 224,
    232, 238
Cassius Longinus, Gaius, 47, 49
Cassius Vecellinus, Spurius, 14
catacombs, 119
Catalaunian Fields, battle of the, 232
Catholic Church, 202, 205, 221, 232
Catalina, Lucius Sergius, 42, 45
Cato 'Censorius', Marcus Portius, 24, 38, 93, 96,
    135–6, 145, 156, 236
Cato Uticensis, Marcus Portius, 142, 235
Catullus, Gaius Valerius, 137–8
cavalry, 10, 12, 29–31, 169, 255
Celsus, Aulus Cornelius, 155, 157; see also
    Origen, Ante Celsum
Celsus, Publius Iuventius, 130
Celts, 15–16, 22, 34, 36, 85, 141, 163
censor, 14 25–9, 53, 191

census, 28–9, 165, 183
centuria, 6, 10, 30–2, 75
ceramics, 93–4; *see also* pottery
Ceres (fertility goddess), 158
Chalcedon, Council of, 205
Chalcis, 224
Châlons, 232
chariot racing, 98, 111
chariot, war, 12, 115
children, 78, 99, 101–3; *see also* infant
Christ, Jesus, 165–6, 201–2, 205, 218–19, 230
Christian(ity), 53, 63, 76, 80, 114, 160, 164–8,
    174–5, 177–9, 187, 189, 192, 201, 205, 211–12,
    218–19, 222, 229, 237
Chrysippus, 108
Chrysostom, St John, 193, 219
Church, churches, 196–7, 202–7, 218, 272, 228
Cicero, Marcus Tullius, 24, 37, 59, 69, 95–6, 103,
    128, 130, 136, 141, 216, 221, 224
Cilicia, 57, 67, 89, 113
Cincinnatus, Lucius Quinctius, 16
Cinna, Lucius Cornelius, 42, 45
Circumcelliones, 197, 203
circus(es), 53, 104, 110–11, 160, 227
Circus Maximus, 111, 113, 117
citizen, Roman, 2, 65, 74–5, 77, 79, 118, 122
citizenship, Latin, 18, 65, 82
citizenship, Roman, 1, 16–20, 29–30, 46, 65,
    82–3, 131, 172; *see also Constitutio Antoniniana*
city, 9, 65, 73–5, 77–9, 82–3, 85–9, 93, 97–8, 114,
    139, 170, 173, 196, 211; council, 13, 86, 189–90;
    prefect, 67, 127, 229
city-state, 9, 17, 21, 86; *see also polis*
civil war(s), 1, 42, 45–8, 53, 60, 63, 83, 161, 170
classical antiquity, 240; education, 179, 210;
    literature, 219; texts, 103, 178
classicism, 152, 208
classis, 30–1, 63
Claudian (Claudius Claudianus), 214–15
Claudius Caecus, Appius, 14
Claudius Nero Germanicus, Tiberius, 52, 60,
    71, 78, 83, 86, 92, 110, 116, 126–7, 136, 143,
    156, 166
Claudius II Gothicus, Marcus Aurelius, 175
Clemens, Titus Flavius (of Alexandria), 217
Cleopatra VII, Queen of Egypt, 50, 54, 59, 142;
    see also Antony, Mark
clergy, 194, 200, 204
client (*cliens*), *clientela*, 10, 12, 23, 41, 45–7, 49,
    50, 63–4, 76, 97, 99, 140, 159, 198
client kings, 64, 67, 127
cloaca maxima, 6, 105
Clodius Pulcher, Publius, 45
clothing, 106–8, 183
Codex Iustinianus, 121
Codex Theodosianus, 121
cognitio extraordinaria, 125–30
coins, coinage, 6, 51, 60, 64, 90, 154, 179, 183–5,
    187–8, 200, 202, 209, 228, 230, 250, 254
collegial(ity), 27, 53, 56
collegium, 2, 77, 184
Collina, regio, 9
Colline Tower, 145
Cologne, 94, 163
colonate, 80, 93, 172, 190, 197
coloni, colons, 92–3, 173, 181, 190, 193, 195,
    197–8

colonia(e), colonies, 19–22, 86–8, 102
colonisation, 1, 17–22, 46, 76, 131
Colosseum, 93, 111, 115, 149, 251
Colossus of Barletta, 229, 252
Columella, Lucius Iunius Moderatus, 91–2
comedy, 96, 117, 134, 208
comitia (assembly), 6, 30, 124
Commodus, Lucius Aelius Aurelius, 55, 114,
    119
compita, compitalia, 162
Comum (Como), 69, 72, 103
concilium, 162
Concord, Temple of, 150
concrete, 147, 155
consilium, 28, 123–7, 129; *principis*, 66, 128, 130
Constans, Emperor, 186, 207, 231
Constantine the Great (Flavius Valerius
    Constantinus), 3, 117, 174–5, 177, 181, 184–9,
    196, 208–9, 211, 214, 219, 231, 237, 254
Constantine II, 185, 189
Constantinople, 111, 153, 176, 188, 204–5, 208–
    10, 214, 219, 228, 232
Constantius Chlorus, Flavius Valerius, 179, 226
Constantius II, Flavius Iulius, 186, 189, 204, 207
Constitutio Antoniniana, 1, 82, 131, 172
constitution, 14, 15, 177
constitutiones, 126
consul, 14, 24–6, 28, 31, 46, 66–8, 122, 124, 130,
    191, 216, 229
consulate, 24, 28, 51, 53, 67, 71, 160
controversies, Christian, 177, 202–5
cook, cookery, 95, 99, 106, 109
Copts, 205
co-regent, 53, 55, 213
Corinth, 36, 116; canal, 53
Coriolanus, Gnaeus Marcius, 16
corn: procurement, 21; ration, 59; Sicilian, 23, 90
Corneille, 236
Corpus Iuris, 132
Corsica, 34, 182
Cos, 107, 157
craftsmen, 1, 78–9, 93–4, 196
craftwork, 76, 154, 195–6, 229
Crassus, Marcus Licinius, 46, 59
creed, 204–6
crime, 123
Crimea, 94
criminal(s), 76, 114, 125
criminal justice, 46, 124
Crisis of Empire, 2, 168, 172, 175, 199, 214
Crispus, 185–6, 211
crucifixion, 80
cult, 9, 73, 77, 87, 133–4, 164, 207
Cumae festival, 62
Cupid, 140; *Cupid and Psyche*, 147
curator, 67, 88, 144, 194
curia, 9–10, 30, 194
curiales, 72, 190, 194–5
currency, 90, 169, 182, 188, 270
cursus honorum, 42, 46, 66–8, 191
customs, 57, 70, 90
Cybele, 160, 164
Cyclades, 91, 139
Cyprian (Thaseius Cecilius Cyprianus), 220
Cyprus, 57
Cyrenaica, 36, 182
Cyrene, Edicts of, 126

Dacia(n), 54, 60, 86, 94, 171
Dalmatia, 57, 86, 88, 182
Damasus, Pope, 120, 206, 224
Danube, 53, 55, 64, 78, 86, 88, 170, 174, 179, 182, 231–2
dead, disposal of the, 77, 119–20, 144, 253–4
death, 119, 212; penalty, 123–5, 129; sentence, 13
debt, 13, 21, 43, 78, 122, 127; see also nexum
decemvir, 13, 121
Decius, Gaius Messius Quintus, 171, 174–5, 217
defensor plebis, 194
deification of ruler, 175
Delos, 44, 153
Delphi, 151
Demeter, 164
Demosthenes, 210
Dexippus, Publius Herennius, 214
diadem, 185, 230, 252
Diana (Latian goddess), 158
dictator(ship), 14, 27–8, 46, 51
Dio Cassius (Cassius Dio Cocceianus), 135, 210
Dio Chrysostom of Prusa (Dio Cocceianus), 135, 209–10
Diocletian(us), Gaius Aurelius Valerius, 3, 90, 117, 174–5, 177, 179, 181, 184, 186, 188, 200–1, 226
Diocletian, Baths of, 120
Diodorus Siculus, 5, 141
dioecesis (diocese), 182, 186–7, 189
Dionysius of Halicarnassus, 5, 31, 135
Dionysus, 160
Dioskurias 94
divorce, 100–1
doctors, 77, 97, 103, 115, 156, 157
dome, 147, 155, 226
Dominate (dominatus), 3, 180
Domitian(us), Titus Flavius, 53–4, 60, 87, 99, 113, 116–17, 137, 144, 150, 152, 166
Domus Aurea, 111, 150
domus principis, 52, 65–6, 74, 107, 145, 162, 199, 253
Domus Tiberiana, 150
donations, public, 73, 206
Donatists, Donatus, 202–4, 205, 225
Donatus, Aelius, 215
Doryphorus of Policlytus, 152
drainage, 6, 105, 147, 150, 157
Drepanius, 209
Drusus, Marcus Livius, 41
Duncan-Jones, R., 69
duumvir, 73
Dyophysites, 205

Ebro, treaty of, 34
economy, 29; barter, 176, 190; managed, 172; money, 23, 42; subsistence, 11
edictum perpetuum, 121, 123, 130
education, 101–4, 134, 210, 215–16; see also schools
Egypt (Aegyptus), 21, 36, 42, 50, 57, 71, 94, 139, 165–6, 179, 182, 185, 198, 206, 216
Elagabalus, Varius Avitus, 211
elections, 42, 87
Eleusinian Mysteries, 207
Emesa, 170
emperor(s), 171, 199, 201, 203, 212, 230; cult (worship), 54, 63, 79, 161–3, 166, 228;

portraits, 228, 245, 252; stories, 137; see also adoptive emperors; Antonine emperors; Flavian emperors; Gracchi; Severan emperors; Soldier Emperors
Engels, Friedrich, 198
Ennius, Quintus, 103, 134
entrails, scrutiny of, 159, 207, 246, 252; see also haruspex
Ephesus, 166
epic, 141–5, 208, 214, 223
Epictetus, 135
Epicurus, 138
Epigrams, see Martial
Epirus, 16, 36, 44
eques, equites (knight), 29, 31, 42–4, 46, 57, 64, 66, 70–2, 75, 78, 87, 108, 124, 127, 140, 163, 173, 193
equestrian order, 70, 72, 181–2
equus publicus, 71, 107
Esquiline, 7, 69, 77, 119
Essenes, 165
Ethiopia, 113
Etruria, 39, 114
Etruscan(s), 5–9, 15, 32, 36, 134, 147, 158
Eugenius Flavus, 177, 207
Eunapius of Sardis, 214
Euripides, 108
Eusebius of Caesarea, 185, 209, 218
Eutropius, 211
Evagrius Scholasticus, 218
execution, 75, 123, 129, 251
exempla, 142, 178, 235
exports, Roman, 94
extortion, 43; see also repetundae

Fabius Pictor, Quintus, 135–6
familia, 9–10, 23, 30, 43, 99–100, 159; see also pater familias
familia Caesaris, 79, 172
family, 65, 97, 101, 119, 158
famine, 197
farm(er), farming, 1, 11–12, 23, 39, 78, 80, 92–3, 195, 198; see also coloni; landowner; latifundia; villa farming
Fausta, Empress, 185
Fayûm, 92
festival(s), 28, 73, 134; see also Cumae festival
feudal system, 190, 198
fides, 11, 37, 50, 128, 159
finance, 26, 58, 87, 186
Finley, M. I., 90
fire, 106; brigade, 77; of Rome, 166
Flaccus, Valerius, 142
Flaminius, Gaius, 24
Flaminius, Titus Quinctius, 35, 38, 114
Flavian emperors, 53, 88, 101, 142, 144, 251
Flavian Amphitheatre (Colosseum), 111, 113
fleet, 33, 138
foederati, 195, 231; see also allies; socii
food, 108–10; supply, 47, 62, 73, 76–7, 192
fortification, 147, 171, 226, 231
formulae, law, 122–3, 126, 133, 156
Fortuna, 158
fortunes, private, 42, 68–9
Forum (forum), 7, 97, 103–4, 106, 109, 147, 150, 180, 188, 201, 227, 229, 252
foundation myth, 5–9

Franks, 171
Frederick the Great, 237
freedmen, 42, 45, 52, 57, 64–6, 69, 72, 74, 78–80, 87, 93, 97, 118–19, 141, 144, 162–3, 195
freedwomen, 103
freight, sea, see Lex Claudia
French Revolution, 236
Friedberg, 164
Frigidus, battle of the, 207
frontier (limes), 41–2, 54, 83, 170, 174, 177, 181, 184, 211, 226, 231
Frontinus, Sextus, Julius, 144
Fronto, Marcus Cornelius, 146
Fucine Lake, 116
Fulvius Nobilior, Marcus, 113
funeral orations, 24, 134; see also dead
Furies, 139

Gainas, 232
Gaiseric, 230
Gaius (jurist), 130, 172
Galatia(ns), 35, 88
Galen, 80, 97, 146, 155–7
Galerius Valerius Maximianus, Gaius, 177, 179, 200–1
Galla Placidia, 228
Gallia, Gaul, 42, 46–7, 55, 57, 62, 64, 86, 90–4, 113, 170–1, 179, 182, 192, 197, 200, 212, 215–16, 232
Gallienus, Publius Licinius Egnatius Augustus, 174–5, 181, 208, 216
Gallus, Gaius Cornelius, 127
games, public, 28, 42, 51, 65, 73–4, 87, 98, 106, 110–11, 114–15, 118, 159–60, 162, 194, 212, 220
games, secular, 160–1
Gellius, Aulus, 108–10, 146
Gemma Augustea (Vienna), 153
gens, 9–11, 51, 107, 134, 136, 159
Geography (Strabo), 141
Georgics (Virgil), 138
German(s), 42, 55, 163, 169, 176–9, 187, 198, 212
Germania, Germany, 59–60, 85, 120, 142, 157, 163, 212
Germanic, 131, 170–1, 176–7, 181, 191, 198–9, 231
Germanicus Julius Caesar, 65
Geta, 130, 174
Gibbon, Edward, 76, 178, 239
girls, 100, 103
Gjerstad, E., 7
gladiators, 55, 102, 110–11, 114–17, 253
glass, 90, 93–4, 154–5
God, 185, 197, 203, 212–13, 219, 225
gods, goddesses, 10, 52, 59, 110, 139, 158–61, 163–4, 218, 235, 252
Goethe, Johann Wolfgang, 120
gold, 71, 115, 143, 196, 229
'Golden House' of Nero, 111, 150
Gordian III, 216
Goths, 171, 214, 228; see also Ostrogoths; Visigoths
governor, 43, 56, 67, 80, 85, 87, 123, 162, 165, 167, 181–2, 187, 191, 199, 223
Gracchus, Gaius Sempronius, 43, 124
Gracchus, Tiberius Sempronius, 39
Gracchi, the, 25, 39, 45–6, 102, 123
Graecia, Magna, 23
grain, 43, 58, 67, 89, 93, 189

grammarians, 96, 103, 215
graves, 7, 114, 119
Great Mother, see Cybele
Greece, 5, 21, 32, 35, 42, 64, 77, 86, 88, 135, 153, 170, 182, 229, 238, 253
Greek, 35–6, 59, 77, 79, 83, 85, 96, 99, 102–3, 107, 116, 129, 133–5, 146–7, 150, 152, 157, 159, 163, 210, 214, 216–17, 221, 224, 253
Greek East, 90, 163, 209, 219, 221, 224
Greek freedom, declaration of, 53
Greeks and Jews, 89
Gregory of Nazianzus, 197, 208, 219
Gregory of Nyssa, 204, 219
Gregory the Great, Pope, 208

Hadrian(us), Publius Aelius, 54, 62, 66, 87–8, 107, 121, 123, 130, 146, 150, 152, 156, 167, 210
Hagia Irene, Church of, 189
Hagia Sophia, Church of, 189
Hamilcar Barca, 33, 35
handicrafts, 43, 90, 93, 150
Hannibal, 25, 34–6, 145
harbours, 57, 59, 94, 150
haruspex, 72, 246, 252
Hasdrubal, 35
heating, domestic, 106, 155
Heddernheim, 164
Hegel, G. W. F., 241
Helena, Empress, 185–6
Heliopolis, 226
Hellenism, -istic, 35–6, 52, 54, 85–6, 89, 103, 128, 131, 137, 152–4, 163, 185, 207, 238
helmets, 116, 202, 248, 253
Heraclius, Emperor, 176
Herakles, Hercules, 54, 164, 180, 200
Herculaneum, 104, 152, 243, 251
Herculius, 179
Herder, J. H., 17, 237
Herennius Modestinus, 131
heresies, 177, 222
hermit(s), 179, 194–5, 206, 224
Herodes Atticus, 146
Herodian of Syria, 210
Hijra, 176
Hilary of Poitiers, 220
Hildesheim Silver Hoard, 154
Hippocrates (of Cos), 157
Hispaniae, 35, 182
Historia Augusta, 146, 211
historians, 5, 49, 135–8, 194, 210–14, 218
Hoffmann, W., 36
Holy Land, 185
Holy Roman Empire, 236
homo novus, 24, 64, 191
honestiores, 63, 129, 190, 195
Honorius, Flavius, 215, 228, 230
honos, 37, 118, 159
Horace (Quintus Horatius Flaccus), 62, 138, 140–2, 161, 251
horse(s), 12, 29, 96, 102, 111, 255
house, housing, 69, 104–6, 251
household, 57, 65, 71, 102, 158
humiliores, 63, 129, 195
Huns, 176, 178, 195, 231–2
hunting, 96, 227
husband(s), 99, 145
hymns, 178, 222

Ides of March, 47
Illyria, *Illyricum*, 174, 197–8
immunitas, 87, 89
imperium, 10, 33, 41, 51, 53–4, 126, 252;
    Galliarum, 226; *Romanum*, 1, 3, 18, 21, 38, 50,
    54–5, 56–60, 62–94, 135, 175, 177, 237, 252
impoverishment, 190, 195
Inchtuthil, Scotland, 157
India, 94, 139, 216
Indo-European origins, 8, 9
infant exposure, 100; mortality, 102, 119
infantry, 10, 30–1
inflation, 169, 182
inscriptions, 24, 76, 78, 98, 101–2, 119–10, 158,
    183, 194, 201, 251
insulae, 104, 106, 109
intercessio, 15, 27, 127
invasions, 169–71, 178, 195–6, 231; *see also*
    migration of peoples
Iranian civilisation, 164, 170
irrigation, 90
Isis, 139, 147, 164
Italia, Italy, 2, 17, 21, 23, 33–4, 39, 47, 86, 91–2,
    106, 120, 139, 154, 170, 182, 192, 232; invasion
    of, 171, 176; northern, 64; southern, 238
Italian, 38–9, 41, 51, 53, 64, 72, 92, 158, 163, 236
Italic, 134, 147
iudex, iudices, 181, 184
Iulianus, Publius Salvius, 123, 130
Iulius Africanus, Sextus, 218
Iulus (founder of Alba Longa), 5
ius, 128; *civile*, 121, 130; *honorarium*, 123;
    Italicum, 87; *Latii*, 18; *Latium maius*, 87; *publice
    respondendi*, 130
ivory, 154, 178, 230, 252

Janus, Temple of, 60
Jerome, St (Eusebius Hieronymus), 218, 220,
    224
Jerusalem, 166, 218
Jesus Christ, *see* Christ
jewels, 107, 154, 230
Jewry, Jews, 54, 60, 89, 165, 218
John the Baptist, 223–4
Jones, A. H. M., 85
Jove (*Iovius*), 179
Judaea, *Iudaea*, 57, 67, 165–6
judge(s), 98, 125, 197
Jugurthine War, 41
Julia, daughter of Augustus, 101, 253
Julia, daughter of Caesar, 100
Julia Domna, 170
Julianus, Flavius Claudius ('Julian the
    Apostate'), 177, 179, 189, 207–8, 210, 229, 231
Juno, 158
Jupiter, 158, 180, 252
Justinian(us) I, Flavius Petrus Sabbatius, 3, 131,
    176, 189, 208, 214, 228
Juvenal (Decimus Iunius Ivenalis), 77, 94, 98,
    145–6, 216
jurisprudence, 123, 127, 129, 132
justice, 13, 46, 67, 73, 121, 125, 127
Africanus, Sextus Julius, 218

Kaser, Max, 132
kings (of Rome), 2, 5–10
koinon, 162

Labeo, Marcus Antistius, 130
Lactantius, 211
ladies, 65, 99, 102, 107
La Graufesenque, 90
Lambaesis, 116
land, 13, 38, 91–2, 95, 190, 199; *see also ager*
landowner(s), 39, 43, 70, 72, 80, 91–2, 173, 193,
    195–6, 198, 202, 212, 232
land settlement, 77
land tax, 192
land workers, 78, 183, 195
Langobardi, 176
Late Antiquity, 2–4, 63, 111, 118, 121, 123, 131,
    137, 152, 165, 169–234, 252, 254
La Tène civilisation, 85
Lateran, St John, 227
latifundia, 39, 78, 91, 171–3, 197
Latin, 6, 15–22, 92, 96, 103, 135, 141–2, 163,
    211–12, 214, 219
Latium, 5–6, 15, 18, 39, 87, 91, 147, 158, 192; *see
    also ius*
law, 68, 102–3, 121–32, 178–9, 217
legacy, -ies, 69, 97–8, 125, 206
legatus, legate, 50, 56–7, 67, 88
leges, lex, 30, 86–7, 122; *de ambitu*, 26; *annales*,
    25–6; *Claudia de nave senatorum*, 29; *Hortensia*,
    13, 15; *de imperio*, 126; *de imperio Vespasiani*, 53;
    Iuliae, 126; *Liciniae-Sextiae*, 14, 24; *Manciana*,
    93; *Poetelia Papiria de nexis*, 13–14, 122;
    reddendorum equorum, 29; *Sempronia iudiciaria*,
    124; *sumptuariae*, 25; *tabellariae*, 12; *venalium
    vendendorum*, 129
legion(s), 19, 32, 53, 57, 67, 157, 173, 181, 200
legionary, -ies, 32, 41, 75, 85
Lentulus Gaetulicus, Gnaeus Cornelius, 68
Leo I, Pope, 192
Leo the Great, Pope, 206
Lepidus, Marcus Aemilius, 49, 161
Leptis Magna, 226, 228
Lérins, 206, 212
lex, see leges
Libanios, 209–10
libertas, 47, 159
Libya, 208
Licinius, Valerius Licinianus, 136, 187–8, 200,
    203
life expectancy, 119
Liguria, 163, 221
limes, 83, 164; *see also* frontier
literacy, 104
literature, 51, 60, 103, 133–47, 178, 208–25
liturgy, 164, 206–7
Livia, wife of Augustus, 65, 71, 253
Livy (Titus Livius), 5, 11, 31, 121, 136, 141, 159,
    235–6
Livius Andronicus, Lucius, 134
logos, 185, 203, 205
London (*Londinium*), 183
love, 98, 140–1, 143–4, 158, 225
love-making, 118
Lucan(us), Marcus Annaeus, 142
Lucania, 39
Lucceius Peculiaris, 155
Lucian, 146
Lucilius, Gaius, 137
Lucretia, 6
Lucretius Carus, Titus, 137

ludi: litterarii, 103; *Romani*, 134; *scaenici*, 134
Lugdunum (Lyons), 94, 162, 183
Luke, St, 165–6, 168
Lusitania, 35, 57
luxury, *luxus*, 25, 38, 43, 90, 108, 121, 144, 146, 150, 184

Macedon(ia), 34–6, 57
Machiavelli, 236
MacMullen, Ramsay, 69, 93
Macrinus, Marcus Opellius, 174
Macrobius, Ambrosius Theodosius, 217
Maecenas, Gaius, 140
magic, 77, 156,207
magister, 28, 180, 186–7, 191
magistracy, 26–9, 56, 74, 216
magistrate, *magistratus*, 10, 13–14, 25, 41, 50, 80, 98, 115, 123, 125, 252
maiestas, 5, 19, 124, 127
Mainz, 174, 232, 253
Mamertines, 33, 37
Malalas, Ioannes, 214
Mani, 224
Manichaeans, 200
Manilius, Manius, 129
Manlius Capitolinus, Marcus, 14
manuscripts, 200, 230
marble, 92, 133, 147, 251, 254
Marcellus, theatre of, 117
Marcian(us), Aelius, 229
Marcian, Emperor, 229, 252
Marciana, Ulpia, 66
Maria (Stilicho), 230
Marius, Gaius, 24, 41–2, 45, 47
Marius Maximus, 211
markets, 28, 73, 90, 147
Marmoutiers, 206
marriage, 100
Mars, 5, 139, 158, 163, 200
Marseilles (*Massilia*), 206, 212
Marsi, 41
Martial(is), Marcus Valerius, 96–8, 100–1, 113, 118, 144–5
Martianus Capella, 215
Martin, St 206
martyrs, 168, 200, 227
Marxist theory, 38, 198
Massinissa, Numidian king, 34
Matthew, St, 168
Mauretania Caesariensis, 182
Mauretania Tingitana, 182
mausoleums, 189, 228
Maxentius, Marcus Aurelius Valerius Augustus, 177, 200–1, 227
Maximianus, Marcus Aurelius Valerius, 179
Maximinus Daia, Gaius Galerius Valerius Augustus, 177
Maximinus Thrax, Gaius Iulius Verus, 174
maximum prices edict, 90, 183, 200
meals, 99, 108–9
Mecca, 176
medical appliances, 156, 249, 254
medicine 95, 144, 154, 156–7; *see also* doctors
Medina, 176
Mediterranean, 33, 35, 42, 93, 121
Melania, 192, 195
Melinno, 135

Melpomene, 140
mercator, merchant(s), 1, 29, 72, 79, 94, 187
Mercury, 158
Messalina, 66
Messana (Messina), 33
Metamorphoses (Ovid), 141
Middle Ages, 137, 141, 155, 176, 183, 206, 218, 223–4
migration of peoples, the, 3, 171, 176, 209, 211, 231
Milan, 180, 189, 205, 214, 221, 228
military: career, 172; command, 67; diplomas, 87; doctors, 157; garrison, 64, 80; hospitals, 157; monarchy, 169; officers, 74, 173; organisation, 10, 30–2, 39; pursuits, 102; reforms, 41; reorganisation, 179–82; service, 39, 76, 86, 181; tactics, 144
Milvian Bridge, battle of the, 201
Minerva, 139, 158
mints, 67, 183, 202, 254
Minucius Felix, Marcus, 220
Mithridates VI, 42
Mithras, 164–5
Mitteis, L., 131
Modestius, Herennius, 134
Moesia(e), 86, 182
Mohammed, 176
Momigliano, A., 304
Mommsen, Theodor, 3, 5, 15, 27, 92–3, 237, 239
monarchies, Hellenistic, 52–3, 85
monarchy, 6, 12, 27, 185
monasteries, 179, 206, 219, 223
Monica, St, 224
monks, 179, 195, 206, 219
Monophysites, 205
monotheism, 164–5
Montanists, 168
Monte Cassino, 206
Montesquieu, C. L. de S., 236
Montmaurin, 92
monuments, 98, 135, 151, 180, 208, 252
mores maiorum, 25, 59, 136
Morocco, 182
mosaics, 147, 150, 153, 178, 196, 227–8, 248, 253
Moscow, 237
municipium, municipality, 41, 86–8, 102
municipal aristocracy, 64, 70, 74, 175; overloading of, 169; *see also curiales; munera*
munus, munera, 73, 114, 117, 190
murder, 114, 116, 122, 124
Muses, 223
museums, 118
Mylae, 33
'Mystery frieze', 153; *see also* Pompeii
mystery religions, 164–5
mythology, 25, 134, 143, 152–3, 214–15

Naevius, Gnaeus, 134
Namatianus, Rutilius Claudius, 215
Napoleon, 37
Naples, 254
Narbonensis (Narbonne), 86, 88, 92, 141, 163
Narcissus, 68
Natural History (*Naturalis Historia*), 144, 155; *see also* Pliny the Elder
Neoplatonism, 208, 217, 224
Neptune, 139, 158

Nero Claudius Caesar, 52–3, 62, 71, 78, 83, 91, 101, 111–12, 115, 119, 142–3, 150, 152, 166
Nerusius Mithres, Lucius, 76
Nerva, Marcus Cocceius, 54, 74, 144, 211
Nestorian, 205
Neuss, Germany, 157
nexum, 13, 122; *see also lex Poetelia*
Nicaea, 88, 203–4, 210
Nicomachus Flavianus, Virius, 215
Nicomedia, 162, 180, 226
Niebuhr, B. G., 5, 239
Nile, river, 139, 145, 168
nimbus, 180, 185, 188, 254
Nîmes (Nemausus), 94, 116
Nobilior, Marcus Fulvius, 113
nobles (*nobiles*), nobility, 14, 16, 23–5, 28–9, 21–2, 39, 49, 70, 101, 107, 118, 159
Noctes Atticae, 146
Noricum, 80, 182
Numantia, 35
Numerian(us), Marcus Aurelius, 211
Numidia, 35, 41, 202, 224

occupations, 95, 98; women's, 102; tied, 172, 187, 196
Octavia (Seneca), 143
Octavian, Octavius, *see* Augustus
Octavius (Minucius Felix), 220
Odoacer, 230
Odyssey, 134
officers, 32, 57, 172
officiales, officials, 118, 193, 197
oikoumene, 59; *see also* world
oil, 90, 94, 118, 142; lamps, 96
Olympia, 111
Olympic Games, 207
omens, 72, 158–9
Optatianus Porfyrius, Publilius, 214
optimates, 38, 45, 63; *see also* aristocrats
optimus princeps, 54, 66, 252; *see also* Trajan
Orders, Struggle of the, 3, 11–15, 23, 26, 41, 43, 63, 121–2
ordo, ordines, 29, 63–4, 72–5, 79, 89, 163
Orestes, Marcus Ulpius, 252
Oriens, 182
Origen, Adamantius, 217
Origines (Cato the Censor), 135
oratory, 103, 136, 141, 144
ornamenta, 71, 78, 79
Orontes, 215
Orosius, Paulus, 211–12
Ostia, 6, 19, 106, 153, 164, 220
Ostrogoths, 111, 232
Otho, Marcus Salvius, 101
Ovid (Publius Ovidius Naso), 101, 138, 140–1

Pachomius, 206
Pacuvius, Marcus, 134
pagan, 63, 136, 175, 177–9, 192, 199–200, 202, 205–8, 210, 214–15, 216–17, 222–3, 228–9
painting, 98, 105, 152, 196, 229
Palatine, 7–9, 111, 150, 187
Palestine, 197; *see also* Jewry
Palladius, Rutilius Taurus Aemilianus, 198
Pallas, 78
Pallio, De, 220; *see also* Tertullian
Palmyra, 171, 226

palaces, 113, 180, 226–7
panegyric, 63, 135, 144, 218
Panegyricus, 146, 209; *see also* Pliny the Younger
panem et circenses, 74, 110
Pannonia(e), 182
papacy, 206
Papinianus, Aemilius, 130
Paris Cameo, 153, 230
Parthia(ns), 54–5, 59–60, 145, 150, 169–70
pater familias, 10, 97, 100, 156, 159, 162
patricians (*patricii*), patriciate, 9–16, 24, 30, 63, 67–8, 107, 122, 145
patron(*us*), 10–12, 14, 63, 71, 76, 93, 97, 134, 159
Paul, St, 81, 166
Paulinus of Nola (Meropius Pontius Paulinus), 223
Paullus, Lucius Aemilius, 151
Paulus, Iulius, 130
Pausanias, 135, 146
Pax (goddess), 62
pax: *Americana*, 237; *Augusta*, 60, 62–3; *deum*, 62, 159; *Romana*, 60, 239
Pelagians, 225
penal system, 125–6
Pergamum, 35–6, 80, 116, 162
periods (of Roman history), 2–4, 175–6, 230
Perseus, king of Macedon, 36
Persian(s), 116, 216, 224
Persius Flaccus, Aulus, 142–3
Petronius Arbiter, Gaius, 78, 98, 109, 142, 144
Peter, St, 205
Pharisees, 165
Pharsalia (Lucan), 142
Philippi, 48
Philippus (Arabus), Iulius Verus, 174
Philip V, king of Macedon, 34–5
philosophers, 207, 220, 224, 229
philosophy, 103, 135, 141, 143, 154, 160, 178, 208, 216–17, 221, 238
Phrygia, 160; *see also* Sabazius
Piazza Armerina, 227
pietas, 10, 51, 159
pirates, 42, 94
Pisidia, 88
Piso, Gaius Calpurnius; *see next entry*
Pisonian conspiracy, 143
Plato, 210, 216–17
Plautus, Titus Maccius, 134
plebei, plebeian, 10–17, 24, 63, 122, 190
plebs, 10, 12–15, 43, 47, 64, 74–7, 158, 163, 196–7
Pliny the Elder (Gaius Plinius Secundus), 80, 91, 94, 98, 144, 154–5, 157–8
Pliny the Younger (Gaius Plinius Caecilius Secundus), 69, 88, 96–7, 103, 146, 166–7, 208–9
Plotina, wife of Trajan, 66
Plotinus, 216–17
Plutarch (Mestrius Plutarchus), 135, 146, 211, 236
poetry, 54, 96, 135, 137–41, 178, 219
Pola, theatre of, 116
police, 73, 123, 177
polis, poleis, 21, 86; *see also* city-state
Pollio, Gaius Asinius, 136
Polybius, 35–7, 135, 236
Polyclitus, 152
Pompeii, 104, 116, 152, 251
Pompeius Magnus Pius, Sextus, 45, 48–51, 60

Pompey (Gnaeus Pompeius Magnus), 41–2, 45–6, 56, 59, 100, 113, 117, 142, 147
Pomponius, Sextus, 130
pontifices, pontifex, 68, 122, 129, 135, 159–60
pontifex maximus, 161, 207
Pontius Pilate (Pilatus), 166–7
Pontus, 57, 167, 182
Popes, city of the, 237
Poppaea Sabina, 66
populares, 38, 45, 47, 63
population, 2, 44, 77, 79, 81, 85, 106, 270
Porphyrius (Porphyry), 216
Porta Nigra (Trier), 226
portraiture, 106, 151, 211, 228, 252
Posidonius, 135
pottery, 93, 154, 194; *see also* ceramics
poverty, 146, 190, 206, 234
praefectus: Aegypti, 71; *annonae*, 59, 71; *classis*, 71; *frumenti dandi*, 59; *Orientis*, 187; *praetorio*, 53, 71, 130–1, 182, 186, 191, 216, 221; *urbi*, 67, 81, 89, 127, 189, 191, 207, 210, 214, 224, 229
Praeneste, 18
praetor, 25, 28, 57–8, 67–8, 99, 123–4, 125, 128, 160, 191
Praetorian Guard, 52, 75, 123, 191
prefects, 19; *see also praefectus*
prices, *see* maximum prices edict
priest(ly), 68, 72, 159–61, 211, 227, 252; *see also pontifex*
Primaporta statue, 150
princeps, principes, 51–3, 54, 55–7, 58, 60, 62, 65–6, 68, 70–1, 73–4, 76, 79, 81, 91, 101, 110, 115, 118–19, 126–30, 136–9, 144–5, 151, 161–3, 166–7, 180, 194, 199
Principate, 2–3, 12, 39, 43, 45, 48, 50, 53, 55–6, 64, 76, 92–3, 97, 111, 117, 124–5, 136–7, 143, 150, 152, 161, 166, 178, 199, 209–10
Probus, Marcus Aurelius, 175
proconsul, 57, 162
Procopius, 214
procurator, 57, 70–1, 93, 101, 173
Propertius, Sextus, 140–1
prorogatio, 29, 50
prostitutes, 107
Provence, 64, 229
province, *provincia*, 26, 36, 41–7, 49–50, 55–7, 61, 68, 70, 72, 77, 85, 87, 90, 92, 102, 123, 150, 162, 181–8, 184, 252
provincial administration, 21, 46
provocatio, 13
Prudentius, Aurelius Clemens, 223
Psychomachia, 225
Ptolemies, 35–6
Ptolemy II, 41
Publilius Philo, Quintus, 14
Punic War(s), 23, 33, 123, 160; First, 19, 37; Second, 3, 28, 34–5, 39, 43, 82, 142, 147; Third, 34
Pydna, battle of, 151
Pylades, 111
Pyrrhus, king of Epirus, 16, 22, 33, 36

Quadi, 232
quaestio(nes), 124, 127–8, 130
quaestor, 28, 67, 73, 186, 191
Quintilian(us), Marcus Fabius, 144
Quirinal, 7, 9

Quirinius, Publius Sulpicius, 165

race, 63, 160
Radagaisus, 232
Raetia, 86, 182
Ranke, Leopold von, 8, 237
Ravenna, 153, 189, 228
recitation, 117
Regillus, battle of Lake, 16
relics, holy, 185, 189, 222
reliefs, 98, 120, 151–2, 228, 246, 252
religion, 6, 14, 63, 110, 133, 147, 157, 159, 161, 165, 180, 199, 206, 252
Remus, 5–6, 151
repetundae, 122, 124, 127
Republic, Roman, 1–3, 6, 15, 24, 27, 36, 38–48, 50, 56, 59, 103, 210
Res Gestae Divi Augusti, 52, 65, 136, 161
res publica, 24, 51, 63, 136
'revolution', Roman, 3, 38
Rhea Silvia, 5, 189
rhetoric, 103, 136, 142, 146, 220, 223
rhetorician, 77, 96, 156, 207, 219
Rhine, 64–5, 90, 170, 179, 182, 186, 231–2
Rhodes, 35, 103, 146
Rhône, river, 94, 215
roads, 67, 99, 147
Roma aeterna, 176, 214–15
Roma, goddess, 199
Roma and Augustus, temples for, 162
Romaioi, 176, 189
Romulus, 5–9, 151
Romulus Augustulus, 3, 230
Romulus (Maxentius), 227
Rostovtzeff, M. I., 39, 239
Rufinus, 218
Rufus, Quintus Curtius, 142; *see also* Alexander

Sabaeans, 113, 139
Sabazius, 164
Sabina, Vibia, 66
Sabines, 6, 39
sacrifice, 106, 114, 151, 158–9, 161–3, 167, 179, 207, 252
Sadducees, 165
Saguntum, 37
St Paul's Outside the Walls (Rome), 228
salary, 71, 91
Sallust(ius) Crispus, Gaius, 66, 136, 236
Salpensa, 87
Salvian(us), 199, 212
Samnite(s), 15–16, 36, 41, 115; wars, 24, 28, 32–4
Santa Maria Maggiore (Rome), 228
Sant' Apollinare Nuovo (Ravenna), 228
Saône, 94, 162
sarcophagus, 120, 151, 229
Sardinia, 34, 57, 182
Sardis, 214
Sarmatians, 113, 169, 171, 231
Sassanids, 170–1, 179
satire, 143, 145
Satiricon, 144
Saturn, 91, 158
Scaevola, Quintus Mucius, 130
Scaurus, Marcus Aemilius, 113
schools, 89, 102–3; *see also* education
Schweitzer, B., 151, 178, 230

science, 132, 154–7, 178, 208
Scipio Africanus Maior, Publius Cornelius, 25, 34–5, 38, 45, 238
scribes, 28, 183
Sejanus, Lucius Aelius, 66, 71
sculpture, 150, 196, 251–3, 255
sea, 94, 153, 158
Sebastopol, 94
Seleucids, 35
Senate, *Senatus*, 1, 9, 11, 25–30, 38–9, 42, 46, 50, 54–8, 60, 66–8, 70, 76, 78, 98, 117, 138, 142, 160, 170, 172, 188–92, 207, 209
senator(s), 24–5, 49, 57, 64, 67–9, 70, 73, 76, 87, 91–2, 97–8, 107, 127, 130, 136, 172, 181, 187, 189, 191–2, 244, 251
senatorial order, 66–70, 130, 172, 181, 192
Seneca, Lucius Annaeus, 52, 71, 83, 98, 116, 142–3, 150
Septimontium, 7
Sertorius, Quintus, 42
Servius, 216
Servius Tullius, king, 6
servus, 198; *see also* slaves
Severan emperors, 3, 106–7, 130, 169, 208, 210, 226
Severus, Lucius Septimius, 60, 125, 170, 174, 188, 226
Severus Alexander, Marcus Aurelius, 210
Shapur I (Sapor), 170
She-Wolf, 6, 254
shields, 115–16, 138, 155, 255
ships, 90, 93, 116, 155, 255
shops, 94, 98–9, 106
shopkeepers, 76, 78–9, 94, 98–9, 158, 183
Sibylline Books, 68, 161
Sicilia, Sicily, 23, 33, 37, 49, 57, 86, 88, 90, 92, 182, 192, 227
Sidonius, Gaius Sollius Apollinaris, 208
Silius Italicus, Tiberius Catius Asconius, 142
silk, 90, 106, 184
Silvanus Cocidius, 163
silver, 7, 23, 78, 154, 196, 229, 254
slaves, 11, 23, 38f., 43–5, 57, 64, 69, 76–81, 83, 87, 89, 91, 93, 100, 102–3, 105, 107, 110, 114, 125, 129, 144, 156, 158, 162, 164, 173, 190, 195–8, 238
smallholders, 23, 35, 41, 77, 93, 196–8
social mobility, 63–4, 79, 81–2, 118, 175, 193
social wars, 1, 18, 41
social welfare, 76, 194, 197, 209–10, 223
socii, 1, 18; *see also* allies; *foederati*
Socrates, 218
sol, 202; *invictus*, 200
Soldier Emperors, 130, 169, 171–2, 175, 180, 214, 228
soldiers, 4, 41, 75, 107, 164, 183
Somme, 92
Sozomenus, 218
Spain, 34–5, 37, 42, 55, 62, 64, 82, 83–5, 146, 182, 192, 197, 211, 223, 232
Spartacus, 45, 115
speeches, 96, 141, 209–10, 219
Split, 226
sport, 251; *see also* games
sportula (patronage), 45, 76, 97
Stalin, 198
Statius, Publius Papinius, 142

statues, 81, 151–2, 188, 227, 229, 244, 251–2, 254
status symbols, 74, 110, 132
Stilicho, Flavius, 209, 214, 230, 232
Stoicism, 54–5, 143, 157
story-telling, popular, 147
Strabo, 135, 141, 147
Strasbourg, 231
streets, 99, 102, 150–1, 243, 251
Suburana, regio, 9
Suetonius, Gaius Tranquillus, 46, 53, 137, 162, 211
Sulla Felix, Lucius Cornelius, 28, 41–2, 45–6, 50, 110, 124–5, 147, 152
Sulpicius Rufus, 130
Syme, Sir Ronald, 3, 239
Symmachus, Quintus Aurelius, 25, 178, 192, 207–9, 215–16, 221, 223
syncretism, 163–4
Synesius, 208–9, 217
Syracuse, 33–4
Syria(n), 37, 53, 55, 57, 64, 66, 86, 94, 153, 165–6, 169, 182, 198, 205, 210, 216, 226

Tacitus, Cornelius, 25, 49–50, 66, 68, 76, 101–3, 136–7, 162, 166, 210, 212
talion, 122
Tarraconensis, 57
taverns, 98–9, 146
tax, 56, 58, 70–1, 73, 87, 182–3, 187, 190–1, 194, 196–9; collector, 95, 197; exemption, 83; farmers, 42, 57–8
teacher, teaching, 78, 95, 101–3
Tellus, 151
temples, 69, 73, 89, 110, 143, 147, 150, 159, 162, 207
tenants, 27, 96; *see also coloni*
tenements, 104, 106
Terence (Publius Terentius Afer), 103, 134
terra sigillata, 154, 247, 253
Tertullian(us), Quintus Septimius Florens, 114, 168, 220
Tetrarchy, 180, 182, 184, 200–1, 208–9, 226
textiles, 183
Thasos, 150
theatres, 71, 73, 104, 117, 134
Themistius, 209–10
Theodoric, 209, 228, 232
Theodosius I, 184, 189, 204–5, 207–10, 221, 223, 229, 231–2
Theodosius II, 131, 189, 194
Theophrastus, 157
Thessalonica, 180, 221, 226
Thraciae, 182
Thracians, 113, 174
Thugga, 226
Tiber, river, 6, 43, 106, 156, 168
Tiberius Iulius Caesar Augustus, 52, 62, 65, 71, 81, 116, 147, 150, 166
Tibullus, Albius, 62, 140–1
Tibur, 18
Ticinum, 202
Titus Flavius Vespasianus, 53, 60, 114, 251
Tivoli, 150
toga, 83, 97, 106, 220, 229, 244, 251
toleration, edict of, 201
tombs, 76, 98, 122, 150–1
Totila, Ostrogoth king, 111

touto nika, 201
Toynbee, Arnold, 34
trade, 42, 76, 93–5, 99
tradition, the Roman, 5–9, 47, 118, 176–7, 199, 235, 237
Trajan (Marcus Ulpius Traianus), 54, 60, 66, 69, 88, 91–2, 97, 106, 113–14, 117, 144, 150–3, 167, 209, 252, 253
transport, 29, 42, 59, 90, 93, 123
tribus, 9, 30, 41
tribuni plebis, 12–15, 30, 51, 67, 122
Trier (Trèves), 94, 163, 180, 183, 186, 202, 212, 221, 226–7, 255
Trimalchio, 78, 109, 144
triumvir, 49, 123
Triumvirate, First, 46
Trogus, Pompeius, 141
Troy, 5, 142
Tullus Hostilius, 6
Tuscan(y), 96, 145
Twelve Tables, Law of the, 11, 13, 121–2, 128
Tyche, 189

Ulpian(us), Domitius, 127–8, 131
urbanisation, 46, 86–7
urns, 7, 249, 253–4
Urso, Spain, 87
U.S.A., 236
usurpations, 169–71, 180, 196; *see also* Soldier Emperors

Vaison-la-Romaine (*Vasio*), 71
Valens, Eastern Emperor, 178, 211, 230
Valentinian I, 184, 191, 194, 196, 231
Valentinian II, 205
Valentinian III, 194
Valerian(us), Publius Licinius, 136, 170, 174
Valerius Flaccus, 142
Valerius Maximus, 142
Vandals, 171, 212, 224, 230, 232
Varro, Marcus Terentius, 6, 108–9, 141
Veii, 16, 159
Velleius Paterculus, 142
Venice, 180
Venus, 5, 118, 139, 143, 164
Venusia, 21
Verus, Lucius, 146
Verona, 116
Vespasian(us), Titus Flavius, 53, 60, 62, 82, 251
Vesta, 7, 158
Vestal Virgins, 139, 158, 207
Vesuvius, 152, 251
vici, 77, 162

Victory altar, 207, 209, 221
Victor of Vita, 212
Vienne, 153, 182
viginitivirate, 67
villa farming, 23, 39, 43, 77, 91–3, 172–3, 198
Villa Hadriana, 150, 153
villas, 72, 92, 104, 192, 198, 253
Vintius Ligurianus, 163
Virgil (Publius Vergilius Maro), 62, 96, 103, 132, 138, 141–2, 151, 217, 221
Viriathus, 35
virtus, 37, 118, 136, 140, 159, 236
Visigoths, 178, 231–2
Vitruvius Pollio, 141
Vogt, Joseph, 59, 180
Völkerwanderung, *see* migration of peoples
Volso, Manlius, 35
Voltaire, 188
voting, 27, 31
Vulcan, 139, 158

war, 12, 14, 26, 145, 158; guilt, 36; prisoners, 43, 114–15, 134, 195; wounded, 157; *see also* civil wars; Goths; Macedon; Punic Wars; Samnite wars; slaves; social wars
water supply, 73, 103–6, 109, 144, 147, 150, 157–8
wealth, 42, 102, 118, 146, 193
weavers, weaving, 89, 99, 187, 196
Weber, Max, 21, 190, 194, 198, 238
wheat, 43, 69
widows, 76, 206
wife, 66, 96, 99, 100
wild-beast baiting, 113
Windisch, Switzerland, 157
wine(s), 91, 94, 99, 108–9, 118, 120, 184, 255
women, 38, 52, 65–6, 99–103, 107, 120, 145, 220
word, the, in law, 128; *see also logos*
work, 95, 98, 105
workshop(s), 43, 89, 93, 95, 106, 150, 157, 198, 219, 229
world: conquest, 146; history, 211; rule, 59, 159; *see also oikoumene*

Xanten, Germany, 157
Xenophon of Cos, 156

Zama, 34
Zanker, P., 150
zealots, 165
Zeus, 163
Zoroastrian, 170